# Plymouth Argyle
# Snakes & Ladders
## Promotions and Relegations
## 1930-2004

DESERT ISLAND FOOTBALL HISTORIES

| CLUB HISTORIES | ISBN |
|---|---|
| Aberdeen: A Centenary History 1903-2003 | 1-874287-57-0 |
| Aberdeen: Champions of Scotland 1954-55 | 1-874287-65-1 |
| Aberdeen: The European Era – A Complete Record | 1-874287-11-2 |
| Bristol City: The Modern Era – A Complete Record | 1-874287-28-7 |
| Bristol City: The Early Years 1894-1915 | 1-874287-74-0 |
| Cambridge United: The League Era – A Complete Record | 1-874287-32-5 |
| Cambridge United: 101 Golden Greats | 1-874287-58-9 |
| The Story of the Celtic 1888-1938 | 1-874287-15-5 |
| Chelsea: Champions of England 1954-55 | 1-874287-77-5 |
| Colchester United: Graham to Whitton – A Complete Record | 1-874287-27-9 |
| Coventry City: The Elite Era – A Complete Record | 1-874287-83-X |
| Coventry City: An Illustrated History | 1-874287-59-7 |
| Dundee: Champions of Scotland 1961-62 | 1-874287-86-4 |
| Dundee United: Champions of Scotland 1982-83 | 1-874287-71-6 |
| History of the Everton Football Club 1878-1928 | 1-874287-14-7 |
| Halifax Town: From Ball to Lillis – A Complete Record | 1-874287-26-0 |
| Hereford United: The League Era – A Complete Record | 1-874287-18-X |
| Huddersfield Town: Champions of England 1923-1926 | 1-874287-88-0 |
| Ipswich Town: The Modern Era – A Complete Record | 1-874287-43-0 |
| Ipswich Town: Champions of England 1961-62 | 1-874287-63-5 |
| Kilmarnock: Champions of Scotland 1964-65 | 1-874287-87-2 |
| Luton Town: The Modern Era – A Complete Record | 1-874287-90-2 |
| Luton Town: An Illustrated History | 1-874287-79-1 |
| Manchester United's Golden Age 1903-1914: Dick Duckworth | 1-874287-80-5 |
| The Matt Busby Chronicles: Manchester United 1946-69 | 1-874287-53-8 |
| Motherwell: Champions of Scotland 1931-32 | 1-874287-73-2 |
| Norwich City: The Modern Era – A Complete Record | 1-874287-67-8 |
| Peterborough United: The Modern Era – A Complete Record | 1-874287-33-3 |
| Peterborough United: Who's Who? | 1-874287-48-1 |
| Plymouth Argyle: The Modern Era – A Complete Record | 1-874287-54-6 |
| Plymouth Argyle: 101 Golden Greats | 1-874287-64-3 |
| Plymouth Argyle: Snakes & Ladders – Promotions and Relegations | 1-874287-82-1 |
| Portsmouth: From Tindall to Ball – A Complete Record | 1-874287-25-2 |
| Portsmouth: Champions of England – 1948-49 & 1949-50 | 1-874287-50-3 |
| The Story of the Rangers 1873-1923 | 1-874287-16-3 |
| The Romance of the Wednesday 1867-1926 | 1-874287-17-1 |
| Seventeen Miles from Paradise – Saints v Pompey | 1-874287-89-9 |
| Stoke City: The Modern Era – A Complete Record | 1-874287-76-7 |
| Stoke City: 101 Golden Greats | 1-874287-55-4 |
| Potters at War: Stoke City 1939-47 | 1-874287-78-3 |
| Tottenham Hotspur: Champions of England 1950-51, 1960-61 | 1-874287-84-8 |
| West Ham: From Greenwood to Redknapp | 1-874287-19-8 |
| West Ham: The Elite Era – A Complete Record | 1-874287-31-7 |
| Wimbledon: From Southern League to Premiership | 1-874287-09-0 |
| Wimbledon: From Wembley to Selhurst | 1-874287-20-1 |
| Wimbledon: The Premiership Years | 1-874287-40-6 |
| Wrexham: The European Era – A Complete Record | 1-874287-52-X |

| WORLD CUP HISTORIES | |
|---|---|
| England's Quest for the World Cup – A Complete Record | 1-874287-61-9 |
| Scotland: The Quest for the World Cup – A Complete Record | 1-897850-50-6 |
| Ireland: The Quest for the World Cup – A Complete Record | 1-897850-80-8 |

| MISCELLANEOUS | |
|---|---|
| Red Dragons in Europe – A Complete Record | 1-874287-01-5 |
| The Book of Football: A History to 1905-06 | 1-874287-13-9 |
| Football's War & Peace: The Tumultuous Season of 1946-47 | 1-874287-70-8 |

# Plymouth Argyle
## Snakes & Ladders
### Promotions and Relegations
### 1930-2004

Series Editor: Clive Leatherdale

Andy Riddle

DESERT ISLAND BOOKS

First published in 2004
by
DESERT ISLAND BOOKS LIMITED
89 Park Street, Westcliff-on-Sea, Essex SS0 7PD
United Kingdom
www.desertislandbooks.com

The right of Andy Riddle to be identified as author of this work has been
asserted under The Copyright Designs and Patents Act 1988

British Library Cataloguing-in-Publication Data
A catalogue record for this book is available from the British Library

ISBN 1-874287-82-1

Printed in Great Britain
by
Biddles Ltd, King's Lynn

# ~ Contents ~

# ~ AUTHOR'S NOTE ~

For the true football fan, there is little to compare the emotion of seeing your team winning promotion or indeed, suffering the indignity of relegation. I like to think that I keep my emotions in check on most occasions, and I have never been one of those who resorts to bursting into tears when the dreaded 'drop' has been confirmed. After all, life goes on. That said, believe me, having supported Argyle through thick, thin and occasionally, very thin, there have been times when I have come close. I must confess, however, that Argyle's Division Three championship triumph in 2001-02 did tug at the heart strings. After the final match of the season at Home Park when the team collected the trophy and 'We Are The Champions' blasted out over the public address system, I do not mind confessing there was a tear in the eye and a lump in the throat. I was not alone.

The Pilgrims' play-off triumph at Wembley in May 1996 was a great day out but, despite winning, deep down there was a feeling that we were not the best. Over the season, other teams had done better. Similarly, there was not quite the same emotion when the Second Division title was captured in 2003-04. Perhaps us Argyle fans are getting a little spoiled.

I hope this book portrays some of those emotions and also reflects on how the game of football itself has evolved, some would say for the worse, over the years.

Of course, there are a few people I would like to thank. Firstly, my publisher, Clive Leatherdale, for his continued enthusiasm and guidance, soccer historian, Leigh Edwards who, if he can't answer a question himself, knows a man who can, and last but, of course, not least, my wife Joy-Anne and children, Sophie and Ben, who in recent months believe their father is a man who disappears to work in the morning, comes back at six o'clock for something to eat and then disappears again for the evening into another room.

ANDY RIDDLE

# ONE

# *1929-30 (Promoted to Division 2)*

As Argyle entered the 1929-30 season, all the signs pointed to another plausible chance of promotion. A glance at the forward line alone – featuring the names of Ray Bowden, Jack Leslie and Sammy Black – gave much cause for optimism. This triumvirate would merit inclusion in any all-time Pilgrims XI but, in modern parlance, manager Robert Jack was a man under some pressure. The loyal Jack had first served Argyle as a player and appeared in the club's first ever match as a professional side in 1903. Two years later he was appointed player-manager but subsequently left for Southend. In 1910, he was lured back to Home Park, combining the duties of secretary and manager, a standard job description in those days. He had masterminded Argyle's progress from the Southern League to a highly respected Football League club.

A healthy mid-table position at the end of that first Football League season in 1920-21 was followed by arguably the most unwanted record still standing. At a time when the English Third Division was split into North and South sections, and thus handing promotion to the respective divisional winners only, Argyle conspired to finish runners-up on six successive occasions. This was followed by third and fourth place finishes.

Understandably, such results gave rise to considerable frustration amongst Pilgrim followers. Most reasonably minded fans put the relative lack of success down to pure bad luck. Some did not. After runners-up spot number six, the conspiracy theorists showed their hand. The club, in their opinion, lacked ambition. Promotion would have meant increased expenditure in the form of higher wages and greater travelling costs. The players, they said, would rather supplement their wages – (£1 per week) with regular win bonuses (ten shillings) – in the Third Division than struggle in the Second.

To substantiate their notion, there were accusations of penalty-kicks being deliberately missed in vital end-of-season games and one match in particular was touted as an example of dubious endeavour. In the final game of the 1925-26 season, a win at mid-table Gillingham would have clinched the title. The Gills had nothing to play for. Argyle had been rattling in goals left, right and centre all season – 107 of them to be precise – yet they came away from Kent with a 0-2 defeat after Black had missed a penalty for the second successive match, allowing Reading to take the championship and promotion.

Matters got so bad that they sparked protest meetings in the city and a call on supporters to boycott matches if promotion was not gained. In

modern times, there would have been calls for the manager's head. The
directors would probably have succumbed to the whims of the fans and
Jack would have been on his way, deemed a failure for not taking the club
out of Division Three. But these were different times. Loyalty was still a
word that featured heavily. None of the accusations of 'match fixing' were
ever founded and the Football League certainly took no interest in them.
To Jack they meant nothing. He was a highly respected figure both locally
and within the game itself on a national level.

The directors refuted the arguments over additional travel costs. They
countered that promotion would mean higher gates at home and away
against such clubs as Chelsea, West Brom and Wolves, who were all regularly attracting attendances in excess of 20,000. Nevertheless, the club's
finances were far from healthy. Debts were reported at £6,000, a substantial figure, although a profit of £216 was declared from the previous campaign. Despite the level of debt, Jack and the directors had resisted the
temptation to sell three unnamed players to equally anonymous First
Division clubs, but they warned that bigger crowds were needed to ensure
this situation remained.

In fact, there was little change to the squad overall, a story not uncommon to many clubs who were as financially embarrassed as Argyle. The
transfer system was embroiled in something of a vicious circle. Clubs were
keen to sell on their best assets but few clubs could afford them. Only half-
back Jimmy Logan had departed the Home Park scene since the conclusion of the previous season, although Fred Forbes had refused the terms
offered to him. The new incumbents came from the local amateur scene,
leaving Jack with a squad of thirty players.

A study of the squad's vital statistics revealed one thing – Argyle's
game-plan would not be based on physicality. Only two players, goalkeeper Fred Craig and centre-half John Pullen reached the 6ft mark. In a time
when bodily contact was permitted to a far greater extent than in the modern game, accurate passing and skill were to be the Pilgrims' main
weapons.

The players would again take to the field in familiar kit – green shirts
with black collar and cuffs and white 'knickers'. The term 'shorts' was not
used for several years hence and would, in any case, have been a totally
inappropriate description, given that the knickers were at least knee length
and contained a considerable quantity of material. Had replica shirts been
available to fans, they would have lasted for years.

Pre-season preparations were limited to two matches involving the
whole squad and titled 'Chiefs' versus 'Reserves'. With a high degree of
anticipation for the new season, large crowds attended both games.

The opening league game, in a season that marked Black's benefit year,
saw a trip to newly relegated Clapton Orient. The Supporters Club were as

active as ever in raising funds and arranged a train excursion to London. Leaving Plymouth at twenty minutes past midnight on Saturday, the train arrived back at quarter past one on Sunday morning. The cost of this twenty-five hour trek was 17s 6d (87½p) and no fewer than 500 supporters shelled out some of their hard-earned cash.

There were few surprises in the team selected jointly by Jack and the directors. The defence was vastly experienced, perhaps too much so. Between the posts was Fred Craig, who had first cemented his place in the Argyle side before the First World War. Craig was virtually an institution and in recent seasons had also made occasional sojourns upfield to take penalties with panache. At 36, he was also appointed captain. Rumour had it that Craig was so confident of his place in the side that he would, on occasions, choose to miss half-time team-talks and briefly retire to the toilet for a cigarette. But he would have to be on his toes. Waiting in the wings was Harry Cann, a brave and agile Cornishman who was highly rated.

The full-backs were both internationals. The unmistakable bald pate of Moses Russell had been a familiar sight in the Argyle side for fifteen years. Despite approaching his fortieth year, he still featured in the full Welsh side and had, indeed, just returned from a summer tour of Canada, where his robust style of play had prompted an enraged spectator to pull a gun on him! Freddie Titmuss was ten years younger and had won two full England caps earlier in his career whilst a Southampton player.

The half-back line featured Norman Mackay, a Scotsman, who would entertain the players on long away trips with his fine singing voice, John Pullen, another Welsh international, and Fred MacKenzie, whose ability had not been impeded by the amputation of one of his toes following blood poisoning.

The forward line consisted of tricky winger Alf Matthews, the ebullient Frank Sloan, local boy-wonder Ray Bowden, who would go on to achieve greatness with Arsenal and England, the mercurial Jack Leslie, and the diminutive Sammy Black, arguably the best winger outside the First Division.

Despite their team having been relegated, Clapton Orient followers were full of optimism. Their club had made a number of new signings, including ex-Spurs and England half-back Arthur Grimsdell, who had been appointed player-manager-secretary. However, shortly before the 3.15pm kick-off, Grimsdell was informed by the Football League that they had not accepted his registration as a player. No reason was cited, leaving Grimsdell furious. He was forced to replace himself with George Eastman, who also doubled as Essex's cricket wicketkeeper.

On a baking hot day, Argyle's half-back's dominated the game. Orient, with their band of new faces, looked understandably disjointed and a two-goal victory for the Pilgrims was well deserved.

Five days later the supporters were on the road again. Fortunately they were not faced with such a marathon journey, as Argyle travelled to Torquay for the first Devon derby of the season. Jack made two changes, bringing in yet another Scotsman, Alec Hardie, to replace Pullen who had injured a shoulder, and Harry Bland who was handed Russell's No 2 shirt with the veteran Welshman being advised that he was being 'rested'.

On the hottest evening of the year, a seven-goal thriller ensued with goalkeeper Craig the hero. Despite conceding three, he pulled off a string of fine saves and also strode upfield to convert a penalty. It was the first time both sets of supporters had seen the implementation of a new penalty rule where goalies were not allowed to move off their line until the ball had been kicked. Custodians did not like the change and former England goalie Dick Pym was particularly vociferous in his criticism, penning an article in which he claimed the new rule would ruin the game.

Brentford were the first visitors of the season to Home Park. They too had won both their opening matches and a keen contest was anticipated. The match however never lived up to expectations. The heatwave continued although it was reported that Brentford looked 'cool' in their silk shorts. Bowden's last-minute goal ensured a share of the spoils. Matthews suffered a knee injury which would ultimately cost him his place for the majority of the season.

A week after the game at Plainmoor, Torquay came to Home Park. The Magpies (their metamorphosis into Gulls was still a few years off) certainly had their feathers ruffled with a 5-0 defeat – their fourth successive loss. Black was imperious and McKenzie scored a rare but spectacular long-range effort to push Argyle into second place with seven points out of eight.

A 3-2 win at Bristol Rovers followed. The local newspaper report was a fine example of the biased reporting prevalent during those days. According to the anonymous 'Pilgrim', Rovers were 'not a good side'.

Jack was forced into another selection change for the visit of Brighton, following the death on the Wednesday of Bowden's father. Tony Bowden, aged 57, had been watching some fishing boats in his home town of Looe when he was accidentally upended by a rope. He was sent crashing onto the deck of the boat some feet below and later died of a fractured skull. Naturally, his son was given compassionate leave and the players wore black armbands as a mark of respect. The game ended in a 1-1 draw with Bowden's replacement, Jack Vidler, scoring.

A midweek trip to Watford resulted in another two points, thanks to two Black goals in the 89th and 90th minutes, despite the winger suffering from an injury. The win took Argyle to the top of the table, a position they consolidated on the following Saturday with victory at Swindon, their fifth in a row away from home. The team stayed away for the remainder of the weekend to fulfil a Monday night fixture at Kettering. Argyle's reserve side had won the previous season's Southern League, Western Division title, with Kettering winning the Eastern equivalent. The match was labelled the 'Championship of the Southern League'. The motive for Argyle fielding their first team was not because of a burning desire to win the title, but rather to support the Kettering club, believing their winning team would entice a larger crowd and swell the Southern League club's coffers.

The strength of the squad was coming to the fore, so much so that Jack was spoilt for choice in who to select for his starting eleven. Bland's consistency at right-back was keeping Russell on the sidelines. Tommy Grozier was proving a more than adequate replacement for Matthews on the right wing, and Vidler would have walked into most teams' first eleven. As it was, he had to be content with filling in for any absentee from the usual forward line. Black was not missed when injury forced him out temporarily. Unusually, a number of players had also seen their names on the scoresheet. In an age when defenders defended and the goalscoring was usually shared primarily among the forwards, by the ninth game of the season no fewer than ten players had already notched a goal when Pullen scored in a 3-0 win over a robust Gillingham. It left Argyle as the only undefeated side in the whole Football League. Nine games, sixteen points.

Things may have been going swimmingly on the field but the main concern to the directors was that Argyle's impressive start had not yet captured the imagination of the Plymouth public. Crowds were healthy enough, with five figures generally the norm, but given the pre-season appeal for greater support, larger numbers could have been expected. As a consequence, the chairman, Mr Elliot-Square, issued a warning over the club's financial position. He revealed the extent of the debt, namely £6,051 to the bank and £1,201 to other creditors, among them a number of local tradesman who were pressing for payment. He stated that barely a day had passed without a bigger club enquiring about one player or another, and if the situation did not improve, the board would have to sell. In desperation, he appealed for 200 benefactors to donate £50 each to ease the crisis and forward their donations directly to Robert Jack at the club's offices in Old Town Street. Ironically, the announcement came two days before the Gillingham game, when the attendance was greatly reduced because of torrential rain.

The appeal worked to an extent. Mr A C Ballard, a Plymouth businessman who would become a future president of the club, immediately pledged the considerable sum of £500 and an anonymous donor gave £100. Jack reported a steady stream of responses with many donating their 'most acceptable half-crowns'.

A second successive home game saw the visit of bottom-of-the-table Merthyr. The result looked a foregone conclusion, but the young Welsh side had a strategy and from the first minute hustled and harried the Argyle players. They went in at half-time with a goal lead and, with the home fans getting restless, it needed a winner via a Pullen penalty to save Argyle's blushes.

The next match was the game-of-the-season so far. Northampton were in second spot and unbeaten at home. It would be the first real test of Argyle's ability. The team set off for London early on the Friday as they were to stay in the capital overnight before going on to Northampton. Black and Grozier both had injuries and did not travel, allowing Matthews a recall on the right wing. The match certainly caught the imagination of the Northampton public. Hundreds were locked out of the ground thirty minutes before kick-off and inside there was such a crush on the terraces that the police had to remove spectators from the playing area. The ambulancemen were also kept busy, with several spectators being overcome by a combination of the crowded conditions and the heat on an untypical October day. The Cobblers were certainly the most impressive side Argyle had encountered to date and they took a first-half lead through the prolific Ted Bowen, but Leslie preserved the unbeaten run with a goal eleven minutes from time.

Next up were great rivals Exeter at Home Park. The Grecians had been struggling and had recently endured a run of five games without scoring, but had then gone berserk, scoring six against Crystal Palace. Nevertheless, Argyle were clear favourites and soon justified the tag with a Bowden goal after just four minutes. City equalised, but two contrasting Pilgrim goals before half-time restored the advantage. Bowden stubbed his toe in shooting, but the ball trickled through the grasp of goalie John Alderson. Black's ferocious volley a few minutes later was more impressive. The second half saw Bowden complete his first ever league hat-trick to increase his burgeoning reputation. The 4-1 margin might even been more emphatic, but Pullen missed a penalty.

Another difficult away game followed. Southend had lost only once. Again, Argyle stayed overnight in London. The supporters could also rest easier in their beds as the board announced that sufficient donations had been received to reduce the immediate threat of selling players.

The game itself was controversial. The first half saw Leslie injured and, with substitutes still a distant thought, he was obliged to limp through the remainder of the game. After a goalless first half, the best chance fell to Leslie himself but he was forced to shoot with his injured foot. Argyle took the lead in the 61st-minute when the referee deemed that the Southend goalie had carried Bowden's shot over the line. Even the normally blinkered Argyle press did not believe the ball to be in, but the referee refused to consult his linesman and the goal stood. Southend eventually equalised, but their fans were so incensed at the earlier decision that a number of them congregated angrily outside the referee's quarters after the game and had to be dispersed by police.

For the second successive home game, Argyle's attendance broke 15,000 for the visit of Luton. The visitors stunned the crowd into silence by taking the lead from a penalty after Pullen had handled. But by half-time, Argyle had responded three times, including an effort from Bowden that ranked among the best goals ever seen at Home Park. He dribbled from the halfway line past several opponents before coolly slotting the ball home. With injury reducing the Hatters to ten men after half-time, Argyle scored three more to leave themselves four points clear at the top ahead of Brentford and Bournemouth.

The Argyle coffers were boosted further when Bristol Rovers paid £750 to secure the signature of 'contract rebel' Fred Forbes who had been sitting on the sidelines since the start of the season.

And so, another top-of-the-table clash ensued as Argyle travelled to Bournemouth. The crowd was boosted by the arrival of around 600 sailors who were based at Portland. They arrived to support Argyle 'gay with Pilgrim green' and carried a huge pasty as a mascot. Sadly, 800 or so Argyle fans didn't make it as their train broke down en route, their 7s 6d fare going to waste. On a treacherous pitch, the game was as tough as expected. Bowden's header had seen sailors' hats being tossed into the air, but Argyle were forced to hang on. Hardie suffered strained ligaments and was forced to play away out of harm's way on the left wing. Black also took a batter-ing. Argyle started the second half with ten men and it was some time later when the wee winger re-emerged from the dressing room to resume bat-tle. Bournemouth capitalised and managed to square things up.

The wet weather showed no signs of abating as Walsall rolled into town. Black had recovered but Hardie was likely to be out until Christmas, so Percy Richards was drafted in for his first game of the season. On this occasion it was Pullen's turn to limp through most of the game. Walsall took a similar approach to Merthyr and harried Argyle out of the game. After being a goal down, Bowden's header with only six minutes remain-ing had supporters swarming onto the pitch to celebrate.

The amateurs of Isthmian League side Dulwich Hamlet had the pick of the first round FA Cup-ties as they were pitched into a home tie against Argyle. The Pilgrims were fast becoming one of the most attractive sides in the country and 11,000 packed the tiny Champion Hill ground to see if Dulwich could pull off one of the great cup shocks. It was not to be. They were no slouches and would have undoubtedly pushed a lesser side closer, but Argyle were simply too good, particularly Black and Bowden who shared four goals.

For several days preceding the home game with Fulham, the country was swept by hurricane conditions, making the pitch extremely heavy.

Once again, the Argyle players adorned black armbands, this time out of respect for a former Plymouth captain, Archie Goodall, whose death had been announced.

The Cottagers had a reputation as a fine footballing side and despite the thick mud, both sides produced some attractive play in an even but goalless first half. Leslie's early second-half goal from virtually on the goal-line dampened Fulham spirits and from then on there was only one winner. Bowden was at his best, beating no fewer than six players before setting up Black, and then winning a penalty which Black again converted. Jim Hammond scored a late consolation.

In preparation for the second round FA Cup-tie at Watford, many of the players were among 400 people who attended a midweek cabaret at the Pier Pavilion on the Hoe, arranged by the Supporters Club to raise funds for the 'Retention of Players' fund, which was still bringing in much needed revenue. The squad travelled to London on the Friday by train and in the evening attended the London Hippodrome to watch 'Mr Cinders.' Neither side was at full strength. Argyle had Sloan and Bowden injured, whilst Watford player-manager Neil McBain declared himself unfit. With a strong wind at their backs, the Hornets almost took the lead in spectacular fashion. A free-kick by full-back George Prior from fully fifty yards almost deceived Craig, who was forced into punching away. Both sides missed good chances and went in at half-time without scoring. In the second period, Watford were in the ascendancy and deserved to go ahead when Arthur Woodward converted a corner. With only six minutes left, a goal from Bland took the tie back to Home Park.

A crowd of almost 19,000 for the replay was substantial, considering the match was played on a Wednesday afternoon. Again Jack had 'ordered' his side to relax prior to the match and a few players enjoyed a round of golf at Yelverton. Some received a lesson from the club's professional, the unfortunately named Mr Hooker. Watford, believing themselves unfortunate not to have won the first game, were confident of beating Argyle and ending their unbeaten record, but it was Vidler, a largely anonymous figure in the earlier game, who stole the show with a superb hat-trick.

With four games in eight days over the Christmas holiday period, three of them at home, players and supporters were in for a hectic time. The question was, how long could Argyle keep up their unbeaten record?

Certainly Crystal Palace never looked likely to threaten. With Bowden fit again, Vidler retained his place and Leslie, still not 100 per cent after his recent injury, was omitted. This time it was Grozier who was the star with a first-half hat-trick. After the break, he scored again to complete a personal triumph. Palace managed a lone consolation, and further strikes from Mackay and Vidler completed the rout as the Palace defence were nonplussed by the speed of Argyle's attacks.

In those days, Christmas Day meant live football, and Argyle travelled to Coventry. After 21 unbeaten games a single goal was enough to defeat Jack's men. It was perhaps a blessing in disguise. There was enough pressure in trying to win the league after so many near misses without everyone talking about how long the run would last.

As soon as the game ended, both teams boarded a train for the journey to Plymouth, to meet again 24 hours later. With the pitch waterlogged in some areas, Jack opted to recall Russell in defence, believing the veteran's robust style would be better suited to the conditions. Bowden was again absent through injury but Argyle barely missed him. In a contrasting performance to the one a day earlier, Coventry were swept aside 3-0, leaving Argyle three points clear of Brentford at the top of the table.

Two days later, Argyle were at home again, but the attendance was 20,000 down on the Coventry game. Three home games in a week was too much for the average working man's pocket and Clapton Orient represented the least attractive opposition of the three. Heavy rain no doubt swayed the minds of a few 'floating voters' as well. It was Orient's first ever visit to Home Park but they put up little resistance. Argyle were three up by half-time, and when the visitors took the field for the second half without the injured Billy Broadbent, another goal-feast looked probable but Argyle tired on a heavy pitch and failed to add to their tally.

Thus the scene was set for the top-of-the-table clash at Brentford, but the headlines the next day were not the ones Plymouth fans' wanted to read. 'A Black Day for Argyle,' was a typical example. It was the Pilgrims' worst performance of the season, with defensive errors gifting their near rivals all three goals. Black was also injured. The Bees were a formidable force on their own ground and would go on to win every home match of the season.

The FA Cup third round threw up an unknown quantity in the form of Second Division strugglers Hull. It would be a good opportunity for Argyle to gauge how they might fare in a higher division. Little was known about their opponents but a local reporter had seen them and made a number of irrelevant observations. His assertion, for example, that the backs 'kick the ball too hard' was hardly likely to help Jack plan his tactics.

The Yorkshire side originally planned an overnight stay in London, prior to continuing their rail journey to Plymouth on matchday. Of course, our ace reporter also had his opinion on this, deciding that they 'feared the relaxing air of the west'. At the last minute, Hull changed their travel plans and arrived in Plymouth on the Friday and spent the evening enjoying a pantomime in the Theatre Royal.

Once again, Bowden was missing, having received a kick on the thigh at Brentford. The heavy rain of recent weeks had continued overnight and had a bearing on the first goal. Within fifty seconds of the start, a Stan

Alexander shot from twenty yards slipped through the hands of Craig. The rain turned to a blizzard of snow and hail but the football continued to flow from end to end in an exhilarating contest. Hull went in at half-time leading by the odd goal in five. Hopes of a Plymouth comeback were dented when Titmuss was unable to resume after suffering a fractured rib. Hardie was moved to full-back and Leslie to half-back, thus weakening Argyle's attacking options. Despite Hull's shoot-on-sight policy, both sides managed only a goal apiece in the second half and Argyle's Cup run was at an end. Brentford, meanwhile, had been in league action but had failed to close the gap after a surprise defeat at Southend.

A familiar face led out Bristol Rovers. Fred Forbes had been appointed their captain and he received a warm welcome from the crowd as he and Craig shook hands in the centre-circle, but Forbes was unable to put one over his old side. Mackay started the scoring with a disputed goal. Rovers' goalie, Jesse Whatley, who performed heroics throughout, plucked the ball away but the referee deemed that it had crossed the line. Leslie added another before Grozier scored the goal of the match with a venomous shot that actually burst the ball!

With no fixture scheduled for the following Saturday, it gave the opportunity for some much-needed rest for Jack's battle-weary players. They had endured a hectic period of matches on very heavy pitches and a number had been carrying injuries. The planned two-week respite extended to three. Argyle were due to play Swindon at Home Park but the rain had still been falling relentlessly. An hour before kick-off, with around 6,000 people already gathered outside, the match was postponed. It was an inevitable decision, with water lying all over the pitch, although there was some consternation that the decision had not been made earlier.

If the break allowed time for injuries to heal, it did little to maintain the momentum that Argyle had built up. Finally back in action at Gillingham, the Pilgrims produced a disjointed performance and were held by a Gills side that were next to bottom and had a dismal home record. On a pitch described as 'lumpy' after a fall of snow, the Greens produced enough chances to win the game but finished badly with Sloan the main culprit.

Argyle were also favourites to take both points from the next game, as they travelled to bottom side Merthyr, who had won only twice all season and conceded 76 goals in their 25 games. The Welsh side were unfairly branded the poor relations of the division and it was reported that many clubs would not be sorry to see them lose their league status to save them a 'long and tiring journey.' Mindful of their opponents' poor defensive record, Argyle adopted a shoot-on-sight policy that only yielded one goal in the first half, from Sloan. In the second half, Bowden converted a Grozier free-kick before Argyle were reduced to ten men when Cosgrove was carried off. Despite this, Argyle scored again, with Bowden chesting in Black's telling cross.

With Cosgrove incapacitated, Titmuss declared himself fit after his rib injury and took his place in the line up for Argyle's first home game for five weeks, with Northampton the visitors. A heavy fall on the frosty pitch took the wind out of Bowden's sails for a while and he sought temporary refuge on the right wing, with Grozier swapping places. Bowden recovered sufficiently to lead the line in the second half, but it was Grozier who struck, firing in from a narrow angle. The goal produced some over exuberant play from both sides and numerous free-kicks punctuated the play. In the end, the one goal was enough, as the Cobblers' slide down the table after a promising start to the season continued.

The Devon derby with Exeter was keenly anticipated. City had taken ten points from a possible twelve during February and over 5,000 Argyle supporters were amongst the 17,000 crowd that somehow crammed into St James Park. The home side took the lead in bizarre fashion as Bob Shanks took a free-kick from wide on the touchline fully fifty yards from goal. Incredibly, no one touched the ball as it tamely entered Craig's net. Vidler equalised after Black collected a scuffed goal-kick from City custodian John Alderson, but the main talking point was the decision to disallow another Vidler effort that appeared to cross the line. The controversy was still being debated in the local press a week later. The draw left Argyle two points behind Brentford, who had played three games more.

A 1-0 home win over Southend followed, thanks to a Grozier header, but the Shrimpers should have gained a point. An unmarked Fred Barnett was poised to score when he slipped over. Argyle were still grinding out victories but, since the recent enforced break, their overall form had dipped and their general play was less dominant than in previous weeks.

A rearranged fixture took Argyle to the capital again to face QPR in a Thursday afternoon game. Rangers went ahead with a dubious penalty but Argyle levelled with a goal that should never have been. Bowden was blatantly offside and the Rangers defenders stood and appealed, but Black continued and scored. A great left-foot shot from Grozier gave Argyle the two points that regained the leadership of the division.

The Argyle party remained in London in readiness for the game at Luton two days later. A first-minute goal by Black gave false hope. The Hatters equalised and then took the lead when Craig and Bland collided. Craig clutched the ball, but was then shoulder-charged into the net by burly centre-forward Jimmy Yardley. In modern times the goal would have been ruled out and Yardley probably sent off, but in 1930 keepers had little protection and the goal was deemed legitimate. Craig had to go off for treatment and Titmuss took his place. The Argyle skipper resumed after ten minutes but was afforded little cover by his defence who chose to have a united off-day. Luton ran riot to inflict a devastating 5-2 defeat. With Brentford winning, the race for the promotion spot was between four sides. The table stood like this: 1st Brentford P 32 Pts 48; 2nd Argyle 30 46; 3rd Brighton 31 43; 4th Northampton 32 40.

Still shaken, both from the physical battering and the ignominy of conceding five goals, Craig was omitted from the eleven that Jack and the directors picked to face Bournemouth. Titmuss was made captain. A fine goal from Black preceded a shout for a penalty when Bowden was brought down. It looked cut and dried but the referee chose to ignore the vociferous claims. There were no histrionics from the gentlemanly Bowden but he 'whispered' something to the referee. Whatever he said convinced the official to consult his linesman but there was no change of mind. A mistake by Bland gifted Bournemouth an equaliser. As the minutes ticked by, it looked a costly mistake, but Black saved the day scoring near the end. In a blatant display of time-wasting, the Argyle players spent the last few minutes kicking the ball far into touch at every opportunity.

A Wednesday evening home game with Swindon saw Argyle regain top form, with Vidler in particular posing a threat which the visiting defence never looked capable of coping with. A 5-0 win kept Argyle neck and neck with Brentford, but more importantly boosted the goal-average, which could still be the decisive factor.

Another comfortable win at Walsall was made more pleasing by the news that Exeter had held Brentford to a draw. The Pilgrims were now a point behind the London club with two games in hand.

Argyle's next opponents, Brighton, were still in the promotion equation, albeit five points behind. With the Brentford players watching the game, having enjoyed a few days break on the south coast, Argyle fielded a twelfth player in Lady Luck. In the third minute, Black intercepted a Harry Marsden back-pass and set up Vidler for an easy goal. In the seventeenth minute Brighton suffered another setback when they lost centre-half Jack Williams to injury. Despite this, the Seagulls put up a spirited showing and it took a superb double save from Cann to maintain the lead and put the Greens back into pole position.

For a time, it appeared the home game with QPR would not take place. With twenty minutes to go before kick-off, the Londoners had still not arrived, having suffered delays leaving their Torquay hotel. They made it in time, but their lack of preparation hardly helped their cause as they were outplayed. Again Vidler was the main man, scoring a hat-trick in a 4-0 win. Grozier hit the woodwork twice, but the biggest cheer came at half-time when it was announced that Brentford were losing at home to Southend. The Bees recovered in the second half to stay on Argyle's tail.

Three train-loads of supporters travelled to London to watch Argyle take on Fulham. The early arrivals took the opportunity to watch the

University Boat Race beforehand. Jack was compelled into making one change, when Grozier was forced to return to his Glasgow home to be with his seriously ill wife. Matthews was given a rare opportunity on the right wing. An end-to-end game ensued, with the Greens coming out on top 3-1. Cann was again in superb form. The news that Luton had defeated Brentford with a last-minute goal made the return journey to Plymouth all the more enjoyable.

The Good Friday game with Newport attracted another big crowd but there was a deathly hush over Home Park. With eleven minutes remaining, Argyle were a goal down. There were murmurings from the doubters. Surely Argyle weren't going to blow their chances again. The answer was an emphatic no. Three goals in the last ten minutes clinched another two points. Brentford had lost again, leaving Argyle needing only four points from the remaining five matches to win the league. Surely this time …

The following day, Argyle took on Norwich, who had been spared a Good Friday game. The directors agreed to allow a 'collection' to be taken for Black's benefit as a gesture of goodwill. There had been talk of a benefit match against Glasgow Rangers, but it never came about.

Argyle had Bowden, Sloan and Leslie all injured. Vidler opened the scoring, but a minute later was carted off to the dressing room with blood pouring from a head wound. Not long afterwards, Black suffered a similar injury. Running repairs were applied to Vidler but trainer Tommy Haynes tried to deter him from resuming his place with the striker clearly concussed and unable to remember that he had scored. Vidler was adamant and returned to huge cheers. It proved a wise decision for Argyle if not Vidler's health. The second half saw him play like a man possessed to score another three times and put his side on the verge of championship glory.

With the next three games scheduled away from Home Park, it was unlikely that the majority of fans would be able to share in the moment promotion was achieved. Nonetheless, there was a fair sprinkling of Argyle followers among the 10,000 crowd at Newport on Easter Monday. Fittingly, in his benefit year, it was Black, so often the catalyst of Argyle's attacking flair, who scored the two goals that finally clinched the title. There was temporary gloom and despondency back at Home Park, though. Supporters watching the corresponding fixture between the two reserve sides were erroneously informed that Argyle had lost!

There was joy across the city now that the long wait was finally over, but there were still three games to play and Jack, a proud man, was keen to maintain the level of performance. Argyle faced another extended stay away, with games against Crystal Palace and Norwich. Still blighted by injuries, Jack was forced to field a weakened side at Selhurst Park. Fred Cosgrove was given a rare opportunity at right-back and Walter Price given his season's debut in the No 3 shirt. It was a case of 'after the Lord Mayor's show' as Palace dominated the game. Argyle looked as though they had other things on their minds.

At Norwich two days later, Jack handed Tavistock-born half-back Bill Fellowes his league debut. In a much more cohesive performance, Argyle inflicted the Canaries' third home defeat of the season with goals from the ever reliable Pullen and Grozier.

Finally, Argyle returned to Home Park and allowed the supporters to pay homage to their heroes. Huge queues formed long before the kick-off, determined not to miss out on such an occasion. Before the start, captain Titmuss was presented with an enormous pasty and watched as it was first laid in the goal net before being moved to a safer position behind the goal. A brass band played with some gusto and the crowd cheered the antics of the Argyle mascot, a young man with his face blackened and wearing a green and black top hat that had seen better days.

The match itself was an anticlimax. Opponents Watford did their best to spoil the party by taking the lead. Sloan equalised. A few minutes later, Black scored what was to prove the winner. The final whistle eventually came, signalling a mass invasion of the playing area.

Various presentations took place with cheques being handed to Black, for his benefit fund, and to Jack from the Supporters Club. The crowd refused to disperse, calling for the appearance of skipper Titmuss. Only when told that Titmuss was in the bath did they slowly but triumphantly drift away to take their places by the roadside, where later they were able to cheer their heroes once again as the team were taken on a coach tour of the city. At last Argyle could call themselves a Second Division side. The doubters had been silenced.

# Two

# 1949-50 (Relegated to Division 3 South)

Since the end of World War Two, life had been a constant struggle for Plymouth Argyle Football Club. But rather than bemoan the fact that relegation had narrowly been avoided for the past three seasons, everyone was merely grateful they had a football team to follow.

The war had had a more devastating effect on Argyle than on almost any other league club. The city, with its naval installations, had been a prime target for enemy bombs. Home Park had not escaped. In early 1941, a bomb had landed nearby, all but destroying the main grandstand. Stories abounded that a crater had ruined the pitch, although this was not true. The reality was that the club had a name, a ruined stadium, no money, the registration of a handful of players, but little else. Thanks, in the main, to the enterprise and endeavour of Jack Tresadern, the man who had succeeded Robert Jack as manager in 1938, the club, quite literally, rose from the ashes.

Tresadern had emerged from the war with the rank of captain and would put his leadership qualities to good use in rebuilding the club and its team. Patience, however, was a not a virtue much in evidence among the directors. They were unimpressed by some of their manager's signings, notably centre-half John Oakes, who was brought to the club on a free transfer from Charlton at the advanced age of 42. Six points from a possible eighteen at the start of the 1947-48 season sounded Tresadern's death knell. Opinions were divided as to whether he jumped or was pushed, although the terseness of the statement announcing his departure suggested the latter.

The appointment of assistant manager Jimmy Rae to the hot seat was a popular one. The Scot had arrived at Home Park in 1932 and became a regular in the full-back berth until the outbreak of war. His skilful and intelligent approach to the art of defending had brought him to the verge of international honours. He was well-liked by players and supporters. Results improved sufficiently to avoid relegation. The following season, 1948-49, saw the side survive an injury crisis to finish twentieth, avoiding the drop by one place.

In his pre-season notes, Rae rightly identified the lack of goals as the main cause of Argyle's struggles. Centre-forward Maurice Tadman and winger Bill Strauss had scored over half of the fairly meagre tally of 49. Four new players arrived in the form of goalkeeper Les Major from Leicester, as cover for the indomitable Bill Shortt, half-back John Porteous from Alloa, inside-forward George Willis from Brighton, and South

African-born forward Stan Williams, a former colleague of Strauss at Aberdeen.

Rae also boosted his backroom staff in an attempt to improve fitness levels. The ever loyal Bill Harper remained in situ as first-team trainer, but joining him were former Argyle half-back George Reed as assistant trainer, and Hugh Ross, a stately, balding figure who looked better suited to a solicitor's office than barking out instructions on the training ground. He had impressive credentials though, being a former trainer to the Welsh side and, more recently, Preston. He was given the rather grand and all encompassing title of 'Supervisor of Training and Coaching'.

Financially, the club still had to watch every penny. The ravages of war would take many years to rectify. The ever active Supporters Club donated £1,000 and urged more fans to pay their one shilling membership fee. From day one, Rae had selection problems. Wing-half Alec Machin had broken a leg the previous April and would be out until Christmas at the earliest, and inside-forward George Dews was still engaged on cricket duties with Worcestershire.

Despite struggling over previous seasons, Argyle pulled in vast crowds. The public, starved of any form of entertainment during the war years, flocked to watch any form of live sport. Many more people were also in employment, particularly in Plymouth, where thousands were utilised in rebuilding the bombed city. It was not only football that was undergoing a boom. Other sports such as cricket and speedway drew levels of support that have never been repeated.

Almost 25,000 attended the opening game of the season against Bradford Park Avenue. Home Park itself had undergone little rebuilding since being devastated by German bombs. There was no covered accommodation for supporters, apart from an area of the Devonport End, and facilities for the players consisted of temporary dressing rooms and very little else. It was an unwelcoming stadium. The Argyle directors had made an application to the Ministry of Works to build a new 2,500-seat grandstand at a cost of £20,000 but the application had been refused as approval was only being given to projects designed to prevent danger to the public. The match itself ended in a 1-1 draw, with Argyle's goal coming off the boot of Bradford full-back Ronnie Hepworth.

The match saw Tadman suffer an injury and render himself unfit for a daunting Monday evening trip to White Hart Lane. Willis was drafted in for his debut against a Spurs side that would, over the next two years, take British football by storm. Under manager Arthur Rowe, the Lilywhites were pioneers of the 'push and run' era, a style which Rowe introduced involving constant movement and passing, although he was not fond of the term. Of course, it still needed players with the ability to carry out such methods and Spurs had them in abundance. Ted Ditchburn, Alf Ramsey,

Len Duquemin, Eddie Baily, Ron Burgess and Bill Nicholson would become legendary figures in Tottenham history. Argyle had no answer, few sides did, and, in front of over 41,000, were defeated 1-4 with Williams getting his first Argyle goal. Spurs would go on to win the Division Two title and, with basically the same squad, the League Championship itself a year later.

Tadman remained on the injured list for the trip to Chesterfield. At least Dews was available again after his cricketing exploits had finished for the season, and Rae also brought in wingers Gordon Astall and Alex Govan. It would be Govan's only appearance of the season due to National Service, something that interrupted many a player's career. Being a footballer was no excuse. How would today's 'superstars' react to a bit of 'square bashing?' Argyle lost 0-2 at Saltergate and already the question was being asked – who would score goals if Tadman was not available?

Few expected much, except thrilling football, from the Bank Holiday visit of Spurs. The visitors ran out 2-0 winners, not a bad result in the context of the rest of the season, particularly as Shortt was also injured and Major given his debut, but a 0-3 defeat at home to West Ham a few days later prompted Rae to ring the changes.

Tadman was fit again but several others were injured. The diminutive Ernie Edds was brought in at inside-forward but made little difference. A single Sheffield Wednesday goal by Eddie Quigley condemned Argyle to a third home defeat in eleven days and bottom place in the league.

A midweek trip to Bury at least saw Argyle score again, but the Shakers replied with five. The defeat cost centre-half and captain Ray Goddard his place and ultimately his Argyle career. It would be his last game in a Pilgrims shirt and he would eventually transfer to Exeter. Stan Dixon, regarded more as a 'stopper', was recalled to the No 5 shirt as Argyle remained up north and travelled to Hull. The Tigers were managed by the legendary Raich Carter and had won the previous season's Third Division (North) title by a country mile. They were a side in a hurry and attracting huge crowds as well. Tadman finally opened his season's account, adding to Strauss's goal, but Hull struck four times to enhance Argyle's quickly growing reputation as the division's whipping boys.

The same Argyle duo found the net again a week later as Rae's side, with Shortt back in the fold, finally won a match, Brentford being the victims. Normal service was resumed at Ewood Park, where Argyle ended up goalless and pointless after the South African Bob Priday scored the only goal needed to give Blackburn the spoils.

Argyle then embarked on what was to prove to be their best run of results for the season. Rae kept faith with the same eleven that was victorious against Brentford for nine consecutive matches, and clearly believed he had found a combination that had gelled. Strauss was again on target as a point was taken from Bramall Lane, where Sheffield United had started the season impressively.

Despite the indifferent start to the season, the crowds were still flocking to Home Park and were finally rewarded as Argyle swept four goals past Grimsby. Once again Strauss and Tadman were on the scoresheet but Dews and half-back George Taylor also found their scoring boots. An aerial photograph of a packed Home Park shows the immediate surroundings have changed little since, but it is strange to note how few cars were parked in the adjoining car park. Motor cars were still considered a luxury item and public transport was still very much the preferred mode of getting from one place to another.

QPR had also started the season badly, and Argyle went to Loftus Road confident of a good result. Two more goals from Tadman, who was now in prime form, secured two points and set up Argyle for what was the most keenly anticipated fixture of the season.

The visit of Preston saw more than 32,000 squeeze into Home Park. The main reason was to see the legendary Tom Finney in the flesh. The England winger was one of the most famous and respected players in the land but, of course, in those days there was no television coverage of matches and supporters in the main were reduced to reading about their heroes in the newspapers. Finney was capable of winning a game on his own but Argyle had a plan hatched by coach Ross, who had recently been in the employ of the Lancashire club. The scheme seemed simple enough. Deny Finney the ball. It was easier said than done but Taylor was asked to clamp down on Finney's main supplier, right-half Bobby Beattie. Should Finney get the ball, his marker, full-back Pat Jones was asked to curb his natural instinct and not tackle, but merely delay Finney from crossing the ball to allow the defence to organise in numbers.

Preston also possessed a threat on the left wing, in the form of another England international, Bobby Langton. There was apparently no such elaborate plan to shackle his talents and if there was it was soon obsolete, as hard-as-nails right-back George Silk clattered into Langton early on and rendered him a virtual passenger for the remainder of the game.

The stop-Finney plan worked perfectly and the icing on the Argyle cake was supplied by Tadman, who scored the only goal of the game with just five minutes remaining. The goal sparked a furious late response from Preston, and the hero of the day, Jones, headed off the line with Shortt beaten.

Jones' display captured the headlines and it was well-deserved. The word 'consistent' was surely invented to describe the rugged full-back. He had broken into the Argyle side in May 1947 and had filled the No 3 shirt every game since. Few wingers got the better of him. He would become an Argyle institution.

After three wins on the trot, few would have believed that Argyle would win only four more games during the season. Tadman maintained his hot streak by scoring again in a draw at Swansea, where Frank Squires registered his first goal of the season against his former club. A week later, Tadman made it five goals in four games by scoring against Leeds, but the Yorkshiremen scored twice as Argyle slid to defeat.

Argyle continued to perform better against top sides. Southampton were potential promotion candidates but Argyle went to The Dell and secured a thrilling 3-3 draw. Tadman again suffered an injury and was omitted for the next game, at home to Coventry, with Eric Bryant brought in for his debut. Bryant was the possible answer to Argyle's goalscoring problem. He had been a member of the Yeovil side that shocked mighty Sunderland in the FA Cup and scored 71 goals for the Somerset side the previous season. He had already scored twenty times in ten games for Yeovil before his transfer to Home Park.

Bryant found Division Two football a different proposition though, and barely got a look in. Williams scored but Coventry struck twice to ensure a winless November for the Greens.

December would prove to be a busy and crucial month. A draw at Luton was reasonable enough. It was the turn of Porteous to open his Argyle account. Then Dews scored both Argyle's goals in a home draw with Barnsley. The blond-haired inside-forward was beginning to show the form Argyle fans knew he was capable of.

There were high hopes of a second away win when Argyle travelled to Bradford. The Yorkshire side had vied for bottom place with Argyle for most of the season and their attack was as goal-shy. Argyle's wingers, Strauss and Williams were on target, but Bradford scored three times to put a dent in the Pilgrims' revival hopes.

In the meantime, Edds had departed the scene. Argyle were delighted to accept an offer of £8,500 for a player who was now no longer in the frame for a regular starting place, despite a successful spell earlier in his Argyle career.

The loss at Bradford convinced Rae that his defence needed tightening. He had been trailing Sheffield United's centre-half Jack Chisholm and eventually secured his services. The cash from the Edds transfer was soon eaten up, with Chisholm costing an Argyle club record fee of £12,000.

Argyle fans got their first glimpse of the new man on Christmas Eve as Chesterfield visited Home Park. They soon realised why Chisholm was more commonly known as 'Jumbo'. At 6ft 2in and weighing 14st, mobility was never likely to be his main asset. He was also bow-legged and had had both cartilages removed from his knees, but he was an imposing figure. He maintained the view that a centre-half was there to defend at all costs and he would rarely stray from his defensive duties.

Chisholm was granted hero status in his first game. Tadman had given Argyle the lead when Jones pumped a high ball into the penalty area and Spireites' keeper Ray Middleton spilled the ball. Just before the interval Chisholm headed a high clearance and the impact of the heavy leather ball left the big man staggering with blood pouring from a head wound. After treatment, he left the field.

The second half started with no sign of Jumbo, but two minutes later, to great cheers, he appeared pitch-side, his head swathed in bandages, having had three stitches inserted in his forehead. Heading the ball only when necessary, Chisholm continued to direct operations, but after 55 minutes dangerous winger Matt Costello equalised. With nine minutes remaining, Squires fired in a shot to secure the points for Argyle.

Also making his debut in the same match was Irishman Tony McShane who had been on trial and impressed sufficiently to be taken on. But Chisholm's bravery had immediately endeared himself to the Home Park crowd. It was to be a quality that would never wane. No one realised it at the time, but his signing would prove to be a major turning point in the fortunes of the club.

Chisholm had little time to recover and took his place for the back-to-back matches with Cardiff. The Bluebirds didn't score many and conceded fewer, so a goalless draw at Home Park was no great surprise. A day later, in front of a massive Ninian Park crowd of 35,000, Argyle went down by a solitary goal. Goals from Strauss and Dews secured a New Year's Eve draw at West Ham, but the supporters' minds were already turning to the FA Cup.

Argyle had been given the plum tie of the third round, a home match with none other than Wolves, one of the country's top sides and current Cup holders. The match had created huge interest since the draw was made and everyone, it appeared, wanted the chance to see international stars such as Billy Wright, Bert Williams and Jesse Pye.

Chisholm, it seems, had quickly settled into his new surroundings. As well as being captain on the field, he soon became spokesman for the team off it. There was a suggestion of the players receiving a bonus if they caused a Cup upset. The board originally refuted the idea, but when confronted by Chisholm, had a change of heart.

Before the match, the famous trophy was paraded around the pitch although, somewhat disrespectfully, it was strapped to a stretcher. It gave the Plymouth fans a unique chance to see the prestigious silverware but at the same time served as a stark reminder of what their side was about to face. By the final whistle it was the Wolves stars who were breathing a sigh of relief. There was a deafening roar from the 40,000 full house when the home side took a shock eighth-minute lead. Squires, full of tricks, cracked a twenty-yard shot onto the crossbar. The ball fell to Tadman and then

Williams, who shot past his namesake. From then on, the Greens worked like Trojans to defend their lead. Dougall and McShane in particular were everywhere. The clock ticked into the last fifteen minutes when, from a corner, a scramble ensued and Sammy Smyth headed past Shortt from close range.

If Rae, the players and fans were disappointed, the directors were not. They saw pound signs flashing in front of their eyes. Receipts for the home tie totalled more than £8,000, a record for a third round FA Cup-tie anywhere, and another windfall was guaranteed from the replay.

Hasty arrangements had to be made, particularly by the fans who intended travelling to Molineux. The replay was scheduled for the following Wednesday afternoon, and more than 2,000 Plymouth supporters set out on the nineteen-hour round trip. From the off, Argyle continued where they left off, as the half-backs, in particular, dictated the play. Despite being without the injured Jones, the Pilgrims' defence rarely looked troubled and Wolves were happy to go in at half-time level.

One man turned the game. England winger Johnny Hancocks was only 5ft 4in and wore Size 2 boots, but on his day he was unstoppable. In the 58th minute he set up Roy Swinbourne for the opening goal. Less than a minute later, Swinbourne was tackled by Dougall and a penalty harshly awarded. Hancocks made no mistake. With the stuffing now knocked out of them, Argyle conceded a third. Again Hancocks was the provider and Smyth the executioner. It was rough justice. Argyle had done themselves proud and won many admirers.

Buoyed by their performances, Argyle continued their impressive form at Hillsborough. Sheffield Wednesday were second in the league but well beaten on the day. Squires was again the man in form with two goals, one of which was out of the ordinary. Despite finding himself in a crowded penalty area, he outwitted four defenders before scoring.

Hopes of pulling away from the basement were dashed a week later as an impressive Hull side went away from Home Park with a 3-1 victory. The fit-again Porteous was preferred to McShane, and again Squires was on target, but remarkably it would be the last goal the Argyle supporters would see their side score at home until Easter Monday, some eleven weeks hence.

With no fixture scheduled for the following week, due to the FA Cup, the players had an opportunity to recharge their batteries before facing a trip to the capital to take on Brentford, where they gained the first of three successive 0-0 draws, proving at least that Chisholm had plugged a gap.

Stalemate at Filbert Street against Leicester was a respectable result in a match that was advanced to ease a hectic Easter schedule. The Foxes were hardly setting the division alight themselves, but the previous week had caused one of the upsets of the season by going to White Hart Lane and beating the all-conquering Spurs 2-0 in their own back yard in front of more than 60,000 fans.

A home draw against Blackburn, who included former Pilgrim Edds in their side, was followed by a 0-1 home defeat by Sheffield United. The Blades were neck and neck with their neighbours Sheffield Wednesday, chasing the second promotion place behind Spurs. Tadman was injured again, but the Argyle No 9 had hardly exuded confidence in front of goal himself, having scored just once since mid-November.

The barren run was ended by Dews, whose two goals at Grimsby were enough to secure a draw. The match marked the debut of centre-forward Harold Dobbie. Small of stature, there were few quicker than Dobbie. His goalscoring record for Middlesbrough reserves had been impressive but his first-team chances at Ayresome Park had been limited. If Argyle's supporters thought that Dews' two goals had ended the drought, they were wrong. It represented no more than a brief shower.

One aspect of the club that could not be criticised was the support. Despite the lack of goals and entertainment, the crowds kept on coming. The next home match, against QPR, attracted more than 23,000, despite the expectation that another scoreless game was on the cards. Rangers had scored even fewer goals than Argyle over the season, but on this occasion had remembered to bring their scoring boots with them as they grabbed a 2-0 win.

With some trepidation, Argyle travelled to Deepdale, no doubt with another plan as to how to subdue Tom Finney. As it was, they didn't have to worry as the England winger was injured and unable to play. One man who was sorry was Jones. The full-back was relishing another opportunity to pit his wits against the great man. Without Finney, North End lacked inventiveness and it was Argyle who were more pleased to come away with a point.

A single-goal defeat at home to Swansea was a bitter blow and the survival chances were growing slimmer by the week. There was still some optimism from Rae, however. As he rightly pointed out, there were still a number of teams involved in the relegation dogfight. Despite the struggles, only a minority of supporters doubted Rae's ability to pull things round, and called for his head. The Scotsman still had the support of the directors and the players.

Argyle had seven games to play, four of them at home. Victory in each match on their own soil and the odd point from the away games would, in all likelihood, ensure survival, but again injuries limited Rae's team selection. Both Squires and Dews were crocked and not considered for the visit to Coventry, where Argyle received a comprehensive 0-3 beating. Local boy Paddy Blatchford was given a rare opportunity on the wing but saw little of the ball.

Luton at home was now a must-win game. The Hatters were not out of the woods themselves and were scrapping for every point. Again, Argyle were woefully short of confidence in front of goal, which was not surprising perhaps, considering their recent tally of just two goals in ten games. Luton were delighted with their goalless draw, the Greens were not. The writing was now on the wall.

A smaller than usual attendance for the Easter Monday clash with Leicester suggested that even some of the faithful fans had lost heart, but the players battled and a Strauss goal boosted confidence. Dews scored another, with Leicester's top scorer, Jack Lee, replying. The two points kept hopes alive but their fellow strugglers also picked up points. The battle to avoid the two relegation places was now between Argyle, Bradford, QPR, and West Ham, with the two London clubs having the dual advantage of more points and better goal-averages.

Argyle travelled to Elland Road and gained a battling point, thanks to a rare goal from right-back Paddy Ratcliffe. It was the Irishman's first for the club and the reward for some consistent performances since he had made the No 2 shirt his own earlier in the season. The draw also put a severe dent in Leeds' promotion hopes. Spurs had already clinched the title but the Yorkshire club were now all but out of the race for Division One status.

One of the sides definitely in contention were Southampton, the next visitors to Home Park. Both sides were desperate for a win for very different reasons, so yet another goalless draw was of no use to anyone. Once the season was over, the Saints would rue the dropped point at Home Park, as they would miss out on promotion by goal-average only. The draw also made it virtually impossible for Argyle to stay up. The following Saturday relegation was confirmed after a dismal showing at Barnsley. Bryant at least showed what he was capable of in front of goal, but the Tykes scored four times in front of a pitifully small crowd.

And so, Argyle returned to Home Park for their final game, for the time being at least, as a Second Division side. Bury were the uninterested visitors, having only recently extricated themselves from the relegation maelstrom. In front of the smallest Home Park crowd of the season, Bryant and Blatchford scored the goals which meant the small consolation of avoiding bottom spot. At the final whistle, the team exited to muted applause.

Argyle's pitiful lack of goals had been the overriding factor in their demise. Tadman, expected to be the main source, had not scored since Christmas. Dews and Strauss had chipped in with useful contributions, but there were times when it was difficult to see where the next goal was coming from. Rae was criticised in some quarters for not signing another forward but, as ever, no one was prepared to sell players who could score goals. He had gambled on the likes of Dobbie and Bryant but they were both inexperienced. A season in a lower league would benefit their development. Certainly Rae had acted expeditiously to plug his leaking defence. The signing of Chisholm had been a masterstroke. The statistics tell their own story. Chisholm arrived at the halfway point of the season. Before then, Argyle had conceded 41 goals compared to 24 in the second half of the campaign. It was not only on the field where his presence was felt. A former guardsman, he was a natural leader and his teammates rallied to him. He was their spokesman when dealing with off-field matters as well, and would go on to be a significant figure in the history of the club.

As for Rae, he vowed to continue in the job. In modern times of course, he would have been on his way out, having paid the ultimate price of relegation, but the directors and the players had faith in him.

# THREE

# 1951-52 (Promoted to Division 2)

The 1950-51 season had started in all too familiar fashion. Argyle won only three of their first ten matches and scored only eight times, but a sudden transformation came over the side. The defence virtually picked itself and the regular selection of wingers Alex Govan and Gordon Astall created chances for Tadman and the goals started to flow. Tadman was like a man possessed. Having been omitted for the early matches he was back with a bang and ended the season with 26 league and Cup goals. The Argyle supporters, starved of the opportunity to cheer a goal for so long, were now reaching for the throat lozenges. Five against Aldershot and Swindon, seven against Colchester and six at Brighton were among the highlights. On two occasions, Tadman scored four in a game. The outcome was fourth place, seven points behind runners-up Norwich. Argyle also reached the third round of the Cup and for the second successive season faced Wolves in front of a full house at Home Park. There was no shock result but Argyle once again gave a good account of themselves before losing by the odd goal in three.

Since relegation, the squad was largely unchanged. Only Frank Squires – sold to Grimsby, and Stan Williams, who had joined Dundee as part of the deal that saw the arrival of inside-forward Peter Rattray – had left. Jimmy Rae was still in charge and retained Bill Harper as one of his coaches. Two former Argyle half-backs, George Reed and George Taylor, were also on the backroom staff as trainers.

One thing that was changing was the appearance of the Home Park stadium. Work had started on the building of a new grandstand to replace the one destroyed during the war. At last, Home Park was beginning to look like a stadium again. The structure was not complete, but one third was deemed safe enough to accommodate spectators. Other improvements were made to the access of the ground, particularly at the Barn Park End, and a donation of £500 from the Supporters Club was utilised on this project.

Confidence was high as Argyle embarked on the 1951-52 season with a visit to Leyton Orient. Bedecked in their familiar green shirts with white sleeves, Argyle started the match as clear favourites, based on the previous season's form, but Rae was without the injured Tadman and the still cricketing Dews. In a disjointed performance, Orient's single goal was enough to settle the result.

The drop to Division Three had affected attendances, and the regular 20,000-plus crowds of the Division Two days were now the exception rather than the rule. But the 14,000 who attended the opening home game against Crystal Palace certainly had their money's worth. With Tadman and Dews available, and Strauss replacing Govan on the left wing, Argyle quickly found the rhythm that made them such an entertaining side to watch. Only Tadman of the forwards failed to score as Palace had little answer to Argyle's attacking flair. Dews in particular took little time reverting to soccer mode, and scored twice as well as covering virtually every blade of the virgin turf.

Three days later, Walsall visited Home Park and again put up little resistance. Tadman made up for missing out against Palace with a brace, and goalkeeper Bill Shortt was a virtual spectator once more, even having time to chat to supporters behind the goal whilst play was in motion.

Another Rattray effort clinched the 'double' over Crystal Palace but just as pleasing was the solidity of the defence. Full-backs Paddy Ratcliffe and Pat Jones, and the imperious Jumbo Chisholm, were quickly dubbed the 'Three Musketeers'. Potential trouble was quickly dampened, while behind them they had Shortt who, at 5ft 8in, was small by goalkeeping standards but had few peers in the lower divisions. Time and again, dangerous crosses would be plucked from the air by his shovel-like hands.

Identical scorelines followed. Argyle won 3-1 at Shrewsbury with goals from Dews, Tadman and a Ratcliffe penalty. Four days later, the same trio scored again in a victory over Colchester, who replied through a Jimmy Elder penalty. Argyle found themselves leading the division.

The momentum continued with a home win over Aldershot. The Plymouth public were wakening to the fact that their city's football side was perhaps a bit special. The attendance rose to over 18,000 for what was hardly the most attractive fixture of the season. By now, Rae's team selection was occupying little of his time. An injury to Rattray allowed Neil Dougall to regain his place but otherwise it was 'as you were'. Dougall, a Scottish international would have walked into most Third Division sides, but his spell on the sidelines only underlined the manner in which Argyle were playing, making it difficult for Rae to leave anyone else out.

With successive games at Colchester and Watford, the match at Layer Road was put back 24 hours to shorten Argyle's time away. The U's were in only their second season of league football, having been elected into the Football League when it was expanded to encompass 92 clubs in 1950, but had made a favourable impression. Nevertheless, victory over Argyle by a single goal scored by Vic Keeble constituted a major surprise.

At Watford, Govan was restored to the No 11 shirt, which he would make his own. The winger was on target too, as were Tadman and fellow flankman Astall, as the Greens maintained their lead at the top.

It was now the turn of the injured Johnny Porteous to miss out, but there was a nasty shock in store for the 25,000 who packed Home Park for the match with Bristol Rovers. Argyle suffered what would prove to be their only home defeat of the season, as Rovers won with goals from Vic Lambden and a disputed penalty by Ray Warren.

A draw at Ipswich would normally be considered a reasonable result, but in the context of the season so far, the players were miffed. Town's goals were scored by Jimmy Roberts and Neil Myles, with Dews and Rattray continuing their impressive strike-rate in reply. Argyle's reputation as a free-flowing attacking side now preceded them, and opposing sides were intent more on stopping the Pilgrims than concentrating on their own game.

Normal service was resumed with an untroubled home win over Port Vale but despite a goal from Chisholm, a collectors' piece in itself, defeat at Northampton still left shreds of doubt in the minds of some that perhaps Argyle were still vulnerable.

The next match, against Reading, was keenly anticipated. The Royals were staking their claim to be Argyle's main rivals and had been banging in goals at will. The real danger-man was Ron Blackman, who cost Reading the princely transfer fee of £10 and the promise of a friendly with his former team, Gosport. Blackman went on to become Reading's greatest ever goalscorer and would end up with 39 goals in this particular campaign alone.

Rae suffered a double blow when Tadman and Shortt were declared unfit. Rattray switched to centre-forward and George Willis was given a rare opportunity at inside-left. In goal, Argyle had an able deputy in Les Major, who was largely kept out of the first-team scene by the consistency of 'Shortty'. The match did not disappoint. Both sides knew nothing other than to play open attacking football and, at the final count, Argyle won by the odd goal in five.

The sick and wounded were back in time for the trip to Newport. The Welsh side were adept at scoring but were also generous in defence. Sure enough, the match proved to be a high-scoring affair with the two sides sharing six goals. Cliff Birch, George Beattie and Beriah Moore were the men on target for the homesters with a Tadman brace and Astall replying.

Southend were comfortably despatched before Argyle went to Dean Court and scraped through a tough encounter with Bournemouth, with goals from Dews and Govan enough to cancel out a Jack Cross effort.

Next up was Millwall. The sides were due to meet again the following week in the FA Cup and when Argyle romped home 5-0 the Cup result looked a foregone conclusion. On their own patch, however, the Lions were a different proposition. The result at Home Park had not reflected their league form, which had seen them move into the top five, and the Pilgrims' Cup record since the war was far from impressive, showing just two wins from the eleven Cup-ties contested since 1945. A single goal was enough to put Millwall through, although Rae perhaps did not despair for long, as it allowed him to concentrate fully on league matters.

Argyle were quickly back on track with a 4-2 win over Gillingham, before they made the short trip to local rivals Torquay. United were a club in turmoil, having won just two of their opening sixteen games. That bad run had left them bottom of the table and without a manager after the resignation of Alex Massie. Eric Webber had been appointed player-manager and had begun to revive their fortunes, but few expected them to do anything except lose to the division's front runners, particularly as they had gone down 0-5 at Bristol Rovers seven days earlier.

Of course, as usual, the form book went out of the window when it came to a local derby. On a Plainmoor mudbath, the Gulls gave everything they had. Rattray scored both Argyle goals, but two strikes from the wonderfully named Marwood Marchant and one from Sammy Collins was enough to ignite Torquay's season. It would see them eventually finish mid-table.

After a week off, Rae's side travelled to struggling Walsall. Porteous was fit again and displaced the unfortunate Tony McShane in the No 6 shirt. McShane had done little wrong but was now the odd man out of a fully fit twelve. Compared to the Walsall pitch, Plainmoor had been a bowling green. The first ten minutes at Walsall was the worst anyone could recall watching. Suddenly Argyle, and in particular wingers Govan and Astall, quite literally found their feet. The wide men were fed a regular diet of passes and in the grassier areas out wide caused havoc. After fifteen minutes, Govan latched onto a misdirected clearance by Henry Walters. Seven minutes later, home centre-half Ron Russon diverted a Tadman cross past his own keeper. Walters, having a match to forget, then blundered again, resulting in Tadman scoring. By half-time, the Argyle No 9 had scored his second.

The Saddlers put up more a fight in the second half with centre-forward John Bridgett scoring. In the 62nd minute, Tadman completed his hat-trick, sidefooting into an empty net after Astall had lured Jack Lewis off his line. Bridgett scored the Saddlers' second near the end but it had been one of Argyle's most dominant performances.

Back in the 1950s, Christmas Day meant football first, roast turkey second. Home and away matches against Bristol City promised more bumper crowds, although the attendance of 17,498 for the home clash was disappointing. Presumably many thought the result a foregone conclusion. City had been inconsistent and hovered around mid-table. By now, of course, Plymouth were clear favourites to win every match they played, but their opponents raised their game. Rattray continued his golden spell with two more, taking his tally to seven in the last five league games, but the match ended 2-2 with young John Atyeo and flying winger Jimmy Rogers scoring for City. At that time, Atyeo was still only a part-timer, studying to become a surveyor, but he would go on to become a Bristol legend. A day later, the points were shared again at Ashton Gate, with City captain Dennis Roberts and Tadman getting the goals.

The final match of 1951 saw Shrewsbury demolished 6-1 at Home Park. Argyle's inside-forwards, Dews and Rattray, ran the show and were both rewarded with a brace of goals. The win set Argyle on a run of victories during which time they played some stunning football with every player in the side on top of his game. Credit, too, had to go to Rae, who was now justified in his decision to keep the team together.

Aldershot provided some stubborn resistance before goals from Dews and Tadman gave the Greens a 2-1 win. Then came the first meeting of the season with great rivals Exeter. The Grecians had won both encounters the previous season and again put up a spirited display. Scotsman Angus Mackay scored the City goal, but Dews and Rattray continued their prolific form with the strikes that maintained Argyle's lead at the top.

The second of three successive home games promised to be one of the toughest tests of the season. Norwich had narrowly missed out on promotion and were now again in contention. For the fourth match in a row, Dews was on target and Astall scored twice. Norwich could only reply once, through top scorer Roy Hollis.

Watford were brushed aside 3-1 before the only home defeat of the season, by Bristol Rovers, was avenged. Goals from Rattray and a typical blockbuster from Dougall reversed the 1-2 scoreline from earlier in the campaign. The Rovers victory completed a record of winning every game in January. If Argyle weren't previously everyone's choice to win the division, they were now. The run continued with successive home victories over Ipswich and Swindon. Argyle weren't just sneaking victories, they were overwhelming opponents. No one, it seemed, had any answer to the all-out attacking style that Rae had instilled. The side could score goals with regularity but, just as significantly, now looked more solid than ever in defence, where Chisholm continued to put the fear of God into opponents and occasionally his own teammates. The return from injury of Porteous had also tightened things up.

The run had to end sometime, and it did so in somewhat farcical circumstances. The squad travelled to Port Vale to find the pitch covered in snow. Mist also began to descend over Vale Park, although referee Mr Griffiths decided that the match would go ahead. The conditions stymied Argyle's usual pacy attack and the home side adapted better, with centre-forward and player-manager Freddie Steele a constant source of danger. A minute before the interval, Albert Mullard gave Vale a deserved lead. During half-time, the fog degenerated into a real pea-souper. As the second half commenced, it was impossible for the spectators to see the whole width, let alone length of the pitch. The fog continued to thicken but Mr Griffiths, seemingly blessed with x-ray vision, let the game continue. Despite Vale's lead, the home fans became increasingly exasperated and annoyed at what they saw as a waste of their admission money and called for the game to be abandoned. It wasn't, and there were no further goals, at least as far as anyone knew, a fact the assembled press corps were at least grateful for, as they were unable to see almost anything from their vantage point in the stand.

There was another minor hiccup when the Pilgrims could only manage a draw at Swindon, with the ever-impressive Dews getting both Argyle goals. Sadly, Dougall suffered a nasty spinal injury that would keep him out for the remainder of the season. Normal service was quickly resumed with a 2-0 win over Northampton, during which Argyle rarely had to get out of second gear. With McShane also injured, Dougall's absence meant a rare appearance for Syd Rundle, who had been a part of the Argyle set up since football resumed after the war, but had been unable to command a regular place.

Rundle retained his place for what appeared to be the most difficult match of the season. Reading had been Argyle's closest rivals since August and had continued to score goals with alarming regularity. With over 28,000 somehow squeezing into the compact if not bijou Elm Park, for what was dubbed the Third Division (South) match of the season, the atmosphere was electric. For once, the Argyle attack was blunted and the 2-0 win for the home side continued to give the Royals renewed hope in their pursuit of the Pilgrims.

That defeat was only Argyle's sixth of the season. One of their great strengths was the ability to bounce back from defeat. A loss only served to strengthen their resolve and they had not lost two games in succession, as Newport found to their cost. The Welsh side were no pushovers, having maintained a top-eight place for much of the season, but found themselves on the end of another Argyle onslaught. In the end they were lucky to have only conceded five.

An easy win over Leyton Orient and a point at Southend left Argyle on the brink of the title. It was now theirs to lose. Bournemouth came to Home Park and put up only minor resistance. The quaintly named Tommy Tippett scored for the Cherries, but Argyle replied with four. Dews continued his remarkable form with two goals and threatened Tadman's mantle as top scorer. Wingers Astall and Govan added the others.

Despite Argyle's comfortable lead, and the end of the season looming ever nearer, there were still a few potential banana skins among the remaining fixtures. An away match at Millwall was, on paper, one of the more difficult. The Lions were one of the sides who, mathematically at least, could still catch Argyle but on the day, cajoled continuously as ever by Chisholm, the Greens were simply too professional and gained ample revenge for their FA Cup exit at the Den back in November.

Boosted by the fact that nearest rivals Reading had lost their previous match, the supporters, at least, believed Argyle were up. Over 31,000 made their way to Home Park to see their heroes take on third-placed Brighton. Argyle were, by now, five points clear of Reading.

If there was a script, Brighton hadn't read it. After 21 minutes, Chisholm was punished for a foul. From the free-kick Johnny McNichol slid the ball past Shortt. A minute later Ratcliffe was penalised for another foul. Another free-kick, and lo and behold another goal, this time via McNichol's head. Argyle were visibly rattled but a Ratcliffe penalty just before the interval settled the nerves. They came out a different side in the second half, but when Tadman missed two easy chances it looked as though it was one of those days. The never-say-die spirit came to the fore fifteen minutes from time. An Astall corner was met by the flying Tadman, whose bullet header registered the 100th goal of Argyle's season.

The loss of a point was tempered by the news that Reading had lost again. The lead was now seven points, with Brighton and Norwich a point further back and the Canaries having a game in hand.

The local derby at Exeter looked a guaranteed two points. The Grecians had struggled for the whole season and were in a fight to avoid the ignominy of finishing last. A month earlier they had appointed a new manager in Norman Kirkham, who had yet to see his side win. As ever, form counted for nothing when near neighbours clash and it was City who gave their new boss his first win with a goal by Douglas Regan.

Victory at Gillingham all but clinched the title. A win at Brighton would remove all doubts, but it would not be easy. In front of the Seagulls' biggest crowd of the season, Argyle started nervously. The home side spurned three easy chances and Jimmy Sirrel hit the woodwork before Billy Reed intercepted a woefully weak Ratcliffe back-pass to leave Shortt no chance. With the next attack, Argyle equalised. Dews headed against the crossbar and then scrambled in the rebound. Govan then scored with a header but after half-time Brighton came back again through Ken Bennett.

The match was still evenly poised. A draw for Argyle would not have been a disaster but with fifteen minutes remaining the moment arrived. In a season when Argyle had scored many fine goals as a result of fast-flowing football, the one that clinched the title was bizarre. Astall collected the ball and, never one to shy away from an effort at goal, struck a full-blooded drive. The ball hit the woodwork but rebounded onto the foot of Brighton goalkeeper John Ball and into the net. The winger was engulfed by his jubilant teammates. Marshalled by Chisholm, the defence held out and the final whistle brought joyous scenes among the Argyle squad and the small band of supporters who had made the midweek trip.

The team returned to Plymouth to a heroes' welcome as thousands lined the route into the city. Two days later, the fans had the opportunity to pay homage to the new champions. Over 28,000 packed into Home Park for the encounter with Torquay. The Gulls lined up to applaud Chisholm and his men onto the pitch and then set out to spoil the party. They were one of the form sides of the division and had taken eighteen points out of a possible 26. The run had seen some strange results, including a 9-0 win over Swindon and 6-1 against Aldershot, before being beaten 0-7 at Norwich two weeks later. After half an hour, the visitors were two goals to the good, through Ron Shaw and former Pilgrim Ernie Edds. After 36 minutes, Dews shot past George Webber in the Torquay goal and it was left to Tadman to level things in the second half with a shot on the turn, a move that was quickly becoming his trademark.

As Chisholm lifted the trophy it was time to reflect on the progress that had been made in such a short time since the end of a war that had left the club as little more than a shell.

It was all too easy to forget that there was still one more match to play, involving the longest trip of the season, to Norwich. Before then, the players said a fond farewell to Dews, who was again off to don the whites for another season of cricket with Worcestershire.

The game at Carrow Road was inevitably something of an anticlimax. Two goals by Ron Ashman and another by Johnny Summers inflicted Argyle's worst defeat of the season, and their failure to score meant they had only equalled, not overtaken, the tally of 107 league goals set by the 1925-26 side.

The tributes flooded in for Rae and his team of coaches and trainers. The manager had been vindicated in his decision to retain the nucleus of the side that had suffered relegation only two seasons earlier. Some clever wheeling and dealing also meant that the team had been assembled at a net cost of just £20,000. The manager was typically reticent. A man of few words, he rebuffed the plaudits and merely paid tribute to the men who had done it out on the pitch. But there was more to it than that. The side was fitter than most and had also suffered little in the way of disruption through injury. Only seventeen players had been used throughout the season, of which five had only been used on a handful of occasions.

Any side that wins a championship is rightly praised and always well remembered. The sign of a truly great side is one whose names trip off the tongue. Most self-respecting soccer fans can name the 1966 England World Cup side, perhaps Manchester United's 1968 European Cup-winners, and the Spurs double side of the early 1960s. Argyle fans of a more mature age can do the same with the 1951-52 side – Shortt, Ratcliffe, Jones, Dougall, Chisholm, Porteous, Astall, Rattray, Tadman, Dews and Govan – with McShane not to be forgotten. It is a line up regarded by many as possibly the greatest Argyle eleven ever, and a team worthy of individual tributes to each player.

Goalkeeper Bill Shortt joined Argyle after the war from Chester for a fee of £1,000, and went on to play over 350 games for the club. Early in his career he won full Welsh honours and his form during this championship season earned him a recall to the Welsh side that shared the Home International crown with England. Renowned for his handling and superb positioning, which often made the art of goalkeeping look easy, he was extremely popular with his colleagues. Sadly, as this is written, his passing has been announced.

Right-back Paddy Ratcliffe was an all-action hero both on and off the field. At the outbreak of war, the Dubliner had volunteered for RAF duties as an air gunner. During one particular raid on Essen, Ratcliffe's bomber had been shot down in flames. Ratcliffe parachuted clear, suffering shrapnel wounds in his left leg and was captured. He spent two years as a prisoner of war. On the field, he was an attacking defender, good with both feet, and became Argyle's regular penalty taker. During the championship season, he was one of three players who played every game. He later retired to the United States.

Another ever present was Ratcliffe's full-back partner Pat Jones. But Jones usually was an ever present. Due to the war, he did not make his debut until the age of 26 in May 1947. Remarkably, he did not miss a league game until November 1953, a run of 279 consecutive matches. He was also only absent for one FA Cup-tie during that period. The supporters adored him, partly because he was a local boy, but also for his whole-hearted displays and commitment.

Neil Dougall was already a Scottish international when he joined Argyle from Birmingham in March 1949 for the not inconsiderable sum of £13,000. He played in a number of positions for the club, but it was at half-back where he was most effective, utilising his speed, excellent passing and occasional mighty shot.

An ever-present in the No 5 shirt was 'Jumbo' Chisholm. A former guardsman, he was a natural leader both on and off the pitch. Some of his antics would have led lesser players into trouble but Jumbo was unique and became known as one of the great characters of the game. He loved a drink, often before a game, and his idea of training was thrashing the living daylights out of a punchbag. He was simply indispensable.

Johnny Porteous was another Scotsman and the quiet man of the team. With fantastic work-rate and energy his no-nonsense approach made him the type of player who was more appreciated by his teammates than by the supporters, but it was noticeable when he wasn't there.

This was the season when right-winger Gordon Astall came of age. Nicknamed 'Flash', due to his speed, he would often outrun his opponents rather than beat them by skill alone, and send low, hard crosses into the box. He was not afraid to have a go himself either, as his tally of eighteen goals in the season testifies. His form was rewarded by a call up to the England 'B' side at the end of the season. Later in his career, he would win full England honours.

Another player loved by the fans was George Dews. A superb all-round sportsman, he was a stalwart in the Worcestershire cricket side for many years. On the soccer pitch, he displayed a prodigious work-rate. His fair hair seemed to pop up wherever the action was, and his championship season tally of 25 goals was remarkable for an inside-forward. Often singled out by opposing sides as the man to stop, he was frequently on the receiving end of some rough treatment, but always remained unflustered, earning himself the nickname 'Gentleman George'. In the event of injury, Dews was usually the man to slot into a different position and even played in goal for the side on one occasion.

As the centre-forward of a successful side, Maurice Tadman was the man who often grabbed the headlines. They were usually well-deserved. His 27 goals were a major factor in the title success. A tall and well-built striker, he relied on skill rather than brawn but was always modest about his achievements. A goal would be acknowledged by a mere nod of the head and a few handshakes. He was the ideal man to have the end of the numerous chances set up by Argyle's free-flowing style of play.

Peter Rattray was the unsung hero of the side. At 6ft 1in, he was the tallest member of the team and posed the greatest aerial threat. A number of his nineteen goals came via his head. The championship was the stellar moment in his career and he never achieved the same success at his other clubs.

Left-winger Alex Govan was a real crowd-pleaser. He loved to tease full-backs with his ball skills and was the archetypal winger of the time. He also scored his fair share of goals and, for a small fellow, was particularly adept with his head. His wing partnership with Astall was regarded as the best outside of the First Division.

Finally there was Tony McShane. The Irishman played in 34 of the championship games and never let anyone down. As a half-back, he loved to attack and his passing skills were his particular strength. His Irish charm and wit made him a popular figure in the dressing room.

It was a squad which bonded well and looked capable of even greater success. Rae's job now was to keep them together.

# FOUR

# 1955-56 (Relegated to Division 3 South)

Since winning the Third Division (South) title in 1952, Argyle had endured a topsy-turvy time. Apart from Peter Rattray, Jimmy Rae had held on to all of the squad who had won it. The following season, back in Division Two, they carried on where they left off. Five wins in the opening six games had the side labelled as promotion candidates. The side were playing so well that George Dews was unable to regain his place until October.

Six defeats in seven games in December and January dented confidence. Combined with the push for promotion was a chance of Cup glory. The draw had been kind to Argyle and Third Division (South) Coventry and Second Division strugglers Barnsley were easily disposed of. The fifth round draw brought a home tie with Gateshead of the Third Division (North) but the rank outsiders provided one of the Cup upsets of the season by winning by a single goal. In later years, Jack Chisholm alluded to the fact that that defeat was the turning point in Argyle's season. Their record after the shock was not materially different from before, but there was no doubt that the side had lost their early-season sparkle. The end result was fourth place, albeit nine points off the promotion places. It remains to this day the highest league position an Argyle side has ever achieved.

It was generally felt that, with some team-strengthening, First Division football was a distinct possibility. In reality, the opposite happened. Alex Govan was allowed to leave for Birmingham and a few weeks later Gordon Astall followed him. Replacing them would be difficult and ultimately never achieved adequately. Furthermore, it became apparent that many of the other stalwarts were past their prime. Numerous points were thrown away in the dying minutes of games as legs became weary. Heavy pitches also took their toll, exemplified particularly at Everton, where Argyle lost 4-8 on a Goodison Park quagmire. Youngsters were thrown into the fray and striker Neil Langman in particular showed promise, scoring nine goals in as many games. Tadman got his usual double-figure quota, but received little other support. Only a late rally, that saw six points gained from the final four matches avoided relegation in 1953-54.

The following season was no different. Chisholm had been forced to retire through injury, and the likes of Tadman and Pat Jones were fading from the scene. By the end of January, only five wins had been racked up. A 1-6 thrashing at West Ham, followed by a home defeat by Blackburn, saw the end of Rae's reign. There were conflicting stories as to whether he had resigned or was dismissed, but whatever the truth, the writing had been on the wall for some time.

The board wasted little time in appointing a high-profile name as Rae's replacement. Jack Rowley had been a star at Manchester United for many years, scoring over 200 goals and playing more than 400 games, not to mention winning six England caps. He also declared his intention to carry on playing. Argyle's goalscoring problems seem to have been solved. Rowley made an instant impact, leading his new side to three successive wins. By the end of the season, his short-term goal had been achieved and relegation was avoided by three points.

Whilst Rowley was seen as the new Messiah by some, he offered a more restrained approach than expected. Knowing that he had a largely inexperienced squad at his disposal, his pre-season address offered words of caution, expectations must not be too high. Prior to his arrival, attendances had dropped. Argyle were still attracting 14,000, but this represented a loss of revenue. Twenty thousand-plus crowds had been the norm for several seasons and gate money was almost the sole source of income. Team sponsors, corporate hospitality and other modern-day money spinners were still years away. Most teams also employed squads of thirty or more professionals. The financial situation at Home Park was tight and there was little available to Rowley for team-building.

The side at Hillsborough on the opening day of the 1955-56 season contained two new faces that, with all respect, hardly gave cause for optimism. American-born half-back Crawford Clelland had been at Aberdeen for five years without ever breaking into the first team at Pittodrie, whilst centre-half Trevor Lawless was a schoolteacher who had been given a match in the reserves whilst holidaying in Devon, and was taken on full time. On his league debut he was also made captain!

Sheffield Wednesday were newly relegated from Division One but still had too much class for Argyle. At half-time it was 1-1, but the Owls ran riot in the second half. Peter Anderson added another to his first-half goal for Argyle but a hat-trick from Jackie Sewell and a double from Albert Quixall saw the home side run out 5-2 winners.

Rowley was quick to ring the changes for the first home game against Doncaster, with Neil Dougall, George Willis and Eric Davis being brought into the fold. Willis got his name on the scoresheet, along with his manager, in a 2-2 draw.

Still not content, Rowley handed the No 9 shirt to Neil Langman for the visit of Nottingham Forest. The youngster certainly knew where the net was, but was still a part-time player, holding down a job with the local electricity board. That meant he was unable to train regularly with the rest of the squad. Despite taking an interval lead through another Willis goal, Forest replied with two in the second half from James Barrett.

One point from three games had hardly induced much confidence into the side as they embarked on a mini-northern tour to play Doncaster and

Hull. Rowley opted for more experience, bringing in Johnny Porteous, now 33, for his first game of the season. Another Anderson goal gave the Greens a half-time lead, but a Rovers fight-back resulted in them scoring three. Two days later, Argyle faced a Hull side that had started the season in a similar losing vein. Defeat at Doncaster cost goalkeeper Les Major his place and veteran Bill Shortt was brought back. Again Argyle held an interval lead through Anderson, but on this occasion they managed to hold on to it to register their first win of the season.

Argyle's third game in five days brought a double blow. Not only did they suffer defeat at home to Stoke, but Anderson – the most consistent player so far – suffered a broken leg and looked likely to miss much of the remainder of the season.

Rowley recalled speedy Welshman Malcolm Davies to cover for Anderson's absence for the visit of Blackburn. Also included for his debut was a young amateur player, Johnny Williams, marking the start of a long and distinguished Argyle career. In a game of few chances, Argyle secured victory via a second-half penalty, with the manager himself taking on the responsibility.

The games were now coming thick and fast, and 48 hours later Argyle visited Stoke, only to be thoroughly beaten. Rowley again scored from the spot, but two goals from Harry Oscroft, plus others from John King and John Lawton, gave the home side an easy two points.

Rowley was certainly not afraid to make changes and there were several victims of the Stoke defeat, notably Lawless. The captain was dropped for the next game at Lincoln and never played for the first team again. His replacement was Peter Langman, older brother of Neil. Another new face was the lanky Reg Wyatt, a Plymothian who had been at the club for five years and was in the midst of National Service. Unsurprisingly, with such disruption to the side, Argyle slumped to another defeat, with Torquay-born Tommy Northcott getting the only goal of the game.

The following week at Home Park, Rowley was on target again. Unfortunately it was Jack's brother, Arthur, who in time would score more goals in league football than anyone else. On this occasion just one was enough to take both points back to Leicester. The match saw the debut of another of Argyle's summer captures, Arthur Stenner on the left wing.

Argyle then faced a trip to Liverpool. The Reds were, at that time, far from the dominant force in football they would become, but still possessed players of the calibre of Ronnie Moran, Alan A'Court and Liverpool legend Billy Liddell. In front of a crowd of more than 34,000, Williams, playing at centre-forward, scored his first goal for the club, but again Argyle were a well-beaten side by the end, losing 1-4. A week later, another four were conceded, this time at West Ham, with Ken Tucker grabbing a hat-trick and a certain Malcolm Allison, future Argyle boss, also scoring.

By this time, it was difficult to see where Argyle's next victory was coming from, a view, judging by his team selections, shared by Rowley. The use of half-backs, such as Porteous and Hugh McJarrow, in forward positions smacked of desperation. With the defence also leaking goals, he brought back another veteran, Paddy Ratcliffe, and handed a debut to winger Charlie Twissell. Still an amateur, Twissell had obtained a discharge from the Royal Navy and was reputed to be the quickest thing seen at Argyle for many a year. He was a highly rated sprinter and long-jumper and, perhaps, Rowley's new secret weapon. Certainly there was an all-round improvement as they took on Port Vale and shared the spoils. Twissell certainly enjoyed a debut to remember. His speed caused havoc in the Vale defence and his powerful shooting almost brought him two goals in the opening quarter of an hour.

The player-manager was also starting to display some of the prowess in front of goal that had brought him so many honours in the game. His strike against Vale was followed by a brace at fellow strugglers Barnsley, giving his side their second away win of the season.

Hopes that the win would signal the start of some sort of revival were soon dashed as Swansea left Home Park with both points, thanks to a goal from future Spurs star Terry Medwin. A week later, Argyle again faded after the break, handing three second-half goals to Notts County.

The game against Leeds provided one of the most entertaining matches seen at Home Park for many a year. The main attraction and danger was John Charles, valued at a massive £40,000 and a real star of the game. Leeds were riding high and Argyle next to bottom. The result seemed hardly in doubt. To make matters worse, Rowley was injured. The powerfully built Eric Davis was handed the No 9 shirt and asked to lock horns with Leeds centre-half, Jack Charlton.

Leeds went one up when George Robertson unluckily deflected the ball past Shortt. The goal stirred Argyle and for the remainder of the half they relentlessly pressurised the United defence. Willis equalised and Williams got a second. After the break, Shortt failed to collect a corner and Harold Williams levelled. Back came Argyle again and Davis and man of the match Dougall added further goals. Charles, superbly policed by Peter Langman, finally broke clear to score but it was too late. Twissell had a hand in three of Argyle's four goals and was beginning to live up to his reputation.

For the first time, Rowley retained the same eleven as Argyle travelled to the capital to face Fulham. A resurgent Dougall scored again, but the Cottagers hit back through England international Bedford Jezzard and Rowley's former Manchester United teammate, Charlie Mitten.

After encouraging attendances during the early part of the season, Argyle's poor form had seen supporters drift away. Fewer than 15,000 attended the home game with Bury. After a goalless first half, the Greens again slumped in the second, as the Shakers ran up a 4-1 win. It was hardly the type of performance required to persuade the stay-aways to return.

After a goalless draw at Millmoor against a Rotherham side just as desperate for points, Argyle finally came to life by destroying Middlesbrough. Argyle scored four times, with Stenner and half-back Ralph Wetton both netting what would be their only goals for the club.

There was an even more unlikely scorer in the creditable draw with front runners Sheffield Wednesday. Full-back Pat Jones had played no fewer than 352 games for the club with barely a sniff of a goalscoring chance. Jones was a defender through and through, and rarely strayed into opposition territory, but his second-half shot was enough to equalise an earlier penalty by Ron Staniforth, who managed only three goals himself in a career spanning almost 500 games.

A Christmas Eve defeat at Nottingham Forest preceded a bizarre two days with back-to-back matches with Bristol City. The Robins had hit a fine spell of form and had led the division for the past five weeks, scoring freely along the way, whilst the Pilgrims remained only one point clear of bottom place. After a lengthy absence, winger Davies and inside-forward Jimmy Crawford were recalled, whilst City were missing their star man, centre-forward John Atyeo, suffering from a toe injury. From the off, Argyle surprised the leaders with the intensity of their play. Despite the heavy conditions, Argyle moved the ball around and Davies in particular proved too hot to handle. By half-time, Davies and Crawford had put Argyle two up. A demoralised City capitulated further in the second half with Crawford, Davis and Williams adding further goals.

Twenty-four hours later, the story couldn't have been more different. Not surprisingly, Rowley fielded the same eleven, but City had Atyeo fit again. Inspired by the return of their talisman, the home side set about exacting revenge, and did – with style. Within two minutes, Atyeo had scored, and seventeen minutes later he scored again. He then set up a third for Jimmy Rogers before half-time. With wingers Davies and Twissell starved of possession, Argyle tried to plough their way through the mud but that only served to tire legs already weary from three games in four days. Defensive mistakes became more frequent and City scored three more times in the second half, with Rogers completing his hat-trick and Tommy Burden getting a sixth.

The thrashing prompted Rowley to tinker with his line up again. For the match with Hull he handed a debut to centre-forward Bob Swiggs, who had been a prolific scorer with Cornish side St Blazey, and was now topping the goal-charts for Argyle's reserves. Also given his first appearance was eighteen-year-old goalkeeper Peter Dyer. Dyer was only 5ft 7in, and his opposite number, Billy Bly, only two inches taller. It is doubtful if any other league game has featured two such vertically challenged custodians. Hull's defence was benevolent, to say the least but, by half-time it was they who led through Tom Martin. Twissell levelled in the second half but it was regarded as a point dropped by Rowley.

As ever there were high hopes of a money-spinning third round FA Cup draw with one of the big guns. Leyton Orient away did not come under that category. The east London side were in the Third Division (South) but looked likely candidates to come up, and their single-goal victory over struggling Argyle did not therefore warrant a 'giant killing' tag.

Argyle travelled to Blackburn wary that their danger-man was Tommy Briggs. The curly-haired former butcher had guested for Argyle during the war years but was never snapped up. Since then he had been a prolific scorer for several clubs. On the day he was well marked by Peter Langman who was fast gaining a reputation for effectively shackling star names. Briggs didn't get his name on the scoresheet, but Plymouth-born Bill Smith and Eddie Crossan did. A Willis reply was not enough.

An abysmal home performance against Lincoln followed and a 1-4 defeat was fully deserved. A week later the side travelled to Leicester and lost by the same scoreline, with Arthur Rowley again showing a liking for playing against his brother's side by scoring two.

Once again, the poor results affected the attendance and only 10,000 turned up for the visit of Liverpool, although no doubt the bitter cold persuaded many to stay at home. It was a dismal day to stand on the terraces. A biting wind and rock-hard pitch suggested the match was hardly likely to be a classic. The temperatures were so low that both keepers wore tracksuit bottoms and Reds centre-half Lawrence Hughes wore gloves. Rowley again sprang a surprise in his team selection by choosing full-back Arthur Morgan as an inside-forward. It was Morgan, relishing a first-team opportunity, who opened the scoring three minutes before half-time by scooping the ball over goalkeeper Dave Underwood's head.

With Liverpool seemingly uninterested and with their minds possibly on the upcoming fifth round FA Cup-tie with Manchester City, the second half belonged to Neil Langman. Six minutes after the interval he shot past Underwood. With ten minutes remaining he scored a second when his downward header bounced off the frozen pitch. Underwood went to grab the ball at shoulder height but his numb fingers failed to function and in the ball went. There was still time for Langman to complete his hat-trick with Underwood slipping as he went to save. Despite Neil grabbing the headlines, brother Peter played an important part in the win, keeping star man Billy Liddell quiet and denying him his 150th league goal.

After such an impressive result, Argyle again frustrated their followers by only drawing at home to Fulham, and then losing at Port Vale, where Argyle were undone by a Ken Griffiths hat-trick.

The Pilgrims got back on the winning trail by easily beating a mediocre Barnsley side. Langman, now fully fit after recent injury problems, was beginning to find the net and hopes that he could be Argyle's saviour were now heaped upon his young if broad shoulders.

Langman scored for the third match in a row as a hard-fought win at Middlesbrough suggested light at the end of the tunnel, but again Argyle demonstrated the frustrating habit of being able to perform better against more highly rated sides, drawing what was a 'must win' game against Notts County, who were also prime candidates for the drop.

Leeds, on the other hand, looked prime candidates for promotion and a trip to Elland Road was not one to relish. Rowley dished out another debut, this time to Ken Mitchell, who was recommended to Argyle by their North Eastern scout. Mitchell had been playing for Whitby Town whilst working for ICI. He became the seventh incumbent of the No 9 shirt for the season and no doubt enjoyed the game rather more than his teammates by scoring both Argyle goals. It rounded off a week to remember, as he had got married only a few days earlier. Peter Langman was unable to shackle John Charles as effectively as he did at Home Park earlier in the season and the giant Welshman scored two of Leeds' four. The defeat left Rowley's side staring into the abyss.

Six matches remained, three at home, which all of which needed to be won. First of all though, there was a Good Friday trip to Bristol Rovers to contend with. Rovers were an impressive side. Mitchell was unavailable and Wyatt asked to slot into an inside-forward role, a position he had filled as a youngster before converting to more defensive duties. Langman scored again but by then Rovers were two up through a brace by Dai Ward.

The following day, Argyle entertained West Ham. The Hammers had suffered yet another disappointing season, having been a mid-table Second Division side since the war. They had won only once on their travels all season but on the day edged out Argyle with a goal from speedy Scotsman Jimmy Andrews.

The situation had now reached crisis point. Argyle and Hull were being cast adrift from the other relegation candidates and time was running out. An Easter Monday defeat at home to Bristol Rovers was, therefore, little short of disastrous. That man Dai Ward was again on target. The match proved to be the last of Bill Shortt's long and distinguished Argyle career. The ever cheery keeper had notched up 356 appearances and won twelve Welsh caps. It was an unfitting way for such a stalwart to bid farewell, but he would always be remembered as one of Argyle's best.

Five days later, Argyle travelled to Bury for the last rites. Defeat would confirm relegation and within the first fifteen minutes it was all over as the Shakers surged into a three-goal lead. It could have been worse but for the recalled Dyer, who made two other brave saves. Mitchell, back in the side, had travelled from Newcastle with his new bride for the game and it was he who gave Argyle a glimmer of hope by supplying the cross from which Wyatt rose high to head home for his first league goal.

It was only a glimmer and that was soon extinguished as Bury came back all guns blazing. They added four more. By the end, Argyle were a dispirited side. Any possession they had was wasted by hopeful punts upfield for Mitchell to chase. Dyer was the only player to emerge with any credit and at the final whistle was congratulated to a man by the Bury players for his bravado.

As often happens, once the pressure is off, struggling teams play better. In front of a pitifully small crowd, Argyle gained only their seventh home win of the season over a Rotherham side that had been saved from the drop by Argyle's dismal spell of form. Langman was again the man who grabbed the headlines, with two goals. With nothing riding on the game, Rowley used the opportunity to cast his eye over two more debutants, Welsh full-back Dennis John and Scotsman Bobby Bell. Bell was actually a Partick Thistle player but was on National Service and stationed at an Army camp in Wiltshire. He was unable to return home each week to turn out for Thistle, so the two clubs came to an agreement to allow him to don the green of Argyle. Such a deal was relatively novel. Loaning players was a far from common practice.

The two new boys retained their places as Argyle travelled into Wales to play their final days as a Second Division side at the Vetch Field against Swansea. The Swans were in mid-table and had nothing to play for, but still attracted a crowd of more than 15,000. Despite a season of underachievement, they were an attractive side to watch, with the likes of Mel Charles, the Allchurch brothers, and flying winger Cliff Jones in their starting line up. In the end, honours remained even, with Bell and Davies bagging the Argyle goals.

And so, after a spell of four seasons, Argyle found themselves back in the Third Division. The heady days of the championship four years earlier seemed an age away. As always, following relegation, there was criticism of the manager. Some of it was undoubtedly justified. The side was chopped and changed from week to week and there was little chance to adopt a cohesive and consistent approach. Players were often asked to perform in unfamiliar positions. Certainly financial constraints had played a major part. No fewer than 32 players were used but the majority were raw and inexperienced, plucked from the reserves or non-league football. Injuries had also played a part and the loss of Anderson early in the season, when he was showing such good form, was a particularly big loss. Several other key players missed games through injuries as well, but the brutal truth was that too many were not up to Second Division standard. The road back from obscurity looked hard and steep.

# FIVE

# 1957-58 (Promoted to Division 3)

The first season back in Division Three (South), 1956-57, merely demonstrated how much the club had regressed. There was still no money and manager Jack Rowley again had to rely on much the same squad. The season started disastrously with five straight defeats, including a 0-6 home drubbing by Reading. Understandably, attendances fell and goals were again at a premium. Rowley finally reverted to centre-forward himself, a position he had filled with style for Manchester United for many seasons, and began to find the net before injury, age and the pressure of his dual responsibilities finally caught up with him. Neil Langman and Eric Davis missed much of the early part of the season, but once reunited began to score regularly. Langman finished with seventeen goals and Davis eleven from just nineteen games. The second half of the season saw an upturn in form that was sufficient at least to avoid the humiliation of finishing bottom, but a final finish of eighteenth was hardly reassuring. On the plus side, players such as George Robertson and Johnny Williams were now firmly established and looked capable of forming the nucleus of the side for several seasons to come.

The summer of 1957 proved to be exciting. Crucially, a new board of directors under the chairmanship of businessman Ron Blindell took control and immediately poured some much-needed cash into the coffers. The financial position was also boosted, not only at Argyle but at every other club, by the Government decreeing that football was to be finally exempt from entertainment tax. Incredibly, the levy had been in place since 1916, when it was introduced as a 'temporary' measure to raise finance for the First World War.

The improved financial position at Home Park allowed Rowley to increase wages and bonus payments, which in turn made it easier to attract new signings. Acknowledging that – no matter his intent in blooding young but untried talent – there was no substitute for experience, Rowley set about revamping his squad. A spate of summer signings saw no fewer than six players make the pilgrimage to the South West. Firstly, Rowley went back to his former club to sign wing-half Tommy Barrett and full-back Bryce Fulton. Neither had been able to break into the first team at Old Trafford, but both clearly had potential. Winger Harry Penk, at 5ft 4in, was one of the smallest players in the game but had earned himself a reputation as a tricky winger who was equally at home on either flank.

Rowley also signed two players from West Brom, goalkeeper Geoff Barnsley, who would provide competition for regular No 1 Harry Brown, who was approaching veteran status, and Wilf Carter, who had started life as a full-back. He had spent six seasons at the Hawthorns but never fully established himself in the side. A fee of £2,500 and the thought of regular first-team soccer was enough to persuade Carter to sign.

The final arrival was young centre-half Jim Nightingale from non-league Irthlingborough, who signed on a part-time basis. The new signings at least allowed Rowley the 'luxury' of ending his own distinguished playing career, enabling him to concentrate on management exclusively.

As usual, pre-season preparations consisted of training, training and more training. Pre-season friendlies were rarely played and Rowley was content to let his players loose in two public practice matches between his squad. Healthy crowds attended both matches and were encouraged by what they saw.

The league season commenced with renewed hope. There was all to play for as the Football League had decided that this would be the final season of the North-South divide in the Third Division. The champions of each league would still gain promotion to Division Two, but the respective top halves of North and South would compete the following season in a combined Third Division, with the bottom halves going into a new Fourth Division. As such, there were in effect *two* promotions to aim for, an easier one to reach Division Three and a much harder one to reach Division Two. Conversely, there was a 50-50 chance of being relegated to the new soccer basement. Such a situation promised an exciting end to the campaign, as many teams would still have something to play for.

Of Argyle's new boys, only Penk and Carter were named for the opening game at Shrewsbury. With the evergreen Pat Jones as captain, Argyle were confident of a winning start. The game was scoreless at half-time, but second-half goals by Colin Whitaker and Bernard Jones condemned Argyle to an opening-day defeat for the third season in a row.

Two days later, in driving rain, the side grabbed their first points of the season, with Neil Langman's first-half goal enough to defeat Reading. Both sides played some stirring football despite the conditions and a crowd of over 20,000 suggested the supporters had renewed faith after the mediocrity they had endured over the past three years.

Such optimism seemed justified a few days later as Argyle swept aside Aldershot, captained by former Pilgrim Ralph Wetton. Some sharp finishing by Carter helped register his first two goals for the club. Langman, perhaps sensing that he had a rival for his top scorer's crown, showed what he was capable of, scooping a hat-trick in the return game at Reading, but much of that work was undone by successive defeats at Swindon and at leaders Brighton, who maintained their unbeaten start to the season.

Despite the double loss, Rowley kept faith with his side, having seemingly learnt a harsh lesson about making sweeping changes after one or two defeats. It paid off. Carter's goal was enough to see off Millwall and maintain Argyle's place in the top half.

Argyle's third game in five days saw them gain revenge on Brighton, but defeat at Gillingham suggested that perhaps they were a Jekyll and Hyde side that would be again blighted by inconsistency. For once, the forwards had an off day and spurned several chances to win the game.

With every side dropping points on a regular basis, a single-goal midweek victory at Southampton was enough to lift Argyle into third place behind Brighton and Southend, who had scored 29 goals in their first ten games. It was a fine win at The Dell, considering that Williams suffered an injury early in the game.

The team was certainly benefiting from having a settled look and home wins over lowly Exeter and a 4-0 demolition of Southampton lifted Argyle into second place. The race for places in the new Third Division was set fair. With most sides having played thirteen games, only eight points separated leaders Brighton from bottom-placed Torquay.

Hopes of attaining the leadership were dashed at QPR. Argyle dominated much of the game but were denied by fine goalkeeping from Ron Springett, and Leslie Locke scored the only goal of the game. An evening game with Colchester at Home Park brought Argyle's first draw. Langman again impressed and scored his seventh goal of the season. It was a performance that would remain in the minds of the Colchester management.

Barrett was finally blooded at Northampton, replacing the injured Peter Kearns, but it was not a game he would remember with relish. The Cobblers had struggled so far and Argyle were expected to take the points, but this was one of those days. At half-time the home side held just a single-goal lead, but Argyle capitulated in the second half as Northampton ran in four more. It would be, by far, Argyle's worst defeat of the season. The side recovered, beating Watford 2-1 at Home Park. Langman scored both, but they would prove to be the final goals of his Argyle career.

The match at Crystal Palace had added interest, in that it marked the debut of Rowley's latest signing – Scottish forward Jimmy Gauld. Gauld had suffered a nomadic career, which began at Aberdeen and then took him to Waterford, where he broke the Irish Free State league scoring record with 46 goals in just 28 games. He subsequently moved to Charlton and then Everton. His signing was completed in London on the Friday evening in time for him to be registered for the Palace match. The deal was apparently completed in just twenty minutes, with Gauld's main concern being that he should be allowed to hold down a second job, something he had done at all his other clubs.

Gauld showed flashes of his potential but by half-time Argyle were two down and without the services of Jones, who had limped off with a torn groin muscle, an injury that would keep him out for several months.

With Carter being moved to Jones' full-back position, Argyle's attack looked lacklustre and Palace added a third before the end. A week later, Gauld marked his home debut with a goal against Torquay, with the Gulls displacing Exeter at the bottom of the division.

Guy Fawkes Night saw Argyle entertain French side Red Star in a friendly. Rowley resisted the temptation to try out a few fringe players and fielded an almost full-strength side, apart from significantly leaving out Langman and replacing him with local boy Bernard Barnes.

Langman was restored to the side for the trip to Brentford. Curiously, Argyle had not yet scored in any Saturday away match this season, and this unwanted record continued as the Bees won 2-0 in controversial circumstances. Len Newcombe gave the home side a seventh-minute lead but Argyle responded in furious fashion. Gauld hit the woodwork twice and Anderson had a shot cleared off the line. In the 64th minute, Argyle keeper Brown came to collect a cross and was felled by a Brentford forward. With the keeper lying prone, George Francis turned the ball into the net. Despite furious Argyle protests, referee Mr Topliss allowed the goal to stand. Brown was hospitalised with concussion and detained overnight, Carter deputising between the posts for the rest of the game.

A few days later, Langman was transferred to Colchester for £6,600. With a number of forwards on his books, Rowley felt the fee reasonable enough to allow the robust forward to leave. Ironically, Langman's brother, Peter, also played his final first-team game for Argyle on the same day. The centre-half had been largely consigned to reserve-team football since Reg Wyatt had slipped into the No 5 shirt. The following Monday saw another friendly against foreign opposition, with West German side Cologne winning an entertaining match 3-2.

The first round of the FA Cup brought a swift return to Home Park for Watford. With Brown incapacitated, Barnsley was handed his Argyle debut. During the week there had been some debate as to Langman's replacement in the No 9 shirt. Argyle were rumoured to be interested in Lincoln's Torquay-born forward, Tommy Northcott, but so were a number of other clubs. Rowley sought a more experienced player in time for the Cup-tie, but was overruled by chairman Blindell, who insisted on Bernard Barnes being selected. It was a wise decision. Within eighteen minutes, Barnes had set up Peter Anderson for Argyle's opener and by the interval had scored two himself. In the second half he forced an error from which Gauld scored. Two from Carter, including a penalty, completed a 6-2 rout. Langman, incidentally, watched the game from the grandstand.

Argyle's dislike of away-Saturdays continued when losing by a single goal at Norwich. They had now played for over eleven and a half hours in Saturday away fixtures without scoring. Gauld had demonstrated the strong, forceful dribbling that would become his trademark. Nevertheless,

Argyle's away from was proving costly. By now they had slipped to tenth place and were perilously close to the bottom half of the table. Winning ways were restored as Bournemouth were beaten 3-1. The Cherries pushed the self-destruct button with own-goals by Alan Rule and Harry Hughes sandwiching another Gauld effort.

Thoughts again turned to cup matters. Argyle were afforded another home draw, this time against non-league Dorchester. Almost 1,000 supporters travelled from Dorset to support their heroes but they would not witness any giant killing. Carter helped himself to a hat-trick. Penk scored his first goal for the club and Gauld continued his fine scoring run. The Dorchester fans at least had something to cheer about, as Derek Stroud and Bobby Barker both found the net.

Carter was now on fire. A week later he scored another three in a 4-0 win over Coventry, and followed up with another goal as Argyle dropped a home point to Shrewsbury. There was also a first Argyle goal for Barrett.

The two Christmas fixtures against Newport promised to be hard-fought affairs, as the Welsh side were just one place below Argyle in the table. That close proximity was not reflected on the pitch, however. In the Christmas Day match at Somerton Park, Argyle handed Newport a 'footballing lesson', according to press reports. George Baker celebrated his recall with a goal and Gauld capped a fine display with another.

The one-sided nature of the game had ramifications for the return encounter the following day. There was little in the way of seasonal goodwill, as Carter and Gauld, clearly earmarked as the danger-men, were subjected to some particularly heavy tackling. It didn't stop Carter, who scored what was to be the only goal of the game in the first half. The loss of a goal only served to rile the Welsh side even more. At one point, Carter was left semi-conscious on the ground. The half-time break failed to quell frayed tempers and the second half would better be described as round two. In the end it all became too much for Gauld. Referee Alf Bond spotted something which few others saw and, to the crowd's astonishment, Gauld was sent off for the first time in his career. He departed to the biggest cheer of the day. Since his arrival he had become an instant favourite. Mr Bond was booed and jeered for the remainder of the game and refused later to discuss the reason for Gauld's dismissal. It was fortunate for him that Argyle held on to win.

These events raised question marks over the wisdom of playing back-to-back matches. If grudges were held, they had little time to dissipate, but the Football League continued the practice for several more seasons. Two days later the same eleven leg-weary players drew 3-3 at Aldershot with Carter scoring two to make him one of the top scorers in the country.

Then came the match of the season, as far as Argyle fans were concerned. The third round FA Cup draw had gifted the Greens a home tie with First Division Newcastle. As soon as the draw was made, the match was made all-ticket with Argyle officials anticipating massive interest in the game. Taking the opportunity to swell the bank balance, ticket prices were increased with supporters being asked to pay 6s 6d for a grandstand seat or 3s 6d to stand. The match was not quite a sell out, but a crowd of over 38,000 was Argyle's biggest for seven years. Fans started queueing at 11.30 in the morning to ensure a place near the front.

For the first twenty minutes, Argyle were the better side. Penk flashed two shots narrowly wide and Gauld hit the crossbar. The difference was the Magpies' ability to exploit mistakes, which they did twice before half-time. Goals then flowed regularly. Len White scored three times and George Eastham twice as Newcastle ran out 6-1 winners, with Carter getting Argyle's only goal from the penalty spot after an infringement by Jimmy Scoular. By the end it was a demonstration of the gap between First and Third Divisions. The spectators certainly couldn't complain about lack of entertainment from Cup matches. Argyle's three ties had seen no fewer than 22 goals scored.

Now free to concentrate on promotion, second-placed Swindon came to Home Park and grabbed a point. Inevitably, Carter was again among the scorers, with Baker getting the other. The Welshman was relishing the opportunity of an extended first-team run. He had been used as a winger since joining Argyle and had been unable to dislodge the consistent Penk and Anderson, but was now demonstrating an eye for goal.

Baker was again on target to give Argyle a vital away win at Millwall and keep the promotion dream alive. With the following week's fixture at Southend falling foul of the weather, Argyle remained fourth, four points behind Swindon, who had played three games more.

Lowly Gillingham put up a fight before losing 1-2. Argyle then continued their poor record at St James Park. Exeter were looking likely candidates to seek re-election, having already conceded 66 goals. They had already conceded five or more goals on four occasions, but they always seemed able to raise their game when Argyle came visiting. Despite the anticipation of a local derby, there was a muted atmosphere with the match coming only two days after the Munich air crash. The news was particularly poignant to Argyle's Barrett and Fulton, who knew most of the victims from their time at Old Trafford.

City's destroyer-in-chief was a former West Brom teammate of Carter's, Johnny Nicholls, a former England international who scored a hat-trick. It was certainly a one-off result for Exeter, who won only two more games, lost 0-9 to Northampton, and eventually finished bottom.

Gauld was now injured, but once again there was no stopping Carter, who scored his third hat-trick of the season as QPR were slain at Home Park. The match saw the debut of Fulton, who had patiently waited for his opportunity in the reserves. Since Jones' injury, the No 3 shirt had been Rowley's one problem position, and Fulton became the sixth player to be given the left-back slot. Frustratingly, pace-setters Reading and Brighton both gained away victories to maintain their advantage over Argyle.

The Pilgrims now struck a rich vein of form. Northampton were despatched easily, and successive 2-0 wins at Watford and in a rearranged game at Walsall saw them climb into second spot, a point behind Reading. After a narrow win at home to Crystal Palace, the Devon derby at Torquay saw Argyle win 2-0. With Reading losing heavily against QPR, Argyle now lay second to the Berkshire club only on goal-average, and with two matches in hand.

Whether realisation that promotion was a distinct possibility struck home cannot be known, but after a run of six successive wins in which they had conceded just once, Argyle lost by a single goal at Home Park to Norwich. Canaries' debutant, Derrick Lythgoe, netted the goal. A collection for the Munich Air Disaster Appeal Fund was made at the game.

A draw at Coventry kept Argyle in the hunt as they entered the vital Easter period. The Good Friday home match with Port Vale saw the welcome return to action of Jones. Fulton had not let anyone down during his recent tenure of the No 3 shirt, but cool heads were now needed and there were none cooler than the veteran Argyle skipper's.

A Kearns goal was enough to take two vital points from Vale but whilst the defence was proving as solid as a rock the goals began to dry up at a vital time. Carter was now a marked man and although Argyle had coped with Gauld's absence, his livewire performances and ability to do the unexpected had certainly been missed. A goalless home draw the following day to Brentford saw Carter injured, forcing him miss the next two games. With an air of inevitability, his absence saw two more stalemates ensue, even though Gauld returned for the game at Bournemouth.

Worse was to follow. A midweek game at Southend resulted in Argyle's first away defeat since early February. A William Morrison own-goal was the sole contribution to Argyle's cause. It could have been worse. The other promotion contenders had all dropped unexpected points and the chase for the single promotion spot remained incredibly tight, with six sides still in with a fighting chance. Reading, Argyle and Brighton all had 54 points, although with two games in hand Brighton held an advantage. Norwich had 53 points, with Swindon on 52 and Brentford 51.

With two home games and an away trip to Colchester remaining, three wins looked a distinct possibility and would give Rowley's men a realistic chance of the title. Argyle overcame nerves to record a 2-1 win over Walsall, with Carter ending his minor goal-drought and Baker getting the other. Two days later, Argyle faced Southend at Home Park. It was a game the Pilgrims were expected to win, despite losing at Roots Hall only five days earlier. It was, however, an evening fraught with controversy and effectively ended the promotion dream.

At the centre of it all was Bristol referee Mr Pullin, who had not been averse in the past to baffling the Home Park crowd with some of his decisions. Carter and Southend's Canadian winger, Errol Crossan, had exchanged first-half goals, but the match sprang to life in the second half with two incidents in particular raising the temperature of both the crowd and the players. First, Argyle looked to have a sure-fire penalty when Baker was brought down but Mr Pullin waved play on, later saying he believed Baker had 'dived'. Then Carter had a goal disallowed for offside, despite the ball coming to him via two Southend defenders. Among the mayhem, the Shrimpers scored twice more with only Baker replying.

At the final whistle, there was fury all around Home Park. The board announced that they would discuss whether or not to protest to the League about the official's performance and there was a demonstration by a number of supporters outside the ground. Mr Pullin needed an escort to extract him safely from the confines of the stadium and wisely decided to cancel his overnight accommodation in the city and to stay instead in Torquay.

The season ended in anticlimactic fashion with victory at Colchester who, by finishing twelfth, had secured the final slot in the revamped Third Division for the following season. For Argyle, it meant a third-place finish and they were left to rue a disappointing run at the end of the season which had yielded only a point a game from the final ten matches. Three more points would have clinched the championship. Several other contenders also succumbed to the pressure, and it was Brighton who eventually emerged as champions by two points from Brentford.

There was a final match at Home Park, with relegated First Division side Sunderland paying a visit for Rowley's benefit match.

So, at least Argyle secured the lesser promotion to the new Third Division and avoided the ignominy of being relegated as founder members of Division Four. Whether technically this qualifies as promotion is open to debate but, as it turned out, the season marked a significant upturn in the fortunes of the club and is worthy of placing on record. It proved to be the coming of age for Rowley as a manager and several of his new signings were unqualified successes, particularly Carter, whose metamorphosis from bit-part West Brom player to one of the most lethal goalscorers in the country was remarkable. Gauld also was an astute capture who thrilled crowds everywhere with his extravagances and showmanship. Penk and Anderson proved themselves as a highly capable wing partnership and Barnsley a safe and reliable goalkeeper. The future again looked bright.

# Six

# 1958-59 (Promoted to Division 2)

Despite the disappointment of narrowly missing out on a place in Division Two at the end of 1957-58, there were high hopes for the new season. The nucleus of the previous campaign's side had been retained, although inevitably a few familiar faces would be missing, notably Pat Jones, who had finally called it a day after 441 appearances for the club. Goalkeeper Harry Brown had also retired and wing-half Rex Tilley was transferred to Swindon. Manager Jack Rowley also reconciled himself to being without Peter Kearns for much of the season, as the inside-forward had been called up for National Service. The club also took the decision to employ all its professional players on a full-time basis, which meant a number of part-timers were released. The ever-reliable Neil Dougall was handed responsibility for looking after the reserve side, which had disappointed. Forty-two players had been used in the 'stiffs' during the previous season and few were of sufficient ability to promote to first-team duties. Dougall was given the task of nurturing more talent.

Rowley had endured a busy close season, signing six players of note. With Geoff Barnsley likely to assume the mantle of first-choice keeper, Scotsman Bob Wyllie was signed as understudy, a role he had already performed at Blackpool and West Ham. Gordon Fincham was a strapping centre-half who had already played over fifty matches for Leicester, whilst the defence was further strengthened by the capture of full-back Eric Doughty. Seen as the natural successor to Jones, Doughty had spent seven years at Highbury without ever breaking into the Gunners' first team, but had received the benefit of playing and training with some great names, such as Tommy Lawton, Wally Barnes and Jimmy Logie.

To add strength and competition to the half-back line, and perhaps to confuse opponents, Argyle also signed John Williams to team up with … John Williams. The newer version was soon dubbed 'Cardiff' by his team-mates in acknowledgment of his previous club, and was more commonly referred to as John L Williams.

Centre-forward Barrie Meyer had been a Bristol Rovers player for ten years although he was perhaps better known for his cricketing exploits as Gloucestershire's wicket-keeper. Rovers were reportedly unhappy with his unavailability for pre-season training and so released him. He would be looking to take over George Baker's No 9 shirt.

Finally, a familiar face returned in the form of winger Alex Govan. The highly popular player had never wanted to leave Plymouth but had achieved great success with Birmingham, in particular, where he had played in an FA Cup final, not to mention several high-profile European matches. He had more recently been with Portsmouth.

Off the field there was also a change. Rowley's backroom staff had remained unchanged under his stewardship, with George Taylor and George Reed as his trusty sidekicks. Former player and trainer Bill Harper was now the head groundsman, whilst ex-winger Bill Strauss was appointed to the newly created position of administrative manager, and would give support to the long-serving club secretary, Bert Cole.

Despite the feeling of confidence that pervaded Home Park, there was still a sense of entering the unknown to a certain extent. This stemmed from the fact that the club would, of course, be playing half of their games against teams from the North, most of whom would be unknown quantities. Sides such as Wrexham, Halifax and Accrington Stanley had never played Argyle before, and it had been many years since the Pilgrims had faced the likes of Stockport and Tranmere.

Of the new boys, only Doughty was selected for the opening game of the season at Hull. It would not be a debut to remember. In the first half, Doughty suffered a cartilage injury. In modern times such injuries are easily treated. In those days they were often career-threatening. In time, he would recover, but he was never able to regain his first-team place and so ended one of the shortest careers on record.

Despite the handicap of playing much of the match with ten men, Argyle gained a creditable draw, with Jimmy Gauld getting their goal.

The fixture list had given Argyle two away games to start the season, and they stayed up north before travelling for the Monday evening game at Rochdale. At least, it made sense to get two of the least attractive fixtures out of the way and not have to endure a mid-winter trip to such places. The evergreen and play-anywhere Dougall was drafted into the left-back slot in preference to Bryce Fulton. Wilf Carter, now the Argyle captain, and Harry Penk scored the goals that gave the side a more than satisfactory start.

Rowley, it seemed, had already stumbled on a successful line up. The first home game proved to be real exhibition stuff. Opponents Tranmere were never in the hunt and Carter was soon demonstrating that he was no one-season wonder by scoring twice to add to strikes from Gauld and George Baker, employed as a deeper lying centre-forward.

Rochdale were also sent packing as Argyle established themselves as early leaders. The squad then undertook another mini-tour of the North West, with matches at Stockport and Bury. Both games ended in draws, leaving Argyle as the only unbeaten side in the Third Division.

Chasing Argyle closely were Reading, who had lost only one match themselves. The Biscuitmen led at half-time through Jimmy Wheeler. The second half saw little to choose between the sides and the match ended up all square, with Bobby Ayre getting a second for the visitors and Carter and Penk replying.

The dropping of a home point for the first time provoked Rowley into making changes. John L Williams came in for his debut, replacing Tommy Barrett at left-half. Meyer was given his first game in place of Baker, and Govan was brought in for the unfortunate Peter Anderson. Penk was asked to switch to the right wing. The changes did little to curb Argyle's attacking style. Despite incessant rain, the Pilgrims played some eye-catching football. Meyer, thriving on the service he was given, grabbed two goals and Gauld another.

Two days later the unbeaten run, together with the leadership of the division, was terminated with a 0-2 defeat at Colchester – inside-forward John Evans getting both goals. The loss of top spot was short-lived. Argyle returned to Home Park for an evening encounter with Doncaster and won handsomely 4-0.

The Argyle supporters were certainly getting their money's worth as another thriller followed, against Bournemouth. A gusty wind made conditions difficult and the Cherries took a tenth-minute lead when Gil Dowsett stuck out an elastic leg to toe-poke the ball past Barnsley. Argyle replied with their usual aplomb. As ever, a number of chances were created, but for once the forwards failed to capitalise, with Meyer in particular being a culprit by missing two easy chances. Argyle's first goal came from an unlikely source. Dougall, whose consistency at left-back had forced him to abandon – temporarily, at least – his plans to look after the reserves, found the net.

Within minutes of the start of the second half, Argyle were awarded a penalty. Up stepped the ever-reliable Carter, but his shot hit the crossbar and flew to safety. Within eight minutes, Argyle were awarded another spot-kick. Surely this time. But, no! Incredibly, Carter's kick struck an upright. The ball rebounded to Penk whose shot seemed destined for the net until Tommy Godwin pulled off a stunning save. Chances continued to go begging. On another day, Argyle might have scored seven or eight. Frustrations continued to mount until Reg Wyatt, scorer of only one goal during his Argyle career so far, put his side in front. A minute from time, Meyer finally got the goal he had strived for all afternoon. The final scoreline, 3-1, looked comfortable but in reality, it was a real nail-biter.

A few days later, the squad set off up north to renew recent acquaintances with Doncaster. Included in the travelling party was Anderson, although he was not expecting to play. Twenty minutes before kick-off Rowley told him to don the No 7 shirt, and thus began one of the most memorable matches of his career.

With no floodlighting, the Thursday evening game kicked off at 5.15pm. Many were still at work, accounting for the crowd of only 5,300.

From the kick-off, Argyle launched an attack and somehow Anderson missed an open goal. It looked an expensive miss when, thirteen minutes later, Ron Walker scored. Almost immediately, Argyle hit back when Gauld hit the crossbar and Penk netted the rebound. The action continued at a relentless pace. George Robertson saved a goalbound shot with his hands and Bill Graham scored from the spot. Meyer equalised after Billy Nimmo had failed to hold a Williams (JL) pile-driver. By half-time, Doncaster had struck twice more, through sixteen-year-old John Meredith and another from Walker.

It looked a lost cause for Argyle, but Gauld for one didn't think so. He came out for the second half like a man possessed. Taking possession from deep positions he frequently embarked on strong-running dribbles to which Rovers had no answer. Twice his tactic conjured up goals for Anderson, plus another for Meyer, and suddenly Argyle found themselves ahead. With six minutes left, Anderson completed his hat-trick and a remarkable turn-around in fortunes. The Pilgrims had won 6-4. It was a pity there were so few people there to witness it.

Yet again the team stayed away, to prepare for the weekend game at Norwich. The Canaries had suffered difficult times in recent years and had again started the season disappointingly. The teams shared a goal apiece and Argyle were again well-pleased with their return from two potentially difficult games.

Argyle's next opponents, Southend, were unlikely to be pushovers. They were scoring freely and were only three points behind the Greens. Their chief threat was posed by former Pilgrim Sam McCrory, who was enjoying the most productive period of his career, despite approaching his mid-thirties. The previous season had seen him notch 31 goals and win his only cap for Northern Ireland at the age of 33. McCrory did indeed score against Argyle, but an own-goal by Shrimpers' Lou Costello set the Greens on their way, with Johnny Williams and Gauld adding further second-half goals.

Next up were third-placed Swindon, boasting one of the best away records in the division. Rowley was forced into a change, with Meyer having taken a knock against Southend, but Baker was a more than capable deputy.

With a wet and muddy playing surface making attractive football difficult, Argyle, not for the first time, found themselves on the end of some robust tackling. Gauld, yet again, was a marked man, with Bert Head's side content to play with 'only four forwards' (how quaint that sounds today) to allow extra defensive cover. The match burst into life when Gauld was felled and Carter stroked home the resultant penalty. Ninety seconds later, Swindon equalised through Andy Micklewright. From the restart, Argyle attacked again and Gauld finished off a move he had started.

The second half started with the visitors in even more determined mood, and a thirty-yard strike from Bob Edwards reinforced their belief that they could continue their excellent away form. They had not bargained for the individual brilliance of Gauld. With hundreds of spectators having already left the ground, believing the game to be destined for a draw, Gauld set about on a trademark run. No one dribbled quite like Jimmy. He never seemed to be fully in control of the ball. Shins, thighs, knees were all used as he blustered his way through scything tackles, using pure strength and the occasional bit of luck. Once he was up to speed he was difficult to stop, as the number of penalties he earned testify. Now, with full-time approaching, he set off on one last ploughing run from the halfway line. Shaking off several tackles, he reached the penalty area and unleashed a shot that keeper Sam Burton couldn't hold. The ball rebounded back to Gauld who had the easy task of scoring into an unguarded net to clinch a sensational 3-2 victory.

Not to be outdone, Carter then produced a hat-trick as another victory was notched up, this time at Mansfield. The Argyle forward was now the Third Division's leading scorer and the Greens were already four points clear of their nearest challengers. The relentless march towards the title continued. Notts County, Chesterfield and Newport were all swept aside. By the time the FA Cup first round arrived, the Greens were six points ahead of second-placed Reading.

Despite the on-field success, a boardroom battle was brewing behind the scenes which threatened to derail the promotion effort. At the centre of the dispute was chairman Ron Blindell. He was attempting to bring in another director in the form of a Mr Hughes, who, it transpired, was the assistant managing director of Blindell's company. Another of Blindell's proposals was to pension off popular secretary Bert Cole. These schemes provoked a stormy response at the AGM, which was held in the YMCA building.

Blindell attempted to pacify his critics by offering Cole a pension of £300 a year in lieu of his service to the club. It did little to calm tempers, with Blindell being accused of running the club as a dictatorship. Two days later, at a board meeting prior to the Newport home match, the directors took just twenty minutes to vote him out of the office he had held for only seven months. Fellow director Harry Deans took over as chairman. Forty-eight hours later, Blindell resigned his directorship, although he remained the largest shareholder.

The Cup draw had given Argyle a seemingly easy passage into the next round, as Gillingham, then a Fourth Division side, came to Devon. With little to lose, they gave an excellent account of themselves and despite goals from Carter and Anderson, took Argyle back to Priestfield on the Wednesday evening for a replay.

With Carter injured, Rowley recalled the fit-again Meyer. The slightly built forward certainly staked his claim for a regular place again with a hat-trick in a 4-1 win. Gauld was again the inspiration, having a hand in all three of Meyer's goals and scoring one himself, despite playing with a broken toe sustained in the first match.

Carter was still injured for the first ever visit of Wrexham to Home Park. He was missed as the Welsh side returned home with an unexpected point following a 2-2 draw. Perhaps the Argyle players' minds were distracted by an appeal carried in the matchday programme for the owner of a lady's pink plastic mac to be reunited with its owner.

The idea of playing friendlies in the midst of a busy season is unthinkable to modern-day managers, keen to protect their players as much as possible. In the 1950s it was common practice, and on the Monday evening Argyle hosted Scunthorpe, managed by former Argyle favourite Tony McShane, with Rowley fielding a full-strength side.

The wisdom of playing a friendly at such a time was certainly questioned by the following Saturday. Argyle travelled to The Dell to take on a Southampton side who were scoring goals almost as prolifically as Argyle. Rowley made the difficult decision to omit Meyer, as Carter was fit again. By the final whistle, Meyer probably regarded the match as a good one to miss. The Saints had been 2-0 up at half-time and never looked back. Argyle were hesitant and their passing abysmal. They had little cause to complain as the Saints ran out 5-1 winners, with future England star Terry Paine scoring twice.

Two nights later, Argyle were committed to another friendly against a British Army XI, with part of the proceeds from the gate money being donated to club secretary Bert Cole, in recognition of his long and loyal service to the club. The Army were able to call on the services of a number of well-known players who were undergoing National Service, including Peter Dobing, Gerry Hitchens and one Lance Corporal John Williams of Plymouth Argyle.

Sadly, a cloud was cast over the excitement of Argyle's winning ways by the sudden death of trainer George Reed, who had been a popular figure at Home Park for many years. Rowley had asked Reed and the injured Govan to travel to Coventry to spy on Argyle's next Cup opponents. At the last minute, Govan was detained in Plymouth and Reed made the trip on his own. While running to catch his train, he suffered a fatal heart attack.

The tie at Coventry presented a potential banana skin, with the Sky Blues in good form and among the promotion candidates in Division Four. The jittery performance at Southampton was quickly forgotten as Argyle soon got into their stride. Baker put them ahead, but Ray Straw equalised before half-time. The second half started with a Coventry onslaught on the Argyle goal, but Barnsley, so often a spectator in previous one-sided affairs, was up to the task, pulling off two superb saves. Gradually, Gauld imposed himself on the match. He had been closely shackled in the first half, but these were methods that had been tried on him before and failed, and so it proved again. A characteristic burst into the area resulted in him being brought down and Carter made no mistake from the penalty spot. Then, another burst saw him square the ball to Baker, who laid it to Carter. The striker had all the time in the world to pick his spot and it was Round Three here we come.

League glory was still uppermost in everyone's minds but a goalless draw at Bradford City saw Argyle's lead reduced to three points. The team now in second place, Hull, were their next opponents.

Rowley decided it was time to reinforce his squad. With the odd exception, he had used the same players for much of the season and was fearful that injuries and fatigue would eventually catch up with them. He made a double swoop on Chelsea players Wally Bellett and Len Casey for a combined fee of £15,000. Bellett was a burly defender, a former England Youth international, whilst Casey was a highly regarded half-back who, within a month of arriving, was appointed as Argyle's new captain. He would be Argyle's third skipper of the season: Carter had earlier asked to be relieved of such duties and Robertson had taken over.

The two newcomers were both included against Hull, with the injured Dougall and JL Williams the ones to miss out. The match was a test of Argyle's character. The Tigers took a first-half lead through tall centre-forward Colin Smith and it took a goal from Carter, his seventeenth of the season, to preserve Argyle's unbeaten home record. A collection on behalf of George Reed's family was taken at the match.

Boxing Day saw Gauld at his imperious best. This time it was the turn of QPR to try, and fail, to suppress his strong running. In front of over 30,000 – Argyle's biggest crowd of the season so far – Rangers took the lead after 24 minutes. Peter Angell sent a free-kick into the Argyle area. With bodies slipping and sliding in the goalmouth mud, the ball somehow struck Les Locke, a Scottish Empire Games half-miler, and flew past a flat-footed Barnsley. Before half-time, Bellett made a Gauld-like surge upfield and set up an equaliser for the prolific Carter.

At one point roars of laughter emanated from the large crowd as a desperate Rangers defender resorted to ripping off Gauld's shorts as the Argyle man was in full flight. Most tactics, legal or otherwise, had been employed over the course of the season to curb him but this was certainly a novel approach.

New shorts were quickly found and Gauld's dignity was restored. For a few minutes, at least, his bottom half stood out like a beacon among his mud-splattered colleagues.

The inside-forward soon exacted revenge. Govan, on the left wing, had been languishing in the reserves for the past three months, but was now relishing his first-team opportunity. In the 53rd minute his cross was met at the near post by Gauld, whose shot left keeper Ray Drinkwater helpless. Eighteen minutes later Gauld scored a sensational goal. Collecting Govan's corner, he beat four defenders along the goal-line before flashing the ball home. Rangers, to their credit, kept plugging away and a late goal from winger Mike Tomkys made it a nervous final five minutes.

The next day, at Loftus Road, Rangers got their revenge. Gauld was again on target but inside-forwards John Pearson and Arthur Longbottom gave the homesters the points.

With the first scheduled match of the New Year, at Tranmere, postponed, it was time for Cup action again. A home tie with mid-table Second Division Cardiff was hardly what the supporters, at least, had hoped for, but it would be a good indicator as to the standard of opponents Argyle would hopefully meet next season. The final result certainly gave Rowley food for thought, as the Welshmen emerged as 3-0 winners. It would be Meyer's last game for Argyle. He had failed to settle in Plymouth and hankered for a move back nearer his Bristol home. An eventual transfer to Newport satisfied his demands. In later years, he would become a familiar figure on TV screens as one of the country's leading Test Match umpires.

The league postponement and Argyle's Cup diversion had seen Hull slip ahead of them in the table. The Tigers were now two points clear but had played four more games than Argyle. The rest of the front runners had made little headway and the chase for the title was beginning to look like a two-horse race. But of course, as the top two would be promoted, the Greens still had high hopes of Second Division football next season.

Winning ways were restored at home to Stockport. Argyle's next scheduled opponents, Accrington Stanley, were surprisingly engaged on FA Cup fifth round duties, so Rowley moved swiftly to bring forward the away fixture with Southend. It was not due to be played until late in the season, but moving it would at least reduce a potential fixture backlog. Roots Hall was not Argyle's happiest hunting ground, and a goalless draw at the home of the third-placed side was a decent enough result.

Although Reading had failed to maintain their early-season form, a trip to Elm Park was still hazardous. A goal in each half from Govan and Baker provided another excellent result in front of a sizeable number of fans who had also made the trip.

Former favourite Neil Langman received a warm reception as he returned to Home Park for the first time with his new club, Colchester. He failed to score the goal he craved, but still had reason to be pleased as the U's stole a point from a 1-1 draw. With the consistent Robertson injured, Fulton was drafted in as right-back. Another draw, at Bournemouth, was chiefly down to excellent work from the defence, but Norwich then came to Home Park and upset the apple cart by condemning Argyle to their first home league defeat of the season. The Canaries had been up and down in the league, leaving them in mid-table, but they were taking the FA Cup by storm. They would eventually reach the semi-finals before losing to Luton. In the meantime, the aforementioned lost property office was becoming overrun. It was now in possession of another plastic mac, a Trilby hat and a set of keys.

That home defeat by Norwich triggered a strange sequence of results. A week later, Argyle went to Swindon and won 4-3, with Gauld getting a hat-trick. Reserve-team striker Reg Jenkins was handed his debut. Then Accrington came to Home Park and defied the odds, and their poor away record, by winning 4-2.

Suddenly, the promotion push was faltering. A visit from Mansfield, who had lost just one of their previous ten games, took on new importance. The Accrington defeat prompted Rowley to hand Wyllie his debut in goal, whilst Fincham, who had waited patiently in the reserves, was also given a belated baptism at centre-half, with Wyatt injured. Within twenty minutes, fears of another home defeat were seemingly dispelled. With less than two minutes on the clock, Town's centre-half, Terry Swinscoe, had turned the ball past his own keeper. Wingers Govan and Penk then got on the scoresheet, but by half-time the visitors were back in it, courtesy of two goals stemming from precision corners taken by veteran Jamaican winger Lindy Delapenha.

The second half started with Argyle looking distinctly shaky and it was no surprise when Mansfield dramatically equalised through John Downie. At 3-3, and sensing that their side's promotion dreams were vanishing before their eyes, some of the crowd began barracking the team. But this Argyle side were a resolute bunch. Gauld scored from the narrowest of angles after bulldozing his way along the goal-line from the left. Then, in a twenty-minute spell, Johnny Williams scored twice, either side of a Carter penalty. There was still time for an eighth, with the hapless Swinscoe again putting past his own goalkeeper to seal one of the most outrageous results, 8-3, in Plymouth's history.

As an aside, Argyle's match programme that day carried a lengthy and detailed breakdown of the potential earnings of a professional footballer of the day. As well as a maximum wage of £20, players were also entitled to a bonus of £4 for a win and £2 for a draw. There were also specified additional payments for appearances in Cup matches and friendlies.

Seven days later, Argyle produced an indifferent display at Notts County but still came away with the points, thanks to two moments of inspiration from that man Gauld. In the eighteenth minute, he astonished everyone by scoring from the narrowest of angles. County's seventeen-year-old goalkeeper, Dick Twigg, later confessed 'I don't know what he did with it'. County equalised through Alan Withers, but a minute before the interval Gauld collected the ball, brushed off two challenges, rounded centre-half Bert Loxley and the hapless Twigg, and planted the ball into an empty net.

A 0-2 defeat in the rearranged match at Tranmere meant Argyle had now used up all their games in hand but were still a point behind leaders Hull, with both sides having played 36 matches. Brentford were third, six points in arrears of Argyle, but with two games in hand.

The defeat of Chesterfield saw Jenkins score his maiden goal. It was one of only three that he scored for Argyle, but he would find great success away from Home Park later in his career, particularly at Rochdale, where he became something of a legend.

Easter began with a worrying 0-3 defeat at Brentford, who were still the most likely side to spoil Argyle's promotion aspirations. It was the London side's twelfth match in a row without defeat and they were on a roll. The manner of the loss moved Rowley into restoring keeper Barnsley and JL Williams for the following day's match at Newport, where Carter's disputed penalty after Gauld had been upended, restored some belief and confidence to the side.

Easter Monday saw a vital match as Argyle again crossed swords with Brentford. It was a game the Bees were more desperate to win than the Pilgrims, but whilst promotion was the initial priority, Rowley still wanted the championship. A goal for each side in the first half was the extent of the scoring, which maintained Argyle's advantage over their opponents.

Fortunately, nerves were also afflicting Hull, who had also dropped points. Argyle led the table again with 54 points from 40 matches. Hull were a point and a game behind, with Brentford on 49 points with two matches in hand over Argyle. Barring the unforeseeable, no other sides were in contention. Perm any two from three for promotion.

Another edgy home draw followed against Halifax, who had little to play for apart from their £4 win bonus. Then came a third successive 1-1 draw at Wrexham. The other leading sides were also faltering. Hull had used up their game in hand and now headed Argyle on goal-average alone. Brentford had collected only two points from their last three games and their odds were now lengthening.

Argyle now sought revenge on Southampton for the 1-5 thrashing inflicted in November. Strangely, since then, the Saints' form had slumped, particularly away from The Dell, where they had captured only four points from their last ten away trips. With goal-average looking likely to decide the destiny of the title, a high-scoring victory for Argyle would have been the ideal scenario, but it wasn't to be. It took Carter's 24th goal of the season to secure the two points.

It was now time for the Argyle players to earn their corn. Away from the 20,000-plus crowds of Home Park, they now faced two away matches in the stark surroundings of Halifax's Shay Ground and Accrington's Peel Park. For the trip to Halifax, Rowley reunited the wing partnership of Anderson and Penk, which had been so successful in the first half of the season. It was an inspired decision, as Anderson scored the only goal, arguably the most important of his career. Brentford were still picking up points but were running out of games.

Argyle arrived at Accrington's ground from their base in Southport to find a quagmire of a pitch. After a prolonged dry spell, the playing surface had been hosed throughout Friday to make it more playable. What hadn't been bargained for was the incessant rain which had swept the North West throughout the Saturday morning and which continued throughout the game. It made for an uncomfortable afternoon for the dozen Argyle supporters who had travelled through the night by train in the hope of seeing their heroes clinch promotion to the Second Division.

They didn't need to wait long to be cheered up. In the fifteenth minute, Stanley's keeper, Bill McInnes, playing his first match for six weeks, sliced an attempted clearance straight to Penk, who blasted the ball into the net. As conditions worsened, so did the standard of play. Argyle held on to their lead until the 57th minute, when Terry Tighe finished off a Stanley move involving the Anders brothers, Jimmy and Harry. Both sides continued to battle their way through the mud but the final whistle brought huge relief as the point was enough to confirm Argyle's promotion.

It was the third time the club had won promotion and on each occasion they had clinched it away from home. The pro-active Supporters Club had made advanced arrangements, in the event of promotion being confirmed, before the final home game. As the team coach arrived back in Devon on the Sunday afternoon it was met at Ivybridge, to be appropriately decorated. It then made its way into Plymouth city centre, where around five hundred cars joined the cavalcade before it returned triumphantly to Home Park.

The final match of the season was scheduled for Wednesday night and over 26,000 turned up to salute the promotion heroes. Of course, the title was still possible. Hull and Argyle both had 61 points. But with a much inferior goal-average, the Pilgrims knew they had to better whatever result Hull achieved at Wrexham.

In keeping with tradition, Argyle's opponents, Bradford City, formed a line to applaud Casey's side out of the tunnel. The match itself was a hard-fought affair with both sides managing a goal apiece in the first half. Just before half-time, Gauld was in the wars and missed the first thirteen minutes of the second half with a back strain. He resumed, but in a right-wing position.

Half-time brought the news that Hull were losing at Wrexham. There were no further goals at Home Park, but there were at the Racecourse Ground, where Hull blew their chances of the championship by being on the wrong end of a 1-5 thrashing. Argyle were the first ever champions of the new Third Division.

# SEVEN

# 1967-68 (Relegated to Division 3)

Since winning promotion in 1959, Argyle had stagnated. Of course, being a Second Division club was nothing to be ashamed of, but apart from 1961-62, when the team had briefly flirted with the possibility of First Division football, the side had generally finished in the lower third of the table. In 1961-62, with Wilf Carter and George Kirby banging in goals, Argyle had finished fifth. It might have been better, but expectation and pressure told, and only one point was gained from the final six games.

Since then, Plymouth had been seen as a footballing backwater, a club lacking ambition and with no obvious direction. As such, it had struggled to attract the calibre of player required to make them competitive. The 1963-64 season had seen the club escape relegation on goal-average. The following year another mediocre league season was brightened by a run to the semi-final of the new League Cup, where Leicester were victorious over two legs. Argyle's manager was the extrovert Malcolm Allison, who had been given his first taste of league management. Before the season was out, relations soured, mainly over team-selection policy, and less than a year after his appointment, Allison was off.

In appointing his successor, Argyle opted for continuity, giving Allison's chief coach, Derek Ufton, the job. It signified that the board approved of Allison's futuristic approach to matters on the field, at least, and it was hoped that Ufton would provide a seamless transition.

Ufton was a distinguished sportsman. He had been Charlton's first-choice centre-half for ten years and had won one England cap. He was also a fine cricketer, having played 149 times for Kent as a wicketkeeper, understudy to the legendary Godfrey Evans.

Ufton's first season in charge was generally uninspiring, with the side finishing eighteenth. His chief claim was that he got the club back on a relatively secure financial footing. Allison was not afraid to spend the club's money, as illustrated by the record fee of £40,000 paid to secure the services of Welsh international winger Barrie Jones. Ufton took a different view. If he could secure a fee for an Argyle player, regardless of how vital that player was to the team effort, he would. Mike Trebilcock and Frank Lord were two prime examples.

The following season was almost a mirror image. A sixteenth place finish barely represented progress and the likes of Barrie Jones and Nicky Jennings had moved on. On a more positive note, local players such as Mike Bickle and Norman Piper had been given their chance and made an immediate impression.

Some of the revenue generated by Ufton was spent on ground improvements. The floodlights had been upgraded and 1,000 extra seats installed below the grandstand, to be known as the Mayflower Enclosure.

There was also a pre-season treat for the players as they embarked on a three-match tour of Holland and West Germany. The Pilgrims won the first and last games, against Groningen and KSV Holstein Kiel, but lost the other game in controversial fashion, with Wuppertal being awarded two penalties and centre-half Andy Nelson getting sent off. The tour also saw a number of players suffer injuries, the most serious being target-man Mike Bickle's cartilage, which necessitated surgery and would mean missing several weeks of the season.

For the fifth successive season, Argyle were handed an opening fixture away from home. Cardiff was the destination, where a last-minute goal from winger John Mitten secured a point, after Cardiff – who included Barrie Jones – had scored from a disputed penalty by former England amateur international Bobby Brown.

Aston Villa provided the attractive opposition as Home Park showed off its new floodlights to a crowd in excess of 20,000. Villa were newly relegated but favourites to make a quick return to Division One. They were upstaged by two of Argyle's young guns, in Steve Davey on the right wing and home debutant, John Tedesco, at inside-right. Both were only eighteen and products of the Plymouth Schools side. The youngsters scored the goals that gave Argyle a 2-0 interval lead. Barry Stobart pulled a goal back but it was a promising start with three points out of four.

Three days later, Portsmouth were the visitors. Unusually for a Saturday game, the match had an evening kick-off so as not to clash with the annual 'Navy Days' event, which would have affected the attendance. Pompey included former Argyle favourite Nicky Jennings and ran out 2-1 winners. The unfortunate Davey suffered a broken collar bone and was substituted by Richard Reynolds. The use of substitutes was still a novelty, with the rule – allowing a replacement for injured players, not for tactical reasons – just two seasons old.

Bank Holiday Monday saw Argyle and Aston Villa quickly renew their acquaintance. The Pilgrims confirmed their new-found status as the Midlanders' bogey side with John Mitten's goal enough to increase the unrest on the Villa Park terraces, following a distinctly unimpressive start to their season.

The fixture planners had been particularly unkind to Argyle, and two more difficult away matches followed, at Norwich and Crystal Palace. Neither match yielded so much as a goal or a point. Carrow Road was proving a difficult place to get any favours and the Canaries were full value for their 2-0 win. Four days later, Argyle suffered a 0-5 thrashing at Selhurst Park. Both games saw Ufton forced to field a makeshift defence, with Nelson suspended after his foreign misdemeanours and Johnny Newman injured. Regular full-backs Mike Everitt and Doug Baird were asked to play in the Nos 5 and 6 shirts, with local lads Tony Rounsevell and Mike Reeves taking their full-back positions.

Supporters hoped the defeats represented only a temporary blip, but a 0-1 home reverse to Rotherham began to set alarm bells ringing. The Millers had started the season abysmally, losing all four games they had played and were rock bottom of the division. Losing to them meant there were now serious concerns that the lack of a predatory goalscorer would prove a severe handicap. Argyle possessed some creative players, such as Mitten and Piper, but at the moment there was no one capable of finishing what they had started. Bickle was the obvious solution, but he was still some weeks away from full fitness.

Attention switched to the League Cup, where Argyle were paired with fellow Second Division side Birmingham. Despite home advantage, Ufton's side faced a tough match. The Blues contained some talented players, notably former England internationals Fred Pickering and Barry Bridges, and were unbeaten after six league games. Goals from Geoff Vowden and Trevor Hockey gave them a relatively easy passage into the next round.

As frustrated as anyone by his side's barren spell, Ufton sprang some surprises in his team selection for the trip to Derby. Centre-forward Keith Etheridge was dropped and his No 9 shirt handed to John Sillett, normally a defender. Davey was declared fit, but Argyle were still firing blanks, except for Everitt, who put past his own keeper to hand Derby victory. To add to the woes, Tedesco's name was added to the injury list.

With the need for more firepower never more obvious, Ufton acted quickly by securing the signing of former England Under-23 left-winger Mike Harrison from Blackburn. With legs of tree-trunk proportions, Harrison had a reputation for possessing one of the fiercest shots in the game, as well as pace and athleticism. There was widespread acclaim for Ufton's enterprise.

The new boy was handed the No 11 shirt for the visit of Preston, ousting Mitten. North End were as inept as Argyle in front of goal, having scored only five times in eight games. Piper, the one Argyle player who had shown any consistency over the season so far, scored the Greens' first goal in six games, but two strikes from Derek Temple consigned Argyle to another defeat.

Even at this relatively early stage, Ufton was beginning to run out of options. Injuries aside, he had little in the way of experience to call upon and there were a few 'I told you so' nods from the wiser old sages in the crowd who had forecast that Ufton would come to regret his decision to allow certain players to be sold.

Ufton again turned to the transfer market and splashed out £9,000 on another winger, Alan Sealey. Sealey was a well-known name in footballing circles, mainly through his exploits in one particular game, when he scored twice in West Ham's European Cup-Winners' Cup final triumph in 1965. Since then he had been blighted by injury, but had notched up over 100 games for the Hammers.

Ufton took his side to his old stomping ground at Charlton, where he continued to tinker with the forward line. Sealey was handed his debut on the right wing and the experiment of using Sillett at centre-forward was quickly abandoned. Reynolds was asked to lead the attack but Argyle were still firing blanks. A goal from Alan Campbell was enough to send them to the bottom of the table. Crowd trouble between the two rival sets of fans contributed to a forgettable day.

Signing wingers to create chances was all well and good, but a waste if there was no one to put those chances away. Anxious to get a new face to fill the No 9 shirt, Ufton again plumped for experience in the form of Alan Peacock. The bearer of six England caps, Peacock was something of a legend at his home town club, Middlesbrough, where he had averaged more than a goal every two games. Described by former England boss Walter Winterbottom as the finest header of a ball in the country, Peacock had spent the previous three seasons at Leeds, where he continued to score his fair share. His agreeing to join Argyle, for a fee of £10,000, was seen as a surprising coup for Ufton. Peacock's arrival attracted such widespread publicity that the actual signing of his contract was televised live on Westward TV. In reality, his capture represented a gamble. Peacock had been dogged by cartilage problems for the past few seasons and had undergone a number of operations.

The new 'dream team' forward line faced mid-table Huddersfield at Home Park. With a touch of irony it was Reynolds who scored the goal that gave Argyle a draw and ended the dismal run of six successive league defeats. In a portent of what was to come, Peacock went off injured and as events transpired, it would be the only game when all three of the new signings lined up together.

A week later, Peacock made a nostalgic return to Middlesbrough. Ufton brought in Alan Banks for his first game of the season. Banks had been a prolific scorer at Exeter prior to becoming a Pilgrim in May 1966, but as so often happens, found life harder at his new club. For the past year he had largely been a peripheral figure at Home Park. It was not a return Peacock would enjoy. Argyle were thrashed 0-5, with Peacock's successor, John Hickton, scoring a hat-trick. Peacock was injured to boot.

Argyle announced an addition to the backroom staff, although it was certainly not a new face. Ellis Stuttard had first played for Argyle during the war years and had since served the club as manager, trainer and coach.

More recently, he had been assisting Arsenal but was back at Home Park now as chief scout.

If the supporters thought it couldn't get any worse on the field, it did. Attendances at Home Park began to fall dramatically. The home game with Hull attracted less than half the number who had attended the opening fixture of the season only two months earlier. Despite being 1-2 down at half-time, Argyle were seemingly still in contention but ended up conceding five for the second successive match. Now Ufton had real problems. Not only was his side not scoring, but the defence was as watertight as a paper tissue.

The following Tuesday saw Argyle win a game, not that anyone was too excited. The match was a friendly against Groningen, one of the Dutch sides Argyle had opposed on their pre-season tour. Only 2,421 bothered to turn up. Argyle fielded a virtually full-strength side, when it seemed an ideal opportunity to blood a few youngsters. In charge for the evening was former favourite Frank Lord, newly appointed as chief coach but also registered as a player.

No one expected much from the next away game. But then no one expected much from a trip to Millwall. The Lions rarely lost at the Den and the hostility of their supporters made The Den an intimidating place. Argyle hardly helped themselves when Baird scored an own-goal, his second of the season. Keith Weller added a second before half-time and Tom Wilson made it three in the second period to increase the pressure on Ufton.

That match was to prove to be Sealey's last in the Football League. He would eventually lose his battle with injury and would see out his playing days at non-league Romford. Another player making his final appearance was Newman. The elegant defender had given great service to Argyle but, along with Banks, joined Exeter in an £8,000 deal. The loss of Newman in particular hardly helped Ufton's popularity rating. The departure of such an experienced player at a crucial time was frowned upon by many.

Due to the inclement weather, the next two games, Blackpool (home) and Blackburn (away), were postponed. As the side ran out for the match with Bristol City at Home Park, there was particularly loud applause for the return of Bickle, seen by many as Argyle's potential saviour, particularly as Peacock was fit again and would take some of the burden off the young-ster's shoulders. Ninety minutes later, any enthusiasm had evaporated. Argyle had drawn a blank again and self-destructed with Everitt's first-half own-goal proving decisive. The Pilgrims' fifteen games had yielded just six meagre points.

Bickle's return coincided with Argyle's best run of the season, starting with a draw at Ipswich. Mitten, recalled for the injured Harrison, once again scored a last-minute equaliser. Then came a heartening 3-1 victory over seventh-placed Carlisle. Bickle was off the mark for the season and Peacock notched his first Argyle goal. In eighteen competitive matches, it was only the third time Argyle had scored more than once in a game.

Another surprise win, at Bolton on an icy pitch, lifted Argyle above Rotherham at the foot of the table. Suddenly there was a new-found confidence in the side. A few of the stay-away supporters returned to watch a goalless draw with Cardiff. The Welsh side, boasting a young John Toshack in their line up, had scored more than double the number of goals Argyle had so far, but the Argyle defence kept them at bay.

Two days later, Ufton's men sprang another surprise by holding leaders Portsmouth to a scoreless draw at Fratton Park. Argyle still weren't scoring many but results were more encouraging.

The Boxing Day clash at home to QPR was keenly anticipated. Not only were Rangers a top-five side but they played attractive football. They had captured the imagination of the public by sweeping to the Third Division title, scoring 103 goals in the process, and by creating history with a famous League Cup final win over West Brom. They possessed a number of skilful players, such as the Morgan twins, Roger and Ian, and more famously, Rodney Marsh. Marsh was an extrovert, idolised by Rangers fans but the type of player opposing supporters loved to hate. He was capable of brilliance but also had developed something of a reputation as a player who, shall we say, fell over with little persuasion when finding himself in opposing penalty areas.

Argyle gave a good account of themselves but in the 73rd minute all hell broke loose. Hore 'tackled' Marsh in the Argyle eighteen-yard box and the Rangers forward went tumbling. To the consternation of the 21,000 crowd a penalty was awarded. The grin on Marsh's face as he got to his feet said it all. A goodly number of the crowd invaded the pitch in protest and it was several minutes before sufficient order could be restored to allow Rangers' skipper Mike Keen to place his penalty out of Pat Dunne's reach. Further protests took place at the final whistle as the players scurried for the tunnel.

Of course, in modern times, a pitch invasion has serious repercussions for the host club. In 1967, it was becoming an all-too-frequent occurrence. Football hooliganism was manifesting itself in the game and fines of up to £250, a considerable sum in those days, had not deterred the perpetrators. On the field, behaviour was little better. Sending offs were more frequent and some star names had been embroiled in fisticuffs. Many blamed the antics of some foreign sides in the 1966 World Cup finals, where the likes of Pele had been given particularly rough treatment in an attempt to overcome skill with brawn.

The small-format, undistinguished Argyle match programme carried a regular warning to would-be trouble makers, informing supporters that 'anyone caught throwing toilet rolls would be evicted and bottle-throwing louts and persons using vile and abusive language similarly dealt with.'

Four days later, Argyle and QPR resumed their acquaintance at Loftus Road. This time the form book was a truer guide. Marsh was on his best behaviour in front of his adoring fans and scored twice in a 4-1 win.

The following Saturday's match with Norwich at Home Park was postponed but hastily rearranged for the following Wednesday. A ding-dong battle ensued with honours even after ninety minutes. A point was better than nothing but Argyle were quickly getting into the position where they could ill-afford to drop home points at all.

A nail-biter against fellow strugglers Rotherham was scheduled, but Britain was enveloped in Arctic conditions and the clash at Millmoor was one of 39 English league games postponed.

There was a dramatic opening to the following match against Derby. Mitten put Argyle ahead with only 36 seconds on the clock. The goals continued to fly in, with County eventually winning 4-3. It was excitement all the way for the spectators, but yet again home points had been frittered away. The match proved to be the last of Peacock's career. He had never been able to shake off the effects of his long-standing injury problems and was eventually forced to call it a day. Ufton's master plan of bringing in experience was falling apart.

Hopes of a lucrative FA Cup run were dashed when the third round draw sent Argyle to meet First Division Sheffield Wednesday. Plymouth's bank manager was rubbing his hands in glee, though. A bumper crowd was ensured regardless of who Wednesday met. The Owls contained a number of players who had played in their losing FA Cup final only two years earlier and simply had too much class as they eased to a 3-0 win. At least another of Ufton's walking wounded was back, veteran Jimmy Bloomfield making his first appearance of the season after injury.

The defeat proved to be one too many. The board decided to act before games ran out and Ufton was sacked. Despite recent struggles, he was a well-liked figure and an excellent coach, but when backsides needed kicking he was probably too nice a chap to do it. He had also, in the eyes of many, lacked ideas on how to extricate his side from its current crisis. Too much emphasis had been placed on the capture of Sealey, Harrison and Peacock, and that had patently backfired. Ufton would never again manage a side, but years later became a director at Charlton.

As the temporary excitement of the Cup passed, Argyle returned to the more serious issue of attempting to avoid the drop. Tough-tackling Bobby Saxton, a player who could play as a defender or half-back, was signed from Derby for £12,000 and his signing completed in a hotel room at 1.30am to enable him to be registered for Argyle's next game, at Preston. Saxton was also appointed as captain. It was not a winning debut, as North

End won 2-0. Bloomfield was injured once more and would be yet another player who would never play for the club again.

The search for a new manager continued. The directors' first choice appeared to be Torquay boss Frank O'Farrell, but with the Gulls looking promotion possibilities, he showed little interest in leaving Plainmoor. Instead, O'Farrell recommended fellow Irishman Billy Bingham. Bingham was manager of Third Division Southport and also of Northern Ireland, a combined role he seemed happy with. But the Argyle board began to make noises his way.

Still managerless, Argyle were thrashed at home by Charlton. Four days later, Bingham was announced as the Pilgrims' new manager although he insisted on retaining his Northern Ireland job as well. Bingham was reported to be on a salary of £5,000 a year and a bonus of £2,000 if he could keep Argyle up. It was a wage that far outweighed anything the club had ever paid before.

His appointment appeared to be a sensible one. Bingham was a genial character but had a reputation of working his players hard. He certainly knew the game inside out, having notched up over 400 league games for Sunderland, Luton, Everton and Port Vale, and earned 56 caps for Northern Ireland, for whom he had appeared in the 1958 World Cup finals. A broken leg had ended his playing career only two years earlier.

Bingham certainly seemed to have the Midas touch. His first two games in charge ended in victories. Goals in the eleventh and 26th minutes gave Argyle a splendid start over Blackburn, and was followed a week later by a single-goal triumph at Huddersfield. These four points again lifted Argyle above Rotherham, but with two sides to be relegated, the Greens were still three points behind the next side, Preston.

Bingham's honeymoon period came to an end with a home defeat by Middlesbrough, Arthur Horsfield getting the only goal after half an hour. The writing looked on the wall a week later, as Blackpool retired to the Home Park dressing room at half-time two goals to the good, but at least there were signs that Bingham had installed some fighting qualities as goals from Reynolds and Tedesco rescued a point.

There was another new face in the Argyle eleven that took the field at Hull. Dave Burnside was a skilful and talented midfielder who had plied his trade with West Brom, Southampton, Crystal Palace and Wolves, and won England Youth and Under-23 honours. Famed for his ball-juggling ability, he was allowed the luxury of regularly commuting from his Bristol home to Plymouth. Burnside more than played his part in gaining a vital two points from Boothferry Park. Hull were relegation candidates themselves and Argyle were now within five points of them.

The squad stayed up North for the rearranged fixture at Rotherham. These two clubs had occupied the bottom two positions for many weeks and defeat for either would be a major blow to survival hopes. As it was, a single goal from Brian Tiler was enough to give the Millers the points. It was a memorable evening for one Argyle player. Colin Sullivan was handed his debut at left-back, and at sixteen years, eight months and 23 days, became the youngest ever player to wear first-team colours for Argyle. It was a bold move by Bingham to thrust the youngster into such a crucial match. Sullivan had only started a handful of games for the reserves but was clearly a talented and level-headed young man who appeared totally unfazed by the burden placed upon him.

There were two departures from Home Park. Bloomfield accepted the position of player-manager at Orient, whilst it was a sad farewell to Neil Dougall, who had served the club as player, manager, scout, coach and manager since 1948. He had recently been assisting with coaching duties.

Two goals from Norman Piper were enough to see off Millwall and at least keep Argyle in touch with their fellow strugglers. Argyle remained bottom with 23 points, one behind Rotherham and two behind Preston. Bristol City held a four-point advantage.

Defeat at Blackpool signalled the end of Harrison's Argyle career. He had regularly occupied the treatment table in recent weeks and would eventually depart for Luton. Ufton's three major signings had managed only 31 league and cup games, and scored four goals between them.

The Easter fixtures looked difficult. Three games in four days were never easy, but the programme commenced with a real four-pointer at Bristol City, followed by home and away fixtures with Birmingham. More than 800 Argyle fans swelled a bumper Ashton Park gate and watched a nervous opening half with both sides knowing that the first goal would be vital. The first 45 minutes passed without a score but two second-half goals from John Galley gave the hosts some breathing space and increased Argyle's plight.

Easter Monday saw Birmingham visit Home Park. The Blues were having a fine season, having remained near the top of the league for the whole campaign, and had just secured an FA Cup semi-final tie with West Brom. They had disposed of Arsenal and Chelsea in previous rounds and were playing with considerable style. On three occasions already, the St Andrews crowd had seen their team score six goals in a match. Barry Bridges had already contributed 22 goals himself, and three other players were in double figures. Injuries had again left Bingham short of options and he was forced into playing striker Keith Etheridge at half-back. The reshuffle didn't upset Argyle's early rhythm and a superb goal from Bickle put them ahead, but strikes from Fred Pickering and Graham Leggatt ensured the form book wasn't upset.

A day later the two sides met at St Andrews. Argyle brought back Andy Nelson to bolster the defence but again the Greens showed spirited form and demonstrated the progress made under Bingham. They were again indebted to Bickle, whose two goals gave the Pilgrims a 2-1 half-time advantage to stun the 30,000 crowd. Birmingham fought back to clinch a draw but it was a blow to their promotion hopes.

The standard of performances since Bingham had taken over had given encouragement, but the harsh fact remained that Argyle probably needed to win all of their five remaining games. When Ipswich won at Home Park on the following Saturday, thanks to a John O'Rourke goal, it all but condemned Argyle to the drop. A draw at Blackburn confirmed relegation and there was little incentive to produce the goods at Carlisle where Argyle suffered a 0-2 defeat.

The two remaining games were both at home and the supporters certainly made their feelings known by staying away. Defeat by Bolton hardly brightened the mood and the final match against Crystal Palace attracted fewer than 5,000 through the turnstiles.

No one could argue that relegation wasn't deserved. At times, Argyle's style of play was not relegation standard, but the 'goals for' column told the story. Thirty-eight goals in 42 matches was a poor effort. Yes, injuries had played a major part in the downfall, and had Bickle been available for the whole season the story may have been different. There were some positive points. A number of youngsters such as Davey, Tedesco and particularly Sullivan had showed considerable promise and would probably benefit from Third Division football. Piper had continued to produce displays which had bigger clubs keeping a watchful eye, whilst goalkeeper Pat Dunne had been a model of consistency and had been rewarded with the player of the year award and a recall to the Republic of Ireland squad. Nevertheless a number of changes would be needed to ensure that the following season would not be another damp squib.

# EIGHT

# 1974-75 (Promoted to Division 2)

Argyle were becoming a Third Division institution. Since relegation six years earlier they had rarely looked like escaping from the division. Billy Bingham had come and gone as manager, unable to effectively juggle the job with managing Northern Ireland at the same time. Ten years after losing the job, Ellis Stuttard was brought back in charge. A personable character and Argyle through-and-through, he was also unable to eke out any improvement.

Determined to be seen as a more forward-thinking board of directors, they appointed Tony Waiters as manager in October 1972. His first priority was to ensure relegation was avoided, which he did. The following season saw Argyle stun the football world by reaching the semi-final of the League Cup, before narrowly losing to Manchester City in a two-legged affair. Despite some glowing football in beating highly rated sides such as QPR and Burnley, Waiters' charges were still unable to translate this form into their league matches, finishing a disappointing seventeenth.

Despite the cup success, a number of players departed the Home Park scene over the summer. Full-back Colin Sullivan had won England Under-23 honours and was always destined for greater things. Nevertheless, his departure to Norwich for £70,000 was hard to take. An even greater blow was perhaps the exit from Home Park of midfield maestro Ernie Machin. The experienced schemer was a class act and the lynchpin of Waiters' side as well as club captain. But Machin was 'unsettled', an all-encompassing colloquialism for not seeing eye to eye with manager-players-directors-Uncle Tom Cobbley. Many years later, Machin revealed the real reason. His wages were considerably less than other players and certainly much lower than his status and experience warranted. He was off to Brighton for £30,000. Also on the move was popular defender Neil Hague, who teamed up with local boy Derek Rickard at Bournemouth.

Waiters had a reputation as a top-class coach. As a goalkeeper he had won five England caps and since retirement had been involved in the coaching set up at Liverpool and the England Youth side. The prospect of working with the relatively young and highly rated coach was a major selling point in attracting the players he wanted to join Plymouth, previously regarded as a soccer outpost and close to the edge of the world by anyone living north of Bristol.

Not that the new faces were household names, but Waiters knew their capabilities. Full-back Phil Burrows was York's Mister Reliable. Bowing to the inevitable departure of Sullivan, Waiters had eyed him as a replacement for some time and tracked Burrows down whilst the player was holidaying in Northumberland to clinch the deal. Defender Clive Griffiths, a fringe player at Manchester United, arrived on loan, suggesting that he was a talent the Red Devils wished to nurture rather than dispose of. John Delve, a blond combative midfielder, was signed from QPR for £30,000, and centre-half Mike Green, fresh from skippering Bristol Rovers to promotion, shunned the idea of higher division football to move south. Green was appointed captain. Another acquisition was Ian Pearson from non-league Goole Town.

Those who bemoaned the departure of Sullivan and Machin in particular nodded a cynical 'told you so' as the pre-season hardly got off to a flying start. Virtually full-strength Argyle sides were defeated by the likes of Stafford Rangers and Burscough. The bookies were also unimpressed by what they viewed as a weaker squad than the season before. Argyle were quoted as 25-1 for the title, well behind the favourites, Crystal Palace.

With Pearson on the bench, the other newcomers were all included for the opening fixture of the season at Preston. The match had received considerable publicity, but it was not the debuts of Green and Griffiths that were stirring up interest. Making his debut as Preston's player-manager was soccer legend Bobby Charlton. There was to be no thirty-yard special, flying into the top corner, but his side did win with the only goal. 'Lucky' was Charlton's full-time verdict. He was right. Johnny Hore hit a post and Delve's shot appeared to go over the line after hitting the crossbar but was disallowed.

Green did not have to wait long to renew acquaintance with his former Bristol Rovers teammates, as Argyle travelled to Eastville for the first leg of the League Cup. In Alan Warboys and Bruce Bannister, a.k.a. 'Smash and Grab', Rovers possessed one of the most lethal strike partnerships in the country, but Green put his detailed knowledge of the deadly duo to good use. He played a starring role in a scoreless draw, spoilt by some over-fussy refereeing which saw five players booked, three of which – Delve, Steve Davey and Green himself – were cautioned for dissent in a fourteen-minute spell.

The same eleven trotted out for a home fixture with Grimsby. A good-sized crowd turned out expecting a comfortable Argyle victory, with Grimsby having lost both of their competitive fixtures so far. They were not disappointed. For the first time, Paul Mariner and Billy Rafferty scored for Argyle in the same match. For Rafferty, now fully fit after being plagued with a knee problem since his arrival at Home Park, it was his first goal for the club and what a beauty it was from fully 25 yards. Grimsby's one goal came with three minutes remaining.

There was to be no repeat of the League Cup run of the previous season. A single goal from Warboys in the second leg ended the dream.

Having endured the joy of a Friday night trip to Southend, Argyle quickly took the lead at Roots Hall with Rafferty striking again. Three minutes later, the Shrimpers equalised in controversial fashion. From a free-kick, David Cunningham scored with Argyle still organising their 'wall'. In the second half, David Worthington scored with an ambitious 25-yard shot which eluded Jim Furnell. It was enough to make it three wins out of three for Arthur Rowley's side and they topped the table.

For the midweek trip to Aldershot, Mariner was relegated to the bench to make way for Peter Hardcastle, a tough-tackling midfield player in the Delve mould who had been signed from Blackpool. Waiters' revised formation looked to have worked as, from the off, Argyle bombarded the Aldershot goal, only for the home side to take the lead against the run of play. Harry Burrows quickly put Argyle back on level terms. Despite his advancing years, the left-winger possessed one of the hardest shots in the game which he ably demonstrated by letting fly from thirty yards. Further goals by Rafferty and Green before half-time looked to have given the Greens a comfortable lead. The Shots came out for the second half a revitalised side. Aided by defensive lapses, they pulled level and then scored again with seven minutes remaining to seal a dramatic 4-3 win.

Argyle's season was threatening to fall apart almost before it had begun. A home match with an inexperienced Tranmere side was the ideal opportunity to get the campaign back on track. Mariner gave Argyle the lead. Shortly afterwards the heavens opened but one player who revelled in the wet conditions was Rafferty. The striker continued his rich vein of form with a hat-trick as Argyle climbed to eleventh place.

Despite the victory, early-season form had convinced Waiters that further strengthening was required. He brought in the vastly experienced Alan Brown as chief coach but the new number two was soon made aware that he had a job on his hands as he watched Argyle succumb meekly at Swindon, who, a week earlier had been beaten 2-6 by Crystal Palace.

Another defeat in midweek, at Colchester, sent Argyle spiralling towards the bottom of the table. Without either of their two Burrows, it was one of those nights. Waiters drafted in the experience of former Scottish international Dave Provan and hard-man Bobby Saxton, but it made little difference. Peter Darke was sent off before half-time for a second booking and the U's scored in injury-time. Argyle had lost five of their first seven games and had just four points on the board.

Fellow strugglers Gillingham were the next visitors. Rafferty missed an opportunity to add to his goal tally when his 34th-minute penalty was saved by Ron Hillyard. Ten minutes later, Keith Lindsey showed him how to do it, scoring from the spot after Darke had handled. In the second half, Colin Randell scored directly from a corner but Argyle had dropped their first home point of the season.

One of the men to suffer from Argyle's indifferent start was Steve Davey. The popular utility player had been part of a three-pronged attack at the start of the season but had lost his place once Waiters adopted a more standard formation.

A fit again Harry Burrows was recalled for the visit of Hereford and set up the only goal of the game for Mariner. Darke, already appealing against his dismissal at Colchester, was again booked for an innocuous challenge, one of several strange decisions from referee Mr Salmon, who incurred the wrath of Waiters to the extent that he reported the official to the Football League.

If Waiters thought his side had turned the corner he had a nasty surprise waiting for him at Wrexham. The Welsh side contained a number of highly regarded players who were also in the 'under achievers' category. They chose Argyle's visit to show what they were capable of. After stalemate in the first 45 minutes, Wrexham ran amok in treacherous conditions. With Arfon Griffiths pulling the strings in midfield, future Manchester United star Mickey Thomas scored a hat-trick, with David Smallman, later to play for Everton, adding two more. In desperation, Argyle threw Green into attack, the position where he started his career. The skipper scored a consolation effort.

Wary that Argyle's next opponents, Huddersfield, possessed an equally dangerous player, Alan Gowling, Waiters left out Griffiths and recalled Saxton to the back four. The move worked perfectly. Gowling never had a sniff and a volley from Randell and a speculative effort from Mariner sent the Terriers back to Yorkshire with their tails between their legs.

The home games were now coming thick and fast, and another two points were gained at the expense of Walsall. The problem was that Argyle's home and away form were chalk and cheese. A defeat at Port Vale was the Pilgrims' seventh away loss on the trot. The game was a niggly affair but then it usually was. There had been no love lost between the two clubs since Argyle had had three players sent off in the corresponding fixture a couple of years earlier.

The supporters were getting mightily disillusioned. It appeared Argyle were again becoming becalmed in the middle of Division Three. The club's seventh lowest crowd since the War turned out to watch a midweek game with Aldershot. Rafferty scored the only goal to lift some of the despondency.

Another newcomer arrived in the form of winger Hugh McAuley, signed from Liverpool for £12,000. McAuley had been on the fringes of the first team at Anfield and was well known to Waiters. With hindsight, it was the turning point of the season. The new signing made a stunning debut against leaders Peterborough and had a hand in both goals scored by Green and Rafferty. With McAuley playing wide on the left and Brian

Johnson a similar role on the opposite flank, Waiters had stumbled upon a new and effective formation.

Part of Waiters' tactical thinking for the trip to Bury was based around how to exploit the lack of inches bestowed on Shakers' goalkeeper, John Forrest. In goalkeeping terms, Forrest was filed under midget and Johnson did not take long to rise in his manager's estimation when, after nine minutes, he attempted a lob. The ball struck the crossbar, hit Forrest on the back and went in. Technically an own-goal, it proved decisive.

Like buses, Argyle had waited two months for an away win and then two came along at once. Victory at Charlton was the first for an Argyle side since 1931. Somewhat fortunately, Johnson's long ball floated over everyone for the opener, and then McAuley scored with a rare header.

Several days of persistent heavy rain preceded the match with Watford at Home Park. A new drainage system had been installed pre-season and did its job, allowing the match to proceed. Once again Johnson was on target, shooting through a ruck of players, but the momentum was lost when an uncharacteristic error from the normally ultra-reliable Jim Furnell allowed Watford a late equaliser.

Coach Brown was, by this stage, leaving his mark. A fiercely competitive character, he could make a regimental sergeant-major look meek and mild. His training methods, on occasion, bordered on the unusual if not eccentric. Runs across Dartmoor, climbing trees, lifting telegraph poles, and dips into a freezing sea were among the range of activities the players had to endure. It made the squad one of the fittest around, though, and in a strange way bonded the team together. Allied to Waiters' technical ability as a coach, Brown's contribution forged a formidable combination. Importantly, the players gelled together off the field as well as on it. They socialised, played golf and were generally a happy unit.

The side faced their toughest test of the season so far as they travelled to Selhurst Park to meet Crystal Palace. The Eagles, under Malcolm Allison, were the glamour side of the division. Champagne Charlies in some eyes. Undoubtedly, though, they possessed some outstanding talent, with Terry Venables the midfield schemer, Alan Whittle and Dave Swindlehurst a formidable front pair, and Peter Taylor, a winger capable of tearing the best of defences apart.

The writing looked on the wall for Argyle when Whittle put Palace ahead after only seventy seconds. Ignoring the vociferous and sometimes hostile home support, Argyle retaliated with goals from Rafferty and Johnson before half-time. The interval brought crowd trouble on the terraces, sparked by five Argyle supporters running the length of the pitch to attempt to infiltrate the end populated by Palace fans. This was the era when football hooliganism was at its height and sadly such stupidity was not uncommon.

Whatever Allison said to his players between puffs on his cigar certainly did the trick. Swindlehurst scored from thirty yards from a twice-taken free-kick, before Mariner regained Argyle's advantage. Martin Hinshelwood then restored parity at 3-3.

The FA Cup draw sent Argyle into unchartered waters and a potential banana skin with a trip to reigning Southern League champions Dartford. It was drama to the end. With just four minutes remaining, Watling Street, already bursting at the seams with over 4,000 inside, went berserk when Henderson's second goal of the game gave the non-leaguers a 2-1 lead. But it was not over. With the wholly inadequate floodlights barely penetrating the gloom, flame-haired substitute Alan Rogers, making his first appearance of the season, set up Randell for his and Argyle's second. With less than a minute remaining, Mariner scored the winner to leave the Kent side distraught.

Back in league action, Argyle continued their surge up the table with yet another away win, this time at Chesterfield. The deadly duo, Mariner and Rafferty, scored again but Darke was out of the side. The wheels of FA justice had turned slowly and taken more than six weeks to decree that his dismissal at Colchester warranted suspension. It was to prove costly for Darke. John Hore claimed his No 2 shirt and proved so consistent that he never relinquished it again for the season. Another man off the Home Park payroll was Griffiths. The defender was recalled to Old Trafford as cover for the injured Jim Holton.

A home win over a Bournemouth side containing three former Pilgrims in their twelve lifted Argyle into the top six. That man Rafferty scored again, taking his season's tally to twelve.

Rivalries with Crystal Palace were quickly renewed, with the sides being paired in the second round FA Cup-tie of the day. It was a close one to call. Argyle had home advantage but Palace were three places above them in the league. There was the usual pre-match bluster from Allison. Swindlehurst gave the former Argyle manager's side a half-time lead. With less than twenty minutes remaining, Green equalised with a deft chip over Tony Burns. Five minutes later, Rafferty volleyed Argyle in front.

Referee Eric Read's watch had already ticked past the ninety minutes when Palace launched one last attack. Green committed himself to tackling the nimble Whittle and was a fraction late. Penalty! Up stepped Terry Venables, former England international and vastly experienced. It wasn't the greatest penalty ever or the greatest save, but Furnell had never made a more important one. Seconds later the final whistle was blown and the grey-haired keeper was mobbed by teammates and supporters. It was a moment still talked about thirty years later.

Argyle's new-found confidence was soon in evidence at Brighton. The south coast club were languishing near the bottom and Ernie Machin only made the subs' bench, suggesting that his move had not turned out as anticipated. After only eleven minutes, Rafferty had scored twice and Argyle had produced a brand of flowing football that had even the home fans applauding. But Brighton had Fred Binney. The striker was born in Plymouth but somehow escaped Argyle's net. He had scored goals wherever he played and turned the match in the last fifteen minutes, scoring himself and setting up Tony Towner for an equaliser. That dropped point meant Argyle slipped to ninth, going into the Christmas period but there was little to choose between the top ten sides.

The Boxing Day visitors were Swindon who, after two successive defeats, had slipped from second place. They boasted the division's top scorer in Peter Eastoe but it was David Moss who did the early damage by scoring twice. No doubt fearful of being subjected to another of Brown's 'special' training sessions, the Greens fought back with Delve and Randell scoring either side of half-time. McLaughlin put Swindon back in front but a strike from Mariner and a penalty from Rafferty – after McAuley had been fouled – sealed a thrilling 4-3 victory.

Now third, Argyle travelled to Halifax. The Shay, an unforgiving ground at the best of times, was lashed by gales. Unwisely, Argyle chose to unveil their new all-white away strip, which quickly transformed into all-brown. Within thirty seconds of the start, Halifax went in front through a Ken Blair header. Rafferty missed an open goal but McAuley later saved his blushes by heading an equaliser.

The FA Cup third round threw up a match to savour for two Argyle players in particular. Rafferty and Hardcastle had been Blackpool players and now had the chance to put one over their old teammates. The game certainly caught the imagination of the Plymouth public, with over 23,000 streaming through the Home Park turnstiles. Rafferty's parents travelled from their Scottish home and it was not a wasted journey as their son was the hero of the day, scoring both goals. For Hardcastle, it was not such a memorable day. He was stretchered off after a clash with Blackpool skipper David Hatton, who was booed relentlessly for the remainder of the game.

Argyle could not have wished for a better fourth round draw – a home tie with First Division leaders Everton. As soon as the draw was made the Home Park telephones went into overload fielding enquiries about the availability of tickets.

The forward-thinking Waiters had introduced many new concepts into the club. A revitalised youth development system was unearthing some real talent and he had masterminded the new training ground at Harper's Park. The commercial department under Bill Pearce was providing much needed additional revenue and for the first time in many years there was a feeling that the club was actually going somewhere. His latest improvement was the purchase of a new state-of-the-art team bus costing £25,000, containing all the latest mod cons. Its first journey was a relatively short one to Dean Court.

Bournemouth were a club in crisis. Early season form had seen them reach the top four but they had taken just three points from their last ten games, prompting them to sack manager Trevor Hartley. They didn't concede many but didn't score many either.

Back at Home Park, an abnormally large crowd of 2,375 had turned out to watch the reserves play Fulham's second string. The main attraction was not the Cottagers, however. Tickets were on sale for the Everton game. Fans were also keeping a keen eye on the score from Bournemouth, which was relayed by numbers attached to a board, cricket scoreboard style. They could barely believe their eyes. By half-time the board read 4-0 in favour of Argyle. Delve soon made it five, before the Cherries hit back with three of their own. Late goals by Mariner, his second of the game, and Randell settled the nerves. It finished an astonishing 7-3.

Those two points moved Argyle into second place behind Blackburn. The Everton game was now uppermost in the minds of supporters but Waiters knew the encounter with Chesterfield was more important. Argyle would not win the FA Cup, they could win the Third Division. The Spireites looked unlikely to provide stiff opposition, having lost seven of their previous nine games, form which had seen them assume bottom place. Argyle won without getting out of second gear, with fringe player Barrie Vassallo scoring his first senior goal.

As the days passed, the excitement over the Everton tie grew to fever pitch, but one man who would not play a part was Davey. He saw little future at Plymouth and was placed on the transfer list.

Much of the focus of the Cup-tie centred around the merits of the two No 9s, Mariner and Bob Latchford, but the Everton man was injured. So too was Mariner. With a capacity 38,000 squeezed into Home Park, there was a stunned silence when the Argyle team was broadcast over the tannoy. Surely there was some mistake, But no. 'Number nine Barrie Vassallo.' Mariner's injury had been kept under wraps but only served as a boost to the Toffees and a demoralising blow to Argyle.

On a pitch bereft of grass and in front of BBC Match of the Day cameras, the game kicked off in an atmosphere of high anticipation, but within seven minutes Jim Pearson had put the visitors ahead. Argyle never really got into their stride and Mick Lyons increased the lead before half-time. After 59 minutes there was renewed hope. Randell's defence-splitting pass found Vassallo, who powered a shot past Welsh international keeper Dai Davies. It was a memorable goal, particularly for the youngster who was making his full debut. Hopes of a comeback were ruined by Lyons' second goal. Argyle had battled vainly but class had told.

The defeat came as something of a relief to Waiters and his players. Now rid of distractions, they could concentrate on the league campaign. There were no post-Blues' blues as Argyle, backed by over 1,000 travelling supporters, went to Watford and comfortably secured another two points that consolidated Argyle's second place. It set the scene for a vital week as they faced home clashes with the two sides sandwiching them.

After Cup fever, it was now promotion fever. Despite it being a midweek game, throngs made their way to Home Park for the match with long-time leaders Blackburn. The streets were packed. Even the players had trouble getting in. Colin Randell recalled how, fearful of reporting late, he abandoned his car by the side of the road and walked a good mile to the ground – not the ideal preparation for such a big game, or any game for that matter.

The attendance was measured at almost 29,000, the biggest in the league at Home Park since 1960. A tense first half ended goalless. Both managers knew the first goal would be vital and, perhaps inevitably, it was Rafferty who broke the deadlock. Another goal, this time from Johnson, with only four minutes left on the clock, brought welcome relief although there was still time for Ken Beamish to score in injury-time.

The win meant Argyle topped the table. It was a remarkable transformation from their indifferent early-season form and there was no doubt that coach Brown's fitness regime had paid off. Argyle were one of the fittest sides around and it was a crucial factor as they ploughed their way through week after week of heavy conditions on pitches that, in modern times, would have been deemed unfit to play on.

Undeterred by the prospect of two games in a week, another healthy crowd turned out to watch the new leaders take on third-placed Charlton. The Valiants' boss, Andy Nelson, a former Argyle player, pledged that his side would come to attack and that they were looking for two points. It was not managerial propaganda. From the off, Charlton attacked and the Argyle defence, relatively underworked in recent weeks, had to be at their best. It took 67 minutes for the first goal to come. Rafferty demonstrated his aerial power to head home. With ten minutes left, Warman equalised but the Greens still had a golden opportunity to win. In the last minute, a handball was awarded against Peter Hunt. Rafferty stepped up but his penalty hit the post and glanced to safety.

Eleven days after their first meeting, the top two clashed again as Argyle travelled to Blackburn. Waiters was again able to name his usual line up. The eleven names were beginning to trip off Argyle supporters' tongues as easily as naming England's World Cup winning side. One interested spectator was England manager Don Revie, rumoured to be watching Mariner, who was being touted in various quarters for future international honours. There was a dream start for Argyle. After sixteen minutes,

McAuley scored. He had yet to experience losing a league match in a green shirt since signing four months earlier. Three minutes later, Rovers' keeper Roger Jones punched a Delve back-header into his own net. The drama continued when Rovers were awarded a penalty. The decision ignited crowd trouble in the Argyle end but when the furore had died down, Furnell, unflustered as ever, saved Don Martin's effort.

Rovers pulled one back before half-time. In the second half it was one-way traffic towards Furnell's goal. Martin made amends for his earlier miss. Rovers' manager, Gordon Lee, sensed victory was there for the taking and stood on the touchline urging his troops forward. Within three minutes, Rovers were ahead through Mike Hickman. From then on there was only one winner. Hickman and Martin added further goals in the last five minutes to deliver a crushing 5-2 psychological blow to their nearest rivals.

Waiters needed to lift his players, but would have wished for an easier game than another duel with Crystal Palace. The Eagles were determined to make amends for their dramatic Cup exit earlier in the season and Allison boasted that his side would end the Pilgrims' unbeaten home record. He was right. Palace were renowned for their elaborate free-kick routines and after 31 minutes a well-rehearsed move resulted in the only goal of the game, from Swindlehurst.

Argyle, with just one point from the last three games, were now out of the top three. With Delve suspended and Johnson injured, Waiters opted to recall Vassallo and Hardcastle. The match against Southend started slowly with Argyle looking shell-shocked after successive defeats. The crowd became restless and called for the inclusion of Davey, who was now obviously out of favour with his manager. It took a Mariner penalty after Rafferty had been fouled to seal a dour victory.

No one could have predicted the result at Hereford. A win was vital and Hardcastle's first Argyle goal gave them the half-time advantage. A Mariner strike increased the lead but the prolific Dixie McNeil, who would finish the season with 32 goals, put Hereford back in the match. Johnson and McAuley moved into top gear, creating havoc down the flanks. With a ready supply of crosses, Rafferty took full advantage, scoring twice in the last nine minutes. Vassallo's last-minute goal completed the rout and helped Argyle's goal figures, possibly a vital factor in the final reckoning given the closeness of the promotion hunt.

With all his personnel fighting fit, Waiters had a difficult selection problem as he pondered his team to take on Wrexham. In the end, he reverted to his first-choice eleven, meaning the unfortunate Hardcastle and Vassallo were omitted. Once again the TV cameras were present at Home Park as the BBC deemed the game worthy of Match of the Day coverage. It was Argyle's opportunity to demonstrate their flowing brand of football to the nation, but Wrexham had other ideas. Despite languishing down in mid-table, they produced their best football of the season, whilst the normally reliable Argyle defence looked jittery. Every team has its 'bogey' side and Wrexham were definitely Argyle's. A 3-0 win was their fourth successive victory over the Greens.

The annual ritual of the selection of the PFA's divisional all-star sides saw the merited inclusion of both Rafferty and Phil Burrows. Several other Pilgrims could feel justly disappointed that they were not included.

Four nights after the Wrexham defeat, another 20,000-plus crowd turned out to watch Argyle take on Preston. Undoubtedly the main attraction was the presence of Bobby Charlton, who included himself in his team's line up. Preston were certainly experienced. Also included were Charlton's former Manchester United teammates Nobby Stiles and Francis Burns.

Once again, Argyle scored early, with an overlapping Hore setting up Mariner, but the home side failed to capitalise on this promising start. With five minutes remaining, Charlton unleashed a trademark thunderbolt past the despairing Furnell. But Argyle weren't finished. With two minutes remaining, Mariner headed his second goal of the night to clinch two vital points.

On a Prenton Park pitch more suited to mud wrestling, McAuley was again in inspired form. The Merseysider had a number of friends and family at the game and the tricky winger was again the main provider as goals from Green, Johnson and Rafferty put the Pilgrims in an unassailable position by half-time. Tranmere scored a consolation effort in the second period but the defeat left them bottom.

A busy Easter period saw Halifax visit Home Park and defend with a mix of tenacity and desperation. The longer the game went on, the more Argyle became frustrated. Even the 50th-minute dismissal of Steve Downes did not dampen Town's resolve. A tackle by Green so incensed the Halifax centre-forward that, despite not being involved in the incident, he ran twenty yards to aim a head-butt at the Argyle skipper. Green later confirmed that no contact had been made but clearly the intent was there. Eventually the deadlock was broken when Mariner's shot was deflected past his own keeper by John Crossley. Six minutes later, McAuley set off on a George Best-type mazy dribble, leaving four opponents dazed before despatching a shot past a helpless Alan Jones. Despite gaining another two points, Waiters was not a happy man. Sitting comfortably in the grandstand, watching the match were Argyle's next-day opponents, Brighton. The Argyle manager branded the fixture planning 'a joke'.

And so, 24 hours later, the same weary Argyle eleven dragged themselves out onto the Home Park pitch again. What would today's players make of such demands? Brighton were enmeshed in a relegation battle but within 29 seconds had taken the lead through Gerry Fell. Green levelled, but Fell was in on the act again before half-time when his shot hit Furnell and rebounded off Burrows' knee into the net. With Machin giving the Argyle supporters a reminder of his silky skills, a surprise result looked on the cards but Mariner rescued the situation with an equalising header.

Argyle's 'day off' was spent sitting on the team coach for several hours as it wound its way to deepest Kent for a fixture at Gillingham. Waiters was forced into making one change. Two games on successive days had finally taken their toll on Randell's Achilles tendon, which had been giving him problems for three months. The midfielder, whose performances had brought him Welsh Under-23 honours, had played on with the aid of cortisone injections. The tendon had been so sore that his leg had been put in plaster between games and fans were astonished at the regular sight of Randell hobbling into the stadium before kick-off, only to watch him sprint out for battle minutes later.

Yet again, Argyle conceded a very early goal from giant centre-half Dave Shipperley who, the previous season, had played one game for the Greens on loan. With Brian Yeo adding a second before the break, it looked another uphill task. Once again, Argyle were grateful to the fitness regime imposed by the coaching staff. With Gillingham visibly wilting in the Priestfield mud, Argyle attacked relentlessly and Green, a one-time Gills centre-forward, scored. The home side now defended in droves but Shipperley was eventually forced to go off injured. With two minutes remaining, Rafferty capitalised on his new-found freedom to equalise.

The following day, leaders Blackburn could only draw at Halifax and third-placed Charlton were defeated at Swindon. Promotion was now a step closer. Results were even more favourable on the following Saturday. Whilst Argyle were beating Bury at Home Park, Charlton slumped to a shock home defeat by lowly Bournemouth, and Blackburn were held to a 3-3 draw at home to Walsall.

With a three-point gap over Charlton, and just one behind Blackburn, Waiters knew his team had to keep picking up points. Huddersfield away looked a banker. The Terriers had suffered one of the most dramatic falls from grace English football had seen. Three years earlier they were a First Division side, but now they looked destined to suffer a third successive relegation. Blizzard conditions threatened to negate any advantage Argyle had in the skill category, but Mariner, brave and strong as ever, scored twice to reinforce calls for his inclusion in England's Under-23 squad. With Blackburn playing the night after, Argyle were briefly back on top of the league table.

A goalless draw at Walsall and similar stalemates for the other two title-chasers meant Argyle were on the cusp of promotion. A win in the next match at home to Colchester would seal Division Two football. With Randell back, over 23,000 poured into Home Park hoping to share in the occasion. The U's were mid-table and their season was effectively dead, but they were no pushovers. Goalkeeper Mike Walker pulled off a string of fine saves but good fortune finally deserted him in the fiftieth minute. Attempting a drop kick, he rifled the ball into the back of Rafferty. The ball could have gone anywhere but dropped invitingly at the feet of Mariner who couldn't miss. A further forty anxious minutes passed without further score and the final whistle signalled a mass pitch invasion of exuberant fans. Initial police attempts to repel invaders proved fruitless and in the end they merely stood and watched.

Now for the title. Blackburn, with a game in hand, clinched promotion by beating Chesterfield. At Home Park, opponents Port Vale complied with tradition and applauded Argyle onto the pitch, but the respect then ended. Determined to be party-poopers, they caused the Argyle defence severe problems and Derek Brownbill headed in when unmarked. With referee Alan Turvey continually baffling all and sundry with his decisions, Randell, never previously booked in his career, was sent off for foul play. The dismissal merely strengthened Argyle's resolve and three minutes later Delve back-headed an equaliser.

The top of the table read: Argyle 58 points with two matches remaining, Blackburn 57 with three to go. Waiters would have wished for an easier finish. On paper, a trip to Grimsby did not look difficult, but they were on a roll, having gone unbeaten in eight games, a run which had seen them dispel fears of relegation. It was Mariner who broke the deadlock, scoring after Rafferty's overhead kick had hit the bar and rebounded to him. A momentary loss of concentration left David Boylen unmarked to level.

The disappointment of conceding a late goal was tempered by the news that Blackburn had been defeated at Colchester. If Argyle won their final match it meant the Lancastrians would need to win both of theirs. It would then come down to goal-figures, which were almost identical.

An estimated 5,000 Argyle fans boarded scores of coaches in the early hours to follow their heroes to Peterborough. Those who purchased the *Daily Express* during their breakfast stop were delighted to read that Rafferty had been voted as the newspaper's Third Division Player of the Year. Sadly, the day was marred by violence in the town before the game. Cars were upturned and other damage caused. Your author remembers having his fish and chips stolen from his hand. Not, admittedly, on a par with having your car wrecked, but nevertheless a traumatic experience for a hungry fifteen-year-old!

On the field, Argyle couldn't quite do it. With both sides in irritable mood, Argyle never found a rhythm and were sunk by a solitary Tommy Robson goal. Blackburn had no such problems, easily dispensing with Port Vale, leaving them needing only a point from their game in hand to lift the Third Division Championship trophy.

Rovers' opponents were Argyle's destroyers in chief, Wrexham. How vital that home defeat by the Welshman now seemed. Regrettably for Argyle, the Robins' form had deserted them since, and a goalless draw was enough for Blackburn.

No one at Home Park could be disappointed though. The club had made tremendous strides in a short space of time and promotion was well deserved. The vital question now was could they retain the services of a number of players, particularly the rising star that was Paul Mariner. Tony Waiters, now widely recognised as a top-class manager, was also being linked with more high-profile clubs, Newcastle for one. Time would tell.

# NINE

# 1976-77 (Relegated to Division 3)

A sixteenth place finish in their first season back in Division Two was satisfactory. Waiters had relied almost totally on the squad that had achieved promotion, but had also blooded youngsters such as Dave Sutton, George Foster and Milija Aleksic as a safeguard for the future. Progress had also continued off the field with the purchase of Elm Cottage, a spacious property on the edge of Home Park, which housed the club's apprentices.

There was, however, unease about the forthcoming season. Firstly, there was no Billy Rafferty. The striker had joined Carlisle for the ludicrous fee of £20,000. It was also only a matter of time before Paul Mariner joined one of any number of First Division clubs pursuing him. Jim Furnell had finally announced his retirement. He was to be employed by the club's commercial department. Phil Burrows and Hugh McAuley were unimpressed with the terms of their new contract and Burrows would leave for Hereford before the start of the league season. Also unlikely to feature was Micky Horswill. The flame-haired former FA Cup winner with Sunderland was a constant menace to referees and Waiters had lost patience with his indiscipline.

To replace Furnell, Waiters signed the experienced Neil Ramsbottom from Sheffield Wednesday, and also Paul Barron, who had been earning rave reviews with non-league Slough. Also arriving was midfield player Doug Collins, who had plenty of experience with Grimsby and Burnley, much of it in the First Division.

But Waiters was also after a bigger fish. Rumours spread that Brian Hall, a fundamental part of Liverpool's great side, was about to sign. It seemed unlikely. The Reds were asking £50,000 and no doubt his wages weren't peanuts either. Argyle simply didn't have the money. Bill Pearce's commercial enterprise raised considerable funds to keep the club afloat but it was still heavily indebted to its bankers to the extent that the directors coughed up loans totalling £60,000.

The prospect of seeing Hall in an Argyle shirt caught the imagination of the supporters. Hall and his wife had travelled down and liked what they saw. Now the fans rallied. A '(H)all for Argyle' campaign was launched with fund-raising functions being arranged throughout the Westcountry. Such enterprise got its reward and Hall signed.

Waiters also added to his backroom staff, appointing former QPR and Birmingham keeper Mike Kelly as reserve-team manager.

Pre-season was low key, with friendlies at Wrexham, Shrewsbury and Bournemouth mixed with home games with Bristol Rovers and Torquay.

The season began with a two-legged League Cup-tie with Fourth Division Exeter. Waiters had mixed and matched his teams during the friendlies but seemed as perplexed as everyone else as to what his strongest eleven would be. The departure of Burrows had left him without a natural left-back, so Horswill earned himself a reprieve by donning the No 3 shirt and promising to be on his best behaviour. Youngster Chris Harrison was preferred to Horswill's fellow miscreant, John Delve, in midfield and Hall was asked to partner Mariner up front. Despite home advantage in the first leg, it was one-way traffic. Argyle never found any cohesion and lost to a solitary goal from Exeter's ace marksman Tony Kellow.

Four days later, it was the same story and same scoreline at St James Park. Hall was restored to his favoured midfield role and Brian Johnson used as a striker alongside Mariner, but the changes gave little cause for optimism about the league season ahead.

The league opened with a tough-looking fixture at Oldham. Away form had been Argyle's nemesis during the previous season. They had failed to win on their travels, and it needed huge improvement if they were to even think of a top-eight finish. The game started encouragingly with Mariner scoring a well-taken goal. Stung into action, the Latics hit back to take the lead midway through the second half, but with Hall showing flashes of his obvious class, Johnson equalised.

Blackburn provided the first home league opposition. Having pipped Argyle to the Third Division title two years earlier, they had fared little better and also fielded a much-changed line up from their title-winning days. Collins wasted little time in opening his Argyle account, scoring after only seven minutes. Rovers' shoulders visibly slumped and another goal on the stroke of half-time, by Johnson, added a few decibels to Rovers' boss Jim Smith's team-talk. Whatever he said made little difference. Hall notched his first Argyle goal and Mariner was also on target, as well as missing a last-minute re-taken penalty. The 4-0 score brooked no argument.

The visit of Notts County looked the ideal opportunity to sustain the momentum. Ron Fenton's side had not had a good start but County had beaten Argyle on their last four meetings. John Sims, a Pilgrim in years to come, hit the bar, and then put County ahead. Mariner replied, but Mick Vinter gave the Magpies a deserved two points. Waiters seemed more concerned by those fans who barracked full-back Peter Darke. Darke suffered a crisis of confidence and was substituted to save further humiliation.

Similarly afflicted were Argyle's next opponents, Orient. The east London team had failed to find the net in three league games but Phil Hoadley soon dispensed with that unwanted record with two goals in a minute. His second was scooped clear from the goal-line and Ramsbottom expressed his displeasure with referee Ron Glasson's decision to award a goal by hurling the ball at the official. He was lucky to escape with only a booking. Green and Mariner levelled things before half-time but Darke was substituted again, this time suffering from blurred vision.

The visit of Chelsea was eagerly anticipated. Aside from veteran goal-keeper Peter Bonetti, they possessed a young but gifted side. Having field-ed an unchanged league eleven so far, Waiters made changes. With Darke and Collins injured, Delve and Colin Randell were recalled. McAuley, still refusing to put pen to paper on a new contract, was left out and Alan Rogers was given a rare chance.

The first half was a turgid affair but there was a complete contrast in the second. An Ian Britton penalty, awarded after Randell upended Ray Lewington, set off a spree of five goals in 28 minutes. Mariner kept up his record of scoring in every league game and the referee added fuel to the fire by collecting five names, including that of Chelsea trainer Norman Medhurst, who had entered the field of play to attend to an injured player before the referee had given him permission.

A 0-3 defeat at Millwall left Argyle in eighteenth place and undid the good work of the first three games. With so much expectation heaped on Hall, there were mutterings that the ex-Liverpool man had not produced the standard of performances he was capable of. In truth, Hall was not a happy man. Years later, he revealed that he knew within a week of signing that he had made a mistake. Central midfield was his best position and yet he had been asked to play on the right or up front. He also had difficulty in adapting to Waiters' style of training. Hall had been brought up under Bill Shankly, never one to conform to the coaching manual. Waiters was a good coach but was too regimented for Hall's liking.

Mariner scored another two goals in the home game with Bolton. Unfortunately, one of them was for the opposition as he lunged at Neil Whatmore's shot and diverted the ball past Ramsbottom. Earlier, he had soared above three defenders to score with a classic header.

Everyone was now resigned to the fact that Mariner's days as a Pilgrim were numbered. Talks had already been held with West Brom and repre-sentatives from both West Ham and Ipswich were at Home Park to observe him in action against Luton. Mariner had little opportunity to shine. The match was dull and it took a disputed penalty from Johnson to break the deadlock. Hatters' boss Harry Haslam was furious with the deci-sion, likening it to the Great Train Robbery.

Argyle's trip to Blackpool was featured on Match of the Day. It was a strange choice. Blackpool were fifth and Argyle couldn't win away. The Pilgrims' normal pre-match routine was severely disrupted when delays on the motorway meant they only arrived at Bloomfield Road thirty minutes before kick-off. It certainly didn't unsettle them. After eight minutes, Collins scored directly from a free-kick and the now-angelic Horswill even got in on the scoring act with a rare goal. The match was interrupted by a phantom whistler in the crowd, but that could not detract from Argyle winning on their travels for the first time in 28 attempts.

The win put Argyle into mid-table. Recent results suggested victory over visiting Cardiff, who had struggled to find any semblance of form. On most fans' minds was the likelihood that this would be Mariner's last game in a green, or, in the case of this particular season, white shirt. The consensus was that he would be a West Ham player in a matter of days. The deal with Hammers boss Ron Greenwood was seemingly done and dusted, with a fee of £200,000 agreed. Mariner, though, had not agreed personal terms and Ipswich were waiting in the wings. At the eleventh hour Bobby Robson gazumped the Hammers and Mariner was bound for East Anglia in a complex deal valued at £220,000. Ipswich fringe players, Terry Austin and John Peddelty, joined Argyle.

Any thoughts that Mariner might take it easy in his last game were wide of the mark. It wasn't his style to give less than 100 per cent and within six minutes he had scored. Four minutes later, Barron, making his league debut in place of the injured Ramsbottom, picked the ball out of the net with almost his first touch as Tony Evans equalised. Early in the second half Hall was sent tumbling but picked himself up to score from the spot. Again the Bluebirds didn't take long to recover and Welsh international Phil Dwyer levelled. The game was marred by crowd trouble and one particular individual who impressed his mates by running onto the pitch was manhandled by Horswill into the arms of a waiting policeman.

The Mariner transfer to Ipswich was all but complete. Expected as it was, it was still hard to take. Bar one or two players, it represented the final throes of the premature break-up of the side that had swept to promotion only eighteen months earlier. The question now on everyone's lips was 'where would the goals come from?' Mariner had already scored seven of Argyle's seventeen goals and looked favourite to finish as leading scorer despite having played for only a quarter of the season.

Although technically still a Pilgrim, Mariner was omitted from the side that travelled to Bristol Rovers and the coveted No 9 shirt was thrust onto the shoulders of seventeen-year-old apprentice Mike Trusson. The youngster had shown promise under the flourishing Argyle youth system and, along with Kevin Smart, John Uzzell and Gary Megson, had recently been selected for England Youth trials. Second Division football on a greasy pitch and against wily old defenders was a different kettle of fish. As it was, Argyle scraped a point thanks to a late deflected goal from Hall.

Twenty-four hours later, Mariner had officially gone. The new arrivals took their place in the side that faced Burnley, with skipper Mike Green dropped to accommodate Peddelty at centre-half and Austin inheriting the No 9 shirt. In a lacklustre performance, a goal from the Clarets' on-loan Malcolm Smith proved decisive.

Terry Austin arrived at Home Park as a makeweight in the deal that took Paul Mariner to Ipswich

David Burnside scores Argyle's first goal in the 3-1 win against Reading in 1968-69

Maurice Tadman in a posed photo. He was a footballing pioneer in doing commercials.
He advertised Quaker Oats porridge

Sammy Black, Argyle's
all-time record goalscorer

Plymouth in action against Tottenham in the FA Cup, January 1962. Argyle lost 1-5

Half-back Johnny Williams
was part of the 1958-59
promotion-winning team

Bradford City clap Argyle's 1958-59 promotion heroes as they take the field

# Argyle Stalwarts of the 50's

**WILLIAM SHORTT**
[Goal]

**TONY McSHANE**
[Left-half]

**WILLIAM STRAUSS**
[Outside-right]

**PADDY RATCLIFFE**
[Right-back]

**PAT JONES**
[Left-back]

**FRANK SQUIRES**
[Inside-right]

**MAURICE TADMAN**
[Centre-forward]

**NEILL DOUGALL**
[Right-half]

**JACK CHISHOLM**
[Centre-half]

**GEORGE DEWS**
[Inside-left]

**STANLEY WILLIAMS**
[Outside-left]

Bristol Rovers' centre-half Mike Green later signed for Argyle and captained their
1974-75 team. Here he is seen tussling with Argyle's Steve Davey

Inside-forward
Jimmy Gauld was
part of the 1958-59
Argyle side

Outside-right Tommy Grozier joined Argyle from Glencairn in 1927

Bobby Saxton in 1969. He played and later managed Argyle

Plymouth Argyle 1958-59:
Back: J L Williams, G Robertson, D Downs, J S Williams, J Rowley (manager),
G Barnsley, R Wyatt, T Barnett, N Dougall, R J Blindell (ex-chairman):
Front: P Anderson, J Gauld, W Carter, G Baker, N Penk

# TWO NEW-COMERS

## "Room for a little one, Mr. Chisholm?"

Jack Chisholm had to go off for stitches to a head-wound on his Argyle debut against Chesterfield in December 1949. His second-half return ensured his hero status

Fred Binney takes the field at Home Park. A goalscoring star with Exeter City,
he became a star with Plymouth Argyle too

George Silk, a hard-tackling full-back, was the only player to appear for Argyle before
and after the Second World War

The date is 7th January 1950, and the FA Cup is stretchered around Home Park.
Holders Wolves brought it down for display. The game ended 1-1

Some of them look like a mob of Al Capone types. Argyle players wait for the train at North Road station. From left: H Bland, G Briggs, F Sloan, T Black, S Black, H Cann, J Cookson, G Reed, N Mackay, T Grozier, H Roberts, T Haynes (trainer)

Argyle's 1929-30 team that won the club's first ever promotion

Tony Waiters, who switched from capable goalkeeper to outstanding manager

Full-back Peter Darke was a member of the 1974-75 promotion team

1968-69 team were more white than green:
Back: N Piper, M Reeves, J Tedesco, D Burnside, C Sullivan. Middle: R Stewart (trainer),
J Hore, P Dunne, A Nelson, M Clamp, E Burgess, F Lord (player-coach).
Front: M Bickle, S Davey, W Bingham (manager), R Saxton, R Reynolds, D Neale

Welsh international Bill Shortt was
one of Argyle's greatest goalkeepers

The 1951-52 promotion team, in the days when Argyle's green shirts had white sleeves

The legendary Bob Jack was secretary-manager at Home Park from 1910 to 1938

Paul Sturrock for Dundee United against Gothenburg in the 1987 UEFA Cup final

Sammy Black, Argyle's goalscoring sensation of the 1920s

Torquay players form a guard of honour as Argyle take the field.
They have just secured promotion in 1951-52

Local lad John
Brimacombe, scored on
his Argyle debut v York
in 1985-86

Harry Bland was posted
to Plymouth with the
Royal Navy in 1927. He
became a stalwart right-
back for the club

Home Park in 2004

**JACK ROWLEY**
*(Manchester United and England)*
One of the hardest shots in the game, as he proved by his record three hat-tricks in the opening month of the season. Comes from the Midlands, and was transferred from Bournemouth to the United in 1937, when eighteen. Has played for England in all three inside-forward positions.

Jack Rowley, who managed Argyle to the 1958-59 Division Three championship

Dave Smith, the Dundonian who achieved promotion with Mansfield Town,
Southend United and Plymouth Argyle

Legendary goalscorer Wilf Carter

Wolves' Bert Williams is beaten by George Dews' shot. The goal made it 1-1, but Argyle lost 1-2 in January 1951

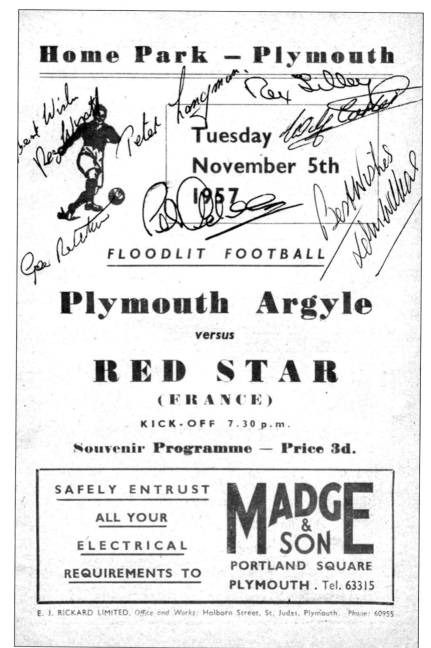

The match programme for this floodlit friendly on Guy Fawkes' Night, 1957

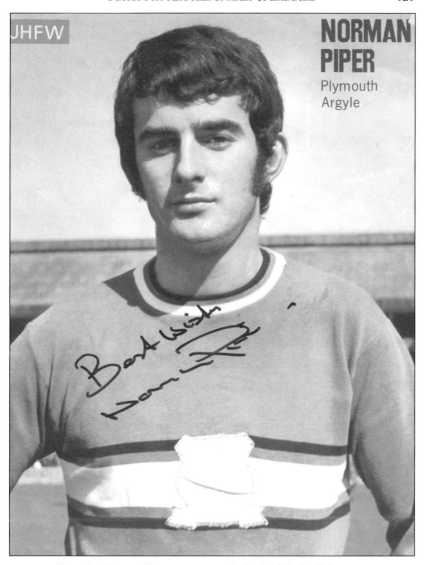

Devonian Norman Piper went on to win England Under-23 honours

Jumbo Chisholm did not have a beard when he joined Argyle. Clean-shaven, he appears almost angelic.

40,000 packed Home Park in January 1948 for the visit of Luton Town in the FA Cup

Home Park. January 10th, 1948.    PLYMOUTH ARGYLE v. LUTON TOWN    3rd Round F.A. Cup.  Attendance  40,000

Goalkeeper Pat Dunne was signed from Manchester United.
He was Argyle's Player of the Year in 1967-68

George Dews and Maurice Tadman are frustrated as Wolves and England goalkeeper
Bert Williams tips this effort over the crossbar

Len Casey joined Argyle midway through the 1958-59 season and captained them to the championship

Fred Craig, in the days when shirts were laced up at the neck like football boots. He was penalty-taker during the 1929-30 promotion-team

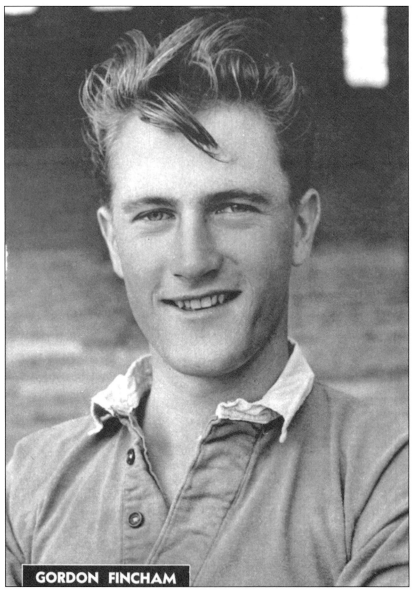

**GORDON FINCHAM**

Centre-half Gordon Fincham was signed from Leicester and came into the Argyle team
towards the end of the 1958-59 championship team

F.A. CUP TIE—PLYMOUTH ARGYLE v. NEWCASTLE UNITED

Plymouth take on Newcastle at Home Park in the FA Cup

Jimmy Rae joined Argyle before the Second World War and managed them to promotion in 1951-52

Winger Barrie Jones signed for Argyle from Swansea for a record £45,000 in 1964

At the Valley, the Argyle defence had a torrid time against the prolific Derek Hales, who notched his fifteenth and sixteenth of the season to enhance his claims of an England call up. Heroics from Ramsbottom kept the score down and a Hall penalty was little consolation.

Argyle's largest crowd of the season turned out to see Fulham's ageing stars. The Cottagers contained an illustrious trio in Bobby Moore, George Best and Rodney Marsh, who gave the occasional glimpse of what used to be. Marsh set up Fulham's opener and Horswill was forced into a Boston stranglehold to bring an ignominious end to a mazy Best run. In the end, four goals were shared in an entertaining game but Argyle's lack of victories was becoming concerning.

Defeat at Hull revealed the first signs that Waiters was becoming frustrated, as he branded his team a 'soft touch'. Poor defensive work contributed to the 1-3 loss, with only Harrison, with his first league goal, having any reason to fondly remember the afternoon.

The loss of both points at home to lowly Carlisle caricatured the fans' frustrations. United, of course, had Billy Rafferty leading their attack, and although he didn't score, he led the home defence a merry dance. The biggest cheer of the day was reserved for McAuley when he entered the fray as substitute. Out of favour, disillusioned and transfer-listed, the winger was considered by many, although not by Waiters, as a solution to the lack of creativity and goalscoring chances.

The loss of Mariner had pervaded Home Park more deeply than imagined. The fans had lost their hero and, on the pitch, he had been a talismanic figure. Not only that, he was a thoroughly down to earth bloke and highly popular with his teammates. One felt sorry for Austin, who was a capable player but on a hiding to nothing.

The trip to Molineux was not one to relish. Wolves had been crashing in goals all season and in John Richards and Alan Sunderland possessed a strike-force that was the envy of many a First Division club. Green was recalled for the concussed Peddelty, but ended up with a headache of his own as the deadly duo demonstrated their fire-power. Richards' second and Wolves' fourth was their team's 41st league goal of the season.

Lack of goals and points had now dragged Argyle into the relegation mire. A goalless draw at home to Sheffield United only served to illustrate the need for a striker. Waiters made his move and snapped up Bruce Bannister from Bristol Rovers. The £15,000 fee, plus under-used striker Jim Hamilton as makeweight, looked a good deal. Bannister was a proven goal-getter whose partnership with Alan Warboys had become the stuff of legend at Eastville. Whether he could do the business without his fellow hit-man was open to conjecture but the fans approved of his arrival.

Bannister's arrival breathed new life into his teammates. His debut at high-flying Nottingham Forest saw him set up Terry Austin for a twelfth-minute goal. It took a Colin Barrett effort two minutes from time to save Forest's blushes, Barrett having had a fourth-minute penalty saved.

After a long Christmas break, a bumper crowd saw Bannister score on his home debut against a star-studded Southampton team, which included debutant Alan Ball as well as former internationals Peter Osgood, Mike Channon and Jim McCalliog. Delve thought he had given Argyle a dream start, 'scoring' after thirty seconds. Having initially allowed the goal, the referee then changed his mind. Ted MacDougall then put the Saints in front. On an increasingly icy pitch, Bannister played the second half in gym shoes. He wouldn't win any fashion prizes, but his choice of footwear allowed him mobility that others struggled to find.

The New Year's Day fixture against Charlton again saw McAuley in action, but it wasn't for Argyle. Instead he was making his debut for the Addicks, although it was not a game he would want to remember. He missed an easy chance and Charlton conceded the only goal of the game from Austin, with Bannister again involved in the assist. It was Argyle's first win in twelve games.

Hopes for the future were renewed with victory at Burnley two days later. The Clarets were in a worse plight than Argyle, having not won for fourteen games and were only two places off the bottom. With Collins dictating the play against his former side, and Bannister in inspired mood, another defeat incurred the wrath of the Turf Moor fans, many of whom staged a protest following the final whistle.

Attention was briefly switched to the FA Cup. The draw had been unkind, sending the Pilgrims to Second Division bedfellows Oldham. Frankly, Argyle were never in the game and a 0-3 defeat was just desserts.

Inclement weather forced a two-week break, so Argyle's next opponents were Oldham again, this time at home. Making his Argyle debut was the burly figure of John Craven, an experienced pro who could play in a variety of positions. £20,000 had been enough to persuade Coventry to let him go. Craven was built for comfort rather than speed, but with pools of water on the surface, he looked better suited than most to cope with the conditions. Within two minutes he had a chance to score but ballooned the ball over the Devonport End roof and into the car park beyond. His aim was better later, as the sides shared four goals.

After another enforced break, Argyle faced three crucial matches, against Notts County – who hadn't won at home since October – Hereford, and Orient, both relegation material. County chose the match to end their dismal run. Again Argyle put up little resistance. The match at Hereford didn't start well either. The bottom side went ahead after a quarter of an hour, and three minutes later the normally placid Green was dismissed for retaliation on veteran Terry Paine. Hall equalised with a diving header but Waiters was left speechless by the performance of the referee.

Another missive from Waiters on the matter was soon winging its way to Football League headquarters.

A home defeat by Orient was an even more bitter pill to swallow. Rising star Laurie Cunningham showed why he was being touted as a future international, rounding off a fine display with a cheeky goal through Ramsbottom's legs for the winner.

Waiters had problems. On the field, his side just wasn't performing as a unit. There were some good individual performances but indiscipline wasn't helping as the bookings mounted. Hall had continued to tread water and Bannister wasn't as prolific around goal as hoped. The last thing Waiters needed, then, was a trip to leaders Chelsea. Within two minutes, the Blues scored, Kenny Swain converting a corner. Remarkably, it was the fifth match in succession that Argyle had conceded from a flag kick. Everyone waited for the floodgates to open but they didn't. Argyle defended resolutely and weren't afraid to counter-attack. Early in the second half, Austin equalised. The two sides then exchanged penalties. With five minutes remaining, Delve chipped in from 25 yards, but an infringement had been spotted and it was disallowed. Nevertheless, Argyle were well pleased with their 2-2 draw.

Hopes that Waiters could field an unchanged line up against Millwall were scuppered as Green and Horswill were suspended. Rumours also abounded that Collins, dropped for the Chelsea match, had requested a transfer. Horswill's unavailability saw Darke recalled at left-back. The match saw Hall at last show flashes of the ability everyone knew he had. He scored twice, but lax defensive work allowed Millwall to secure a draw. Craven and Delve were both booked, not an uncommon occurrence, and they too now faced suspensions.

Pressure was now beginning to mount on Waiters, and rifts between him and the board began to appear. The directors were dismayed at the poor performances on the pitch, whilst Waiters felt he was not getting the backing he deserved. He cited the vetoing of the appointment of a new youth-team coach and the refusal to improve the contract of assistant manager Keith Blunt. It was a familiar scenario at many clubs and one that rarely ended amicably.

The squad now faced a few days in the North West, with matches against Blackburn and Bolton. It was perhaps fortunate that Horswill was suspended. Unable to rid himself of his 'bad boy' tag, he made it known that he wanted to return north himself on a permanent basis, but the opportunity to seek asylum had been lost.

Lady Luck certainly didn't accompany Argyle. At Ewood Park, Rovers were awarded a penalty despite Bobby Svarc only appearing to slip over. Late in the game, Ramsbottom, one of the few successes over the season, let a Svarc shot through his legs.

At Bolton, three nights later, Argyle were never in the hunt after Neil Whatmore's second-minute goal. Cue another penalty and another Waiters rant, with the Argyle boss suggesting in his post-match press conference that Garry Jones had spent most of his spare time on the high board in his local swimming pool, so good was his diving. Late in the game, Whatmore added a cracker, flicking the ball over Green and beating two more defenders before planting the ball past Ramsbottom. One man who did have a memorable evening was Randell. Injured against Blackburn and unable to play, he was forbidden from returning to Plymouth despite the fact that his wife was due to give birth imminently. At half-time, a message was relayed to him that he was the father of a baby daughter.

Such a poor run of form prompted Waiters into changes for a third successive away game, this time at Luton. Youngster Kevin Smart was handed his debut at right-back and warmed to the task of marking former Manchester United European Cup-winner John Aston. George Foster staked a claim for a regular place with a goal, as a draw ended Luton's run of nine successive wins. The biggest talking point, and the one which would have the most serious long-term repercussions, was the omission of Brian Hall from the starting line up. The former Liverpool man's form on the pitch characterised his increasing disillusionment with life in Devon. It was clear he had no future and, after seeking talks with Waiters, he made the poignant gesture of putting his house on the market.

This was hardly the ideal backdrop to an increasingly fraught battle against relegation. Nevertheless, the side performed bravely at home to Blackpool, with Foster getting a morale-boosting goal after four minutes. The match originally looked unlikely to go ahead. Heavy rain had left the pitch resembling a swamp and Waiters opted for bare feet to make his pre-match inspection. Despite the mud, Randell, shaking off the effects of sleepless nights, stood out like a beacon and dictated play. Bannister scored a second from the spot after Rogers was upended to secure Argyle's first win since early January.

Off the pitch, the Waiters versus directors battle hotted up. Perhaps inspired by Hall's show of defiance, Waiters put his own house on the market but went one better by circulating the availability of himself and four backroom staff to other clubs. He confirmed he had not consulted the board over his actions as it was 'nothing to do with them'.

Ignoring the in-fighting, the team clinched a crucial win at Cardiff courtesy of a late Austin goal. The side were playing better without Hall.

Despite indifferent form and the shenanigans from within, crowd levels remained, by and large, in five figures. Honours remained even in the home game with Bristol Rovers, a match Argyle expected, and needed to win. Peddelty scored on his 22nd birthday, but an error by Darke led to the equaliser. Referee Alan Robinson could have been forgiven for not always keeping up with play. The night before, he had spotted a French sailor vandalising his car outside his hotel and given chase in his pyjamas. Whether he was successful in his pursuit was never known.

Easter brought three games in four days, commencing with a trip to Southampton. With Craven available after suspension, Waiters selected him as sweeper, believing it would curb the considerable attacking threat posed by the Saints stars. It didn't work. Bannister briefly lifted the hearts of the large travelling support by giving Argyle the lead, but Peach scored a 'peach' from thirty yards. The second half saw Southampton take charge. Two goals from Ted MacDougall took his season's tally to twenty and Mick Channon demonstrated his famous arm-twirling goal celebration after beating four defenders before scoring.

The following day, Argyle, including the restored Hall, faced bottom side Hereford at Home Park. Steve Davey was eager to put one across his former side and equalised Bannister's early goal but was later replaced after suffering a fractured cheekbone. Bannister scored again before Hereford were awarded a penalty. Ramsbottom barely had to move to save Dixie McNeil's feeble effort. A minute from time, Craven was sent off for persistent misconduct, a charge that could legitimately have been levelled at him in most games.

Argyle's 'day off' was taken up by travelling to London in preparation for the game with Fulham. Despite their high-profile if ageing stars, the Cottagers had endured a difficult season and stood just below Argyle in the table. The Greens started brightly, with Delve striking the post in a goalless first half. Amid howls of protest from Argyle players and fans, Fulham took the lead through John Mitchell, despite Ramsbottom being impeded. Vintage George Best magic set up a second for Teddy Maybank. The win saw Fulham leapfrog Argyle in the table.

Five games remained and two wins looked sufficient to stave off relegation worries. Hull at home looked as good a chance as any of picking up two points. The Tigers had not won on their travels for the season and were in the midst of a major injury crisis, forcing manager Bobby Collins to select four eighteen-year-olds. In front of the lowest crowd of the season, the ninety minutes that followed proved to be the low point of the season. The first two goals of Ian Dobson's career sunk Argyle. Waiters, a hero only two years earlier, was jeered by the crowd, the players slow handclapped, and by the time Hall scored an 89th-minute goal the terraces were populated only by those determined to vent their spleen.

Chairman Robert Daniel and his fellow directors now faced a dilemma. It was clear to all that Waiters had no future at the club, but to dismiss him at such a critical stage, with relegation still a possibility, was a high-risk tactic. The board acted in what they felt was in the best interest of the club and announced the sacking of Waiters. It was a sad end to a managerial reign that had promised so much. Assistant Blunt resigned and Kelly was handed command.

Kelly's first game in charge involved the long trek to Carlisle, who were also fighting for their lives. Within eight minutes, Rafferty put them ahead. Before half-time he was brought down by Peddelty and Mike McCartney converted the resultant penalty. Any hopes of a comeback were dispelled by Mick Tait, who sidefooted past Ramsbottom. A last-minute goal from Hall was scant consolation.

Argyle now faced two critical home games in three days and they did-n't come much tougher than Wolves and Nottingham Forest. Sammy Chung's Wolves had continued to score freely and headed the table, need-ing only a point to guarantee promotion. Hundreds of their supporters swelled the attendance, hoping to celebrate a return to top-flight football. A goalless draw gave them reason to celebrate. For Argyle, a point and a clean sheet against the leaders constituted a minor triumph.

The battle for promotion was as keenly contested as the fight at the wrong end of the table, and Brian Clough's Forest were in the thick of it. The match was preceded by the customary presentation of the Argyle Player of the Year award. There were few contenders and the long depart-ed Mariner was touted as the likely recipient. In the end, Ramsbottom got the vote. It was well deserved. He alone had displayed a consistency in his performances which none of his teammates had matched. It represented a personal triumph for a player who had been vilified by some sections of the crowd early in the season.

Bannister raised hopes by scoring against Forest, but Tony Woodcock and Peter Withe took their joint goal tally to 33 for the season to keep Forest's promotion hopes alive and all but condemn Argyle to the drop.

Argyle travelled to Sheffield United for their final game knowing that not even a win could determine their own destiny. Hereford, with 27 points, looked doomed. Cardiff had 31 points, Argyle and Orient 32, and Carlisle 33, but all had games in hand over the Pilgrims. Kelly again rele-gated Hall to the subs' bench, with winger Rogers recalled to give width to the attack. Argyle created chances but it was a familiar tale as they were squandered. Ramsbottom made several fine stops but was powerless to prevent Keith Edwards' fourteenth goal in as many games. News filtered through that other results had conspired against Argyle and that they had been relegated.

It was the end of a sorry season. Waiters and Mariner had gone. The club had one of the worst disciplinary records in the league and a number of players made it clear they no longer wanted to play for Plymouth Argyle. Bannister and Randell were the latest to join the ranks of the unsettled. Despite the drop, Kelly was handed the manager's role on a per-manent basis but faced a busy and difficult summer.

# TEN

# 1985-86 (Promoted to Division 2)

Argyle had become a Third Division fixture. Since relegation, they had rarely challenged at the top. Even the heady FA Cup run to the semi-finals in 1983-84 had failed to spark a revival. Managers and players had come and gone, some good, some bad, but the X-factor was missing.

In Dave Smith, fans hoped and indeed expected that he would be the man to deliver. Canny is an adjective all too readily used when describing Scotsmen, but in Smith's case it seemed apt. He had been in the game as player, coach and manager for more than thirty years and had built a reputation as someone capable of getting provincial clubs – Mansfield and Southend – promoted. He had soon become popular with supporters with his approachable manner and eccentric quirks. He quickly became the self-styled 'Ciderman' and his programme notes were worth the purchase price alone, offering snippets of poetry and replies to supporters' letters, rather than the usual 'we was unlucky in the last game' drivel.

There was much to keep Smith occupied over the summer of 1985. Physio Jimmy Goodfellow had quit and several players also sought pastures new. Leigh Cooper and winger Andy Rogers – two of the FA Cup heroes – both felt they needed fresh challenges. Stalwart defender Chris Harrison would be released following his pre-season testimonial, and striker Gordon Staniforth rejected new contract terms.

If all this wasn't bad enough, Tommy Tynan, goalscorer extraordinaire, Player of the Year and living Argyle legend, wanted to move north. Fans pleaded with Tynan to stay, but his mind was made up. He signed for Rotherham for a paltry £25,000. The other 'escapees' also eventually got their way, with the exception of Cooper, whose talks with Orient came to nothing. Rogers went to Reading, Harrison to Swansea, and Staniforth to Newport in exchange for Steve Cooper and £15,000.

Joining Cooper among the new faces were ex-Arsenal midfielder John Matthews, who had tasted success with Sheffield United and Chesterfield, and Garry Nelson, a pacy forward who had been given his first league opportunity by Smith at Southend.

On the eve of the season, Chairman Stuart Dawe stepped down, to be succeeded by fellow director Peter Bloom. Bloom had run the club's finances and would no doubt watch the cashflow, but he promised not to interfere in team affairs – which was welcomed by Smith.

After the usual pre-season training under the watchful eye of coach Martin Harvey, the friendlies had a more attractive look than usual. With English clubs banned from Europe, following the Heysel Stadium tragedy, some big-name clubs chose to sample the delights of the Westcountry. Tottenham, Aston Villa, Chelsea, Luton and Southampton provided some top-class opposition.

It was soon back to reality with an opening game at York. The pundits had few worries about the defence. Gordon Nisbet, Gerry McElhinney, Clive Goodyear and John Uzzell looked secure. Kevin Hodges and Russell Coughlin would provide the midfield guile, but it was the front line that caused most concern. It was difficult to see how Tynan's goals would be replaced. Smith had warned that Cooper was not a direct replacement, and that burden should not be put upon him. It would be a case of 'wait and see' what impact the other new signings would have.

So much for opinions. Fancied York ran out easy 3-1 winners and the Greens' defence looked uncertain against the strongly built Keith Walwyn. Argyle had to rely on a penalty from McElhinney.

There was little time for Smith to sort things out before the first leg of the Milk Cup-tie against Exeter. The 2-1 win gave little cause for optimism. The recalled Kevin Summerfield was the star man, but suffered a fractured cheekbone and would be missing for eight weeks.

Reading were the first league visitors. The crowd got a soaking from an un-August-like cloudburst just before kick-off. Trevor Senior, touted as a summer Tynan replacement, gave Reading a first-half lead. Argyle again looked toothless in front of goal. In the second half, ever-smiling referee Roger Milford said Nelson had been fouled in the area but McElhinney's spot-kick was saved, prompting cries of 'rubbish' from the sodden fans. It was not the kind of start Smith had envisaged.

Convinced that a striker was a priority, Smith missed the match at Swansea. He was after Tranmere striker John Clayton who, statistically at least, was as prolific as Tynan, having equalled his tally of 31 goals in the season just past. Clayton's boss, Frank Worthington, understandably want-ed to keep him, but Smith gambled on a Football League valuation to secure his fellow Scot. The fee was later set at £24,000, which numbed the pain of Tynan's knock-down price. Smith missed Argyle's first win. Steve Cooper's first Argyle goal trumped a penalty from McElhinney.

Clayton was signed in time to make his debut in the Bank Holiday clash with Notts County at Home Park. Central defender Adrian Burrows was also recalled to add some stability. Again Argyle dominated, but could not retrieve Rachid Harkouk's early goal. The Pilgrims had lost three of their first four league games, and worse was to follow when injury-blight-ed Exeter went through 3-2 on aggregate in the Milk Cup.

An easier fixture than a trip to high-flying Brentford would have been welcome, but Argyle battled for a point earned by another penalty, this time converted by Steve Cooper. The last-minute award hardly delighted the hosts. Referee Baker was yards behind the action when future Pilgrim

Danis Salman impeded Nelson. Bees' boss, Frank McLintock, was so exasperated that at the final whistle the official needed a police escort to reach the dressing room. Former boxer McElhinney suffered his eighth broken nose, although such was the battered appearance of the Irish snozzle, no one would have known.

The result left the Greens floundering in 20th position as they entertained a Newport outfit containing former favourite Staniforth. The league table must have told the popular striker he had made the right decision. The Welsh side were second, but an acrobatic header from Burrows, followed by Nelson's first goal for Argyle, secured a second away win. The attendance was under 4,000.

Despite a broken finger, Clayton made the side for the midweek trip to Doncaster and was granted permitted to play wearing a plaster cast. A single goal was enough to give the Yorkshiremen all three points (since 1981, wins earned three points instead of two). In a miserable game, Smith used a substitute for the first time this season.

The visit of once-mighty Wolves failed to ignite interest in the Plymouth public. Admittedly, Bill McGarry's side were young, inexperienced, and hit by injuries and their naivete was exploited by Nelson, who was beginning to show what a shrewd signing he had been. His two second-half goals were preceded by another Cooper penalty. The defeat left Wolves rock bottom.

A 1-3 defeat by a physical Bolton side was at least an improvement on the 2-7 debacle from the previous season. The result left Argyle near the bottom, but Smith still uttered enthusiastic words, believing that, given a fair wind, his side wasn't too far short of producing the goods.

The next two games, both at home, went some way to vindicating Smith. Gillingham were despatched 3-0, and naturally there was a penalty given, Argyle's seventh of the season. Bristol Rovers then felt the brunt of Argyle's new-found confidence in front of goal. Argyle showed no mercy against opponents down to twelve fit players. Hodges and Nelson, operating in their familiar wide positions, created havoc and the front pairing of Clayton and Cooper, thriving on regular service, finally worked in tandem. Two late defensive errors brought the score back from 4-0 to 4-2, but Smith's post-match comment that his side could have scored nine illustrated Argyle's dominance.

Walsall away. That would provide a more accurate measure of Argyle's recent progress. The Saddlers had won every home game, and two goals from Mark Rees suggested that run would continue. The second provoked Smith to bring on Summerfield – making a welcome return from injury – against one of his former clubs. With under five minutes left, Nelson pulled a goal back, and in the second minute of injury-time scored another, squeezing the ball past Steve Cherry from almost on the dead-ball line.

In the overall scheme of things, it would prove a significant moment in the season, a catalyst for greater things.

For the fourth successive game, Argyle were unchanged as they travelled to Rotherham. After a dull as dishwater first half, a low Hodges shot put Argyle ahead. Ten minutes later they were down to ten men. Matthews, already booked and the subject of several 'conversations' with referee Mr Hendrick, was expelled for a late tackle. From then on it was backs to the wall stuff until, inevitably, one Tommy Tynan grabbed a late equaliser.

A last-gasp goal from Nelson clinched all three points at home to Lincoln in midweek, which set up a daunting trip to Derby. The Rams' side was packed with experience and big-money signings. Smith's pre-match message was clear: concentrate on your own game and don't be overawed by the opposition. It worked a treat, although two errors by Derby keeper Mark Wallington helped. The final whistle was the cue for Smith to embark on a previously unseen version of the Highland Fling.

After such an impressive win, it was a case of after the Lord Mayor's show at home to Chesterfield. Matthews' suspension meant he was unable to feature against his former side and how Argyle missed his midfield guile. It was all too easy for Spireites' keeper, Chris Marples, whose safe handling demonstrated why he was also Derbyshire's wicket-keeper. Argyle could not score and Chesterfield were so uninterested that it was seventy minutes before they registered their first shot.

With wretched weather putting paid to planned firework displays, 5th November saw a bigger than expected crowd to witness another Argyle victory, lifting them to fifth position. Bournemouth provided stiff opposition but Cooper's first Argyle goal from open play proved crucial.

Overcoming the loss of McElhinney at half-time with a head injury, the Pilgrims' win at Bury pushed them up to third, a fact that would not have gone unnoticed by Aldershot, languishing in the bowels of the Fourth Division and unlikely to be relishing an FA Cup first round trip to Home Park. The tie produced the largest Cup attendance of the day, and although the Shots made a game of it, Coughlin capped a man of the match performance with a fine individual goal.

Back in league action, a win over resolute Wigan saw the Greens move up to second. It was the highest position they could realistically hope for. Reading had come out of the traps by winning their first thirteen matches of the season and were uncatchable. The Wigan match was never likely to flow, as referee Hedges awarded no fewer than 58 free-kicks. Inevitably, with so many infringements, a penalty was among them. With Cooper already subbed, it was left to Coughlin to score the winner with five minutes remaining.

Just for a change, Argyle were on the receiving end of a penalty when they travelled to Blackpool to face a team unbeaten at home. Paul Stewart's cross was blasted at McElhinney's arm. The defender was unable to take evasive action and the award looked harsh, but there was hardly cause to complain, given that the Greens had enjoyed more than their fair share of dodgy penalty decisions. Now fast becoming a specialist in the art of late goalscoring, Nelson slotted the equaliser from a flowing move with seven minutes left. Such was the congestion at the top (Reading excepted), that the draw meant Argyle dropped to fifth place.

Once again, the 'magic' of the Cup enticed a handy crowd to Home Park. Call a game an 'FA Cup-tie' and for some reason it lifts people out of their armchairs. Certainly the quality of the opposition was not responsible: Maidstone were not only a non-league side, but a struggling one. They were managed by the ebullient Barry Fry, who had got his side fired up. Hefty tackles flew in but, in truth, Maidstone were no match for Argyle who were buoyed by a superb opener from Cooper, this time the Leigh variety. Maidstone had a glimmer when another handball by McElhinney led to a penalty, but Crudgington smothered Barnes' kick.

Argyle were now firing on all cylinders, as Darlington discovered to their cost. The Pilgrims went four up and it could have been more. Steve Cooper recovered from the disappointment of failing his driving test for the second time by smashing in the goal of the game from 25 yards. Cyril Knowles' side played their part in an entertaining contest and were rewarded with two goals of their own. There were red faces in the Argyle dugout as substitute Darren Rowbotham entered the fray wearing a No 11 shirt. Several minutes passed before the elusive No 12 was located.

The scene was thus set for the trip to Reading. The creaking old Elm Park stadium creaked a little louder as 8,512 formed the Royals' biggest crowd of the season, eager to see the runaway leaders pit their skills against a side now unbeaten for fourteen matches. Those Pilgrimites who had secured tickets looked uneasily at their programmes. The home side contained the likes of former Pilgrim Andy Rogers who, on his day was capable of turning any match, and Trevor Senior, Berkshire's equivalent to Tommy Tynan. There was also Kevin Bremner, who had spent a month on loan at Home Park three years earlier. That was long enough to make an impact on the Plymouth fans and his teammates. As his nickname, 'Mad Max' suggested, Bremner was not one to shirk a challenge, whether in the heat of battle or in a five-a-side training match. Those who anticipated an irresistible force (Mad Max) meeting an immovable object (McElhinney) were disappointed as 'Mad' played in midfield. This meant fireworks were instead expected with the irascible Coughlin.

With 48 minutes gone, all pre-match concerns seemed irrelevant. Argyle, oozing confidence, had swept into a three-goal lead. Reading were more invisible than invincible. Inevitably, manager Ian Branfoot ordered, well, probably politely asked, Bremner to play up front and 'put himself about'. That he did, and within minutes Goodyear had illegally made contact. Dean Horrix converted from the spot. Max was now in full cry. Ten minutes later he set up Senior for a goal, a scene repeated a minute later. At 3-3 Reading were a different side and, unlikely as it had seemed, there was now going to be only one winner. Three minutes later the comeback was complete with Bremner himself tapping in. Could it get any worse? Well, yes. In the final minute Rogers played that favourite time-wasting game of keep-ball by the corner flag. It was all too much for the normally placid Nisbet, who lashed out at Rogers' shins and was sent to the dressing room a few seconds ahead of everyone else.

The loss of three points was disappointing but the main concern was what effect the manner of such a defeat would have on the players. A 0-2 Boxing Day defeat by Bristol City five days later suggested the worst, particularly with Nelson wasting no fewer than four good chances.

If Smith could have chosen his opposition to recover some confidence, Swansea would probably have been high on his list. The Swans were struggling both on and off the field. Next to bottom, they had all but gone out of business and had been saved only by the High Court. There were a couple of familiar faces in their line up, with ex-Pilgrims Chris Harrison and Colin Sullivan in defence. A frosty pitch helped the Greens, forcing them to adopt a close-passing game. Clayton scored twice and was afforded the opportunity of a hat-trick when Cooper allowed him to take over spot-kick duties, but Mike Hughes pulled off a save to ensure there was no match ball in the Clayton kit bag.

There followed one of the more bizarre and exciting games of the season. Almost 9,000 supporters dragged themselves out of their New Year's Day hangovers for a morning kick-off against Cardiff. Argyle were expected to comfortably dispose of the lowly Bluebirds, although Alan Durban's side had shown better form away from home in recent weeks. Nelson scored the opener but Cardiff replied when Robbie Turner demonstrated the aerial power which Argyle fans would appreciate in years to come. Three minutes later came an incident that threw Argyle's plans into chaos. Crudgington's cheekbone collided with Tarki Micallef's boot. The wound required twelve stitches, rendering 'Crudgie' unable to return to the match. With only one substitute available, Nisbet was the logical choice to take over, having started his league career at West Brom as a goalkeeper. His first touch was to pick the ball out of his net, but from the restart Summerfield equalised at 2-2. The half-time whistle afforded players and spectators a breather.

It did not take long for the goals to flow again. Nigel Vaughan headed Cardiff back in front. Then, with Nisbet beaten, Hodges handled on the goal-line. Such an offence in those days was not deemed worthy of dismissal. Jimmy Mullen converted the penalty and at 2-4 Argyle were staring defeat in the face. Again, Argyle scored late on, twice. Clayton pounced on a rebound and Hodges made amends for his earlier indiscretion with an 88th-minute leveller.

With only three days to recover, Crudgington was declared unfit to take his place in the third round of the FA Cup, which meant a rare call up for understudy Dave Philp. Nisbet was suspended, denying him a return to one of his old stomping grounds. The anticipated glamour tie had conjured up a trip to Second Division Hull. In temperatures that would have kept penguins indoors, Hull scored first when Philp floundered and Flounders pounced. Argyle again showed an appetite for a fight and retreated to the relative warmth of the dressing room at half-time in the lead. A second Flounders goal took the tie to a replay but it could have been different. Steve Cooper rose high, but his header found woodwork. Argyle, though, were well pleased with their day's work and fancied their chances in the replay three days later.

Tigers' manager, Brian Horton recalled himself at Home Park. In driving rain, a remarkably large crowd saw his side take an early lead, which they tried to hang on to. Hull's powerfully built defence ably soaked up Argyle pressure to move into the fourth round.

A disappointing defensive display at Notts County saw the two sides swap places in the table. A draw at home to York followed. It was not a memorable game to anyone except John Brimacombe, who combined playing part-time with working in Devonport Dockyard. Playing as a central defender, it took only six minutes for his Andy Warhol moment to arrive, when he hooked in a corner. Again, it took a penalty to extract Argyle from the mire.

A Keystone Cops performance at Newport threatened to undo all the good work. After Clayton had given Argyle an early lead, some Staniforth magic evened things up. Goodyear's boot connected with nothing more than thin Welsh air, allowing Mercer an easy chance. In the second half, Hodges passed back to where he thought Crudgington was. He wasn't. In fact, he was practically standing next to Hodges and the duo watched the ball trickle into the net. Of course, there was the obligatory Argyle penalty, but Steve Cooper's shot was saved.

This poor run of two points from a possible twelve convinced Dave Smith that the forward line still needed strengthening and he spent much of the week preceding the Brentford game spying on various possibilities. Jokingly, he suggested that he should stay away from the club more often as a Nelson double sank the Bees in front of the watching England manager, Bobby Robson.

A fortnight's break from competition did little to change Smith's opinion over recruitment, as abysmal finishing cost Argyle dearly in the home defeat by Doncaster. Smith had publicly announced a target of 85 points, which he believed would secure promotion. The 'floating' fans weren't convinced. Attendances were still generally below 5,000. Performances such as the Doncaster one did little to lure back the sceptics. Smith had recently put pen to paper on a new two-year contract as a reward for transforming Argyle's prospects.

Now even the elements were conspiring against Argyle. A lengthy spell of icy weather caused a number of postponements, thereby creating a potential end-of-season fixture pile up. Other promotion candidates were luckier, with most able to play the odd game here and there to extend the points gap between Argyle and themselves. It was not just postponed games that were causing inconvenience. Training was disrupted, with outdoor practice virtually impossible.

Three weeks elapsed before the Greens found themselves in meaningful action with a hazardous-looking trip to the unwelcoming Priestfield stadium. The hosts, Gillingham, were lying second. A few (fool)hardy Argyle souls made the trip. A goal from danger-man Tony Cascarino did little to warm their spirits, or anything else come to that. But, of course, by now, the Green Army, well, platoon in this case, knew full well that a game lasts for ninety minutes and anyone habitually leaving a few minutes before the end of matches had, by this stage of the season, missed a fair number of goals. This time Summerfield, in for the suspended Matthews, equalised with four minutes left. The match saw the debut of Orient's bearded forward Kevin Godfrey, who arrived on loan.

The new man made a vital contribution to the next game, scoring the winner against a Bristol Rovers side that had not conceded a goal in five games. Coughlin had given Argyle an early lead with another penalty.

Little did anyone know, but that win proved the catalyst for a remarkable sequence of results. The win took Argyle to the 50-point mark, still, it seemed, a long way off Smith's 85-point target. It meant just seven points could be dropped in the final fourteen games. Furthermore, those games had to be squeezed into a seven-week period.

Three of those required points seemed guaranteed at Wolves. The Old Golds were a sorrowful bunch, bottom of the table and with little hope of escaping. Their supporters had little hope either. A paltry crowd was dotted around a Molyneux stadium that had seen so many great games in the past. After another Coughlin spot-kick, Godfrey again made his mark, laying on goals for Summerfield and Clayton.

The following game would be a tougher test, or so everyone thought. Nelson was not considered, suffering from a virus. Walsall were one of Argyle's main rivals for a promotion slot but they failed to register a single shot on target in the ninety minutes as the Pilgrims won 2-0.

A fourth successive win was chalked up at Chesterfield and, finally, a decent-sized crowd turned up for a league fixture at Home Park to see the crunch game against third-placed Derby. It didn't start too well. County took a twelfth-minute lead after poor defending, Coughlin limped off, and Argyle failed to get into their stride during the first half.

Whatever poetry or other words of wisdom Smith uttered at half-time, they clearly inspired his side. Within two minutes Clayton scored. Nine minutes later he was at it again. It was particularly satisfying to inflict such punishment on one of his former clubs, where he had failed to make much of an impression. Rowbotham scored his first league goal and Hodges rounded off a fine individual performance with a fourth. It was only County's fifth defeat of the season and a tremendous psychological boost for the Pilgrims.

Good Friday turned into very Good Friday as 2,000 travelling Argyle fans constituted more than half of the Ninian Park crowd to see the Pilgrims grab another three points. There was widespread relief when the game kicked off. Torrential rain had put it in doubt and a pitch inspection was required with most of the crowd already in the ground. With Coughlin missing and Cooper on the bench, young Rowbotham took responsibility for a dubiously awarded tenth-minute penalty, when goalkeeper Lee Smelt dived at the feet of Hodges. Smelt required lengthy treatment but recovered sufficiently to block the spot-kick, only for Hodges to put away the rebound. A rare Matthews goal from an even rarer Matthews header increased the gap, and although Cardiff nicked a goal, it was not enough. The result finally convinced Smith that something special was happening, to the extent that the final whistle saw him toss his beloved flat cap into the crowd. When the euphoria had subsided, he regretted his impulsive action. Desperate to be reunited with his close companion, an appeal was launched for its safe return. Forty-eight hours later it was returned, none the worse from its brief excursion.

The Cardiff match also marked the end of Godfrey's loan period. He had limped out of the action after typically giving his all. He had quickly become popular with fans and colleagues, and Smith was now left to find an adequate replacement.

York's Keith Houchen and Archie Stephens of Middlesbrough were rumoured to be on Smith's shopping list, but he also had his eye on another out-of-favour striker. Up north, at Millmoor, Tommy Tynan was not seeing eye to eye with manager Norman Hunter. With transfer deadline day approaching, Tynan was reported to have been involved in a training ground bust-up with teammate Phil Crosby. Deemed to be the guilty party, Tynan had been banished to the reserves, igniting a chase for his signature by no fewer than nine clubs.

Sensationally, Smith got his man. The news leaked out before the scheduled Easter Monday morning game against Bristol City. The rain had barely stopped for the whole of the Easter weekend. Fans began arriving early at Home Park. A large crowd was expected but there was to be no match. Pitch waterlogged. The early arrivals were turned back, the later ones were still arriving. Chaos reigned in the streets. In the event, a mutiny might have been unwittingly averted. Unbeknown to supporters, Tynan's registration was somewhere in the post and he would not have played. Clayton was also injured and he too would have missed out.

The postman delivered in time for Tynan to play at Bournemouth. Nisbet, as excited as anyone about the homecoming, put himself in line for 'rash statement of the year' award. 'No one will be more pleased than me if Tommy scores ten goals and we win promotion'. With Clayton still out, Steve Cooper was recalled to form an ex-Newport front pairing with Tynan, and it was Cooper who played a starring role, opening the scoring and then winning a penalty, which Coughlin converted. John Beck pulled one back, but Hodges scored another late one to send the large travelling contingent home happy. Five away victories in a row had set a new Argyle club record.

The situation at the top of the table was still tight. Reading had not faltered and looked certainties for promotion, but only four points separated Gillingham, Wigan, Argyle and Derby, with County still having eleven games to play compared to Plymouth's eight.

Tuesday night, and 13,000 poured into Home Park to see the return of the prodigal son. What's more, the opponents were Rotherham. The loan agreement for Tynan had involved some discussion as to whether the striker should be chosen for this particular game. According to Smith, the matter had been left in abeyance. Hunter begged to differ, but there he was in the familiar No 9 shirt. Nelson was also recalled after a five-game absence, despite not being 100 per cent fit.

From the start it was one-way traffic. A Pickering own-goal contributed to Rotherham's downfall, but not as much as two goals from the man himself. Never has anyone so enjoyed scoring against their own club. A last-minute effort from Summerfield completed the 4-0 rout, sealing another three points and, perhaps just as importantly, improving the goal-difference. Hunter continued to rant about the 'gentleman's agreement'. Previously famed for biting legs, the former Leeds hard-man was now biting heads, but Smith refused to become embroiled in the dispute.

The following match, at home to lowly Bury, was preceded by the presentation of 'manager of the month' to Smith, the Scotsman probably appreciating the gallon of whisky more than most. On this occasion, the defeat which traditionally accompanied such an award, was never likely. Hodges scored early on, and two typical Tynanesque goals from inside six yards proved more than adequate to clinch a remarkable ninth successive win, equalling the feat of Argyle's promotion side of 1930. The crowd were buoyant. At one point, a dog wandered onto the playing area. An impromptu chorus of 'there's only one Jack Russell' broke out with impressive quick-wittedness.

The winning sequence was broken at a rainy Sincil Bank, where Lincoln were fighting to avoid the drop. The hosts scored early, in the third minute, but Argyle equalised in the second half with 'you know who' scoring the goal.

A glance at the remaining fixtures suggested the next game against promotion rivals Wigan could be crucial. Over 5,000 travelled from the Westcountry to more than double Springfield Park's usual attendance figure. From the off, tension was high and the game niggly. Wigan began to impose their authority and what followed was one of Argyle's worst performances of the season, prompting fears that fatigue was now a factor.

Smith asked his men to put the 0-3 defeat out of their minds, but it obviously preyed on his, to the extent that before the following game, at home to Bolton, he publicly apologised to the crowd over the PA system for the performance at Wigan.

From the off, Argyle were up for it, but it was Bolton who went in at half-time leading through ex-Pilgrim Dave Sutton. Wanderers keeper David Felgate was in inspirational form until Hodges finally made the breakthrough in the 72nd minute. It was going to need another late, late show and so it proved. Coughlin from the spot, Tynan, of course, and Burrows, deputising for the absent McElhinney, all scored in the final five minutes to record a 4-1 victory.

No one could quantify what effect Plymouth's remarkable run was having on their rivals, but one by one they were dropping points here and there. Even Reading were having a shaky spell.

Four days later, Blackpool came a visiting and again threatened to spoil the party when Paul Stewart gave them a first-half lead. Nelson ended his personal goal-drought to level before a Coughlin penalty, Argyle's fourteenth of the season, and a Tynan goal from all of two inches, hoisted the team up to second, two points ahead of Wigan.

The situation was now more clear cut. Victory over Bristol City, coupled with anything less for Wigan at Darlington, would seal promotion. On that Tuesday evening, fans arrived at Home Park in droves. The official capacity of the stadium was 19,900, a miserly figure to those who remembered the days of 38,000 crowds not that many years earlier. Somehow, everyone got in. The official attendance was announced as – surprise, surprise – 19,900. Estimates put the figure at nearer 25,000 but don't tell the Football League.

It was little surprise that the start had to be delayed. When the game did commence, Argyle were magnificent. If the players were nervous, they didn't show it. Tynan broke the ice in the 22nd minute – 1-0 at half-time. The night air buzzed to the sound of transistor radios pressed nervously to ears. A cheer broke out with the news that Wigan were losing. Whether those cheers infiltrated the dressing room and inspired the players, only they will know, but with adrenalin flowing, they overran City. Nelson, still 'bugged by his bug', was at his best and scored a great second. Coughlin then scored directly from a corner. Tynan bagged his second with a flying header. The three points were not in doubt. It now all hinged on events 400 miles away. Then the news came. Wigan had only drawn and Argyle were up. Within seconds of the final whistle the pitch was flooded with fans. Somewhere in there were eleven green-shirted players. For a second time, Smith's cap was sent into orbit, this time never to return.

With Reading uncatchable, runners-up was the best Argyle could hope for. If the players and supporters had over-indulged in celebrations over the past few days, a trip to Darlington for the final game was a sobering solution. Smith was again named as 'manager of the month' and was determined to ensure his players also finished the season on a high note. The early loss of McElhinney through injury saw Matthews revert to centre-half, a position he had played in during his early Arsenal days. Matthews was magnificent. Over one thousand Argyle fans urged the team on, and after a goalless first 45 minutes Hodges scored a beauty. With six minutes left, Tynan scored his tenth in nine games, to fulfil the prophecy according to Saint Nisbet.

The win saw Smith's unlikely points target exceeded. Back home, the players were rewarded with an open-top bus tour through the city and a civic reception. It poured with rain, everyone was soaked, but no one really cared. It was time to celebrate a promotion that, in October, was unthinkable. Certain individuals played starring roles. Hodges was rightly named Player of the Year for a season that was undoubtedly the best of his long stint in a green shirt. His fellow wide-man, Nelson, had an equal claim, and the pair contributed 29 goals between them. McElhinney was a rock in defence. There were few better full-backs than Nisbet and few safer goalkeepers than Crudgington. Matthews and Coughlin had pulled the strings in midfield and there was, of course, the masterstroke of Tynan's late-season return. When the loan had been agreed, some questioned the likely commitment of a player who had wanted away only a few months earlier. The answer was obvious. The question now was, would he return permanently?

Another important factor was the ability of fringe players to come in when required without disrupting the side. It was a testimony to the coaching methods of Smith and Harvey. Was this the dawn of a new era?

# ELEVEN

# 1991-92 (Relegated to New Division 2)

Under Dave Smith, top-division football, never before seen at Home Park, was a distinct possibility. Despite still having an unfashionable tag, Argyle had more than held their own against more glamorous teams such as Leeds and Sunderland. In the first season after promotion in 1985-86, Smith retained the nucleus of that side. Most fans considered a mid-table position acceptable, but the Pilgrims started where they had left off and were rarely out of the top six. In the end, they finished seventh, having endured a barren spell away from home and the loss of the final three games of the season.

The following season was anticlimactic. After briefly topping the table in late August, a steady slide ensued. Tynan was still knocking them in but other favourites, such as Garry Nelson and Gordon Nisbet, had moved on and the years were catching up with Geoff Crudgington and John Matthews. Once again, away form proved problematic and, with only four wins on the road, seventeenth place was a disappointment. The close season saw the departure of Dave Smith, for whom the chance to return to his native Tayside and manage Dundee in the Scottish Premier League was too much to resist.

In Smith's place, Argyle again opted for experience, in the shape of Ken Brown, who had led Norwich to two promotions and a League Cup victory. Brown was one of the game's 'nice guys', but he failed to ignite the Pilgrims in his first season and they finished eighteenth.

Following another indifferent start to the following season, supporters became restless and Brown paid the ultimate price. By early February 1990, he was sacked, replaced, briefly, by John Gregory and then permanently by former Pilgrim goalscoring hero David Kemp, who succeeded in his initial task of avoiding relegation.

Kemp's first full season saw little improvement. His long-ball style of play proved unpopular with the fans and a some of his signings were clearly not up to Second Division football. Tynan had finally departed and his regular supply of goals were badly missed. As the 1991-92 season began, Kemp knew he was under pressure to deliver the goods. Off the field matters were also proving a distraction. Kemp had already fallen out with the local press, who had lambasted his style of play, and a consortium of local businessmen had put forward proposals to revamp Home Park into a new 20,000-seat stadium.

There was little money available to strengthen the squad and, in the circumstances, Argyle were among the favourites for the drop. Kemp's new signings – such as they were – hardly inspired confidence, if only on the basis that few supporters had even heard of Morrys Scott, Mark Quamina and Steve Morris. These three had notched up barely a handful of league appearances between them. Add to that list, striker Dwight Marshall, an expensive buy in Pilgrim currency. Non-league Grays Athletic were £35,000 richer for selling him.

The one experienced newcomer was Tony Spearing, formerly of Norwich and Leicester. Kemp hoped Spearing would fill the left-back spot which had not seen an adequate successor to John Uzzell.

Pre-season saw a rare 'double' of testimonial matches. Arsenal provided attractive opposition for Graham Little's benefit. Little had been the long-serving and popular secretary of Argyle through thick and thin. Tynan also made a nostalgic return for his testimonial against Aston Villa.

Little's departure saw the club seek to modernise its image by renaming the secretary 'chief executive'. The role was filled by Liz Baker, the clubs' first female in the job.

The league season started encouragingly with a win over Barnsley. Marshall made an instant impact by scoring with a spectacular overhead kick after just nineteen minutes of his debut.

It was then on to Rumbelows Cup action, with a first round, first leg tie at Third Division Shrewsbury. Former Pilgrim Kevin Summerfield didn't take long to exact revenge on Argyle and, in particular, Kemp – who had shown him the door – scoring controversially after seven minutes. Mick Heathcote, a familiar face to Argyle followers in years to come – saw his header saved by Rhys Wilmot, but Summerfield appeared to bundle the ball from the keeper's grasp. The goal was allowed to stand. A thunderous late volley from Andy Morrison levelled the tie, leaving Argyle favourites for the second leg.

Back in league action, Argyle never looked likely to prosper from their trip to Leicester, where the defence failed to cope with the long-ball tactics of the home side. More disappointment followed, with Shrewsbury dashing Argyle's Rumbelows Cup hopes on the away-goals rule. Once again, Summerfield scored, while Robbie Turner was sent off in extra-time.

Argyle returned to winning ways in the league with an exciting performance over a costly Millwall side. Adrian Burrows scored for both sides. His 84th-minute own-goal appeared to have shared the points until substitute Steve Wood returned the compliment in the fourth minute of injury-time.

Midweek saw an action-packed visit to Newcastle. With Argyle's green and white stripes clashing with United's famous black and white, the Pilgrims donned unfamiliar blue shirts, bereft of a sponsor's name. After half an hour, Wilmot collided with the bulky frame of Micky Quinn and was incapacitated. Nicky Marker took over the goalkeepers's jersey and substitute Danis Salman came off the bench to score with his first touch. Argyle defended fiercely to protect Marker, and when Marshall added a second goal it seemed like they had succeeded. The Toon Army were in unforgiving mood and Turner was attacked for celebrating Marshall's strike and required three stitches in a head wound. Two goals in the final eight minutes salvaged the Magpies' wounded pride.

With Wilmot having failed to recover, reserve custodian and occasional sheep farmer, Dave Walter, was thrust into action for the home game with Charlton. Walter was not a total stranger to league action, having deputised for Wilmot before. He could feel well pleased with his first 45 minutes against the Addicks as the game was goalless. That didn't take long to change. Garry Nelson, relishing his return to the Home Park stage, won a penalty after his heels were clipped by Nicky Marker. Darren Pitcher converted. Then Nelson scored himself and in post-match interviews revealed that he almost re-signed for the Greens during the summer. With Kemp's side now sliding towards the bottom of the table, Pilgrim followers were beginning to wish Nelson had.

Defeat at Grimsby a week later did little to lighten Kemp's normally sombre mood. He was critical of his defence and also began to speak out over the lack of cash available to him. It was apparent to all that the squad needed ballast. A few players were Division Two quality, some, clearly were not. It was also difficult to see where a regular supply of goals would come from. Marshall was showing promise, but understandably was still adjusting to the tempo of league football, and Turner was bearing the brunt of the attacking options, but he was now suspended.

Tactical changes, including the deployment of Marker as a sweeper, failed to halt the slide at Southend, where Walter was hero and villain, pulling off a number of fine saves and then needlessly conceding a corner from which Ian Benjamin netted the winner.

With Argyle in the bottom four, a visit from leaders Middlesbrough was the last thing Kemp and his players wanted. There was little cause for optimism. Boro had won their last six games, Wilmot was still injured, and Morrison was also sidelined by an injury picked up in training. Boro, though, chose to have an off-day. Burrows, showing a rare penchant for scoring, gave Argyle an interval lead. Barlow than had a golden opportunity to tie the game up, but his penalty, given for handball, was well saved by Stephen Pears. Paul Wilkinson equalised to preserve his side's leadership of the division.

Much-needed points were on offer in the next match at bottom side Oxford. Wilmot was fit again, but Kemp chose to retain Walter. With hindsight, it was a decision he would regret. Argyle looked the likely recipients of three welcome points when Martin Barlow put them 2-1 ahead with only eight minutes remaining, but poor Walter then suffered a disastrous sixty seconds. Firstly he flapped at a cross and allowed Paul Simpson to equalise. From the kick-off, Oxford regained possession, Walter fumbled a through ball, and David Penney pounced. The hapless keeper had earlier suffered a blow to the head, which perhaps contributed to his errors but, nevertheless, the pressure on Kemp intensified.

With Walters' confidence in tatters, it was not the most difficult decision of Kemp's career to recall Wilmot for the next game against Swindon. A larger than usual Home Park crowd were, no doubt, lured by the prospect of seeing the mercurial Glenn Hoddle in action. The former England man did not disappoint. Turning back the clock, he was head and shoulders above everyone, but it was Duncan Shearer who grabbed the headlines. Two goals in each half from the Swindon forward sunk Argyle without trace. Shearer even 'scored' a fifth, which was disallowed for offside, although this was not noticed by the Argyle PA announcer who glumly informed the crowd of a fifth goal. His embarrassment was matched only by that of the Argyle defence.

A daunting trip to Blackburn followed. This was 'rich man, poor man' stuff. Despite their appalling form, Kemp was forced to field virtually an unchanged side. Rovers, on the other hand, were being bankrolled by steel magnate Jack Walker. They already boasted the likes of half million pound man David Speedie in attack, and 45 minutes before kick-off announced to an astounded press corps that former Liverpool legend Kenny Dalglish would be their new manager. It was the ultimate psychological blow. From that moment, Argyle were only ever going to be bit-part players.

An early goal had an already vibrant Ewood Park in raptures. Then Turner was sent off for elbowing Kevin Moran. On the stroke of half-time, Simon Garner, onside in the eyes of the linesman if not anyone else, increased the lead. It was all too much for Kemp who became embroiled with the referee as they left the pitch at the interval. His manner did not suggest he was congratulating Mr Holbrook on his first-half performance. Rovers added three more goals in the second half. Argyle scored twice but the defeat left them rock bottom. One point from the last seven games deserved little else.

In desperation, Kemp switched Turner to central defence for the trip to Bristol Rovers, one place above Argyle and without a manager. He knew the switch would weaken the attack, but realised Argyle need to stop conceding goals before they could consider winning. The move worked to an extent. Argyle didn't concede but, perhaps inevitably, didn't score either. To add to Kemp's woes, Morrison, coming back from injury, lasted just 35 minutes before being carted off to hospital for X-rays on an ankle. The injury would keep him out for a few weeks.

Despite the doom and gloom on the pitch, and dwindling attendances, there were still interested parties throwing together takeover packages.

Local businessman Steve Tiller went public on his proposed £2 million 'rescue' package. The proposal only served to split the board, some of who backed the idea. Then, from nowhere, millionaire entrepreneur Dan McCauley announced that he had taken a controlling interest in the club. McCauley had previously been involved with both Torquay and Exeter. His arrival would launch a turbulent but, ultimately club-saving reign. The outgoing chairman, Peter Bloom, and two other directors remained on the board.

McCauley was away on business as Argyle played their first game under his chairmanship. This was, perhaps, just as well, as he might have questioned the wisdom of his involvement. Barely 4,000 turned up to witness another dismal display against Watford, who secured victory despite playing for 75 minutes a man short. An uncharacteristic rush of blood by Wilmot gifted the Hornets the only goal. Turner's flirtation with the central defensive role was temporarily put on hold as he served his second suspension of the season. Former Welsh international Jeff Hopkins was drafted in on loan to provide defensive cover.

Argyle won for the first time in eleven games, scraping through by a single Marshall goal against a Wolves side denied the services of their lethal strike force, Steve Bull and Andy Mutch, who both failed late fitness tests. At Bristol City, however, the hosts were already two up when Mark Aizlewood was dismissed for aiming a head-butt at Andy Clement.

McCauley gave notice of his commitment by promptly splashing out a club record £200,000 for Notts County striker Dave Regis, who had scored a hat-trick against the Pilgrims the previous season. The new man made his debut at Tranmere, where a John Aldridge penalty consigned Argyle to another defeat, although the overall performance was somewhat improved.

Regis's arrival meant Turner, available again, could be restored to his defensive role. The big man's presence certainly plugged some holes at the back, and two wins and two clean sheets followed against Port Vale and Sunderland. Another loan signing, winger Michael Meaker, had arrived from QPR as McCauley vowed to continue team-strengthening.

An injury-time goal at Brighton sent Argyle back to the bottom, but spirits were lifted as Morrison was declared fit and donned the substitute's shirt for the visit of Ipswich. Mark Fiore's goal was enough to take the points and Turner was again in the wars, this time as the victim in a clash with Steve Whitton, that saw the Ipswich man sent off.

The main worry now was the form of Regis, whose performances had been lackadaisical at best, but a scrappy albeit much-needed goal against Newcastle was hopefully the catalyst for improved performances. Barlow added a second with a shot that went through the legs of Northern Irish international keeper Tommy Wright to seal a second successive win.

Christmas brought another present for Kemp in the shape of winger David Smith, a £185,000 buy from Bristol City. The new man made his debut as a substitute on Boxing day at Cambridge, where Turner's late penalty cancelled out Dion Dublin's header. It was to be a rare appearance from Smith, who was destined to spend more time in the physio's room than on the pitch. Two days later, Argyle travelled to Millwall, who had been on the end of a 0-4 Boxing Day thrashing by Watford. When Steve Morgan headed Argyle ahead it looked as though the Lions would roll over, but they came back to score twice to leave Argyle in the relegation zone. Good riddance 1991.

The New Year started in brighter fashion. An exciting 3-2 win over old rivals Portsmouth saw Marshall make a welcome return to the scoresheet after six goalless games. The victory saw Argyle move out of the bottom four for the first time since September.

The FA Cup draw had also been relatively kind, or so everyone thought. A trip to Bristol Rovers was hardly the money-spinning glamour tie that everyone hoped for from the third round, but it appeared to represent a reasonable chance of progressing. Rovers were only a place above the Greens in the league and Argyle had drawn there earlier in the season. But it was to be one of those days, again! Ian Alexander opened the scoring with a header that went through Wilmot's legs. Rovers' Carl Saunders had one of those games that every striker dreams about. Every time a chance came to him he scored. Four times in fact. Kemp labelled his players 'brainless'. The pain of the defeat was worsened when the fourth round draw was made. Argyle had missed out on a plum home tie against Liverpool. The defeat, or more precisely the manner of it, was quite enough as far as certain directors were concerned. The manager had to go. But McCauley persevered with Kemp, believing that perhaps a recovery was on the way. Yes, the Cup defeat was demoralising, but league form, and results, had shown an upturn in recent weeks.

Against Leicester, Argyle blew a two-goal lead. Yet another 'loan ranger' arrived on the scene, in the form of defender Tony Witter. Two minutes into his debut he scored with his first touch. Fiore added a second, but a Turner own-goal sparked a Leicester revival.

Witter's arrival allowed Kemp the luxury of restoring Turner to the attack against Barnsley, and he soon showed his worth by creating all manner of problems for the home defence. He played a major part in helping Marshall to his first ever league hat-trick and also a rare away victory for Argyle. Barnsley had problems of their own. Some of their supporters staged a post-match demonstration calling for the sacking of manager Mel Machin. Argyle's victory had done little to sweeten their mood.

Four weeks after the FA Cup debacle, Bristol Rovers came visiting and, no doubt, much of Argyle's focus was on Carl Saunders. The need to stop him at all costs was matched only by Rovers' apparent uninterest in gaining anything more than a point. All this added up to a game as interesting as last week's newspapers. A remote-controlled jeep was sent scurrying around the penalty area at half-time. It was the highlight of the afternoon. Spearing was sent off for persistent misconduct.

The clock was now ticking on Kemp. Another poor midweek performance at Portsmouth did little to help his cause. Regis, still woefully lacking in confidence did manage to score but Pompey, by that time, had already hit four. Sadly, the rest of the side were mirroring Regis. Kemp made three changes for the visit to Watford but they made little difference. David James demonstrated the form that would eventually bring him England honours, and old hand Luther Blissett showed he still had an eye for goal.

Kemp knew he was on borrowed time. A Tuesday evening fixture against Cambridge suddenly took on huge significance. The visitors, under the leadership of John Beck, were also exponents of the long-ball game, but they had mastered it to a degree that Kemp had always strived to attain but never succeeded. Cambridge had achieved a top-four place with limited resources, but in Dion Dublin and John Taylor possessed a top-drawer strike duo. Again Kemp made changes, dropping record signing Regis to the bench. Kemp even had the luxury of a fit David Smith, who made his full home debut some six weeks after signing. Also included was another loan signing, Erik van Rossum, a Dutch Under-21 international.

Within fourteen minutes Cambridge had the lead as Dublin flicked on a corner to leave Michael Cheetham an easy chance. Argyle came back and twice Marker hit the woodwork. Frustration got the better of Kemp in the second half as he was sent from the dug-out for remarks made to a linesman. As he trudged to the grandstand it was a symbolic moment. Two days later, he was sacked, a sad ending for someone who, as a player, was the hero of the Home Park terraces.

Assistant manager Alan Gillett survived, and along with youth team manager Gordon Nisbet, was put in temporary charge. But McCauley had already named his number one target – former Argentinian World Cup star, Ossie Ardiles. Ardiles declined the bait. Ray Wilkins was also mentioned but was keen to continue a top-flight playing career.

Gillett and Nisbet took charge for the first time and could not have wished for an easier beginning. Brighton were bottom of the table and missing six regulars. With Kemp's long-ball style quickly abandoned, all seemed to be going to plan when Smith scored his first Argyle goal, but Mark Gall equalised with eight minutes left and two more vital home points went begging.

Worse was to follow at high-flying Ipswich. Shortly after half-time, Wilmot and Turner collided and Chris Kiwomya scored. More seriously,

Turner lay prone on the ground. After several minutes of treatment he was stretchered off with a double fracture of the leg. His season and possibly Argyle's were over.

On the following Monday, some of the resultant gloom was lifted as McCauley called a press conference to announce the new manager. It was a closely guarded secret but the chairman seemed intent on a high-profile name. In walked England's most capped footballer, Peter Shilton, who had still been playing, for Derby, at the age of 42. The appointment generated intense publicity, but there was a nagging doubt that Shilton was untried at managerial level. Success as a player did not necessarily mean instant success as a manager. Bobby Moore and Bobby Charlton were two prime examples.

Shilton wasted little time in appointing his assistant, John McGovern, who had shared some great moments as a teammate at Nottingham Forest. At the same time, Shilton confirmed that he still intended to play. This prompted a transfer request from Wilmot, who clearly thought that he would no longer be first choice. Morgan had also already decided that his future lay elsewhere, so there was much to occupy the mind of the new boss.

Ironically, Derby provided the opposition for the first match of the new managerial 'dream team'. A larger than usual attendance gave a rapturous greeting to the duo as they were introduced to the crowd but the excitement quickly faded as Paul Simpson gave Derby the lead. Morrison equalised but another home draw was barely sufficient. Winning the remaining home games was now a must, given the continued poor away results. Three days later, Argyle grabbed three vital points against Bristol City through a Marshall effort, at the same time heightening the relegation crisis for City. The two 'want aways', Wilmot and Morgan were playing at the top of their game.

Much of the pre-match publicity for the visit to Wolves centred on ace striker Steve Bull, who needed one goal to break the all-time Wolves scoring record. He was to be denied, but the home side still grabbed the win, thanks to a 25-yard effort by full-back Mark Venus. With two sides of the redeveloped Molineux ground closed, neither team was capable of raising their game. It was not one to remain in the memory bank for long.

With transfer deadline day approaching, Shilton missed the home game against Tranmere, deciding his time would be better spent spying on potential new signings. Once again, Wilmot and Morgan were the heroes, with the goalkeeper saving John Aldridge's penalty and Morgan bagging the only goal.

The fruit of Shilton's labours was revealed when he made a swift but unhappy return to Derby. With Argyle a goal down, new striker Kevin Nugent, a £200,000 purchase from Leyton Orient, came on for the final half hour, only to see Derby extend their lead. Steve Sutton, Shilton's successor in the Derby goal, was barely tested.

Transfer deadline day saw two more arrivals. David Lee, a lanky midfielder, arrived on loan from Chelsea, and the vastly experienced Steve McCall signed from Sheffield Wednesday for £25,000. The acquisition of McCall represented a major gamble. Having gained European experience during the salad days of Ipswich, he appeared to be the ideal type of player to help extricate Argyle from their present crisis, but he had been blighted by injuries and had managed a total of only 29 appearances in the past five seasons.

All three new boys were included in the starting line up for a vital relegation clash at bottom of the table Port Vale, with Regis and Smith on the bench. McCall in particular was impressive but Wilmot, for once, was the villain, bringing down David Lowe. Ray Walker converted the resultant penalty to deal another blow to Argyle's survival hopes. Thanks to defensive errors, a home defeat by Grimsby, who were hardly setting the division alight, saw the season reach crisis point. To make matters worse, Nugent suffered a broken bone in his foot. He would miss the remainder of the campaign.

For the trip to Charlton, Shilton opted for experience. In recent weeks, many of Kemp's bargain bucket signings had been discarded and older hands such as Burrows and Kevin Hodges restored to the first team. Now, for the first time, Shilton picked himself and played his part in a sturdier defensive performance to seal an unlikely scoreless draw.

Perhaps this would be the turning point. It certainly needed to be, with games running out. The euphoria of Shilton's appointment had quickly evaporated. Argyle's standard of play might have improved, but results had not. The manager now needed to earn his corn and show that he could inspire his players to fight for everything. A home game against a Southend side harbouring faint hopes of a play-off place was the ideal opportunity to start amassing the points needed to climb away, but Marker's own-goal demoralised the players and the crowd. The 0-2 defeat left Argyle bottom of the table with the escape route narrowing. The only ray of hope was that just four points separated the bottom seven clubs.

With little to lose, youngsters Ryan Cross and Michael Evans were drafted in for the daunting trip to Sunderland. Morrison was assigned the task of shackling 21-goal John Byrne and did so with style. Evans set up Marshall to score the only goal and clinch the Pilgrims' first ever victory at Roker Park.

Remaining in the North East, Argyle faced Middlesbrough but injuries forced more changes which disrupted the side. Again, Marshall gave Plymouth the lead, but Boro quickly responded. Falconer put the home side ahead and then Hodges was sent off for instinctively thrusting out a hand to stop a goal-bound shot. Shilton saved the penalty but the damage had been done.

Three games remained, two at home. Seven points might be sufficient. Fellow strugglers Oxford were dismissed without difficulty, and as other results panned out, Argyle realised they needed one win from the remaining two games to stay up.

The only problem was that those games were against Swindon and Blackburn, both still encamped in play-off country. Once again the fates would conspire against Shilton and his men. Marshall had been injured against Oxford and was not available. Morgan tweaked a hamstring at Swindon, forcing McCall to switch to left-back, thus depriving the side of any midfield creativity. Argyle were sunk by a goal scored by Plymouth-born Shaun Taylor, who had just been voted Swindon's player of the year.

Three points, no less, was now needed in the final game at home to Blackburn. Even then, Argyle's fate would be down to how the others performed. At least there was a strong show of support, as over 17,000 turned up, forcing a fifteen-minute delay to the kick-off. Nugent was surprisingly declared fit and took his place on the bench, while Marshall was fit enough to make the starting eleven. Argyle enjoyed the start they craved when Smith scored after twelve minutes, but the wily David Speedie then came into his own, giving a peerless display of finishing. Two goals before half-time and a third after 67 minutes finished Argyle off and sealed Rovers' play-off spot.

Hard as it was to take, relegation had seemed almost inevitable for a number of weeks. A number of factors had contributed to Argyle's downfall. The squad had been short on quality and experience, and injuries to key players such as Turner and Morrison had not helped. McCauley's takeover had provided much-needed funds but the quality of the signings were questionable, particularly Regis and Smith, who had provided minimal return on the outlay.

Perhaps relegation would be a blessing in disguise. A number of promising youngsters – Evans, Cross and Marc Edworthy – were chomping at the bit, and with Marker, Morrison and Marshall there was hope.

# TWELVE

# 1994-95 (Relegated to Division 3)

There was an air of confidence around Home Park as Argyle entered the 1994-95 season. The previous campaign had seen the team perish in the play-off semi-finals to Burnley, after Argyle had finished third in the division, missing out on automatic promotion by three points. Compared to the season before, that was a huge improvement. Fourteenth place in 1992-93 had seen the season peter out into a non-event due, in the main, to wretched away form. Now, with many of the play-off squad retained, the main question was whether, psychologically, they could put that nightmare behind them.

Compared to that of the previous season, the summer transfer activities was almost non-existent. Jittery goalkeeper Ray Newland and veteran defender Adrian Burrows had, not unexpectedly, been released and striker Dwight Marshall had sought pastures new at Luton. The one new arrival was experienced centre-half Peter Swan, who cost a club record £300,000 from Port Vale. Swan was immediately installed as captain in preference to Steve Castle, who had remained a Pilgrim but didn't want to, publicly stating his desire to quit Home Park. The loss of Castle would have been a significant blow to manager Peter Shilton's plans. The goalscoring midfielder was the club's prize asset and would undoubtedly command a healthy fee, but his value to the team was greater than any transfer fee. Shilton was determined to dissuade him from going.

The Home Park stadium had been spruced up. A lick of paint here and there, and new-style goal nets were more pleasing to the eye, although there was still no sign of the major improvements, such as seating in the Devonport End, or installing a new roof on the grandstand. There were other changes too, not as noticeable, but certainly necessary. Head groundsman or 'Park Superintendent' to give him his official title, Colin Wheatcroft, had discovered that the corner flags were not regulation size and that the wooden crossbars on each goal were not true. Metal versions were installed.

There was also a new strip, with green and black striped shirts back in vogue. It was a similar design to the 1974-75 promotion season. A good omen perhaps. Despite the feelgood factor, deep down there was still unease over the relationship between chairman Dan McCauley and Shilton. The two had been involved in various public spats and the working relationship was strained. Many felt it was a ticking time-bomb.

Apart from that against Coventry, the pre-season friendlies had less appeal than usual, and other than build up fitness levels, did little except crock a few players. Castle and goalkeeper Alan Nicholls were among a number of players who picked up knocks. The injury to Nicholls in particular caused much head-scratching. With Shilton not looking to play himself, a number of goalkeepers, among them Jonathan Gould and Ian Andrews, were tried out. Eventually, Shilton had to turn to YTS youngster James Dungey. Shilton also had his eye on former Pilgrim Martin Hodge, who at 35 was no spring chicken himself. At first the board vetoed the notion, but on the eve of the season relented and Shilton got his man.

The injury count stood at five as Shilton prepared his team for the first match of the season, at home to Brentford. In front of a healthy and optimistic crowd, things couldn't have started better, as Swan marked his debut with a goal after just eighteen minutes. But then it started to go horribly wrong. By half-time the Bees had scored three times and added two more in the second half. Their new forward, Nicky Forster, was rampant. Moreover, it could have been worse, as illustrated by the fact that Hodge picked up the man of the match award. Not surprisingly, it was the Greens' worst ever opening day home defeat.

Insisting that the 1-5 thrashing was a one-off, Shilton named a largely unchanged line up for the Coca-Cola Cup visit to Walsall three days later. A meagre crowd turned up to watch Argyle's first ever visit to the Bescot Stadium. The good news was that Hodge was again in sparkling form. The bad news – well there was plenty. Craig Skinner went off injured and Andy Comyn (foul) and Martin Barlow (dissent) were both sent off. Oh yes, and Argyle also lost 0-4 after holding out until half-time. And all this against a team a division below them.

Shilton moved quickly to bolster his ever diminishing squad by bringing in the experienced Darren Bradshaw from Peterborough on loan. The new man made his mark by getting Argyle's equaliser at Brighton, after ex-England winger Mark Chamberlain had come on at half-time for his Seagulls debut and scored. But at least one of the sick and wounded, Paul Dalton, was back.

After the first leg shambles at Walsall there was little hope of progression in the Coca-Cola Cup, hence the small crowd for the second leg at Home Park. The Pilgrims welcomed back Castle into midfield, and he was instrumental in securing Argyle's first win of the season, albeit by the odd goal in three.

Another loan signing, Stoke striker Graham Shaw, arrived in time to join the Argyle attack for the visit of Bradford City. By half-time he was probably wishing he hadn't. By then, City were four up with Paul Jewell enjoying a thirteen-minute hat-trick. After ninety minutes the opening day scoreline had been repeated. Argyle were quickly becoming the laughing stock of the Football League. McCauley publicly derided the team's performance. For once, there were no dissenters to the chairman's views.

Shilton had five regulars unavailable as he took his side for a tough-looking midweek match at Hull. Mind you, the way they were playing, Argyle would have been underdogs against The Pig and Whistle Veterans' XI. A proposed Travel Club trip to Boothferry Park was cancelled due to lack of interest. The handful of foolhardy fans who did make the long trip had a brief moment of excitement when Shaw latched onto a Castle through ball but shot straight at the keeper. A misunderstanding between Hodge and Mark Patterson gifted Neil Mann his first ever league goal and Alan Lee headed a second to give the Tigers their expected win. Following the loss, wider cracks began appearing in the relationship between manager and chairman. In a veiled attack on the board, Shilton demanded support 'from everyone in the club'.

An even more daunting trip to Birmingham ensued. Shilton would have rung the changes, but simply didn't have the personnel available. The injury dilemma worsened when Patterson was carted off to hospital with a head injury. Naturally, Argyle lost. The Blues' destroyer-in-chief was Dave Regis who, on two occasions, found the back of the net, a concept largely alien to him during his unsuccessful spell at Home Park.

It was not just the fans who were becoming disillusioned. In the space of a few matches Argyle, with basically the same set of players, had gone from being one of the most free-scoring sides in the country to strugglers, and the board wanted to know why. McCauley concluded that it wasn't a 'happy squad'. As soon as the previous season had ended, Shilton had agreed a new two-year contract but hadn't signed it as certain minutia had to be finalised. Despite the board's displeasure, the finer points were now ironed out and the contract completed.

After such an abysmal start it was amazing that more than 5,000 turned up to watch the next match against high-riding Huddersfield, managed by Neil Warnock. Perhaps those who arrived believed it couldn't get any worse. It did. Within nine minutes, Andy Booth – already earmarked for greater things – scored twice. At half-time Shilton made an unusual tactical switch, replacing Hodge with substitute goalkeeper Nicholls. The young keeper's first appearance of the season lasted just 32 minutes before he was sent off, denying Booth a hat-trick by bringing him down. Castle took over but was unable to prevent Booth from claiming the match ball as he completed his hat-trick a minute from the end. Perhaps the most amazing statistic was that, given such a dismal start, Argyle weren't bottom. Yes, there was a worst side in the division – Chester.

With a touch of irony, the midweek game against Cambridge saw Argyle keep their first clean sheet of the season. Swan was absent due to the birth of his child and was not particularly missed. The record signing had not settled and had borne the brunt of the fans' ire. For the money, they expected more and Swan hadn't yet delivered.

Of course, a match couldn't pass without another crisis rearing its head. Shilton's assistant, John McGovern, announced his resignation, citing 'personal reasons'. Many felt the real reason was that his name had been linked with a similar post at Rotherham, where another former Nottingham Forest teammate, Archie Gemmill, had recently been appointed manager.

Youth team manager Ian Bowyer stood in for McGovern and at first appeared to have the Midas touch. Argyle won, not once but three times. Swan could not regain his place and was left on the bench for the trip to Cardiff as Shilton kept faith with his defensive pairing of Comyn and the permanently dishevelled Keith Hill. Nicholls, now installed as first choice between the posts, saved a weak Carl Dale penalty. Castle, back to something like his best, dominated the midfield battle and his 25-yard shot provided the only goal. There was, of course, a downside. Shaw suffered a serious knee injury and limped away from his loan spell.

With Nicholls suspended as a consequence of his Huddersfield misdemeanour, Hodge was reinstated for the visit of hapless Chester, who had the grand total of one point to their name. Even Argyle were expected to win comfortably but in the end only Chris Twiddy's first senior goal after four minutes separated the sides.

Realising that just one of Argyle's nine goals to date had come from a striker, Shilton omitted Kevin Nugent for the trip to Leyton Orient. In came Richard Landon, who had made six appearances towards the end of the previous season and scored five times. His impressive strike-rate continued, for by half-time the former Bedworth striker had netted with two long-range efforts. But victory was overshadowed by revelations in a national newspaper over Shilton's personal financial position. McCauley alleged that on a number of occasions Shilton had requested an advance of his salary, to the tune of about £100,000. Equally damning were McCauley's comments that he didn't like Shilton as a person and that the former England goalkeeper didn't have a friend on the board.

With the recent upturn in form, Shilton was keen to appoint Bowyer as his number two, but the chairman did not feel an assistant was warranted, questioning why his manager needed one when he was 'only working an eight-hour week'. Shilton demanded a meeting with his chairman but McCauley refused to retract his eight-hour week comment or sanction a new loan signing.

A 1-3 defeat by Exeter at an eerily empty Home Park in the Auto Windscreens Shield was the least of Shilton's worries. To add to his woes, his talisman on the field, Castle, was suffering from an illness, later diagnosed as jaundice and would be missing for weeks. Argyle's mini-revival ended at Oxford, where Irish international John Byrne scored the only goal.

A rare event occurred in the home match against Wycombe. Matt Crossley's handball gifted Argyle a penalty and the players could have been forgiven for wondering who their official penalty taker was. It was the Pilgrims' first spot-kick for almost a year. As it was, Skinner stepped up to give the Greens the lead. Almost at once, Martin O'Neill's side responded through veteran Cyrille Regis who, despite his advancing years, outpaced Comyn. It was all-action, as a minute later Barlow scored. The pace receded and Argyle looked to be heading for victory until Regis struck again despite pleas for a foul on Nicholls.

Shilton did not have to ponder over his squad for the trip to Stockport. Only fourteen players were fit. The *Evening Herald* criticised the way in which the club was being run. McCauley took umbrage and banned the paper's football correspondent from the press box. For a time the hack was forced to file his reports from the relative comfort of the Lyndhurst Stand. McCauley also barred club officials, including Shilton, from talking to the paper's representatives.

The match at Edgeley Park was certainly full of incident. Stockport scored within 31 seconds, Hill was stretchered off with a dislocated shoulder, and Nicholls sent off for receiving two yellow cards in the space of a few seconds. The hot-head had been booked for time-wasting and promptly flung the ball down in disgust at the decision. Despite these obstacles, Argyle won the game 4-2, with Landon on the mark twice.

Temporarily, at least, McCauley and Shilton put a halt to their playground antics with the chairman agreeing to a verbal ceasefire in what he succinctly described as a 'zero relationship'.

Once again, home form let Argyle down. Having climbed to the heady heights of seventeenth after the win at Stockport, two home games in succession provided an excellent opportunity to open the gap over their fellow relegation contenders. If only. Firstly, Argyle lost to Blackpool, whose Tony Ellis scored one of the goals of the season. His long-range strike flew in off the underside of the crossbar. Peterborough then came and left with all three points. Shilton fielded his most inexperienced side, and it showed. Only Nicholls prevented a heavier defeat and the Argyle attack was virtually non-existent.

The visit to Rotherham saw Shilton and McGovern reacquainted for the first time since the latter's acrimonious departure. As expected, he had joined the Millers as joint manager only two days after his departure from Home Park. He had the last laugh as two goals from Shaun Goater helped Rotherham to victory.

Considering Argyle's current plight, being paired at a non-league side in the first round of the FA Cup was the last thing they wanted. Kettering were flying high in the Vauxhall Conference, and with the match a prime candidate for a 'giant killing', Sky TV cameras were there to beam the action live to the nation. Fortunately, Shilton's men got their act together sufficiently for Skinner's goal to take them through. For once, a 1-0 score did not reflect the relative ease of the win.

Despite McCauley's earlier misgivings about loan signings, another arrived in the not inconsiderable shape of Mick Quinn, whose physique suggested a permanent place in the aforementioned Pig and Whistle side. Although he was in the twilight of his career, the ace goalscorer – seemingly the answer to the perennial question 'Who ate all the pies?' – lifted spirits around Home Park. Youngsters such as Marcus Crocker, Dungey and Danny O'Hagan had been plunged into first-team action in recent weeks before they were ready, and Quinn's experience was vital.

Quinn's debut certainly had a positive effect. Although he didn't score, Argyle easily cast Wrexham aside, 4-1, although the Welsh side pressed the self-destruct button by scoring two own-goals, one a spectacular Bryan Hughes header from twenty yards.

Shilton's personal finances had by now become a matter of national intrigue, and further revelations again hit the press. A bankruptcy petition had been issued against the former England keeper in respect of unpaid bills to a racehorse trainer. Shilton cleared the debt, only to become embroiled in another mess as Argyle received an Inland Revenue demand for £50,000 in respect of taxes due on Shilton's signing-on fee. McCauley insisted it was Shilton's responsibility and was furious that the demand had now come to the club.

On the field, the Wrexham magic was not repeated a week later at York. Micky Ross, a free transfer from Exeter, came off the bench for his debut, replacing Twiddy who had been concussed after the ball hit him in the face. The only goal came from York's Jon McCarthy, who headed in unmarked. The frustration got the better of the normally placid Edworthy, who was dismissed near the end for aiming a kick at an opponent.

Despite the indifferent league form, the Cup was bringing out the best in Argyle. Pitted against Bournemouth at Home Park, Ross soon endeared himself to his new supporters by scoring twice in the first half. The Cherries managed one of their own, but with his side bottom of Division Two and now out of the Cup, manager Mel Machin felt the world pressing upon his shoulders and it was an hour before his battered side emerged from the dressing room. A new Argyle record had been created when Shilton's son, Sam, became the youngest ever Argyle player. The second half also saw Swan and Comyn both wearing No 5 shirts.

Back in the league, Argyle suffered a comprehensive home defeat by Brighton. Liam Brady's side had not won for twelve matches but were far superior. Shilton gave a debut to seventeen-year-old YTS lad Simon Dawe. He was assigned to mark Robert Codner, singled out as the Seagulls' danger-man. Dawe did a sterling job but when Shilton decided to take him off,

Codner made the most of his new-found freedom to score twice, with Adi Akinbiyi scoring a third.

The match marked the end of Quinn's all too brief loan spell. He hadn't scored but the fans were appreciative of his efforts. A few years later, when his autobiography was published, his spell as a Pilgrim merited only scant mention. He did, however, ridicule the management style of Shilton who, he claimed, barely discussed tactics but was more interested obtaining horse-racing tips. Quinn was well-placed to oblige, as his deep knowledge of the gee-gees led him into a career as a racing trainer.

It wasn't long before lurid headlines detailed the explanation behind John McGovern's departure. In July 1993, he had personally lent Shilton £7,000. According to McGovern, the loan plus interest was to be repaid in six months, only it wasn't. Eighteen months later, McGovern claimed almost half the debt was still outstanding. Meanwhile, at Home Park, it was clear that make-or-break time for Shilton was fast approaching. The board told him he had four games to improve results. Shilton branded it a negative intervention.

The first of those games saw Argyle visit Brentford. The Bees' opening day thrashing of the Pilgrims had flattered to deceive, and David Webb's side were lying in mid-table. Ninety minutes later, the Bees had walloped Argyle 7-0, the club's worst defeat for 34 years.

It was difficult to imagine how matters could get any worse. Certainly record signing Peter Swan didn't think they could. Lack of form, injury, and off the field problems had made his life as a Plymouth Argyle player a living nightmare. Being the pivot of the most generous defence in the league had hardly endeared him to the Home Park faithful either. By now, he had moved home to Staffordshire, trained in Plymouth during the week, and then escaped back home as soon as possible after matches.

A 0-3 Boxing Day defeat at Swansea heaped more pressure on Shilton. The next scheduled home match, against Bristol Rovers, was postponed due to a waterlogged pitch but allowed the directors to have another pow-wow over the deteriorating situation on and off the pitch. They considered sacking Shilton, on the twin grounds of poor results and for bringing the club into disrepute over his financial problems. In the end they settled on issuing a solicitors letter threatening him with dismissal if the outstanding tax bill was not settled within a week.

Shilton, for his part, appeared not to deny liability over the debt, but merely pleaded for more time to pay it. Time though, was not on his side. A 3-2 win over Crewe in the first match of 1995 was not enough. Two days later, Shilton was no longer managing. Strictly speaking, McCauley did actually fire him, preferring to suspend him on full pay.

Either way, it was ignominious end to Shilton's term of office. As a player, he had made his mark as one of the greatest goalkeepers of all time, with a dedicated work ethic that carried him to the top. Now he was a broken man, vilified in the press and publicly humiliated.

McCauley wasted little time in naming Steve McCall as Shilton's successor. Twice Argyle player of the year, the experienced midfielder was a highly popular figure around Home Park, although injury had blighted much of his later years. McCall's first match in charge was a daunting prospect. Amid the doom and gloom it was easy to overlook the fact that Argyle had reached the third round of the FA Cup, where they would visit Premiership Nottingham Forest, a club Shilton had helped to two European Cup triumphs. No one gave Argyle much hope, nor had any reason to alter their way of thinking as Forest took a two-goal lead after sixteen minutes, but Argyle's players showed enough grit to prevent any further score.

McCall's job description was simple. Keep Argyle up. A goalless draw at fellow strugglers Bournemouth hardly represented the onset of a revival, but a point was a point. Another no-score draw followed at home to Rotherham. That match was one of only sixteen in the country to survive torrential rain. McCall could have been forgiven for doing a private rain dance. His squad was now so threadbare, he was forced to name a far from fit Dalton as a substitute.

A disastrous 2-5 defeat at Blackpool followed. The home side had fallen behind to a thirty-yard Patterson special and were jeered off the pitch at half-time. The second half was a different matter. With the help of some sloppy defending, former Pilgrim Andy Morrison inspired his side to victory. How Argyle could have done with his drive and enthusiasm.

Defeats at home to York and away to Shrewsbury, where striker Kevin Nugent scored his first goal for almost a year, then got himself sent off, left McCall's side stranded in relegation country. To make matters worse, five teams would go down this season, as part of the restructuring that followed the trimming of the Premiership from 22 clubs to twenty. The one glimmer of hope was that Castle was on his way back to full fitness.

It was left to McCall himself to show his players the way, giving his side a third-minute lead at Peterborough. Posh equalised but a late Nugent goal clinched a precious away win. It was the first victory under McCall's stewardship.

Prior to the must-win home game against Bournemouth, Swan went public on his desire to leave Home Park. It was not unexpected. Despite the bonus of having Castle back in the starting line up, Argyle were undone by a single Cherries goal. Nicholls came for, but missed, a corner. McCall was forced off after half an hour with blurred vision.

It looked as though the players now preferred playing away from Home Park, where performances had been nervous. At Wrexham, Argyle took the lead – through Castle – for the fourth successive away game. It took an hour for Wrexham to equalise and it came as no surprise that it came from Gary Bennett, who had been unable to stop scoring all season. Six minutes later Bryan Hughes put the home side in front with the softest of goals. His tame shot somehow trickled past three players and nestled in the corner of the net. In injury-time, that man Bennett scored again, his 37th of the season.

The next two games were real six pointers, as Orient and Chester filled the bottom two places. Orient looked inept, as befitted a side that had gained just one away point all season. It took a Landon goal to win the game, making him Argyle's top scorer with a meagre five goals.

Chester, cast adrift at the bottom, announced Derek Mann as their new manager prior to the Pilgrims' visit. The match was played in front of fewer than 2,000 people. The announcement sparked new life into Chester and it took only two minutes for Stuart Rimmer to score. Argyle lacked creativity and failed to carve out any clear-cut chances. A few long-range efforts were the best they could muster.

Eleven games into the McCall era, results had barely improved. The board, realising time was running out, suggested that an experienced coach be recruited to assist McCall, but the temporary player-manager, to give him his official title, declined.

Two goals by substitute Lee Power, who in years to come would briefly become an ineffective Argyle forward, sunk the Greens at Bradford City. The second goal came from the spot, after John Taylor dropped like a sack of potatoes, despite no obvious contact from the ostensibly guilty Comyn. McCall branded the decision a joke.

The game against Hull started with a flurry. Argyle were 2-1 up within nineteen minutes but that was to be the extent of the scoring. Strangely, Hull were given permission to wear their usual away strip of green shirts! In a bid to encourage more people through the turnstiles, Argyle introduced a 'Kids for a Quid' scheme. The attendance of under 5,000 suggested the idea was not a roaring success.

The day before a daunting trip to Huddersfield, McCall brought in his former Ipswich teammate, Russell Osman, on a non-contract playing basis, believing the former England international's experience would be invaluable during the run in. Little did Osman know what lay in store.

Few expected much from the trip to Yorkshire, and the doubters were right. Huddersfield scored in the first minute from a 25-yard effort by Jon Dyson. Andy Booth notched a second shortly after half-time, his 26th of the season and that was enough for the Terriers to regain top spot.

Facing two home games in four days, McCall knew anything less than six points could be fatal. Cardiff were first up. Their abject record suggested little resistance, but the Bluebirds shut up shop and yet again Argyle lacked the imagination to break them down. More players were also in the wars. Nugent came out for the second half with his head swathed in bandages and Patterson was taken off with blood pouring from a head wound.

Worse was to follow with a defeat by Stockport. In relegation terms, crisis point was on the horizon. The board reiterated their suggestion to McCall that some help may be appropriate. Again McCall refuted the idea, but this time reacted by resigning as manager whilst vowing to stay on as a player.

The board appeared to be taken aback by his reaction to what they believed to be a genuine offer of help. With just nine games remaining they were again left with the task of finding someone to take charge. Former manager Dave Smith was immediately installed as favourite, particularly as he was the man the board had in mind to assist McCall, but Ciderman declined the offer to save the world, believing that, at 62, his best days were behind him.

A replacement was soon found and just eight days after arriving at the club Russell Osman was put in charge of team affairs. The appointment had a touch of irony. After the sacking of David Kemp early in 1992, Osman had been short-listed for the manager's job but lost out to Shilton. Now here he was trying to sort out the mess. Osman was also in dispute with his former club, Bristol City, who had sacked him as player-manager in November. So as not to jeopardise any compensation claim, Osman agreed to be paid expenses only. He was not given any official title either, although having had a manager and a temporary player-manager it was probably difficult to think of a new one anyway.

Osman's first game in charge saw Argyle secure a point at Cambridge. Landon was again on target but Steve Butler equalised from the spot after Carlo Corazzin had been pulled down. Castle, in particular, was unimpressed with the referee's decision and was cautioned for dissent. The matter continued to rile him and after the final whistle he continued his futile protests only to be shown the red card.

Osman kept faith with the same eleven as Argyle did battle with Bristol Rovers. Nugent scored early and Nicholls was enjoying a rare quiet afternoon in the Argyle goal until the hour mark, when he tangled with Swan in attempting to cut out a cross and Rovers equalised. It meant more vital home points lost.

Now without the suspended Castle, Osman recalled his old friend McCall for the midweek clash with Shrewsbury. To his credit, the former manager gave his all, and one moment of genius from Patterson was enough to give Argyle victory. The full-back swept past two players and despatched a powerful shot past the Shrews keeper.

Eleven days after their first meeting, Argyle travelled to Twerton Park for the second instalment against Bristol Rovers. It was a ground at which Argyle had never scored, and frankly they never threatened to break that sequence. Rovers were in the promotion hunt and slack defending was responsible for both goals.

The crucial and busy Easter period continued with a home game with Swansea. Nicholls, prone to recent errors, made another when he attempted to fly-hack a clearance but miskicked to John Hodge, who was left confronting an empty net. Swan quickly equalised and Nugent staked his claim to be Argyle's top scorer with his sixth of the season.

Two wins out of three was encouraging but the league position hadn't improved. Fellow strugglers Cambridge and Bournemouth were also stringing together a few results and it looked as though either of those two, or Argyle, would survive. Chester and Orient looked doomed and Cardiff also needed help from above.

Over 8,500, Argyle's biggest crowd of the season, turned up to watch an attractive fixture with Birmingham. Although he didn't score, the gangly 6ft 7in Kevin Francis was the focal point of much of the action. Chris Whyte had given the Blues the lead shortly after half-time. Francis then trod accidentally on Nicholls, leaving the Argyle custodian feeling as if a ton of bricks had landed on him. Swan, struggling to contain his giant adversary, then committed two fouls in quick succession and was off. In an ill-disciplined season, he was the eighth sending off Argyle had suffered. Birmingham were quick to exploit their man advantage. Steve Claridge scored twice in nine minutes and only a last-gasp goal from Dalton gave the scoreline meagre respectability from an Argyle perspective.

With just three matches remaining – all against sides harbouring play-off hopes – things looked bleak. Matters were not helped when it was learned that Nicholls would not recover from being used as Francis's doormat and would be out for the season. That left the inexperienced Dungey as Osman's only goalkeeper. With the transfer deadline long gone, Argyle applied to the League for special dispensation to sign another keeper, but were refused, and so the youngster took his place between the posts for a nerve-wracking trip to Crewe.

Dungey was not the tallest keeper in the land and it did not take Crewe long to adapt accordingly. Neil Lennon lobbed him after just seven minutes. Argyle then had to thank Crewe's Mark Gardiner for giving them a lifeline as he diverted Nugent's header past his own keeper. With nine minutes remaining, the same player handled in the box to allow Dalton to score from the spot. Argyle had barely regrouped when Dele Adebola equalised. Nevertheless it was a point few had predicted.

An equally tricky match at Wycombe a week later was turned by a rare Hill effort after only four minutes. The goal inspired Argyle and Dungey in particular, as the youngster performed heroically. He had little chance with Mickey Bell's leveller, but Landon's prod gave Argyle three points and severely dented Martin O'Neill's play-off hopes.

The joy of victory was tarnished by the news of Bournemouth's even more unlikely victory. The south coast side had gone to championship hopefuls Brentford and won. Since thrashing Argyle, the Bees had gone from strength to strength and this was only their second home defeat in 26 games. To complicate matters even more, Cambridge had grabbed an unlikely point at Huddersfield.

In the course of normal events, all the final league games would be played on the same day. But not this year. With the matches falling on a Bank Holiday weekend, the Football League had heeded police advice and brought forward Bournemouth's home game with Shrewsbury to the Tuesday night. Three seasons earlier, thousands of Leeds fans had converged on the seaside town desperate to see their side clinch the First Division title. Apparently a game against an injury-hit, out of form and mid-table Shrewsbury – who would have been fortunate to fill one supporters' coach – represented a threat of similar public disruption.

A win for the Cherries meant there was no escape for either Argyle or Cambridge. Any glimmer of hope was quickly extinguished. Within twenty minutes Bournemouth were three up.

Thus the final game of the season against Oxford was rendered meaningless. Nugent scored to finish as joint-top scorer with Landon. The tally of seven goals, though, was hardly one to proudly tell the grandchildren about. Argyle were condemned to the league's basement for the first time in their history. Frankly, it was little more than they deserved. The whole season from start to finish, on and off the field, had been a shambles.

# THIRTEEN

# 1995-96 (Promoted to Division 2)

The club was at an all-time low. There was much to sort out, but the first priority was a new manager. Chairman McCauley had not ruled out Russell Osman, who had left a good impression, despite failing to keep Argyle up. Inevitably, virtually every out-of-work manager was linked with the job, among them, Plymouth-born Trevor Francis, Brian Horton, Steve Perryman, Roy McFarland and Gary Megson. Argyle super-hero Tommy Tynan and another former Pilgrim, Danis Salman, also threw their hats into the ring. They appear to have been ruled out by McCauley's statement that he had had enough of first-time managers.

But, deep down, McCauley knew who he wanted. Neil Warnock was manager of Huddersfield but the two had become pals through Warnock's brief spell as a management consultant at Torquay, when McCauley was involved with the Plainmoor club. There was an added complication in that Warnock had guided the Terriers to a Wembley play-off place, something of a Warnock speciality, as he had achieved a similar feat on two occasions when with Notts County. Rumours abounded, however, that all was not well in the relationship between Warnock and his current chairman, Terry Fisher, although their disagreements had remained behind closed doors, unlike the public spats between McCauley and Peter Shilton.

Sure enough, Warnock masterminded another Wembley victory to secure First Division football, but eight days later, resigned. To the footballing world it seemed an odd decision, but he knew he was Plymouth-bound before jetting off for a holiday in the Maldives. McCauley, for his part, was so keen to obtain Warnock's signature that he arranged to meet up at the airport. Nothing was signed but arrangements were made for the two to be in contact during Warnock's holidays. Various faxes and phone calls were exchanged and the deal was all but done. Warnock even received a list of available players to scour through.

Back in Blighty, rumours abounded that Warnock was the man, but all McCauley could do was confirm his interest. After all, nothing had been signed. Three days after the end of Warnock's 'restful' holiday he was named as Argyle's 24th manager. It looked an astute move on McCauley's part and one had to admire Warnock's commitment. He had left a club bound for the First Division, with a superb new stadium and a number of highly sought-after players, for a Third Division club in chaos.

Warnock had professed his love of the area but there was to be no time to laze on beaches or ramble on Dartmoor. There was a team to build. Already, several players had baled out. Marc Edworthy was the biggest loss, but when Crystal Palace offered £350,000 for the promising defender it was tough to turn it down. Richard Landon and Craig Skinner had also gone, record signing Peter Swan was transfer-listed, and Steve Castle and Martin Barlow were unimpressed with the deals offered to them.

Within days of Warnock's arrival, Castle had gone to Birmingham, despite the new boss saying he was an integral part of his plans. Warnock's building began by acquiring an assistant and a physio. His chosen number two was no surprise. Mick Jones had been a trusty sidekick to Warnock at both Notts County and Huddersfield. The two complemented each other. Warnock, ebullient and chirpy, Jones the straight man. In new physio, Norman Medhurst, he acquired someone who had worked with the England set up for twenty years.

With the financial backing of the chairman, Warnock began signing players. Like a child dipping into a bag of sweets, he knew which ones were his favourites. Warnock knew their qualities. Speculative buys were not on the agenda. For many years, it had been a common complaint that it was difficult to attract players to Plymouth. To many, it might have been another planet. Modern transportation had, of course, helped but with five new players signing in the space of ten days that myth was finally put to bed. It was hoped that Warnock's reputation also helped.

First to arrive was left-footed full-back Paul Williams from Coventry. He had been on loan at Huddersfield and Warnock had tried to sign him then, but the asking price of £250,000 had killed the deal. Now he was snapped up for a fifth of that. The midfield was bolstered by the £40,000 arrival of Ronnie Mauge, a chirpy Cockney who had ended up at Bury, and Chris Leadbitter, a 'free' from Bournemouth. Striker, Adrian Littlejohn cost £200,000 but Warnock was not put off by the price. Convinced he was good for fifteen goals, he worked hard on convincing Littlejohn that it was the right move. Also in was Geordie centre-half Mick Heathcote from Cambridge United. He cost £70,000 and was made captain.

The substantial outlay, on Littlejohn in particular, was offset by a Football League tribunal ruling that Argyle would receive £225,000 for Steve Castle and £30,000 for Richard Landon. It wasn't as much as Argyle had hoped for, but that was usually the way.

Both the playing and coaching staff were boosted by Kevin Blackwell, who took on the youth team duties and, at 36, also provided experience as goalkeeping cover. He had played for Warnock at three previous clubs. Blackwell joined Alan Nicholls and the inexperienced James Dungey in the goalkeeper's union, but Warnock wasn't enamoured with Nicholls' increasingly wayward off-field antics. A number of keepers came for trials but Warnock eventually paid out £40,000 for Swindon's Nicky Hammond.

Pre-season friendlies gave supporters the first look at Argyle's gawdy new strip. It was green, black and white, of course, but defied accurate description. It was easy to imagine the designer poring over various sketch-es before asking his baby son to come up with the finished product. The design prompted one supporter to pen a letter to a local paper complain-ing that the diagonal stripes 'disturbed the mind'.

Still keen to run the rule over possible new recruits, Warnock used no fewer than 42 players during pre-season, which included matches against Spanish side, Real Oviedo and the might of Ruud Gullit's Chelsea.

The upshot was another bout of new signings, namely Mark Saunders from Tiverton, Aussie Doug Hodgson, on loan from Sheffield United, and Chris Billy and Gary Clayton, former Warnockites at Huddersfield. Indeed, Billy had scored the winning goal at Wembley only a few weeks before. An exchange for Paul Dalton, who was determined to return north, formed part of the deal. Others were also dithering over new offers and, as a result, Martin Barlow, Chris Twiddy, Wayne Burnett and injured defender Andy Comyn were all on weekly contracts.

Disregarding Argyle's team of total strangers, the bookies listed them as favourites for promotion. Warnock was not making any predictions other than a promise that his team would work hard.

A visit to Colchester was the unkind welcome to the new league. With seven debutants, fast-flowing football was hardly likely to be in the Argyle repertoire, but defensive failings contributed to a 1-2 defeat despite the U's being reduced to ten men and Warnock making full use of the new rule allowing three substitutes.

The Coca-Cola Cup threw up the previous season's Second Division champions Birmingham. At St Andrew's, slipshod defending was punished when Blues defender Gary Cooper waltzed around flimsy tackles to score the only goal. It was, nevertheless, a reasonable result which owed much to some fine goalkeeping by Hammond.

Further inroads into the transfer deficit were made when record sign-ing Peter Swan was offloaded to Burnley for a third of Argyle's outlay of £300,000. As investments went, it was the equivalent of a stock market crash. Swan didn't like Argyle and, frankly, the feeling was mutual. Twiddy also finally agreed terms and put pen to paper on a new contract.

The first home league game pitted Argyle against Preston, judged by Warnock as most likely to win the division. The Argyle eleven ran out, not to the familiar *Semper Fidelis* but to the strains of Tina Turner's *Simply the Best*. Given the events of the previous term, a more inappropriate tune was hard to imagine.

Ninety minutes later, Preston strode off with a 2-0 win under their belt. There was no doubting the main culprit: after 64 minutes Hammond collected a Jamie Squires corner kick but inexplicably threw the ball into his own net. Twelve minutes later Ian Bryson was given the freedom of Home Park to slide in the second. Given the Argyle defence's reluctance to venture near him, more goals looked likely. Mind you, Argyle's forward line hardly gave cause to believe that the goals would start rattling in at the other end. The defeat left Argyle rock bottom of the whole Football League. Statistically, at least, they were simply the worst.

Warnock kept faith with Hammond for the return game with Birmingham. 'I wouldn't swap him with anyone in our division,' was the normally astute Warnock's ill-judged verdict on his new keeper. Again a corner proved Hammond's undoing, as Steve Hunt's inswinger eluded both keeper and Burnett, allegedly defending the near post. Heathcote had already levelled the tie before Andy Edwards equalised on the night.

Such was Hammond's almost comical baptism that Warnock must have considered recalling Nicholls, but more off the field misdeeds terminated the youngster's Home Park career. A drink-driving charge was one indiscretion too many, and he was off to Gillingham, who had already declared an interest in the close season.

And so, Hammond kept his place for the trip to Chester. A 1-3 defeat ensued, with veteran striker Cyrille Regis among the scorers. Hammond was exonerated but there was little else to get excited about.

There was no respite for the shell-shocked Greens. Warnock called them in for Sunday training to prepare for Tuesday night's clash with Hereford, then axed Burnett, Twiddy and Keith Hill, all ex-Shilton signings. In fact, Kevin Nugent was the only non-Warnock recruit in the line up. It made little difference. Hammond came to collect a Richard Wilkins long throw, but merely ended up waving at nothing. The ball fell to Steve White, allowing him one of the easiest goals of his career. It would be forty minutes before ironic cheers greeted Argyle's first shot on target. Yes, it was that bad.

Six games. Six defeats. That was it for Nicky Hammond. Warnock washed his hands of the goalkeeper and omitted him from the side that travelled to Bury. A glance at the league table hardly had the Shakers shaking. Warnock drafted in Blackwell between the posts. Pre-season, he had said the youth team boss would only play in emergencies. Well, this was one but not the type Warnock had envisaged. The match itself was totally one sided. No surprise there then. Well hold on. Argyle ran riot, winning 5-0. Mickey Evans, brought in for Nugent – who had failed to click with Littlejohn – scored twice, Clayton creamed one from 25 yards, and Mauge, captain for the day against his former side, was inspired. Despite the margin of victory, Argyle remained bottom, a stark reminder of how bad the start of the season had been.

Warnock kept the same team for the visit of Leyton Orient. Another Evans goal failed to ignite the side and a stuttering draw resulted. Warnock raged at referee Clive Wilkes who, in his eyes had denied Argyle a blatant penalty and then awarded Orient a dubious one which Blackwell saved.

There were enforced changes for the midweek visit of Doncaster. Injury-hit Sheffield United had recalled Hodgson from his loan spell, meaning a return for Keith Hill. Hill had been on the transfer list at his own request, believing he did not feature in his manager's long-term plans. An injury to Clayton also meant a recall for Burnett, who had been on trial at Premiership Bolton.

With eleven minutes gone there were signs that Hammonditis was still prevalent at Home Park. Hill shepherded a harmless through-ball back to Blackwell. The keeper unleashed a well-aimed boot at the ball at the precise moment that Hill decided another touch was required. As a result, Blackwell, boot, and ball went their separate ways and it was one up to the Tykes. Displaying new-found confidence, Argyle fought back with Evans and Billy, from a sitting position, putting them in front by half-time. A well-worked free-kick saw Littlejohn get a late third.

The Pilgrims now travelled to Barnet. Despite their woeful start to the season, the Argyle fans were out in force. By the time the players emerged for their pre-match warm up, everyone was drenched by a thunderstorm. Warnock was so concerned about the lightning flashing around the ground that he quickly abandoned the warm up and the players dashed back to the dressing room.

The truncated preparation may have explained a disjointed first half, but after the interval Billy was brought down and Evans scored the resultant penalty. Barnet equalised following lax defending. With two minutes remaining the tannoy announced that Barnet defender Linvoy Primus was man of the match. Seconds later, Littlejohn escaped Primus's clutches for the first time to score a winner. Primus's champagne no doubt lost some of its sparkle.

Hammonditis was now replaced by common or garden flu. Several players went down with the virus during the week leading up to the game at Wigan. Fortunately, all had recovered sufficiently to allow Warnock to name an unchanged side. It wasn't a pretty game, but another Littlejohn effort was enough to lift the Greens into the top half of the table and seal the fate of Latics' manager Graham Barrow, who was subsequently sacked.

Midweek saw an AutoWindscreens Shield visit from Peterborough. Amazingly, as many as 1,600 people chose to watch the match on a miserable evening. Warnock was not among them, opting instead to run the rule over Bristol City striker Ian Baird. A second-string Argyle side lost 0-3. Nobody cared.

By Friday lunchtime, Baird was a Pilgrim. Nugent was not, as the two players swapped clubs with £75,000 also boosting the Argyle bank balance. The move suited both players. Nugent looked unlikely to displace the in-form Evans, and Baird had been transfer listed after reacting angrily to crowd barracking during a pre-season friendly.

There was another new face in the Argyle dressing room, as winger Kevin Magee had joined on a month's trial. Warnock had already seen what the Scot was capable of when he gave Mark Patterson a torrid time in Preston's early season win at Home Park. Fearing that the performance was a one-off, Preston had not renewed his contract but Warnock thought he was worth a try out. Both new boys played in the victory over bottom of the table Lincoln, albeit for just two minutes in Magee's case. Argyle's second goal was the 4,500th of the club's league existence.

Warnock's wheeling and dealing continued with Burnett finally signing for Bolton. His loss was tempered by the rejuvenation of Martin Barlow, who had broken into the first team reckoning after an unsettled period which had looked likely to end with his departure. Baird was soon demonstrating what a shrewd acquisition he was, scoring twice in an easy win against Fulham. This fifth league win on the trot lifted Argyle to fourth place.

So content was Warnock with the performance of what was clearly now his first-choice eleven that he named his side as early as Monday for the next match, a visit to Mansfield, who had attempted to shed their tag as the division's draw specialists by trouncing Wigan 6-2. For twenty minutes Argyle looked superb and led by a Heathcote header. The Stags forced their way back into the game and levelled after half an hour. By the end Argyle were hanging on.

Of course, an Argyle season wouldn't be complete without some off-the-field dispute. McCauley was in conflict with fellow director Denis Angilley who, it was alleged, had reclaimed a £50,000 guarantee and was therefore no longer a director. Angilley disputed this, claiming he had been attempting to meet with the chairman for several weeks. McCauley also fired a broadside at the other directors, claiming they were not putting in enough work or money. The protagonists took their places in the directors' box for the first local derby of the season, against Torquay.

On paper, Argyle were clear favourites. Torquay were struggling near the bottom and had come off the back of a 4-0 defeat. But local derbies are different and a seven-goal thriller ensued in front of Home Park's biggest attendance of the season so far. Littlejohn was the star of the show, scoring a hat-trick, all from his lethal left boot, although referee Rob Harris did his best to upstage him by booking eight players, including Gulls boss Don O'Riordan for 'waving an imaginary flag at a linesman' and sending off Ian Gore.

The momentum was halted a week later at Darlington. Argyle never got going, with Heathcote giving a rare below-par performance after suffering for several days with his wisdom tooth. The match saw the debut as substitute of former brickie Richard Logan, another of Warnock's former storm troopers at Huddersfield who had signed in the week for £20,000.

Argyle remained in the North East for a Tuesday night match at Scarborough, another of Warnock's old stomping grounds. Not wishing to subject his players to excessive travel, Warnock gained agreement from McCauley that the players could stay away. No doubt the chairman was swayed by the players' offer to pay for their own accommodation for one night. On Third Division wages, it was never likely to be the Ritz, so a Scarborough guest house at £13 a night for B&B found itself unusually fully booked for early November.

The bargain-break appeared to do the trick as Argyle swept into a two-goal lead at the McCain stadium. Scarborough pulled one back and then equalised deep into the six minutes of injury-time. Warnock was furious with his players for throwing away points. It left his side four points behind the top three teams.

Littlejohn was beginning to get himself a reputation. Cardiff were the visitors and their game-plan was based on stopping the in-form striker at any cost. Sadly for Argyle and the frustrated fans it worked. Nil-nil was the inevitable result, prompting Warnock to apologise to the supporters for the worst game he had seen for several seasons. The following Tuesday, Argyle were knocked out of the Auto Windscreens Shield after losing at Northampton. Logan was sent off and Hill, skipper for the night, was substituted after only 26 minutes after a dismal start to the match.

The boardroom rumblings continued to rumble. Director Ivor Jones resigned after taking umbrage at McCauley's earlier remarks.

The FA Cup draw saw Argyle break new ground with a visit to Wexham Park, home of GM Vauxhall Conference Slough, whose team contained two former Argyle men, Mark Fiore and Andy Clement. With TV cameras poised vulture-like, hoping to capture an upset, Argyle displayed the right attitude and ran out 2-0 winners.

With league action the main focus, Argyle travelled north again, this time to Hartlepool, where they again proceeded to throw away a two-goal lead. Warnock, a former Hartlepool player of the year, was not smiling. Four league games had now passed without a win and silly points had been dropped against lowly sides. Argyle were still sixth but it could have been much better.

Things got back on track with a home win over Rochdale, one of the sides above Argyle. The first 45 minutes were not quite in the Cardiff boredom league, but not far from it. Warnock went to town on his players at half-time. Whatever was said, worked. Littlejohn quickly notched his twelfth of the season. A late Evans strike moved Argyle up a place.

Monday's headlines were not about Argyle's return to form but the death of former keeper Alan Nicholls in a motorcycle accident. The tributes poured in for the youngster who, for all his misdemeanours, was well liked and not a bad goalkeeper either.

The reward for a cup victory at a non-league ground was a visit to another non-league ground. This time it was Kingstonian. Again the TV companies smelt blood and the match was chosen for live Sky TV coverage, necessitating a switch to a Sunday kick-off. The coverage swelled the Pilgrims' coffers by £60,000. It was just as well. The club's annual financial statement revealed a loss of more than half a million pounds with liabilities of £2.5 million. An exquisite late goal from Littlejohn clinched a 2-1 win to set pulses racing over the prospect of a plum third round tie.

On the eve of the home game against Wigan, the annual shareholders meeting had seen Angilley removed from the board, thanks purely to McCauley's massive personal shareholding having the deciding vote. The chairman was duly re-elected and then refused to bow to demands from Ivor Jones for an apology over previous remarks. Angilley described the club as an autocracy.

Warnock had attended the meeting but his mind was focused on Wigan who, under new manager John Deehan, had undergone something of a resurgence and were unbeaten for eight games. Littlejohn was again the main man. The fleet-footed striker was made captain for the day in the absence of the injured Mauge. Heathcote was the natural choice to lead the side, but the ultra-superstitious Warnock believed Argyle always lost when 'Hector' was skipper. After an early goal apiece, Littlejohn added to his burgeoning reputation with two goals.

Although Angilley had been removed from the board, he refused to go away and publicly stated that he would launch a hostile bid to take over McCauley's 75 per cent shareholding if the chairman did not sell the club to him willingly. Warnock declared that if McCauley went, he would too. Yet again, it seemed as though off-field wranglings would derail any success on the playing side.

The news broke on the morning of the match at Lincoln. The Imps had a new manager in John Beck and almost a new team, fielding only two players who had appeared in the corresponding fixture at Home Park only ten weeks earlier. Lincoln were lying next to bottom and it looked a good opportunity for Argyle to take another three points, but neither set of players looked particularly interested and they managed just six shots at goal between them for the entire match.

Warnock was soon back in the transfer market, bringing in versatile defender Chris Curran from Torquay. Curran made his debut when coming off the bench in a single-goal victory over Cambridge, courtesy of a dipping shot from Mauge.

Accepting that Boxing Day derbies were now a thing of the past, it still seemed extreme to send Argyle on a trek to Gillingham over the Festive Period. Moreover, Gillingham boasted the most miserly defence in the country having conceded just seven goals in twenty matches.

The frostiness of the pitch was matched by the mood of the players. The Christmas spirit had not infiltrated Kent. Leadbitter was booked in the first minute and Mauge was subjected to racial abuse by an unnamed opponent. Warnock suggested that spirit was something the referee had by the gallon, blaming him for the defeat via a Steve Butler penalty, awarded after Clayton had palmed away Leo Fortune-West's header off the goal-line. Clayton received the obligatory red card. To cap it all, Warnock was involved in a late-night minor car accident near his home when he skidded on ice. It was a day to forget. At least the defeat allowed the manager to get his hair cut. Another Warnock foible.

Three days later, the scheduled game at Northampton was postponed with the pitch frost-bound. It gave the players extra time to prepare for the New Year's Day derby clash at home to Exeter. Warnock's ill-fortune continued as he was stricken with flu. He made it to Home Park and croaked his pre-match message. He wanted his players to perform to the extent that he wouldn't have to raise his voice at half-time.

Wishful thinking. Within 94 seconds of the morning kick-off, Mark Came scored the first league goal of 1996. Paul Buckle increased the Grecians' lead on half-time and Warnock's temperature, already reading 102 degrees, threatened to reach boiling point. The interval rollocking had the desired effect as Baird and Mauge both laid claim to the first Argyle goal. Baird scored a second. A 2-2 home draw in front of the largest Third Division crowd of the season was disappointing but not disastrous.

The next match was keenly anticipated, by the supporters anyway. The FA Cup had thrown up a home tie with Premiership Coventry. Ron Atkinson's side had not exactly set the footballing world alight and many tipped Argyle to go through. As far as Warnock was concerned, it was merely a respite from league action. To exemplify this, he left out Clayton and Patterson, both suspended for the next league match.

In front of a rain-soaked crowd of well over 17,000, a giant-killing act looked on the cards after twenty minutes. Evans bore down on goal and was hoiked to the ground by David Busst. It was a definite red card and, from the free-kick, Baird blasted in via Dion Dublin's shoulder. In the second half, the game turned in a five-minute spell. Ally Pickering's cross looped over Blackwell. Man of the match John Salako and Paul Telfer also scored and it was game, set and match.

The unfortunate Nicky Hammond was the next to leave Home Park. Reading signed him for £40,000, meaning Warnock had recouped his initial outlay. It seemed liked a good deal.

Lady Luck again failed to accompany Argyle on their trip to promotion rivals Preston. After Heathcote had robustly given the Pilgrims the lead, Preston scored three times. To exacerbate matters, Littlejohn was sent off for remarks made to a linesman. Whatever he said, presumably not complimentary, represented the consensus of opinion of all persons green, but it was not his place to say it. Five minutes later Evans had a penalty saved by John Vaughan. Saunders headed his first league goal with two minutes remaining but it was all too late and Argyle lost further ground on the teams above them.

Warnock had long thought about bringing in another goalkeeper and now decided it was the right time. On a month's loan, he signed Australian Andy Petterson from Charlton. The new keeper was thrust into immediate first-team action for the visit of Colchester and was soon making his mark, firstly on Paul Abrahams, and then on the home fans by saving the resultant penalty by Simon Betts. With Baird scoring with another deflected free-kick and Petterson making more great saves, a win looked on the cards, but Colchester were in the running for a play-off spot and pushed everyone forward. The ploy worked. With two minutes to go, centre-half David Greene powered in an equaliser.

Worse was to follow. Scunthorpe at home on a Tuesday evening in January is, admittedly not the most attractive fixture in the football calendar, but perhaps the 13,000 'fans' who had deserted their side since the Coventry Cup-tie had a portent of what was to unfold. Wearing Argyle's second-choice yellow kit after realising too late that their own white shirts clashed – in a strange sort of way – with Argyle's, Scunny swept into a two-goal half-time lead. Warnock introduced his latest employee, Scott Partridge, on loan from Bristol City. Partridge had been one of Torquay's scorers at Home Park earlier in the season when on loan. Confused? It made little difference. Scunthorpe scored a third. Logan scored late on, by which time a goodly portion of the crowd had gone home. A day later, Littlejohn underwent a hernia operation and was likely to be missing for four or five weeks.

Away to Hereford was postponed, so Partridge's full debut came in the rearranged game at Northampton a week later. It was Argyle's best performance for several weeks, but Ian Sampson's goal consigned them to another defeat.

Without a win in six league games, there was little optimism for the visit of third-placed Chester. In desperation, Warnock even broke with superstition and handed the captain's armband back to Heathcote. For the first time in a while, Argyle really looked 'up for it'. Within thirteen minutes they were two up and had added another, by Partridge, by the break. Heathcote had also posted his entry for 'miss of the season' by failing to convert from a yard out.

Argyle relaxed in the second period and Chester scored twice but they were interspersed by a rare Williams goal to ensure the Warnock fingernails remained at standard length. In the last minute, Petterson saved a second successive Home Park penalty, boosting his chances of a permanent place.

A visit to Scunthorpe came just eighteen days after the hosts had blown Argyle apart at Home Park. It looked a case of déjà vu. Andy McFarlane had scored after just four minutes when Logan generously placed an attempted clearance at the feet of the lanky striker. Evans, celebrating the signing of a new two-and-a-half-year contract, quickly restored parity. There were no more goals, but in the final minute Evans was dismissed in controversial fashion. Having been booked earlier for a tackle, the striker was involved in an aerial challenge with Paul Wilson. The Scunthorpe man fell to the ground with the grace of a clay pigeon. The referee was clearly unsure what had happened but brandished a red card in Evans' face anyway.

A drab 0-0 draw at Doncaster had Warnock conceding that automatic promotion was now unlikely. If promotion was to be achieved, he would again have to guide his side through the play-off minefield. The Doncaster game proved to be Petterson's swansong as Charlton needed him as emergency cover and Warnock decided to let him go. A familiar sight returned in goal – former Argyle player of the year Steve Cherry, borrowed from Watford. Warnock knew Cherry from old and also knew that his experience would be invaluable in the run in. He was not wide of the mark in describing his new signing as 'He's overweight, always has been'.

Cherry donned the No 1 jersey for the visit of Bury. Also making a welcome return, after surgery, was Littlejohn, in his case a place on the bench. The striker was now suffering from a broken toe, after a horse trod on it, not an everyday hazard in the life of a professional footballer. Bury were no pushovers, having scored seven themselves in their previous match and been undefeated on their travels since September. In front of Argyle's lowest and coldest crowd of the season, it took a Heathcote goal to take the points, with an overhead kick would you believe. A goal as spectacular as it was unlikely. There was more good news. Close rivals Chester had lost at Hereford. Argyle were now within a point of third place.

Another player signed a new contract. Martin Barlow's life as a Pilgrim had seemed destined to end early in the season. Out of favour, he had spoken to various clubs but no deal had been done. To his credit, he fought for his place and was now showing the kind of form that made it difficult to leave him out.

Barnet, on the fringes of a play-off place, were the next visitors and sneaked away with a point. With Evans suspended, Partridge had retained his place and scored within seven minutes. In the second half, Littlejohn, through on goal, was hauled back. The referee played advantage when patently there wasn't one, and then declined to send off Littlejohn's assailant, Alan Pardew. Warnock was incensed and when Cherry's weak punch was returned over his head for an equaliser, the manager's mood did not lighten.

With Evans again available and Littlejohn, one toe excepted, back to full fitness, Partridge was deemed surplus to requirements and returned to Ashton Gate, although the lively striker had done a worthy job during his short spell.

A Logan header gave Argyle all three points at Orient, after Warnock had kicked backsides for the full fifteen minutes of the half-time break.

A clash with the league leaders is normally highly anticipated. True, there was a decent crowd for the visit of Gillingham, but no one was expecting to see any flashy football. The Gills' brand of play was ugly. There was no other word to describe it. Stop the opposition at all costs and hump it up to their big forwards. It worked. They were, after all, top of the league and had let in only thirteen goals. They also had, by far, the worst disciplinary record in the league and possibly the universe. The fact that Barlow infiltrated the Kentish Iron Curtain to score the only goal of the match had more than the usual tinge of satisfaction. Gills boss Tony Pulis described his side's performance as one of the best for some time. It defied imagination as to how bad the worst was.

Another player leaving Plymouth was defender, Andy Comyn. A costly Shilton purchase, he had suffered a serious back injury and become one of the forgotten men of Home Park. Now recovered, he was offered a new two-year contract but felt a better one was merited. A free transfer was his reward.

A 3-2 win at Cambridge put the Pilgrims third. There was now a feeling that the wheel of fortune had turned. A flukey goal, finally credited to Evans' hip after detouring via a defender's back and Heathcote's arm, was enough to defeat a Northampton side that had clearly read the Gillingham guide to non-adventurous football.

Devon derby time again. A glue-pot pitch didn't matter to Clayton, who sweetly struck the opener after just nine minutes. By the final whistle, the shot-count read Argyle 21, Exeter 4, but the result read 1-1. One of City's rare efforts from Mark Cooper was heading wide until Logan decided to fling a leg at it and divert it past Cherry. Warnock declared himself satisfied by the overall performance but with transfer deadline day looming was still looking to strengthen the squad.

Two players on the periphery, Micky Ross and Ian Payne, sought pastures new in Canada, whilst the forward line was boosted by two new arrivals, Neil Illman, a £5,000 buy from non-league Eastwood Town, and Carlo Corazzin of Cambridge and Canada. Illman, one for the future, was immediately loaned to Cambridge for the rest of the season to allow him some experience of league football.

The trip to Fulham saw a change from the normal routine, as the players, staff and around 400 fans travelled to the capital by train. Had it been a British Rail XI there would, no doubt, have been a number of excuses for a crushing 0-4 defeat. Leaves on the goal-line, wrong type of grass, that sort of thing. Warnock could only come up with, 'a total disgrace' and 'an utter shambles'. True, he was less than enamoured with his away day, claiming the trip had too many distractions. It was not an exercise he would repeat.

The main concern now was what effect the Craven Cottage debacle would have, as Mansfield arrived for a midweek game. Lack of confidence in front of goal was the verdict. Stags keeper Ian Bowling was also having a blinder. With three minutes remaining, Corazzin was sent into the fray. His first touch was a header saved on the line. His second saw him brought down for a penalty, and his third was to finally defy Bowling from the spot. Prior to that, the biggest cheer of the night was reserved for the appearance of Steve McCall as a substitute, reminding Argyle fans that he was still on the books after an injury-plagued season. His experience and sublime skill was another boost to the promotion challenge.

A few days later it looked as though Lady Luck had been upset again. Darlington's long trip back to the North East was accompanied by all three points, courtesy of a contentious goal. With Robbie Painter, possibly, and Robert Blake, definitely offside, the Argyle defence stopped. Cherry made a half-hearted attempt to stop Painter's scuffed shot. Everyone waited for a flag or a whistle. There was the latter but only to signal a goal. The referee's verdict was that Blake had not been interfering with play. He was certainly interfering with Painter, who was forced to push his teammate out of the way to get his shot in. McCall started the game and was quickly back to his imperious best. Sadly his ten teammates weren't.

Things were still tight at the top. A glance at the remaining fixtures suggested Argyle had the easiest run in. Only Hereford were in the top half of the table. If the form book was to be believed, five wins from the remaining six matches looked feasible. Argyle certainly had to win the first of those. Torquay were hopelessly adrift at the bottom. An early Mauge goal settled the nerves and Argyle ran out 2-0 winners. It wasn't pretty but it was three points.

Plymouth City Council announced ambitious plans to redevelop the Home Park site into a £25 million superstadium. The 'Tradium' would be the epicentre of Plymouth sporting life and also create hundreds of jobs.

Scarborough made the long trip to Devon and must have wondered why. They were awful. Even the ball boys were glancing at the Scarborough bench wondering whether they would get the nod to come on. A 5-1 win not only boosted confidences, but perhaps, vitally, the goal-difference.

Three days later, Plymouth were undone by 37-year-old striker Steve White. Despite his advancing years, White was still one of the best in the game. Only two years earlier, Argyle had tried to sign him. Now, here he was scoring a hat-trick. Warnock was so embarrassed by his side's display that he personally went to the Argyle section of the crowd after the final whistle to apologise. Bury won, meaning automatic promotion was now highly unlikely.

If Warnock could have chosen ideal opponents to get the promotion push back on track, he would probably have picked Cardiff. The Bluebirds had not won for ten games and had tumbled into the bottom four. Nevertheless, it took an Evans goal and a penalty save by Cherry to seal the expected victory.

Rochdale needed to be overcome next. The Spotland ground was less than spotless. The pitch had more sand than Bigbury beach with the tide out. It was not a case of which stud but which sandal. Again Evans was the saviour, scoring the only goal after seventy minutes. Having been booed incessantly since his fifth-minute clattering of Dale keeper Lance Key, he was hardly in line for Rochdale's most popular visitor award. Sadly, Clayton suffered a knee injury early in the match which effectively ruled him out for the season.

After the various permutations which had arisen over the past few weeks, the equation had now simplified. Argyle needed to win at home to Hartlepool and hope that both Bury and Darlington failed to win. Such a combination would ensure promotion. Anything else would ensure Warnock's annual ritual of the play-offs. Preston and Gillingham were already up.

Chris Billy soon settled Argyle nerves with the fastest goal of the day. Argyle never looked like losing and didn't, thanks to further goals from player of the year Heathcote and Logan. With Darlington going 0-2 down at Scunthorpe, and Bury, for a time, drawing at Cardiff, Argyle momentarily held third position, but the Shakers eventually overcame the Bluebirds and Argyle finished in fourth place, a measly one point behind Bury. It was frustrating but bearing in mind the start they had, still a splendid effort.

Colchester lay in wait in the play-off semi-finals. The U's would be at home in the first leg due to their inferior finishing position. If you wanted anyone to guide you through play-offs, Warnock was yer man, having completed a managerial hat-trick of Wembley victories.

There was huge interest from the Argyle followers, but with Layer Road as spacious as a broom cupboard, only 1,200 tickets were sent to Plymouth. They were quickly snapped up, with the unlucky ones having to console themselves with watching the match live on a giant TV screen erected on the Home Park pitch.

Prior to the match, both managers indulged in some psychological skulduggery. Steve Wignall played on the fact that his side – which had cost a total of just £2,000 – were competing with Warnock's expensively assembled outfit. Warnock retorted cruelly: 'Little teams like Colchester shouldn't even be on the same pitch as us.'

Well, they were on the same pitch and Argyle knew it. It was a far from vintage performance from the Pilgrims and they were grateful that a Mark Kinsella thunderbolt from thirty yards was the only thing to separate the sides as the full-time whistle blew. Three nights later, the teams faced each other again. Warnock urged the Home Park faithful to recreate the intimidating atmosphere that his team had experienced at Layer Road, barring the apples, coins and other assorted objects which had been aimed at his players. The locals responded magnificently with 500 Colchester fans being outnumbered by 14,000 green 'uns.

Wignall kept faith with the eleven he had sent into battle in the first leg, although he had his previously suspended top scorer, Tony Adcock, lurking on the bench. Warnock made just one change, replacing Billy – who was partly at fault for Kinsella's goal – with Mauge. Warnock knew he needed an early goal. How about three minutes? Cherry's skewed clearance was nodded on by Leadbitter into the path of Evans, who swung his left boot at the ball and sent it past Carl Emberson. Four minutes before half-time Argyle were in front. Future Pilgrim Paul Gibbs was adjudged, harshly it seemed, to have fouled Patterson. Gibbs was booked for airing his opinion to the referee. From the free-kick, Leadbitter's sweet left foot curled the ball, Brazilian like, past a stranded Emberson.

On the hour, the game threatened to boil over. Littlejohn and opposition defender Tony McCarthy chased a through ball. It was never an even contest and as Littlejohn raced ahead his heels were clipped. It was surely a red-card offence but referee Mr Kirkby brandished only yellow. Warnock was beside himself with rage and also beside the linesman, who had found himself in the wrong place at the wrong time by patrolling in front of the Argyle dug-out. Warnock let rip at the linesman and then Mr Kirkby, who promptly sent the Argyle manager packing.

Refusing to take the traditional route to the directors' box for such misdemeanours, Warnock instead plonked himself on the Mayflower Terrace and directed operations surrounded by yellow-coated stewards and several hundred fired-up supporters. Within two minutes of the furore, Kinsella repeated his first-leg feat by scoring from 25 yards. The U's were now ahead on away goals.

Argyle had to score. They pushed forward with the U's content to defend their slender advantage. With five minutes remaining, Barlow took possession on the right wing and swung in a cross. Was it a bird, was it a plane? No, it was the unlikely figure of Paul Williams launching himself to head the ball in. A Williams appearance in an opposition penalty area was almost unheard of, but no one deserved the goal more. He was the only player to have played in every game of the season.

Five minutes later the final whistle blew. Please Keep off the Pitch? No chance mate. Green and white swamped the playing area. Warnock and

McCauley were both in tears. For the first time in the club's history, an Argyle side would step on to the hallowed Wembley turf. Euphoria swept the Westcountry. Everyone, it seemed, wanted a ticket, although Warnock was keen to remind everyone that nobody had won anything yet.

As the big day approached, Warnock took his men to the Belfry golf complex in the Midlands, partly to relax and also to remove them from the frantic goings on at Home Park. Late May Bank Holiday dawned and the usual trail of holiday-makers made their way, snail-like, to Devon and Cornwall. This year, something was different. There were more vehicles going the other way. Radios were swiftly re-tuned as the emmets and grockles sought news of some disaster to hit the South West. In truth, it was the sight of 30,000 people Wembley bound. Other Argyle exiles flew in from all corners of the globe. It was a day not to be missed. Of course, Argyle still had to do the business on the pitch, otherwise it would be the biggest anticlimax of all time. Darlington would be their opponents and certainly no pushovers.

At 2.55 the squads marched side by side onto the pitch. The National Anthem never stirred the heart so much. The game started nervously and rarely reached the heights such an occasion deserved. Had it been a league clash it would have been quickly consigned to the memory dustbin. Stalemate ensued for 65 minutes. Then Argyle won a corner on their right-hand side. Leadbitter shaped to take an inswinger but in a well-rehearsed routine played the ball short to Patterson, who had feigned indifference. The full-back swung the ball in and, arriving late, Ronnie Mauge cement-ed his place in Argyle history by looping a header past the leaden-footed Paul Newell.

Darlington threatened only once in those final long 25 minutes. With the clock counting down, Argyle played keep-ball as if to send out a defi-ant message to those who branded Warnock sides as long-ball merchants. The final whistle was greeted by a gamut of emotions. Thirty thousand tear-filled eyes watched Heathcote climb the famous steps to collect the trophy. Simply the Best? You bet.

# FOURTEEN

# 1997-98 (Relegated to Division 3)

The heady days of the Wembley play-off triumph seemed a distant memory as the 1996-97 season began. There was no Warnock, sacked by chairman McCauley after an increasingly fraught relationship between the two. The chances are Warnock would have left, in time, of his own accord, such was his frustration with the way the club was being run. The general atmosphere around Home Park also pervaded the pitch. Second Division football was a different proposition and that 1996-97 season was a struggle from day one. Relegation looked on the cards, but Warnock's trusty sidekick, Mick Jones, had taken the hot seat and succeeded in his given task of avoiding the drop.

It was enough to keep Jones's name on the manager's office door. He was under no illusions, however, as to the task he faced. After a season of struggle it is normal for clubs to strengthen their squads in order to avoid a repetition. It was not so at Home Park. McCauley's spend, spend, spend philosophy of the early Shilton and Warnock eras had fallen by the wayside, partly through the club's lack of cashflow, and also because of the chairman's own disillusionment with, it seemed, all things Plymouth Argyle. There was no Mickey Evans, who had signed for Southampton in a big-money deal before the end of the previous season, and no second season for the controversial Bruce Grobbelaar, who had spent as much time in a Crown Court over match-fixing allegations as he had between the sticks. Experienced defender Chris Curran had joined Exeter, while young striker Lee Phillips and defenders Tony James and Jason Rowbotham were long-term injury victims. The chairman's 'hand stays in the pocket' attitude had also seen Wembley hero Ronnie Mauge and midfielder Mark Saunders refuse to sign new contracts, believing the proposed terms were less than generous. Mark Patterson was also refusing to sign for 'personal reasons'.

Grobbelaar's replacement was the well-travelled Peterborough goalkeeper, Jon Sheffield, who had cost £45,000. The remaining new faces were non-league striker Padi Wilson, midfield player Graham Anthony, and small but chunky striker Earl Jean. Hardly household names except, perhaps, in St Lucia, where Jean was a regular in the international side.

There were also changes backstage. Jones appointed youth-team manager and erstwhile reserve custodian Kevin Blackwell as his assistant, and brought back former player Kevin Summerfield to take charge of the youngsters. Also given a 'reprieve' was Gary Clayton, who had been released as a player due to a serious knee injury but then brought back as reserve-team manager.

Jones was keen to get on with the job, to the extent that the first friendly of the season, at St Blazey, had to be postponed when the Football League interjected, pointing out that the game was due to be played before the official start of the season. Another friendly at Falmouth saw the injury list lengthen with Simon Collins adjourning to the treatment room. Pre-season's main attraction was the visit of Premiership Sheffield Wednesday. The game saw an appearance in an Argyle shirt of Nottingham Forest striker Steve Guinan. The front man impressed sufficiently for Jones to attempt to sign him, but Forest were reluctant to release him.

The league started in earnest with a relatively short trip to Bristol Rovers and a reminder of what might have been. Rovers had splashed out £200,000 on striker Barry Hayles over the summer. Twelve months earlier, Warnock had wanted to bring the forward to Home Park, together with future Premiership and international stars Dean Kiely and Mark Kinsella. The threesome would have cost a combined £400,000, but McCauley was having none of it. Inevitably, Hayles scored the opening goal, but the match proved that, if nothing else, Jones had instilled some fighting spirit in the side. Argyle's Canadian international goalscorer Carlo Corazzin uncharacteristically lost his rag after being clattered from behind and was sent off for elbowing his assailant, Steve Foster. Six minutes later, the ever reliable Micky Heathcote levelled the scores and some tough rearguard action saw out a satisfactory draw.

The Coca-Cola Cup pitted Argyle against First Division Oxford. Given the Pilgrims' dire recent record in this particular trophy, the supporters had become overwhelmed by their own indifference. The first leg away from home was not one to remember. A Richard Logan own-goal contributed to a 0-2 defeat. To make matters worse, Collins was in the wars again, carried off with a feared broken leg after colliding with Sheffield, although the later prognosis was severe bruising. The game was watched by Formula One star Jean Alesi who looked suitably unimpressed throughout. At least Mauge was back, having agreed his new contract.

Spirits were lifted by half-time in the first home league game. At 0-2 down, Grimsby looked well beaten. As an added bonus, the once prolific Adrian Littlejohn scored his first goal at Home Park for sixteen months, but Logan – having scored the opener – turned villain, tripping Jack Lester to concede a penalty. Suddenly inspired, Grimsby equalised.

With Corazzin suspended, Jean was given the opportunity to compare the delights of St Lucia with Wigan. Logan, mindful of his early-season contribution to the opposition, changed his pre-match preparations by despatching his wife and newly born offspring to his parents for the week, allowing him to catch up on some much-needed sleep. The ploy worked as his late equaliser cancelled out Wigan's freak goal, scored by David Lowe, whose attempted cross sliced off his shin past a startled Sheffield.

With Argyle conceding a two-goal lead in the previous home game, Oxford's comeback in the second leg of the Coca-Cola Cup had more fizz than the sponsors' product. The Greens quickly wiped out the first-leg deficit, with Wilson's first goal for the club and that man Logan finding the net again. David Smith's own-goal immediately after half-time also helped matters, but within a minute the dangerous Joey Beauchamp scored from 25 yards. Suddenly the goals flowed thick and fast, sadly past Sheffield. Five of them in fact. At least the steadfast 3,000 who turned out had value for money.

The 3-5 defeat prompted demands for contract rebels Patterson and Saunders to be included, but they remained on the sidelines as another draw was notched up, at home to Chesterfield. Jean scored his first goal for the club and was determined to celebrate the fact, despite it being in front of the away fans. Such was his delight, even the referee received a cuddle after attempting to cut short the St Lucian's one-man show.

September dawned with the nation in sombre mood after the death of the Princess of Wales. The glumness around Home Park was exacerbated by McCauley's announcement that he was prepared to sell the club. To back up his claim, he brandished plans to build a supermarket on the Home Park site if the City Council did not renew the lease on the ground which had only thirteen years remaining. McCauley named his price – £3 million. Quite where that valuation came from baffled most. With such a small number of years on the lease there was little value in the ground itself, and with respect to the players, their overall valuation would not contribute much of the figure in question. The price did not, however, deter former hero Tommy Tynan, who announced his intention to form a 'Pilgrims for the People' consortium in an attempt to wrestle control.

Such events did little to help on-field matters and it was no great surprise that a home defeat to Watford resulted. Those who promote the 'there should be more ex-players as referees' theory would be forgiven for revising their opinions had they been at Craven Cottage to witness another Argyle defeat. In charge was Steve Baines, a man with well over 400 league games to his credit, but some of his decisions left both sets of fans incredulous. Firstly, Littlejohn was scythed down by Mark Blake as he bore down on goal. Blake expected to see red but saw only yellow. Then, with Sheffield clearly impeded, Paul Moody's goal was allowed to stand. Even Moody expressed surprise.

Off-field matters continued to dominate. The local *Evening Herald*, not for the first time, was highly critical of the chairman's actions. It led to McCauley banning their reporters from the ground. The editor responded with some initiative by hiring a fifty-foot crane which was erected outside the ground for the clash with Brentford. With fortitude, the hack and his photographer did their job, although a scoreless draw ensued.

By this stage it was easy to overlook that the team had not won any of their first seven games and were now languishing one place off the bottom. Crowds had drained away, with fewer than 5,000 attending the Brentford game. There was an inkling of good news, with Saunders agreeing a month-to-month contract. His reward for such commitment was a seat on the bus and the bench for the trek to Carlisle, where Argyle kept the pools pundits happy with another score draw. The final game of September finally allowed the new signings to taste victory in an Argyle shirt. Fellow strugglers Walsall were despatched thanks to two goals from an inspired Martin Barlow.

Any signs that the belated first win might inspire more of the same were dashed over the next three games, which resulted in three defeats. A dire game at York was followed by a 0-3 loss at Luton, where Hatters striker Tony Thorpe scored his sixth and seventh goals against the Pilgrims in three games. The game at Kenilworth Road saw manager Jones dismissed in bizarre circumstances. Luton debutant Matthew Spring was red-carded for a bone-crunching tackle on Barlow, but Jones then followed him down the tunnel for trying to intervene and have the youngster reprieved!

The home game against Southend signalled one of the low points in Argyle history, such was the mess the club were now in. Understandably, crowds had dropped and the financial position was worsening. In a cost-cutting exercise, four players – Anthony, reserve keeper James Dungey, local student Steve Perkins, and the experienced Chris Leadbitter – were to be released and four office staff made redundant. Rebel Patterson had also been transferred to Gillingham. For the Southend game, the Lyndhurst and Mayflower stands were empty, their closure forced by Devon County Council prohibition notices that demanded safety improvements to the roof and the public address system.

The circumstances attending the 2-3 reverse to Southend at least exacted an apology from McCauley, who by now had chosen to stay away from Home Park in response to the verbal abuse he and his wife had been subjected to by a section of supporters.

The midweek game against Burnley, the only side below Argyle in the table, saw the attendance creep above the 3,000 mark. The Clarets were the happier side after a draw inspired by some magic by former England international Chris Waddle, their player-manager.

A trip to high-flying Gillingham was hardly one to inspire confidence but when Jean scored after just four minutes a shock looked possible. Then it all went wrong. Heathcote was stretchered off after an awkward fall and the Gills immediately equalised. In the second half, an indisciplined Wilson was sent off for kicking the ball away and a thirty-yard effort from Leo Fortune-West three minutes from time consigned the Greens to yet another defeat. Fourteen games had produced just ten points.

A few victories were now much needed, and they came. Three of them on the trot, in fact. An unlikely win at Preston was followed by a thriller at home to Wycombe, although there were fewer than 3,000 there to witness it, despite the ground being fully opened again. Corazzin was finding his scoring boots and a number of others finally showing some semblance of form. The Canadian striker was missing through international duty for the visit of Bournemouth, his place taken by Danny O'Hagan, who had been released by Argyle the previous season and was more recently plying his trade in Division Three of the local Sunday League. Lee Hodges, on loan from West Ham, made his debut and soon endeared himself to the crowd with some neat touches. With Littlejohn looking more and more like the player of old, a comfortable 3-0 win over the Cherries lifted the Pilgrims clear of relegation country.

A first round FA Cup-tie at home to Cambridge looked a kindly draw. The U's were loitering in the lower reaches of Division Three, but Argyle never seemed to adapt to the pressure of being favourites to win, and in the end were lucky to hang on for a replay as mist symbolically hung over Home Park.

After being undone by two superb Mickey Bell free-kicks at Ashton Gate, a hard-earned point was gained at Wrexham, where Argyle played for over an hour with ten men, after Littlejohn was dismissed for spitting at an opponent.

Argyle's AutoWindscreen Shield aspirations were already ended after coming second best in a penalty shoot-out at Northampton by the time of the much-anticipated return of Neil Warnock, now Oldham manager. Fans arriving for the game were asked to sign a 'Save Argyle' petition which was to be forwarded to the Football League to highlight the plight the club was in. Of course, it was the same Warnock of old, cajoling his players, berating officials and living every second of the game. He received a warm reception from the home crowd, who had been sad to see his departure. He was also smiling broadly at the end with a 2-0 victory under his belt, which consolidated the Latics' promotion push.

After a decent draw at Blackpool, Argyle's players seemed to benefit from an eleven-day break. They produced one of their best performances of the season to defeat Billy Bonds' highly rated Millwall, but a defeat at Northampton undid all the good work.

The approach of Christmas had a mellowing effect on the chairman. Having been re-elected at the end of year shareholders meeting, he made a number of important announcements. Crucially, his Rotolok company would continue to finance the club until the end of the season, although he stressed that the club was still for sale and he intended to write to the Football League to give provisional notice of Argyle's resignation. He also confirmed that a major sponsorship deal with a multinational company was in the pipeline. That deal with whoever-it-was never came to fruition. Even the local press were given a 'pressie' from Santa Dan as their Home Park ban was lifted.

There were still parties interested in buying McCauley out. The Tynan consortium was doomed to fail when insufficient finance was raised. Other businessmen expressed good intentions but talk was cheap. There was nothing in the way of concrete proposals.

The biggest crowd of the season filed through the Home Park turnstiles for the Boxing Day clash with Kevin Keegan's expensively assembled Fulham, who were in danger of winning the 'under-achievers of the year' award. Barlow's tame free-kick somehow found the back of the net after just five minutes, but the Cottagers hit back and in the end were comprehensive winners.

Few expected anything from the next game, as Argyle visited leaders Watford. Saunders' late goal saw many home fans streaming for the exits, fearing the worst. They missed Tommy Mooney's last-minute equaliser as the Pilgrims went into the New Year in the bottom four Successive defeats against Bristol Rovers at home and at Chesterfield increased the pressure and put added significance on the next three games, all against sides who were in the bottom six themselves.

A spirited display against Wigan saw Jones's side retrieve a two-goal deficit and Collins' late winner completed a fine comeback. There was no joy at Brentford, but McCauley was back from his self-imposed exile to see three vital points gained against Carlisle, for whom Ian Stevens scored his twelfth goal in eleven games.

The next visitors were York, who had just been thrashed 2-7 at Burnley, of all places. Determined not to suffer a repeat performance, City put up the shutters from the first minute. Argyle were sufficiently bereft of ideas to break them down and no one was sorry to hear the final whistle.

After a much-needed win at Walsall, where the Saddlers' manager Jan Sorensen was sent from the dug-out after offering choice words to the referee, it was the same old story. Any hopes that a victory away from Home Park would give the season some momentum were soon dashed. Argyle were never in contention during the midweek match at Southend and were beaten 0-3. Even more of a blow was the next defeat, at home to fellow strugglers Luton. Jones had been busy attempting to sign an experienced striker on loan. Enquiries were made about Kevin Francis, Marco Gabbiadini, Mark Stein and the aforementioned Fortune-West, but to no avail. Instead, the match saw the debut of striker Barry Conlon, hardly a household name, except to those who closely followed the fortunes of Manchester City reserves.

Time was beginning to run out for Argyle and the signs were not good. Performances had consistently been below par. Defensive mistakes had proved costly, and the fact that only one goal had been scored in the last four games hardly inspired confidence.

A rain-soaked pitch at Bournemouth contributed to an entertaining game with six goals shared. Perhaps thinking that he had found the answer to his problems, Jones ordered the groundsman to water the pitch for the match against Preston, despite torrential overnight rain. The ploy seemed to work. Paul Wotton gave an early indication of the shooting ability that would become legendary in the coming years by blasting home from thirty yards, and Conlon opened his account. Logan was later sent off, but Argyle held on. The game saw the absence of left-back Paul Williams, for the first time in 127 matches. 'Charlie' had picked up an injury at Dean Court.

Typically, after some minor cause for optimism, it all went wrong again in the next game, and badly. A distraught Logan was sent off for the second time in a week, this time for a 'professional' foul on Mark Stallard. Mid-table Wycombe took advantage of Argyle's new habit of playing with ten men, scoring five, with only Corazzin managing a reply. A token substitute appearance by Littlejohn was to prove his final appearance in an Argyle shirt. Once the darling of the Home Park faithful, in the past two years he had all too often been firing on only one cylinder. Lack of goals led to lack of confidence, and he undoubtedly needed a transfer to refresh his career.

The man who snapped him up, perhaps not surprisingly, was Neil Warnock. He believed he knew how to get the best out of the pacy striker. Oldham's promotion charge had faltered and needed a boost. Moving from the Latics as part of the deal was the experienced Phil Starbuck. It was hardly a signing with the longer term in mind, but Jones felt his know-how would be invaluable for the run in. Starbuck's debut came in a real pressure cooker atmosphere against Bristol City, who were flying high in second place. The City fans almost outnumbered the locals but weren't 'singing any more' by the end, as two second-half goals from Saunders and Conlon stunned them into silence.

Once again, Argyle had pulled clear of the bottom four as they travelled north for a Tuesday night game at Grimsby. Already without injured top scorer Corazzin, they lined up against a Mariners side that had kept a clean sheet in no fewer than 28 matches. The 'loan rangers' of Conlon and Starbuck had little joy and a solitary goal was enough to make the journey pointless.

Corazzin was back, earlier than expected, for another tough home encounter, this time with Wrexham, who were also in the top four. The Canadian put the Pilgrims ahead with a first-half header. With Saunders scoring a second after the break, another unexpected win was notched up. The game saw two more new faces make their bow, Stephen Woods, a young versatile defender from Stoke, and the more experienced Darren Currie, released by Shrewsbury and signed on a short-term contract until the end of the season.

Despite all this, results had conspired against Argyle and the trip to Oldham again saw them back in the bottom four. Of course, there was one 'A Littlejohn' in the opposition line up. As his name was announced over the PA, he was roundly jeered by the travelling Green Army. This lack of appreciation had continued for 43 minutes when the inevitable happened. The ex-Pilgrim fired into the roof of the net past a less than fit Sheffield, struggling with bruised ribs. Nine minutes into the second half, the Argyle fans were transported back in time. Littlejohn received the ball. Tricky, elusive and direct, he waltzed past several defenders to score his second. Why couldn't he have done more of that for Argyle?

By this stage of the season, a number of managers were studying the remaining fixtures with a calculator at their side. The bottom placings had become incredibly congested. Carlisle and Southend looked likely candidates for the drop, but a poor run would drag any number of others into the drop zone. Jones believed that three wins from the final five games would probably be enough to stay up.

Heathcote – own-goal 28 minutes. Rowbotham – sent off 41 minutes. Hardly the ideal start to the must-win home game against Blackpool, but rather than wilt, the Jones boys were now fighting. In the second half, Saunders' header struck the crossbar and for reasons known only to himself, Tony Butler blasted the ball past his own keeper. The incident reduced the Tangerines to pulp. Logan scored a second and Corazzin's last-minute penalty made it four home wins on the trot.

A trip to Millwall was traditionally one to fear for both players and supporters alike, but the current season had seen the Lions give a number of toothless displays. Expected by many pundits to be challenging for honours, they now found themselves embroiled in the relegation dogfight. Three points would all but guarantee their safety and Danny Hockton's fourth-minute goal gave them a dream start. Corazzin's sixteenth of the season soon cancelled the advantage, and from then on, Argyle looked the most likely winners. Billy Bonds' side were hesitant and nervous. The home crowd did little to help as they vented their frustration on a number of their own players. Unfortunately, Argyle could not capitalise further but a valuable point had been gained.

With the next two games at home, a four-point haul seemed sufficient to avoid a nail-biting last-day decider at Burnley. Unfortunately, opponents Northampton and Gillingham were not middle of the table, nothing to play for sides, but were both sniffing around the play-off zone.

Jones spent much of the preceding days working on defending corners and other dead-ball situations. He was not then, best pleased, when, after just eight minutes, the Cobblers' lively forward Chris Freestone headed in unhindered from a John Frain flag-kick. Saunders, again showing a penchant for drifting into the penalty area, levelled on the stroke of half-time. Within two minutes of the turnaround sloppy defending again allowed Freestone to slot home. Argyle had little option but to press forward, but it was to be one of those nightmare days. Three times they struck the woodwork before the inevitable happened. With virtually every green shirt forward, Dean Peer broke clear on a counter-attack and set up Freestone for his hat-trick.

An anxious week followed before Gillingham arrived in town, followed everywhere by a film crew who were recording their push for promotion for a fly-on-the-wall documentary. Included in their line up was early-season contract rebel Mark Patterson.

Before the start, the traditional player of the year award was made. For the first time, there were joint winners, namely Barlow and Corazzin. Both players were rumoured to be on their way out of Home Park and there were suggestions that the award was made jointly as part of the master plan to persuade them to stay.

From the start, both sides were patently nervous with so much at stake and the match was largely uninspiring. With a scoreless draw looking likely, Gillingham launched one final attack. The ball came to Paul Smith, a one-time Argyle trialist. His shot was not struck sweetly, but goalkeeper Sheffield was unsighted and he was powerless to prevent the ball finding the net. Players and fans alike were stunned. The only noise came from the open spaces of the Barn Park End where the Kentish men had gathered.

Such a morale-sapping defeat was difficult to stomach. The task for Jones was to lift his side. Ironically, after involving so many sides, the relegation battle was now more clear cut. Carlisle and Southend were already down, and only one of Argyle, Burnley and Brentford would survive. The Bees had a difficult trip to Bristol Rovers, who were embroiled in an equally tight race for play-off positions. If, as expected, they lost, the victors of the Argyle-Burnley match would stay up.

So a large travelling contingent of fans swelled the attendance to the second largest in the division that season, in the knowledge that nothing but three points would suffice. The Clarets had kept faith with Chris Waddle and he had steered them away from the bottom after a dismal start that had seen their first win delayed until mid-October. With Chris Billy injured, Jones opted for experience and recalled Starbuck.

The danger-man, as far as Argyle were concerned, was Andy Cooke. His eighteen goals had played a large part in his side's revival and he made it nineteen with a header after twelve minutes. Fortunately, Argyle heads didn't drop and Saunders headed past Chris Woods, formerly of England, leaving a gaggle of Burnley defenders staring accusingly at each other.

Minutes before half-time Cooke struck again, reacting more quickly than Heathcote, and guided another header past Sheffield.

Jones knew he had 45 minutes to save Argyle's season and possibly his job. Mauge replaced the anonymous Starbuck, and Barlow and defender Williams were sacrificed to allow a more attacking formation. Burnley were content to sit back and soak up the pressure but it looked a dangerous ploy, particularly when Jean fizzed a twenty-yarder just over and then missed a sitter by shooting straight at Woods.

In the end, it was another case of 'if only'. The final whistle signalled a jubilant pitch invasion by Burnley fans. News had filtered through that they had stayed up, with Brentford, as expected, losing. Argyle were down. Jones, a hardened northerner, kept his emotions in check and consoled his players. Wotton needed more consoling than most as tears streamed down his face in the knowledge that his home-town team would be playing in the bottom division of the Football League. Sadly, a mindless minority of home 'fans' threw missiles at the Green Army and trouble followed outside the ground.

It was time for reflection. No one wanted relegation but in the overall scheme of things, it was of little surprise. There were too many off the field distractions and no money to spend on players, leaving Jones to rely on largely uncommitted loan signings. Of the regulars, Sheffield had proved a decent signing, Heathcote and Williams were as reliable as ever, Saunders was developing into a useful player, and Barlow gave his all. Corazzin's goals proved important, but he lacked an able assistant up front to carry some of the burden.

Assistant manager Kevin Blackwell, having suffered relegation for the first time in his long career, summed it up for many, describing the club as a 'rudderless ship'. The much-vaunted major sponsorship deal never materialised. Chairman McCauley announced that he had no intention of abandoning the club, but would be prepared to sell some of his monopoly shareholding if a wealthy investor could be found. Ten players were out of contract. The future was not bright but Jones would not be around. During his summer holidays he took a phone call informing him that his contract had been terminated. It was an ignominious end to an inglorious season.

# FIFTEEN

# 2001-02 (Promoted to Division 2)

Since relegation in 1998, the club had been in the doldrums. Mick Jones had paid the price and had been replaced by former Argyle playing legends, Kevin Hodges as manager, and Steve McCall as his assistant. Both had enjoyed some success at Torquay by dragging them away from the bottom of the Football League and into play-off territory. Playing wise, the duo could not have been more popular. Hodges was the club's appearance record holder and had given sterling service in a number of positions over the years. McCall had joined in the twilight of his career, but his experience of top-flight and European football was plain to see. There were few classier acts in an Argyle shirt.

But management, of course, was a different proposition. The likes of Johnny Hore and David Kemp, former star players in their time, had once returned as managers and failed. Sadly, Hodges and McCall could be added to that list. In the first season in Division Three, a thirteenth-place finish had cemented a place in Argyle record books as their lowest ever finishing position. An improvement of one place the following year was hardly cause for optimism. The style of football was less than exhilarating, new signings had under-performed, and a string of loanees showed little commitment. The club was at a low ebb, and not only on the field. There was still uncertainty over the development of the new stadium and the Home Park pitch itself had drainage problems that had caused several unnecessary postponements.

Another poor start had inevitably led to Hodges' and McCall's dismissal. After a caretaker spell from youth-team boss Kevin Summerfield, former Scottish international striker Paul Sturrock became the surprise choice to take over the hot seat. He watched his first match in charge from the directors' box at Plainmoor, where a 1-1 draw with Torquay left Argyle in a lowly twentieth position and Sturrock under no illusions as to the task ahead.

The new man moved quickly in the transfer market, bringing in a number of players, including unknown French duo David Friio and Romain Larrieu, and tempting 'local boy made good' Mickey Evans, back to his home city. Results improved sufficiently to ward off any thoughts of relegation to the Conference and mid-table mediocrity at least allowed Sturrock the luxury of assessing his squad and forming future plans.

Sturrock showed little mercy in preparing his new squad. Long-serving players such as Martin Barlow and Jon Sheffield were allowed to leave. Fringe players and under-performers alike were included in the cull, although Craig Taylor and player of the year Wayne O'Sullivan – who were safe bets to play a part in the future – were also out of the equation. Taylor suffered a late-season broken ankle and O'Sullivan decided his future lay in Australia.

The summer months saw another arrival. Central defender Graham Coughlan arrived on a free transfer but with a sound pedigree having captained Livingston to two successive Scottish divisional titles. Strangely the club did not see him as Scottish Premier League material, a decision they would come to regret.

Off the pitch there were other developments that would have significant long-term impacts. Oft-criticised chairman Dan McCauley was never one to show patience, as many had found to their cost, but in this instance everyone benefited. Fed up with the deliberating, he took a massive gamble and forked out half a million of his own money to ensure work began on revamping Home Park. And a gamble it was. At that stage, a new lease with the City Council had not been signed although, with their hand forced, it was a few days later. It gave Argyle the security of a new 125-year lease and ended years of speculation over the future of the site.

It was to prove the last significant contribution of McCauley. Vilified by many, he could, in the cold light of day be considered the saviour of Argyle. He had ploughed millions of his own money into the club over the years and kept them afloat. Yes, he had upset managers, supporters, players and fellow directors alike over the years with some of his antics, but there was now grudging admiration for his commitment to the stadium project. On the eve of the season, the announcement came that McCauley was prepared to sell his shares to a new five-man consortium headed by director Paul Stapleton, who would become the new chairman. Also in on the act was the 88-year-old former Labour Party leader, Michael Foot, a lifelong Argyle fan who had never missed an opportunity during his public life to extol the virtues of being a Pilgrim. McCauley would remain on the board until the liabilities to his company, Rotolok, and to the club's bankers, had been repaid.

Sturrock began the season leaving no one in doubt as to who was the boss. Pre-season training is universally detested by players but Sturrock's promise that it would be the hardest pre-season they had ever faced must have tinged their summer breaks with a degree of trepidation. Certainly one player was not happy. Striker Steve Guinan, who had only sporadically shown any sort of form, was not among Sturrock's favourites. He was exiled from the first-team squad and forced to train with the youth team. He cut a forlorn figure around Home Park.

Some of the pre-season was spent north of the border, with four friendlies interspersing training, mixing socially with a number of fans who also made the trip, and visits to some of Sturrock's favourite haunts. Once back home, Premiership side Sunderland came visiting to provide attractive opposition for Argyle stalwart and one-time Rokerite Mick Heathcote. 'Hector' was a great favourite among the Argyle faithful but had been dogged with injury for much of the previous season. With veteran status also fast approaching, his future looked uncertain but Sturrock allowed him the pre-season to prove himself. He seemed to pass the test and a one-year contract lay in wait. But another of his former clubs, Shrewsbury, offered him two years and reluctantly, but understandably, the former skipper was off, only three days after his benefit game. Sadly, injury would force his retirement midway through his second year.

The league programme commenced, ironically, against Shrewsbury at home. Heathcote received warm applause and was left with the last laugh as the Shrews nicked a single-goal victory despite the first-half dismissal of Karl Murray. The match was played in a strange atmosphere. The stadium redevelopment was now in full swing and three sides of the ground resembled, nay was, a building site. The 5,000 or so were all assembled on the grandstand side of the ground and, despite the weary and dilapidated condition of the old stadium, there was still a tinge of sadness that such familiar sights as the Devonport End, and even the exposed open space of the Barn Park End, were gone forever. Some people had stood on the same spot for years. It was like losing an old friend. Memories flooded back to great matches of the past. The friendly against Santos, Everton in the FA Cup, and Manchester United against St Etienne when Home Park was packed to the rafters. Now where thousands had stood, rattling rattles and waving scarves, sat a few hard-hatted demolition workers, doubling for the day as ball 'boys'. Never before had the ball been returned from the terraces with such velocity.

The match also saw one of the briefest Home Park careers. On the eve of the season, diminutive Stoke striker Dean Crowe arrived on a one-month loan deal. He played the final 24 minutes against the Shrews but within days was back in Pottery country citing family problems.

Two tough away games now lay in prospect. A trip to Hull is never one to relish. The Tigers' manager, Brian Little, had been busy increasing BT profits over the summer and had spent a small fortune assembling a side which was universally expected to win promotion. But Sturrock had done his homework. Jamaican playmaker Theodore Whitmore was shackled and a stalemate ensued. Returning to the Argyle squad was Lee Hodges, who had a brief loan spell eight years earlier. He had made a favourable impression during that time although his career had somewhat drifted since, but he knew his way around the lower leagues.

It was then on to First Division Watford for the toughest imaginable first round Worthington Cup-tie. Managed by former Chelsea and Italy star Gianluca Vialli, the Hornets had a particularly cosmopolitan line up but for eighty minutes Argyle gave as good as they got, before Marcus Gayle's free-kick sealed the Pilgrims' traditional first round exit from the competition.

Sturrock had been delighted with the performance at Vicarage Road and was convinced that things were about to come right. Another loan signing was added to the squad. Striker Nicky Banger had been around a bit and would put pressure on the other strikers who had not yet come up with the goods, although a match against Rochdale at an ever-changing Home Park seemed a good place to start. Argyle did score, thanks to an own-goal, but within a minute Rochdale had equalised. The match saw a welcome return for full-back David Worrell, who had missed six months with a broken ankle. The tiring Worrell was replaced after 75 minutes by eighteen-year-old Joe Broad, but within three minutes a suicidal pass from the youngster on the edge of the penalty area was intercepted and Paul Connor scored a winner.

Little more than 4,000 witnessed the defeat. Suddenly a new stadium didn't seem quite such a good idea, if the fans weren't going to fill it. Argyle were languishing in 22nd position. It was little consolation that they were still the best team in Devon. Exeter and Torquay occupied the remaining two places below them in the league.

Few expected the position to improve after a Bank Holiday trip to league newcomers Rushden & Diamonds, an opinion that seemed eminently sensible after Duane Darby struck twice before half-time. Mickey Evans' goal just before the interval did not prevent a half-time 'Sturrocking' which the manager later admitted involved generous use of Anglo-Saxon and from which a number of tea cups failed to survive. With the players no doubt fearful for their lives if they did not deliver the goods, two second-half goals completed a fine comeback, although goalkeeper Larrieu played an important part with a number of fine saves.

Frustratingly, the next match was postponed, with opponents Swansea having a number of players on Welsh international duty. Argyle managed to bag an international of their own, when dreadlocked Canadian Jason Bent agreed to sign. The deal was subject to a work permit being obtained, which was no foregone conclusion as Preston had discovered when they tried to sign the same player.

The directors revealed a five-year plan for the club which was based around the desire to reach the First Division before it elapsed. A tall order? With crowds at 4,000 and the side treading water in the depths of the Third Division, what would you think?

After an unusually long-term early-season break, the first Devon derby of the season took place at Torquay. The Plainmoor pitch was as soft and smooth as, well, a walnut actually and did much to contribute to a dire game. But a win is a win and Friio's second-half goal was enough.

The Swansea game was rearranged for 11th September, a date inexorably linked with the terrorist atrocities in the USA. In view of those events it seemed likely at one stage that the game would be postponed, but it went ahead and provided some relief from the unbelievable scenes that had been constantly beamed from our TV screens. A less than strenuous 3-1 win brought welcome home points, with Banger a constant menace on his full debut and Martin Phillips on song. The defeat cost Swans boss John Hollins his job.

A point was taken from the trip to Kidderminster, although the performance was a tad better than dreadful. Could Sturrock raise the level of performance for the midweek trip to deadly rivals Exeter? Phillips and Chris Curran exchanged early goals, each against one of their former sides, before City regained the lead through the tricky Christian Roberts. He had been giving Jon Beswetherick a torrid evening, to the extent that the tousle-haired full-back was hauled off at half-time. It would be some time before 'Bezzie' would see first-team duty again. Sturrock, sensing that the game was slipping away, also made other changes, detailing Steve Adams to closely mark Martin Barlow, who was keen to show the Argyle manager that he had been hasty in releasing him. Evans equalised, but with a draw seeming probable, a great last-minute finish by Ian Stonebridge nicked three points. A win over City always brought a warm glow, but to do it in such a fashion was just that little bit more satisfying. Argyle's reputation as the grim reapers was also enhanced. The defeat cost Exeter manager Noel Blake his job by the end of the week.

As icing on the cake, Bent's transfer was finally confirmed after much hard work behind the scenes. A player that Sturrock had long been interested in was finally a Pilgrim. The Canadian made his debut as a substitute in the next game, a 2-0 home win over Macclesfield. Then it was back on the road again for another midweek trip, this time to York. The game was goalless but the performance pleasing.

Plymouth versus Luton. A fixture that had taken place many times over the years without any particular significance. But suddenly Joe Kinnear's Hatters were rivalling Exeter as the most unpopular opponents. The Hertfordshire boys were favourites for the title and had started impressively, topping the table. Furthermore, they weren't afraid of telling everyone either. Striker Steve Howard didn't foresee 'any problems in beating Argyle' and the Luton website suggested that Argyle were no more than average. Come 4.40pm, well it seems to have drifted to about 4.55 these days, they were to revise their opinions.

The dominant factor in the first half was referee Andy Hall, who brandished six yellows and one red card. The man who saw red was Evans for allowing Chris Coyne the opportunity to closely examine his elbow. The score at the time was 1-1. Inevitably, Dean 'haven't I seen him somewhere before?' Crowe opened the scoring. Yes, the same Crowe who had flown from the Argyle nest earlier in the season. Phillips had equalised, making him an unlikely top scorer for the season, and a Friio header seconds before half-time at least gave Argyle something to hang on to.

Evans' dismissal did not prove as disruptive as expected. Stonebridge was now the lone striker, a formation Argyle had been used to playing in away games. Inevitably Luton had their chances but Larrieu was more than up to it. Bent greatly impressed on his full debut, nullifying the threat of French wide-man Jean-Louis Valois, the best player in the division, according to Luton anyway. The second period saw the Hatters run out of ideas and, perhaps more surprisingly, Mr Hall's cards remain in his pocket. And so, Luton lost top spot and Argyle climbed to fourth. Kinnear remained unimpressed, and some derogatory remarks, which included describing Coughlan as a 'Joe Soap centre half' in the post-match press conference only exacerbated his unpopularity. 'Are you watching Joe Kinnear?' became a favourite chant for the remainder of the season.

A run which had seemed unthinkable at the start of the season earned Sturrock the divisional Manager of the Month award. The team spirit was becoming more evident with every game. A disputed penalty at Oxford with only sixteen minutes remaining failed to rattle the side, and Banger equalised against one of his former clubs after a twenty-yard run.

Things were coming together generally. On his 45th birthday, Sturrock signed an extension to his contract that would take him to the end of the 2005-06 season. The FA upheld Argyle's appeal against Evans' sending off against Luton, and another member of the Sturrock clan moved south. Twenty-year-old Blair Sturrock joined the club on a six-week trial and dad promised no favours.

The in-form team of the moment versus dismal Halifax produced the expected result. Argyle went three up after 25 minutes and treated the rest of the afternoon as a training session.

After a 1-2 LDV Vans Trophy defeat at Cheltenham, blamed on a rare Larrieu error, a trip to Mansfield was predicted to provide Argyle's biggest test to date. The Stags had won five home games on the trot. Evans, spared from suspension, opened the scoring in the second half, whereupon the defence's 'they shall not pass' mentality came to the fore. Two goals in the last minute provided a result which made every other side suddenly sit up and notice.

A Tuesday night win over Lincoln saw top spot attained. Yet another clean sheet, but the Imps could count themselves unfortunate. The downside of Argyle's rapid rise was that opposing teams were now intent on stopping them, instead of going on the offensive themselves, and Alan Buckley had prepared his side well. From the fans' point of view, Argyle had attained an air of invincibility. But Sturrock had seen it all before and kept his and his players' feet firmly on the ground. There was a long way to go.

The leadership was lost temporarily to Luton, but only because Argyle's game at Bristol Rovers was deferred for 24 hours to allow live TV coverage. Phillips, never previously renowned for his goalscoring prowess, was now in danger of being described as prolific as his fifth of the season after just two minutes set the ball rolling, as it were. As a TV spectacle the match was a non-event, but another goal from Hodges at least stirred Rovers into some sort of action. Evans was the pick of the bunch but he did have a point to prove. The ex-Rover was described by his former chairman as 'the worst signing I've ever made'.

The victory set a new club record for successive away matches without defeat. The fact that the previous record was eight was hardly a staggering statistic and only served to remind everyone what poor travellers the club had been for many a year. For Sturrock, it meant a second successive manager of the month accolade.

The joy of a single-goal victory over a resolute Hartlepool was compounded by the news that Luton had failed to claim all three points at Mansfield.

It was time for more movement on the personnel front. Striker Martin Gritton, having signed a two-year contract a few months earlier, was deemed surplus to requirements. Marino Keith, surely it should be Keith Marino? arrived from Scottish football, where he had been a teammate of Coughlan, and the club announced they were prepared to offload midfielder Sean Evers, who would probably go down as Sturrock's most ineffective signing. His arrival had prompted 'Luggy' to state that the side would be built around the highly rated player, but injuries and a failure to settle had seen him reduced to a bit-part role.

A Saturday afternoon England international prompted the trip to Cheltenham to be brought forward to a freezing Friday evening, and once again the referee was the central figure. The first half was, shall we say, feisty. Referee Mr Curson was not only oblivious to some of the 'tackles' which were flying about but also, it seemed, his watch, as the first half lasted an incredible 55 minutes. The shenanigans continued down the tunnel at half-time. Perhaps inevitably, the second half saw a sending off, when the already booked Mark Yates left the imprint of his studs on Larrieu's chest. Scorewise, the game ended goalless. At least Argyle were still grinding out results on those occasions when they did not play well.

The next game was also in front of TV cameras, no doubt hoping to capture another 'giant killing' act. The FA Cup had thrown up probably the worst draw Argyle could have received – a trip to Whitby Town of the Unibond Premier League. The directors saw fit to sanction a flight north rather than clocking up another few hundred 'bus miles'. With a narrow and bumpy pitch to contend with, the Pilgrims fell behind shortly before half-time, but Phillips again proved to be the saviour with an equaliser. The players were home in time to watch their efforts on 'Match of the Day'.

After the luxury of the flight to Whitby, the team bus was rolled out again for the midweek trip to Southend, who had just disposed of Luton in the Cup. There was not even an overnight stay, and a 7am start on the morning of the match constituted something of a gamble. However, Steve Adams' first ever Argyle goal proved one of the most crucial of the season and the league momentum was maintained.

Carlisle came and went. The 3-0 score said it all, and the visitors gave an ample demonstration as to why they hadn't won an away match all season. They also made tetchy Cheltenham look angelic, as Steve Soley was sent off after 33 minutes and Mark Birch substituted minutes later when it was obvious he would shortly follow suit. The win created a post-war club record for an unbeaten run and created a list of statistics that made Argyle the best club in the country for points gained, most wins, best goal-difference, most clean-sheets, the list went on. And it was to get longer.

The replay with Whitby saw the non-leaguers determine to enjoy a rare visit to a league ground. Evans did little to endear himself to Sturrock by getting sent off for raising an arm at Dave Goodchild, who had prevented him from taking a free-kick quickly. The 37th-minute dismissal failed to derail the home side who were three up by half-time. Seemingly content with their evening's work, a number of feet came off gas pedals and two Whitby goals in three minutes gave Argyle a rude re-awakening. They held out, but it was Whitby who were the recipients of the warmest applause at the final whistle.

Sturrock junior passed his six-week test and was offered a year's contract. He was on the substitutes' bench for a goalless draw at Orient, which saw top spot retained, although Sturrock was less than pleased with the overall performance.

The first week of December saw Argyle's final new signing of the season. Neil Heaney was a talented wide player who had pulled on first-team jerseys for Arsenal and Southampton, among others. Sturrock had signed him for £200,000 whilst at Dundee United, but had now got him for nothing. Heaney was ineligible for the next game, a second round home FA Cup-tie with Bristol Rovers. The main interest focused on the return to Home Park of former hero Ronnie Mauge. Always a popular figure, he still showed that he could put himself about. Argyle twice tested the strength of the woodwork early on, and a Wotton special put them ahead. At half-time, Rovers introduced their secret weapon, former England man Mark Walters. He was now 37 but you wouldn't have guessed it. All the old skill and quite a bit of his pace was still there and his presence turned the tide. His goal on the hour saw another replay pencilled into the diary.

After a 1-0 victory over Darlington, when Sturrock the younger came off the bench to set up Friio's late winner, a busy period ensued, although it could have been busier. A 2-3 defeat at Bristol Rovers in the Cup replay meant missing out on a lucrative trip to Premiership Derby.

The unbeaten league run had stretched to nineteen games and had to end sometime. An uncharacteristically poor defensive performance brought defeat on a snow-covered pitch at Scunthorpe, where Argyle were sunk by two goals from Lee Hodges. No, not Argyle's version, but his wee namesake who had also had a loan spell at Home Park. Confused?

The Boxing Day visit of Torquay had extra significance. Over many weeks, Home Park had gone through a transformation as remarkable as Argyle's form. The stadium wasn't complete, but for this match both ends were open and over 13,000 poured in. The Gulls seemed equally inspired by the occasion and looked, by far, the most impressive visitors so far. Argyle went two up, but Brian McGlinchey turned an own-goal past Larrieu and then conceded a last-minute penalty which no one argued about. Thoughts were also with Evans, on compassionate leave after his wife had been involved in a serious car accident.

In the context of the season overall, the past few weeks constituted a loss of form but pole position had been retained. A single goal was enough to see off Rushden, and more pleasingly the performance was back to normal. With the matches at Swansea and Rochdale called off due to frozen pitches, a full scale 'Blues' versus 'Greens' practice match was arranged, which remarkably attracted around 1,000 fans through the turnstiles, boosting the coffers of the club's Youth Development Trust. The match saw Larrieu's understudy, Luke McCormick, suffer a torn thigh muscle, which necessitated a search for a replacement keeper. In came West Brom's third choice, Chris Adamson, as an on-loan bench-warmer.

Early-season favourites Hull came to Home Park with that tag firmly removed. Failure to win in the last five games had seen them drop to sixth. Only a series of impressive stops from Paul Musslewhite saved them from further embarrassment after Stonebridge's goal.

It was déjà vu at Shrewsbury. Cast your minds back to the opening game of the season. The Shrews have a man sent off in the first half and go on to take all three points. Well, it happened again. Down to ten men after just sixteen minutes and a goal down, the home side came back with three goals. What's more, Sturrock was taken ill with a virus and spent most of the second half in the dressing room. He was driven home in the chairman's car to avoid contaminating the rest of the squad.

There was to be no Sunday lie-in for anyone else. After the Gay Meadow effort, they probably would have been called in for extra training anyway but there was a midweek game to prepare for. Sturrock was still laid low for the visit of Scunthorpe. So, too, was his son and Larrieu. The latter was still named as a substitute, but spent the whole game in solitary confinement in physio Paul Maxwell's medical room. That meant an unexpected appearance for Adamson, who through no fault of his own found himself retrieving the ball from the back of his net after only thirteen minutes. Three minutes later, McGlinchey hobbled off with what was subsequently found to be a broken ankle. He was out for the season. Argyle were grateful for Wotton's penalty just before half-time, and Keith added to his growing reputation with the winner.

The remaining 'new' side of the ground was opened for the visit of Oxford, raising the official capacity of the stadium to around 20,000. A highly entertaining game followed and there was added cheer when it was announced that Darlington had beaten Luton. Argyle were now seven points clear. With a trip to Luton next on the agenda, the two results were significant. Without trying to be negative, a loss at Kenilworth Road would not be so disastrous.

There was also an important item on the directors' agenda. The consortium finally relieved McCauley of his financial commitments to the club and the controversial former chairman resigned as a director.

The Luton game was pretty much one-way traffic in favour of the Hatters, although perhaps not quite the 'massacre' that Kinnear described. Joe Soap hit the bar with a header, but two late goals revived Luton hopes that they could still catch the leaders.

After the previous invincible away form, this was the fourth defeat on the trot on Argyle's travels. It prompted an amicable meeting between players and management, from which a number of ideas over training, travel and the such-like emerged. What did become clear was that the players felt totally comfortable playing with a lone striker in away games. It was a formation which Sturrock had begun to shy away from. The rearranged game at Swansea saw the away form restored, with full debutant Heaney setting up another full debutant, Sturrock, for the only goal.

Plymouth's paying public now sensed that something special was on the horizon. Over 14,000 arrived for the encounter with promotion-chasing Mansfield, prompting a fifteen-minute delay to the kick-off. The first 45 minutes were tedious. The Stags were also a free-scoring side, but showed little attacking inclination. With the minutes ticking away, Beswetherick, looking more like the 'Bezzie' of old, won a corner after a surging run. Wotton's inswinger was met by Friio. It was enough. Luton blew it at Rochdale. Ten points clear. Surely that was enough.

The forgotten man of Home Park, Steve Guinan, finally had his contract paid up and was free to search for a game elsewhere. One team who could have done with him, or anyone else for that matter, were Argyle's next opponents, Halifax, a full 42 points behind the Greens and rock bottom. It looked an obvious victory but, it's a funny old game as someone once said. Two first-half goals were sufficient to ensure everyone slept easily on the trip home, particularly as Luton had blown it again by losing to a last-minute goal at home to Scunthorpe.

The re-arranged match at Rochdale had to be re-arranged again, with the Spotland pitch waterlogged. It was the fifth time in two seasons that this particular fixture had been called off. Few who attended the next game, at home to Kidderminster, will forget the afternoon. Not for the standard of play, you understand, but that the game finished at about 6.15pm. Not bad for a 3pm kick-off. At around 2.30 a power failure caused chaos. The main problem was that the electronic turnstiles in the new part of the ground could not operate. So, those who were in couldn't get out, and those who were out couldn't get in. The former were better off. At least they had a prolonged warm up to watch and could wave sympathetically at those outside during a heavy shower. The match finally kicked off at 4.30. A disjointed first-half performance saw the leaders go in at half-time one down, but two goals from the central defenders saved the day.

Perhaps minds were on the Tuesday night derby with Exeter. The Grecians had shown some decent form under new boss John Cornforth and still harboured play-off ambitions, but on the night they were totally outclassed. It was 2-0 at half-time, although the biggest cheer was reserved for a streaker of the male variety who, on a bitterly cold night, was clearly not too bothered by personal appearance. A stunning thirty-yard strike from Keith with fifteen minutes left finished the game as a contest, but gave City the excuse to introduce twice ex-Pilgrim Sean McCarthy. Within seven minutes, the burly striker was back down the tunnel, having elbowed an already battle-scarred Coughlan in front of the referee.

On the eve of the trip to Macclesfield, Sturrock was awarded his third manager of the month award of the season. At Moss Rose, he was again forced to read the riot act at half-time, after a less than inspiring first 45 minutes. Coughlan, more a Joe Frazier than a Joe Soap after his Exeter battering, headed Argyle into the lead in his bid to be the unlikeliest top scorer in the club's history, but one-time Sturrock target Chris Priest sneaked a last-minute equaliser. With Luton winning, the lead was now cut to eight points.

The next four games were against sides in the bottom half of the table. First up were York, but Argyle had to rely on a Graham Potter own-goal to reap the points. The biggest cheer of the evening was reserved for Craig Taylor, who was brought on as a sub almost twelve months after breaking his ankle. The normally mild-mannered Worrell was the unlikely recipient of a red card. Having already been booked for encroachment, he petulantly threw the ball away in disgust and was off. The glare from Sturrock as his full-back went down the tunnel did not suggest Worrell would be receiving a consoling pat on the back after the game.

With the players and most of the travelling fans already having arrived at Darlington, the game was called off only two hours before kick-off, when heavy rain and then snow put paid to any possibility of football on the Feethams ground. The postponement allowed Luton to move within two points. The Hatters had played two games more, but were currently winning and scoring with abandon.

A week later, the unbeaten home run was stretched to twenty games, as Orient were despatched by a performance described by Sturrock as the worst at home of the season. The high point was a memorable double save by Larrieu, that had O's striker Steve Watts shaking his head in disbelief. A single goal victory at Lincoln the following Saturday all but confirmed promotion. In any other season, the championship would have been wrapped up as well, but the spectre of Luton still loomed large as Kinnear's men kept on winning.

Sturrock had carefully avoided the 'p' word so far, but the fact that he took the whole first-team squad to the re-arranged match at Rochdale suggested that even he thought Argyle were now over the line. Unusually for Spotland, it was a dry and sunny evening. The large travelling contingent of the Green Army had to endure seeing their heroes on the back foot for most of the first hour. Two saves from Larrieu had the numerous big club scouts scribbling notes, but he could not prevent a thirty-yard dipper from veteran Paul Simpson flying past him. Sensing an anticlimax, Sturrock threw on three substitutes, and within two minutes Keith had equalised. Two more in the final ten minutes ensured promotion and, of course, the appropriate celebrations on and off the pitch. Never was a late night coach journey home from Rochdale so enjoyable.

But the job wasn't finished. Everyone wanted the championship, and a home game against Bristol Rovers seemed a safe bet for another three points. Keith, going through a hot spell, scored in the first minute but Rovers, to their credit, did not capitulate despite having debutant Wayne Carlisle sent off. Another 89 minutes followed without further score and the final whistle saw the players indulge in a lap of honour. Meanwhile, Luton won again to seal their own promotion.

The players would have welcomed a break but there was to be none. The fixtures had played a cruel April Fool's trick and dictated a trip to Hartlepool just two days later. Sturrock's fear that fatigue could be his side's most difficult opponent seemed well founded, as his leg-weary troops lost to a late goal. Luton won again, scoring an impressive five against third-placed Mansfield.

To aid recovery, Sturrock gave his players the next three days off, before preparing for battle at home to Southend. It didn't work. Another lacklustre performance, resulting in a scoreless draw, combined with Luton's 4-0 drubbing of Hull, saw the Pilgrims overtaken by the Hatters.

The momentum had suddenly changed in favour of Joe Kinnear's men. Both sides had racked up a mighty 93 points, but Luton's terrific form meant they had not only caught the Greens but effectively gained a one-point advantage through their superior goal-difference. Perhaps crucially, Argyle had played a game less.

If asked to select their least favourable away trip, Sturrock's battle-weary army would have placed Carlisle near the top of the list, but that was the next stop. The Green Army was boosted in numbers by a contingent of kilt-clad Dundee United fans. They made the journey to Brunton Park to pay homage to Sturrock, who enjoyed god-like status at Tannadice to an even greater extent than at Home Park. Sturrock, fittingly, chose the game to reveal next season's away strip – tangerine shirts, of course. There was perhaps a stuttering uncertainty in the familiar 'Come on you Greens' chant, but the new kit seemed to receive favourable reviews.

Now desperate for the title, Sturrock fielded a more attacking formation at Carlisle. It soon paid off, with Keith continuing his impressive end of season form with a superb volley. A trademark Wotton free-kick from thirty yards sealed it. What was more remarkable was the result from Kenilworth Road, where Macclesfield had derailed Luton with a goalless draw. It meant Argyle needed two points to clinch the championship.

With the re-arranged game at Darlington, Argyle unsurprisingly stayed 'up north'. If the fans were filled with tension it didn't filter through to the players. Three up in 28 minutes was a dream start. That man Keith was on target twice. Ian Clark's penalty increased the pulse rates again, but Bent's second-half goal all but killed the game. The final whistle signalled Argyle's first championship since 1959, when legendary names such as Wilf Carter, Jimmy Gauld and Johnny Williams were Argyle's heroes. On a Monday evening in Darlington, new legends were created.

Home Park was set for its biggest ever party. The floor loading of the new stadium was tested to its limits for the final game against Cheltenham, who needed a point themselves to gain the final promotion spot and were determined to play the role of party-poopers. They didn't get the chance. A thoroughly professional Argyle performance condemned them to the play-offs, which they surmounted to gain promotion.

Then came the main event of the day as each player was introduced to the crowd. Finally, *the* moment, when skipper Wotton lifted some silver-ware for the first time in 43 years. There were all sorts of records, 102 points, 27 clean sheets. The list went on. Who would have thought it after the first two home games of the season had ended in defeat?

There were individual accolades as well. Coughlan was rightly voted as the club's player of the year. A colossus in defence, he had also finished as top scorer with eleven. Not bad for someone whose pre-Pilgrim days had seen him find the net only twice before.

Four players were voted by their fellow professionals into the PFA divisional team of the year – Larrieu, now talked of in the £1 million class, his fellow Frenchman Friio, Coughlan, of course, and captain Wotton. A key to the season had been the consistency of the last two. Both had been ever present. Was there ever a previous example of a centre-back pairing going through a season without injury or, more remarkably, suspension?

Of course, Sturrock was manager of the season. He had built a side from almost nothing. Astute signings, master tactician, great motivator. He seemed to have it all. The five-year plan was retrieved from the waste bin.

# SIXTEEN

# 2003-04 (Promoted to Championship)

The first season back in Division Two had seen a highly respectable eighth-place finish. A keen start saw the Pilgrims into the top two by the end of August, but by Christmas only a further three wins had been forthcoming. The side was never able to put together a consistent run of results, particularly in the latter third of the season, when a winning burst would have made the play-offs a genuine possibility. All was eventually revealed when manager Paul Sturrock, canny as ever, made the frank admission that he had chopped and changed in the closing weeks, not only to experiment with fringe players, but also in the belief that the team was not quite ready for another promotion.

Chairman Paul Stapleton pronounced his objective for 2003-04 to be 'to finish higher than last year'. Sturrock, never one to make rash predictions, kept his thoughts private, but one sensed a quiet confidence, partly due to his relative inactivity during the usual close-season transfer mayhem. Only two new faces arrived. Left-sider Tony Capaldi, who had impressed in the final game of the previous season, was secured on a free transfer from Birmingham, along with his Blues teammate and fellow 'leftie' Peter Gilbert, who arrived initially on a three-month loan deal.

The aforementioned fringe players presumably did not shine sufficiently brightly and went off to pastures new. With only 21 players realistically in contention for first-team places, the squad looked short on numbers but Sturrock placed greater trust in quality than quantity.

Instead of pre-seasoning in Scotland, the squad went to the Austrian resort of Obertraun, where the beauty of the surrounding scenery was matched by the quality of the facilities. A goodly number of supporters went along and mingled with the players. Matches were arranged against foreign opposition, although the term 'friendly' could not be applied to the confrontation with German Second Division side SV Wacker Burghausen. In a tetchy affair, both sides made challenges and young defender Paul Connolly was sent off shortly after half-time. Results abroad were disappointing but, on home soil, draws against Charlton and West Brom were more encouraging.

A sweltering August afternoon in Devon saw the league campaign start against relegated Grimsby, who many fancied to be promotion contenders. A 2-2 draw was reasonable enough. Days later came the now-traditional first round exit from the League Cup, now sponsored by Carling. The draw had been ungenerous, giving the Pilgrims a mind-numbing midweek trip to Colchester.

Back in the league, an uncharacteristic error by Lee Hodges handed Rushden & Diamonds all three points as the Argyle team bus racked up a few hundred more miles. A week later, the first win was achieved against an unimpressive Stockport. A draw at Chesterfield was followed by a further share of the spoils at home to Brighton. That game saw the league introduction of the aforementioned Connolly. He was quickly on target, but sadly it was for the Gulls, as his bizarre long-range own-goal helped the visitors to a 3-1 lead with ten minutes remaining. Argyle's comeback to 3-3 gave the first indications of the fighting spirit that would be manifested over the coming months, but the defence – solid as Dartmoor granite over the past two years – was creaking. The team was languishing in fifteenth place.

A first away victory, at Brentford, was tempered by goalkeeper Romain Larrieu sustaining a serious knee injury. For several days it was kept secret. Fans arriving for the home game against Luton were surprised that the familiar figure of the tall Frenchman was not in the team. Larrieu had, in fact, completed the game at Griffin Park, and Argyle had closed ranks to leave the Hatters as much in the dark as everyone else. But word spread quickly that the injury was so serous it might mean the end of the Frenchman's season. Indeed, much of Sturrock's week had been taken up vainly trying to sign a replacement.

Understudy Luke McCormick was drafted in and performed admirably in a 2-1 win over Luton, thanks to two late goals, but doom and gloom was settling in some supporters' minds. The team were not playing particularly well and the small squad had suddenly lost one of its main cogs. A new goalkeeper was a must but Sturrock, never one to panic, was in no rush.

Late goals were becoming a speciality, and another from Capaldi clinched a midweek draw at Peterborough. Sturrock seemed more concerned about his team's form than the so-called goalkeeper crisis, particularly as McCormick was faring better than even he dared hope. Congo international defender Eugene Kangualungu arrived on a three-month deal. He was not a goalkeeper, but a midfielder.

Tactically, Sturrock had employed a twin strike-force, but the trip to Peterborough saw him revert to using warhorse Mickey Evans as the lone striker, a ploy he had employed successfully on a number of away games over the past two seasons. Perhaps Sturrock was unimpressed, because Evans was dropped from the next match, at Wrexham, which also ended 2-2. A 2-0 home win over Barnsley eased Argyle into the top five, setting the scene for the 'derby' match with Bristol City. The biggest crowd to date, almost 14,000, converged on Home Park for the Tuesday night clash, but City had done their homework. Argyle's 'up and at 'em' style was stifled and one of Bristol's few attacks saw Lee Peacock evade the attentions of Peter Gilbert to score the only goal. It was the last thing the young defender needed. He had been thrust into regular league action for the first time in his fledgling career, and his inexperience had been cruelly exposed. When later substituted, he was the target of some verbals from the mindless minority, an act which understandably angered Sturrock.

A sleep-inducing goalless draw at Wycombe gave little indication of what would transpire over the next few weeks. Tranmere were the next to visit. Rovers were struggling and seemed likely to present themselves as lambs to the slaughter. No one, however, expected them to be crushed so emphatically. Bereft of a manager, and seemingly any notion of how the game should be played, they allowed Argyle to score six. The return of midfield maestro David Friio seemed to inspire the Pilgrims. The tousle-haired Frenchman seemed refreshed by an enforced four-match absence through injury and produced the sort of display which everyone knew he was capable of, but which had rarely been seen this season. Sturrock had tinkered with his line up again, employing striker Ian Stonebridge in a wide left role. The youngster gave the impression he had played there all his life, which he hadn't, and linked well with Gilbert. A trademark piledriver from skipper Paul Wotton was the most memorable of the six goals but no one received heartier congratulations than the previously vilified Gilbert, who finished off a slick move to notch his first senior goal.

That rout sparked a sequence that would capture the attentions of supporters nationwide. Bristol City made a quick return, this time to begin the defence of the LDV Vans Trophy. Cup holders or not, fewer than 5,000 turned out to see two virtually full-strength sides in action. Argyle fired another four goals as City capitulated. Flame-haired striker Nathan Lowndes took the eye by scoring twice and Gilbert once.

Ten goals in two games. A trip to Port Vale seemed a more daunting prospect. They had been expected to be divisional whipping boys but had surprised everyone by maintaining a top-five position. Yet four Argyle goals in twelve minutes either side of half-time had the 'Green Army' in raptures. Well, some of them anyway. Others were still stranded on coaches with little to do other than to admire the beauty of the M6. They eventually made it in time to see Friio score one of the goals of the season. The game ended on a sour note. Pilgrims substitute Jason Bent was allegedly the victim of racial abuse from the home side's Andreas Lipa. The incident was bad enough in itself, but was made worse by the the fact that it took place on Vale's anti-racism action day. Lipa later sent a letter of apology to Bent who, to his credit, did not take the matter further.

The midweek matches were coming thick and fast. Next up was a trip to Sheffield Wednesday. In days gone by, a visit to Hillsborough was as big as they came, but the Owls, having just been relegated, were now struggling to adjust to Second Division football and had shown abysmal form at home. Over 20,000 still poured through the turnstiles but they only served to motivate the Pilgrims, who cruised to a 3-1 win – two more goals from Friio. The three points took Argyle to the top.

Knowing that his side would face the new leaders, Blackpool manager Steve McMahon played a few mind games ahead of the Tangerines' visit to Home Park, boasting that his team were better, man for man, than Sturrock's. Come 3pm, however, his team-selection did little to back up his claims. He left top-scorer Scott Taylor on the bench with the obvious intention of shutting up shop. McMahon might have succeeded, but for a strike from Marino Keith which sent Argyle three points clear at the top, although the scoreline did flatter Blackpool.

Argyle's winning ways made Sturrock a sure bet for October's Manager of the Month. Friio was named Second Division player of the month, and the team's LDV Vans victory over Bristol City won them the sponsors' Performance of Round One award.

November arrived with a visit from feisty Oldham. Ian Dowie's side had shown mixed form but were clearly fired up for this one. Another long-range Wotton effort cancelled out the visitors' early goal but the game exploded shortly before half-time. Friio, clearly earmarked as the man to stop, was the subject of a bad tackle from veteran John Sheridan. Friio retaliated with raised hands and both were sent packing by referee Warren. As Friio disconsolately made his way down the tunnel, his assailant gave chase, clearly intent on continuing the feud. Stewards and the fourth official intervened, preventing further trouble. Even though the Latics were reduced to nine men in the second half, they held out for a 2-2 draw which, on reflection, they probably deserved. Argyle immediately signalled their intention to appeal against Friio's red card, although the decision was later upheld.

With a promotion push now a probability, Sturrock finally decided that some goalkeeping cover was required. Not that the chosen man would see immediate first-team action, as McCormick seemed to improve with every game. In came Finnish international Jani Viander on a one-month contract. Heading out of the club was diminutive winger David Beresford, who had rarely been given a look-in. Beresford was one of the quickest players seen at Home Park for many a year, but even in reserve-team football he had only occasionally suggested there were other facets to his game. He joined Tranmere, perhaps remembering their inept performance at Home Park earlier in the season, which suggested he would walk unopposed into the side.

Thoughts now turned to cup action. Struggling Wycombe came to Home Park in the LDV and took an early two-goal lead through the wonderfully named Jermaine McSporran. Argyle fought back and extra-time failed to produce a clear winner. Wanderers' went through 4-2 on penalties, not that anyone would lose too much sleep over the result.

The FA Cup had given the Greens a tricky tie at Northampton, but the swashbuckling manner in which opponents were now being cast aside suggested that the Cobblers would be no real match. This was the Cup, however, and the Third Division side raised their game. Former Pilgrim Chris Hargreaves found the net and a further, late goal saw the home side notch up a mini giant-killing. A home draw with Manchester United in the next round was ample reward.

Clearly, the league had been Argyle's main priority, and now it was the only one. Further squad-building seemed on the cards as Sturrock declared an interest in Torquay's talented striker David Graham. The Scots' wages were apparently burning a hole in the Plainmoor pocket, a rumour seemingly justified when the transfer fell through on the grounds that Graham's wages would have breached Sturrock's strict salary cap. Reading's striker Nathan Tyson was rumoured to be another target.

A trip to Loftus Road beckoned as league action was resumed. QPR were riding high and looked to be among Argyle's main rivals for a promotion slot. They were also virtually unbeatable at home. Aware of Rangers' attacking threat, and minus the suspended Friio, Sturrock juggled his formation but to little effect. One of the worst performances of the season ended in a 0-3 defeat, toppling Argyle from first to third.

Successive 2-0 wins over Hartlepool at home and at Colchester got things back on track and saw second place regained. Viander had been released. Unable to dislodge McCormick, he had little opportunity to impress. The home win over Hartlepool had seen Sturrock freshen his side with a number of changes. Connolly was given another chance, replacing David Worrell at right-back. Bent was injured in a midweek outing for Canada, and Evans suspended. Perhaps most surprising was the omission of captain and dead-ball specialist Wotton. He was replaced by Hasney Aljofree, who had looked comfortable in a central-defensive position but was becoming increasingly frustrated with his lack of opportunity. Wotton was back in the side at Colchester, but in midfield, covering for the injured Steve Adams. Sturrock's message was clear. Being top of the division did not give reason for complacency and no one was ever likely to be certain of their place.

December began with the club parting company with chief executive John McNulty. He had been absent through illness and the directors felt the club could do without his position. McNulty had been instrumental in overseeing the rebuilding of the stadium and was distraught at the manner of his departure. He was later successful at an industrial tribunal, which ruled that he had been unfairly dismissed.

With Sturrock anxious to maintain the on-field momentum, a friendly with Torquay was arranged as both sides were out of the FA Cup. Several fringe players were given an opportunity in a keenly contested match. The

Gulls came out on top by a single goal scored, not surprisingly, by the recently targeted Graham.

Canadian international Lars Hirschfeld, third-choice goalkeeper at Tottenham, impressed sufficiently in an Argyle reserve game to be offered a loan deal. But no sooner did he realise he would not be first choice than he was on his way back to London.

A trip to Swindon proved the pivotal point of the season. Friio was available after suspension but was kept on the bench. Andy King's side were similar in style to Argyle. Big and strong, their football was rarely pretty to watch, but in Sam Parkin and Tommy Mooney they possessed probably the most effective front pair in the division. Nevertheless, Argyle seemed to be cruising when David Norris put them 2-0 up with only fifteen minutes remaining. But Swindon weren't finished and looked set for a share of the spoils with goals in the eightieth and ninetieth minutes. This was the moment where the Pilgrims' spirit and desire shone through. Not content with a point, they launched one final attack and Keith pounced to grab a vital win.

A 3-0 win over struggling Notts County ensured that the Greens went into Christmas in pole position, but there was to be another present for the supporters. On 23rd December, a midday press conference announced an exciting new signing. Even the name of Paul Gascoigne was bandied around. But the 'new' face turned out to belong to Paul Sturrock, who had agreed to extend his contract to 2008. The manner in which the announcement was made only served to illustrate the deep satisfaction of the directors in securing his services for a longer period. The fans were equally content in the knowledge that their man was now seemingly off-limits as far as being head-hunted by bigger clubs.

Frenchman Abdallah Bah was the next nomadic goalkeeper to arrive and depart. Boxing Day brought a relatively short trip along the south coast to Bournemouth. A gale-force wind proved to be the decisive element. Paul Wotton's opener was the 5,000th league goal scored by Argyle and there could have been few better. Cherries' keeper Neil Moss had hurriedly cleared the ball straight to the Argyle skipper. Never one to shy away from chancing his aim, Wotton belted the ball back past the startled custodian from all of forty yards.

If Wotton's was one of the best of the 5,000, number 5,001 was one of the strangest. Another wind-assisted long-range effort from David Norris struck the crossbar, ballooned twenty yards into the air, spun back to the ground and into the net behind the hapless Moss. Stubborn second-half defending by Argyle meant another three points were in the bag.

2004 began with yet more plaudits. Sturrock was again the choice of Second Division manager of the month. He also won the Tissot Managers Performance League, which rewards the most successful manager over a three-month period. Sturrock travelled to Stamford Bridge to receive his trophy from the previous holder, Claudio Ranieri of Chelsea.

The first game of the new year saw Chesterfield as the visitors. Roy McFarland's side had struggled to claw themselves away from the relegation dogfight, and it was soon clear to see why. From Argyle's first attack, Lee Hodges scored. Capaldi quickly added another, as did Lowndes, then Friio, then Lowndes again. After seventeen minutes it was 5-0. It was the most remarkable start to a game that anyone present had probably ever witnessed. Every time the ball was pumped into the Spireites' penalty area, a green shirt was on the end of it. Friio added a sixth before half-time and the majority of half-time discussions centred around the threat to Argyle's record score. McFarland's team-talk was presumably on different lines, but whatever he did say seemed to sink in, as his side tightened up in the second half. There was only one more goal, a minute from time, which saw Friio complete his hat-trick to seal the Pilgrims' biggest home victory since 1936.

After such a run of results, it was hardly a surprise that Sturrock saw little need to bolster his squad. Indeed, it merely proved that certain players were unlikely to feature. The tenacious Brian McGlinchey, recently returned from a three-month loan spell at Torquay, now joined the ever-increasing throng of ex-Pilgrims at Plainmoor on a permanent basis. Also leaving was Kangualungu who, with his cheery smile and 'thumbs up' gestures, had developed something of a cult following with the diehards who attended the reserve-team games.

Over 700 of the 'Green Army' plucked up the courage to undertake a day trip to Grimsby. After the 7-0 thrashing of Chesterfield, expectations were high but a dreary game ended goalless.

The visit of Rushden & Diamonds saw an added attraction for the crowd. Argyle's legendary former strike-force, Billy Rafferty and Paul Mariner, were reunited for the first time in several years. Besieged by autograph hunters from the moment they entered Home Park, the pair were greeted with rapturous applause as they were introduced to the 13,000 crowd. A stagnant 45 minutes ensued, with Aljofree, in the absence of substitute Wotton, missing from the spot. During the interval the former heroes came back out and, for old times' sake, belted a few balls into the net at the Devonport End. Despite the fact that many in the crowd weren't even old enough to have seen them play, they were acknowledged with a standing ovation. The refrain of 'Oh Billy, Billy' and 'There's only one Paul Mariner' echoed around the stadium for the first time in almost thirty years. It was a hair-bristling moment.

The 'old boys' were still signing autographs as the second half got under way. Within two minutes, Graham Coughlan scored. This seemed to settle Argyle and the Diamonds began to lose their sparkle. Stonebridge scored a second and within a minute the visitors were down to ten men. Wotton came on for the last ten minutes and left his mark with a 35-yard free-kick that was ferocious even by Wottonian standards.

An industrious performance at Stockport saw another 2-0 victory and created a new club record of seven consecutive clean sheets. The early season defensive fragility was a distant memory, with much of the credit going to defensive coach John Blackley. As an added bonus, closest rivals QPR were surprisingly defeated at Bournemouth, allowing the Pilgrims to open up a five-point gap at the top.

Brighton versus Argyle was the choice of Sky TV for live coverage, which meant a later Saturday kick-off than usual. It appeared to be a good choice. The Seagulls were an attractive side that had hovered around the play-off zone for much of the season and now lived up to their billing. Argyle sadly didn't. Brighton scored early on, with McCormick conceding his first goal for 642 minutes. The diminutive but tricky Leon Knight scored a second before half-time. For once, Sturrock's team-talk failed to light the fuse. A late goal by Lowndes was hardly deserved, all of which meant that Argyle had reserved their worst performance of the season for a large TV audience.

One point from the next two games constituted, in the context of the season to date, a mini-crisis. At home to Bournemouth, it was one of those days as the woodwork was struck four times and Wotton missed a penalty. Next up came a midweek trip to Tranmere. Rovers, under the guidance of new manager Brian Little, had been transformed from the clueless rag-bag that had turned over so easily at Home Park some months back. They had now reached the FA Cup quarter-finals and were climbing the league. With a sickly Sturrock tucked up in bed at home, proceedings started in a sombre mood. A minute's silence was observed for Steve Cooper, who had served both clubs but had died suddenly at the weekend at the young age of 39. Once play began, uncharacteristic defensive errors contributed to a 0-3 defeat. Even worse, there was a new enemy in the camp. Bristol City notched up their tenth straight win to take over top spot.

It didn't take long for a few 'fair weather' supporters to stay away. The visit of Port Vale saw the attendance dip by 2,000. Vale's confidence had not been shaken by their crushing home defeat by Argyle earlier in the season and they had maintained their push for a play-off slot. The prolific Steve McPhee gave them a second-half lead, but substitutions proved crucial. Firstly Martin Phillips came on to equalise with his first goal for more than a year. A draw seemed probable, but in the fifth minute of injury-time another replacement, Ian Stonebridge, sneaked a winner. Bristol had won again, but Argyle's season was back on track. City's run couldn't last for ever, and they went down at Sheffield Wednesday. This meant that supersub Stoney's solitary goal at Blackpool saw Argyle regain top spot.

More than 17,000 packed into Home Park for the Tuesday night visit of Sheffield Wednesday, but Chris Turner's injury-ravaged side were no match for Argyle. Two-nil was fast becoming a favourite scoreline, not that anyone was complaining.

Top of the league, scoring goals a-plenty, and not letting them in. Life seemed rosy in the Pilgrim garden, but the following day news emerged that would shake Home Park to the core. Manager Sturrock had been given permission to 'talk' to Southampton. Despite the razzmatazz over the signing of his extended contract a few weeks earlier, it emerged that it contained a clause allowing him to discuss terms with a Premiership club should he wish to do so. Former Saints manager Glenn Hoddle had bowed to public pressure and decided not to seek his old job back. It was this that prompted the approach to Sturrock. No one was immediately confirming that he was on his way, but increasingly the signs were that a deal had been done. By Thursday, everything had been confirmed. Sturrock emerged at a Saints press conference brandishing a red and white scarf.

Emotions were mixed among the Argyle faithful, to say the least. Some felt hoodwinked by the board, given the fuss made over the extended contract. There was anger against Southampton. Money had spoken the loudest and the timing of the departure couldn't have been worse. There was also a sense of panic. Would this derail the season at such a critical time? But no one was blaming Sturrock himself. He was held in high esteem, and who could blame him for making himself a millionaire with one stroke of the pen. Argyle naturally, negotiated a compensation package, the details of which were kept secret. Figures from £250,000 to £500,000 were mentioned, but whatever it was could not replace the contribution the former Scottish international had made to the club, having dragged it up from the lower reaches of the Third Division.

Not surprisingly, Sturrock's trusty sidekick, Kevin Summerfield – together with Blackley – were placed in charge. Questions were asked about whether they would follow Sturrock to St Mary's, although Sturrock confirmed that, should any approach be made, it would be after the end of the season.

Various names were bandied about as to who the new man in charge would be. Local boy Trevor Francis was one, but Peter Reid, John Gregory and Frenchman Alain Perrin were all allegedly 'favourites' for the job at one point or another. Each of the above had certain qualities, but none was likely to come cheap.

Despite all these distractions, the team had a job to do. Summerfield's first game in charge during this, his second stint as 'caretaker', saw Notts County invaded by more than 2,000 of the Green Army, a fantastic show of support for the team. They didn't see any goals, but McCormick added to his burgeoning reputation with a penalty save.

Swindon at home was next up. Andy King's side had been going well and now proved redoubtable opponents. Argyle again had Evans, oh, and Evans, to thank for a hard-earned victory. Swindon's version, Rhys Evans, fielded a back-pass, then allowed Argyle's Mickey to snatch the ball from him. Quickly taking the indirect free-kick, Mickey guided the ball towards the corner of the net. Had it remained untouched it would have resulted in a goal-kick, but Rhys instinctively stuck out a hand and got a touch as it sped past him. The 'goal' counted, Swindon lost their cool, and then had Andy Gurney sent off.

Three days later, Peterborough came to visit. There was to be no familiar celebratory touchline dash from ebullient Posh boss Barry Fry, as '2-0 to Argyle' cropped up again. The team had bagged seven points from three games since Paul Sturrock's departure and had a seven-point lead at the top. No problem?

A 1-1 draw at Luton felt like a victory, as it was earned by another injury-time goal, this time from Steve Adams. Wrexham's visit was preceded by a parade of more than seventy former Argyle greats, all part of the club's centenary celebrations. Former legends were out in force – Tommy Tynan, Billy Rafferty again, Jim Furnell, Gordon Astall, Ernie Machin, Johnny Williams. A real Who's Who of Pilgrim history. But a 'new' star was about to emerge. Marcus Murphy, 89 years old and believed to be the oldest surviving Pilgrim, was delighted to attend.

Your author had the pleasure of organising this event and on more than one occasion enquired whether Marcus was capable of completing a lap of honour around the pitch. 'Well, he's still fairly mobile,' confirmed the delightful Mrs Murphy. It proved to be the understatement of the year. As soon as Marcus was introduced to the crowd he was off and running, and running, and running. He made the whole length of the pitch before being besieged by photographers and autograph-hunters in one corner. Afforded a brief respite, he was then off again, leaving an assortment of overweight cameramen in his wake. The crowd were in raptures and even the current squad broke off from their pre-match warm-up routines to join in the applause. Unfortunately, Marcus's exertions proved to be the high point of the day. Resolute defending secured Wrexham's limited ambition of going home with a point, despite their finishing the game with nine men.

The last day of March saw a small piece of Argyle history made when Tony Capaldi became the first Pilgrim to win full international honours for Northern Ireland. Despite playing in a midfield role all season for Argyle, he was selected at left-back but at least played his part in a rare Irish win over Estonia.

Perhaps feeling that his side had gone off the boil, Summerfield adjusted his formation for the trip to Barnsley. It didn't pay off. A 0-1 defeat suddenly had everyone looking over their shoulders. The two promotion spots were being contested by three teams. QPR had remained invincible at home and Bristol City were looking ominous. Argyle had taken just two points out of nine, reinforcing the view that a new boss was needed quickly. The previously mentioned 'big' names now seemed out of the equation. If speculation was to be believed, the vacancy rested between two candidates, Walsall manager Colin Lee and Hibernian boss Bobby Williamson. The latter came recommended to Argyle by no less an authority than Paul Sturrock.

At least there was ink on some contracts. Gilbert made his move from Birmingham permanent, while Connolly, McCormick, Coughlan and Wotton signed extended deals, although in the light of the Sturrock affair few paid much heed to the power of contracts.

Easter Saturday's 2-1 home win over Wycombe brought some welcome relief, except for Wanderers' fans. The loss all but sealed relegation, although Tony Adams' side was by no means the worst opposition seen at Home Park.

A vital midweek trip to Bristol City ensued. A win for Argyle would all but guarantee promotion, but City were equally desperate for the points to keep them in the race. Summerfield employed Evans as a lone striker, a tactic successfully employed in previous seasons. The outcome was a surge of City pressure which, with five minutes left, paid off with the only goal. The slim line between success and failure was never more evident. Had Argyle held out, Summerfield would have been praised for his tactical nous. As it was, he was criticised in some quarters.

Speculation continued to mount over the identity of the new manager. Colin Lee was given permission by his chairman to speak to Argyle and then duly sacked when he did so! It was little wonder there was sparse sympathy for the Saddlers when they were relegated at the end of the season, after such bizarre treatment of their manager.

The way seemed open for Bobby Williamson, but the team needed to concentrate on a trip to Oldham, whose form had been lifted by the recent arrival of a new manager of their own, Brian Talbot. It was not a good day for Argyle. A 1-4 thrashing was compounded by the seemingly ludicrous dismissal of Wotton. Already booked, he was given permission to take a quick free-kick and then received a second yellow card for doing so. It epitomised one of the worst refereeing performances seen in many a year. Even Talbot was prompted to query the decision. There was not total despondency at the result. Argyle's rivals had also dropped points. A win from the next game would clinch promotion.

That same day, the local press 'leaked' the news that Williamson was the new boss. The board denied everything until the official press conference confirmed what everyone seemed to know. Once again, Argyle had gone north of the border to get their man, a recurring theme throughout the history of the club and one that had usually held them in good stead.

Williamson's pedigree seemed ideal for Argyle. Following a playing career which had included Rangers, West Brom and Rotherham, he had been appointed coach and then manager of another of his former clubs, Kilmarnock. Despite their limited resources, he took 'Killie' into Europe on five occasions and also nurtured some fine young talent. He then took charge at Hibernian, another club not exactly awash with cash, saved them from relegation, and had recently guided them to the Scottish League Cup final, defeating both Rangers and Celtic on the way. The Argyle board were clearly impressed by his knowledge of the game and ability to work on small budgets, qualities also common to Sturrock.

And so, the moment had arrived. QPR saw the first full house for the revamped Home Park. The match had been sold out for weeks and a gloriously sunny day illuminated a sea of green and white. If Williamson had any doubts about his move, they were surely dispelled. The match, unsurprisingly, was a tense affair but with less than ten minutes remaining Evans' bullet header broke the deadlock. Friio added another near the end, and for the second time in three years 'We Are The Champions' blasted from the tannoy. Rangers were gracious in defeat (but their time would come when clinching the second promotion spot as runners up). Everyone else savoured the moment. Friio was in tears. He was not alone.

The triumph captured the public imagination far more than the 2001-02 championship had done. Everyone seemed to be talking about Argyle. All of a sudden, half of the Westcountry had apparently been supporting the Greens all their lives.

Whilst the QPR game was a glorious moment, the following encounter epitomised the spirit within the club. A trip to Hartlepool is never one to savour and the home side were striving for the play-offs. It would have been all too easy for Argyle to ease back on the throttle, but pride and professionalism drove the team to a deserved 3-1 victory.

Home Park was again packed for the final game of the season, against Colchester. The U's had little to play for except perhaps, in a few cases, new contracts. From around noon, there was a cup final atmosphere outside the ground. The tension of the last few months had been lifted and everyone was determined to enjoy the day. The match was preceded by the usual end-of-season presentations, with Mickey Evans deservedly winning the player of the year award. With Evans now into his thirties, many supporters back in August had forecast a bit-part role for him, but a leaner and meaner 'Trigger' had been a revelation. Few defences had managed to subdue him, and he proved to be the fulcrum of Argyle's attacking style. Week after week, opposing managers had expressed their admiration for his valiant contribution to Argyle's cause.

There were, of course, many other successes. McCormick had been outstanding. It was not so long before that he feared being released. Not even a fit Larrieu could displace him. Connolly had displaced the steady Worrell and looked as though he had played league football for years. Gilbert had improved match after match. Coughlan was again a colossus in defence and contributed some vital goals. Yet again his disciplined style had seen him go through a season without suspension, and he was rewarded with the Second Division Player of the Year accolade. Aljofree had looked assured when he finally cemented his place in the side and kept skipper Wotton out. Friio finished as top scorer and few would forget his mid-season golden spell. Norris's non-stop endeavour and quick feet had caused numerous problems for the opposition. Summerfield and Blackley deserve mention for keeping the show on the road after Sturrock's departure. One other factor was barely mentioned – the Home Park pitch. Thanks to stadium manager Colin Wheatcroft and his team, it remained in immaculate condition from August to May.

There was also a downside. Two players, Phillips and Bent, would be released into the uncertain world of the transfer list. Both had been unfortunate with injuries, but it was sad to see two of football's nice guys leaving the club.

That final match against Colchester seemed almost secondary. To their credit, the players maintained their standards and ran out winners by, yes you've guessed it, 2-0. The trophy presentation was made, yet it somehow seemed a trifle flat. It had lacked the dramatic spontaneity of the QPR game, or maybe – following two championships in three seasons – the supporters were becoming a trifle blasé. Fittingly, among all the celebrations, the crowd chanted the name of Paul Sturrock, his immense contribution rightly not forgotten. For Williamson, it was three games, three wins and a championship. What an easy way to make a living.

And so, the Coca-Cola Championship beckons. The club had been at that level before, but this seems different. With some team-strengthening, there is a genuine belief that something special is around the corner. Let the good times roll.

# LEAGUE DIVISION 3 (SOUTH) — Manager: Robert Jack — SEASON 1929-30

| # | | Date | Opponents | Att | F-A | Scorers | 1 | 2 | 3 | 4 | 5 | 6 | 7 | 8 | 9 | 10 | 11 |
|---|---|---|---|---|---|---|---|---|---|---|---|---|---|---|---|---|---|
| 1 | A | 31/8 | Clapton Orient | 18,054 | W 2-0 | Bowden, Black | Craig | Russell | Titmuss | Mackay | Pullen | McKenzie | Matthews | Sloan | Bowden | Leslie | Black |
| 2 | A | 4/9 | Torquay | 8,299 | W 4-3 | Craig, Matthews, Bowden, Leslie | Craig | Bland | Titmuss | Mackay | McKenzie | Hardie | Matthews | Sloan | Bowden | Leslie | Black |
| 3 | H | 7/9 | BRENTFORD | 12,161 | D 1-1 | Bowden | Craig | Russell | Titmuss | Mackay | McKenzie | Hardie | Matthews | Sloan | Bowden | Leslie | Black |
| 4 | H | 11/9 | TORQUAY | 9,827 | W 5-0 | Leslie 2, McKenzie, Sloan, Black | Craig | Bland | Titmuss | Mackay | McKenzie | Hardie | Healy | Sloan | Bowden | Leslie | Black |
| 5 | A | 14/9 | Bristol Rov | 11,787 | W 3-2 | Bowden, Leslie, Black | Craig | Bland | Titmuss | Mackay | McKenzie | Hardie | Healy | Sloan | Bowden | Leslie | Black |
| 6 | H | 21/9 | BRIGHTON | 11,530 | D 1-1 | Vidler | Craig | Bland | Titmuss | Mackay | McKenzie | Hardie | Grozier | Sloan | Vidler | Leslie | Black |
| 7 | A | 25/9 | Watford | 7,015 | W 2-0 | Black 2 | Craig | Bland | Titmuss | McKenzie | Pullen | Hardie | Grozier | Sloan | Vidler | Leslie | Black |
| 8 | A | 28/9 | Swindon | 8,663 | W 2-1 | Grozier, Bowden | Craig | Bland | Titmuss | McKenzie | Pullen | Hardie | Grozier | Sloan | Bowden | Leslie | Vidler |
| 9 | H | 5/10 | GILLINGHAM | 5,777 | W 3-0 | Pullen, Grozier, Bowden | Craig | Bland | Titmuss | McKenzie | Pullen | Hardie | Grozier | Sloan | Bowden | Leslie | Vidler |
| 10 | H | 12/10 | MERTHYR | 12,392 | W 2-1 | Pullen, Black | Craig | Bland | Titmuss | Mackay | Pullen | Hardie | Grozier | Sloan | Bowden | Leslie | Vidler |
| 11 | A | 19/10 | Northampton | 21,102 | D 1-1 | Leslie | Craig | Bland | Titmuss | Mackay | Pullen | Hardie | Matthews | Sloan | Bowden | Leslie | Black |
| 12 | H | 26/10 | EXETER | 15,427 | W 4-1 | Bowden 3, Black | Craig | Bland | Titmuss | Mackay | Pullen | Hardie | Grozier | Sloan | Bowden | Leslie | Black |
| 13 | A | 2/11 | Southend | 10,966 | D 1-1 | Bowden | Craig | Bland | Titmuss | Mackay | Pullen | Hardie | Grozier | Sloan | Bowden | Leslie | Black |
| 14 | H | 9/11 | LUTON | 15,073 | W 6-1 | Vidler 2, Groz', Sloan, Bow', Black | Craig | Bland | Titmuss | Mackay | Pullen | Hardie | Grozier | Sloan | Bowden | Vidler | Black |
| 15 | A | 16/11 | Bournemouth | 13,667 | D 1-1 | Bowden | Craig | Bland | Titmuss | McKenzie | Pullen | Hardie | Grozier | Mackay | Bowden | Vidler | Black |
| 16 | A | 23/11 | WALSALL | 12,543 | D 1-1 | Bowden | Craig | Bland | Titmuss | Mackay | Pullen | McKenzie | Grozier | Richards | Bowden | Vidler | Black |
| 17 | H | 7/12 | FULHAM | 15,653 | W 3-1 | Black 2, Leslie | Craig | Price | Titmuss | Mackay | McKenzie | Bland | Grozier | Vidler | Bowden | Leslie | Black |
| 18 | H | 21/12 | CRYSTAL PALACE | 15,728 | W 6-1 | Grozier 4, Mackay, Vidler | Craig | Price | Titmuss | Bland | McKenzie | Hardie | Grozier | Mackay | Bowden | Vidler | Black |
| 19 | A | 25/12 | Coventry | 26,400 | L 0-1 | | Craig | Price | Titmuss | Bland | McKenzie | Hardie | Grozier | Vidler | Bowden | Leslie | Vidler |
| 20 | H | 26/12 | COVENTRY | 27,975 | W 3-0 | Mackay, Leslie, Black | Craig | Russell | Titmuss | Mackay | McKenzie | Hardie | Grozier | Vidler | Bowden | Leslie | Black |
| 21 | H | 28/12 | CLAPTON ORIENT | 7,001 | W 3-0 | Black 2, Vidler | Craig | Russell | Titmuss | Mackay | McKenzie | Hardie | Healy | Mackay | Vidler | Grozier | Black |
| 22 | A | 4/1 | Brentford | 20,511 | L 0-3 | | Craig | Russell | Titmuss | Bland | McKenzie | Hardie | Grozier | Mackay | Bowden | Leslie | Vidler |
| 23 | H | 18/1 | BRISTOL ROV | 11,610 | W 3-0 | Mackay, Grozier, Leslie | Craig | Bland | Russell | Mackay | McKenzie | Hardie | Grozier | Sloan | Bowden | Leslie | Black |
| 24 | A | 8/2 | Gillingham | 4,905 | D 0-0 | | Craig | Bland | Russell | Mackay | McKenzie | Hardie | Grozier | Sloan | Bowden | Leslie | Black |
| 25 | A | 15/2 | Merthyr | 2,968 | W 3-0 | Bowden 2, Sloan | Craig | Cosgrove | Bland | Mackay | McKenzie | Hardie | Grozier | Sloan | Bowden | Leslie | Black |
| 26 | H | 22/2 | NORTHAMPTON | 15,376 | W 1-0 | Grozier | Craig | Bland | Titmuss | Mackay | McKenzie | Hardie | Grozier | Sloan | Bowden | Leslie | Black |
| 27 | A | 1/3 | Exeter | 17,742 | D 1-1 | Vidler | Craig | Bland | Titmuss | Mackay | McKenzie | Hardie | Grozier | Sloan | Vidler | Leslie | Black |
| 28 | H | 8/3 | SOUTHEND | 13,998 | W 2-1 | Grozier, Black | Craig | Bland | Titmuss | Mackay | McKenzie | Hardie | Grozier | Sloan | Vidler | Leslie | Black |
| 29 | A | 13/3 | QP Rangers | 8,758 | L 2-5 | Grozier, Black | Craig | Bland | Titmuss | Mackay | McKenzie | Hardie | Grozier | Sloan | Bowden | Leslie | Black |
| 30 | A | 15/3 | Luton | 9,051 | W 2-1 | Black, Miller (og) | Cann | Bland | Titmuss | McKenzie | Pullen | Hardie | Grozier | Sloan | Bowden | Leslie | Black |
| 31 | H | 22/3 | BOURNEMOUTH | 14,226 | W 5-0 | Bowden 2, Pullen, Sloan, Vidler | Cann | Bland | Titmuss | McKenzie | Pullen | Hardie | Grozier | Sloan | Bowden | Vidler | Black |
| 32 | H | 26/3 | SWINDON | 14,931 | W 3-1 | Grozier, Bowden, Black | Cann | Bland | Titmuss | McKenzie | Pullen | Hardie | Grozier | Sloan | Bowden | Leslie | Black |
| 33 | A | 29/3 | Walsall | 7,213 | W 1-0 | Vidler | Cann | Bland | Titmuss | McKenzie | Pullen | Hardie | Grozier | Sloan | Vidler | Leslie | Black |
| 34 | A | 2/4 | Brighton | 9,791 | W 4-0 | Vidler 3, Pullen | Cann | Bland | Titmuss | McKenzie | Pullen | Hardie | Grozier | Sloan | Vidler | Leslie | Black |
| 35 | H | 5/4 | QP RANGERS | 18,897 | W 3-1 | Pullen 2, Sloan | Cann | Bland | Titmuss | McKenzie | Pullen | Hardie | Grozier | Sloan | Bowden | Vidler | Black |
| 36 | A | 12/4 | Fulham | 22,994 | W 3-1 | Sloan 2, Mackay | Cann | Bland | Titmuss | McKenzie | Pullen | Hardie | Matthews | Sloan | Bowden | Leslie | Black |
| 37 | H | 18/4 | NEWPORT | 26,409 | W 4-1 | Vidler 4 | Cann | Bland | Titmuss | McKenzie | Pullen | Hardie | Grozier | Sloan | Mackay | Vidler | Black |
| 38 | H | 19/4 | NORWICH | 19,899 | W 2-0 | Black 2 | Cann | Bland | Titmuss | McKenzie | Pullen | Hardie | Matthews | Mackay | Vidler | Grozier | Black |
| 39 | A | 21/4 | Newport | 10,766 | W 2-0 | Black 2 | Cann | Bland | Titmuss | McKenzie | Pullen | Mackay | Grozier | Sloan | Vidler | Leslie | Black |
| 40 | A | 26/4 | Crystal Palace | 18,649 | L 0-3 | | Cann | Cosgrove | Price | McKenzie | Pullen | Bland | Grozier | Sloan | Vidler | Leslie | Black |
| 41 | A | 28/4 | Norwich | 13,736 | W 2-1 | Pullen, Grozier | Cann | Bland | Price | McKenzie | Pullen | Fellowes | Grozier | Sloan | Vidler | Leslie | Black |
| 42 | H | 3/5 | WATFORD | 23,459 | W 2-1 | Sloan, Black | Cann | Bland | Titmuss | McKenzie | Pullen | Fellowes | Grozier | Sloan | Vidler | Leslie | Black |

## FA Cup

| | | Date | Opponent | Att. | Res | Score | Scorers |
|---|---|---|---|---|---|---|---|
| 1 | A | 30/11 | Dulwich H | *11,000* | W | 4-1 | Bowden 2, Black 2 |
| 2 | A | 14/12 | Watford | 9,235 | D | 1-1 | Bland |
| 2R | H | 18/12 | WATFORD | 18,929 | W | 3-1 | Vidler 3 |
| 3 | H | 11/1 | HULL | 28,929 | L | 3-4 | Vidler, Leslie, Black |

| Match | 1 | 2 | 3 | 4 | 5 | 6 | 7 | 8 | 9 | 10 | 11 |
|---|---|---|---|---|---|---|---|---|---|---|---|
| Dulwich H | Craig | Bland | Price | Titmuss | Mackay | McKenzie | Grozier | Sloan | Bowden | Leslie | Black |
| Watford | Craig | Bland | Price | Titmuss | Mackay | McKenzie | Grozier | Matthews | Vidler | Leslie | Black |
| Watford | Craig | Hardie | Price | Titmuss | Bland | McKenzie | Grozier | Mackay | Vidler | Leslie | Black |
| Hull | Craig | Hardie | Bland | Titmuss | Mackay | McKenzie | Grozier | Sloan | Vidler | Leslie | Black |

## League Table

| | | P | Home W | D | L | F | A | Away W | D | L | F | A | Pts |
|---|---|---|---|---|---|---|---|---|---|---|---|---|---|
| 1 | PLYMOUTH | 42 | 18 | 3 | 0 | 63 | 12 | 12 | 5 | 4 | 35 | 26 | 68 |
| 2 | Brentford | 42 | 21 | 0 | 0 | 66 | 12 | 7 | 5 | 9 | 28 | 32 | 61 |
| 3 | QP Rangers | 42 | 13 | 5 | 3 | 46 | 26 | 8 | 4 | 9 | 34 | 42 | 51 |
| 4 | Northampton | 42 | 14 | 6 | 1 | 53 | 20 | 7 | 2 | 12 | 29 | 38 | 50 |
| 5 | Brighton | 42 | 16 | 2 | 3 | 54 | 20 | 5 | 6 | 10 | 33 | 43 | 50 |
| 6 | Coventry | 42 | 14 | 3 | 4 | 54 | 25 | 5 | 6 | 10 | 34 | 48 | 47 |
| 7 | Fulham | 42 | 12 | 6 | 3 | 54 | 33 | 6 | 5 | 10 | 33 | 50 | 47 |
| 8 | Norwich | 42 | 14 | 4 | 3 | 55 | 28 | 4 | 6 | 11 | 33 | 49 | 46 |
| 9 | Crys Palace | 42 | 14 | 5 | 2 | 56 | 26 | 3 | 7 | 11 | 25 | 48 | 46 |
| 10 | Bournemouth | 42 | 11 | 6 | 4 | 47 | 24 | 4 | 7 | 10 | 25 | 37 | 43 |
| 11 | Southend | 42 | 11 | 6 | 4 | 41 | 19 | 4 | 7 | 10 | 28 | 40 | 43 |
| 12 | Clapton 0 | 42 | 10 | 8 | 3 | 38 | 21 | 4 | 5 | 12 | 22 | 41 | 41 |
| 13 | Luton | 42 | 13 | 4 | 4 | 42 | 25 | 2 | 6 | 13 | 17 | 53 | 40 |
| 14 | Swindon | 42 | 10 | 7 | 4 | 42 | 25 | 3 | 5 | 13 | 31 | 58 | 38 |
| 15 | Watford | 42 | 10 | 4 | 7 | 37 | 30 | 4 | 6 | 11 | 23 | 43 | 38 |
| 16 | Exeter | 42 | 10 | 6 | 5 | 45 | 29 | 2 | 5 | 14 | 22 | 44 | 35 |
| 17 | Walsall | 42 | 10 | 4 | 7 | 45 | 24 | 3 | 4 | 14 | 26 | 54 | 34 |
| 18 | Newport | 42 | 9 | 9 | 3 | 48 | 29 | 1 | 5 | 15 | 26 | 56 | 34 |
| 19 | Torquay | 42 | 9 | 6 | 6 | 50 | 38 | 2 | 3 | 16 | 14 | 56 | 31 |
| 20 | Bristol Rov | 42 | 11 | 3 | 7 | 45 | 31 | 1 | 3 | 17 | 22 | 62 | 30 |
| 21 | Gillingham | 42 | 9 | 5 | 7 | 38 | 28 | 1 | 5 | 15 | 13 | 52 | 30 |
| 22 | Merthyr | 42 | 5 | 6 | 10 | 39 | 49 | 2 | 1 | 18 | 21 | 86 | 21 |
| | | 924 | 264 | 108 | 90 | 1058 | 574 | 90 | 108 | 264 | 574 | 1058 | 924 |

## Appearances and Goals

| | Appearances Lge | FAC | Goals Lge | FAC | Tot |
|---|---|---|---|---|---|
| Black, Sammy | 37 | 4 | 21 | 3 | 24 |
| Bland, Harry | 40 | 4 | | 1 | 1 |
| Bowden, Ray | 28 | 1 | 18 | 2 | 20 |
| Cann, Harry | 12 | | | | |
| Cosgrove, Fred | 2 | | | | |
| Craig, Fred | 30 | 4 | 1 | | 1 |
| Fellowes, Bill | 2 | | | | |
| Grozier, Tommy | 35 | 4 | 13 | | 13 |
| Hardie, Alec | 35 | 2 | | | |
| Healy, Jimmy | 3 | | | | |
| Leslie, Jack | 32 | 4 | 8 | 1 | 9 |
| Mackay, Norman | 30 | 4 | 4 | | 4 |
| Matthews, Alf | 6 | 1 | 1 | | 1 |
| McKenzie, Fred | 37 | 4 | 1 | | 1 |
| Price, Walter | 5 | 3 | | | |
| Pullen, Jack | 22 | | 7 | | 7 |
| Richards, Percy | 1 | | | | |
| Russell, Moses | 7 | | | | |
| Sloan, Frank | 33 | 2 | 8 | | 8 |
| Titmuss, Fred | 37 | 4 | | | |
| Vidler, Jack | 28 | 3 | 15 | 4 | 19 |
| (own-goals) | | | 1 | | 1 |
| 21 players used | 462 | 44 | 98 | 11 | 109 |

# LEAGUE DIVISION 2

## Manager: Jimmy Rae

### SEASON 1949-50

| # | H/A | Date | Opponents | Att | F-A | Scorers | 1 | 2 | 3 | 4 | 5 | 6 | 7 | 8 | 9 | 10 | 11 |
|---|-----|------|-----------|-----|-----|---------|---|---|---|---|---|---|---|---|---|----|----|
| 1 | H | 20/8 | BRADFORD P A | 24,767 | D 1-1 | Hepworth (og) | Shortt | Silk | Jones | Porteous | Goddard | Taylor | Squires | Dougall | Tadman | Williams | Strauss |
| 2 | A | 22/8 | Tottenham | 41,882 | L 1-4 | Williams | Shortt | Silk | Jones | Porteous | Goddard | Taylor | Squires | Dougall | Williams | Willis | Strauss |
| 3 | A | 27/8 | Chesterfield | 14,805 | L 0-2 | | Shortt | Silk | Jones | Porteous | Goddard | Taylor | Astall | Dougall | Williams | Dews | Govan |
| 4 | H | 31/8 | TOTTENHAM | 25,242 | L 0-2 | | Major | Silk | Jones | Porteous | Goddard | Pengelly | Strauss | Taylor | Squires | Dews | Williams |
| 5 | H | 3/9 | WEST HAM | 23,521 | L 0-3 | | Major | Silk | Jones | Porteous | Goddard | Pengelly | Strauss | Taylor | Dougall | Dews | Williams |
| 6 | H | 10/9 | SHEFFIELD WED | 20,008 | L 0-1 | | Major | Hartery | Jones | Porteous | Dixon | Taylor | Strauss | Dews | Tadman | Edds | Williams |
| 7 | A | 14/9 | Bury | 12,614 | L 1-5 | Strauss | Major | Ratcliffe | Jones | Porteous | Goddard | Taylor | Strauss | Dougall | Tadman | Williams | Edds |
| 8 | A | 17/9 | Hull | 40,000 | L 2-4 | Strauss, Tadman | Shortt | Ratcliffe | Jones | Porteous | Dixon | Taylor | Strauss | Squires | Tadman | Dews | Williams |
| 9 | H | 24/9 | BRENTFORD | 17,810 | W 2-0 | Strauss, Tadman | Shortt | Silk | Jones | Porteous | Dixon | Taylor | Strauss | Squires | Tadman | Dews | Williams |
| 10 | A | 1/10 | Blackburn | 24,300 | L 0-1 | | Shortt | Silk | Jones | Porteous | Dixon | Taylor | Strauss | Squires | Tadman | Dews | Williams |
| 11 | A | 8/10 | Sheffield Utd | 26,134 | D 1-1 | Strauss | Shortt | Silk | Jones | Porteous | Dixon | Taylor | Strauss | Squires | Tadman | Dews | Williams |
| 12 | H | 15/10 | GRIMSBY | 24,276 | W 4-2 | Strauss, Tadman, Dews, Taylor | Shortt | Silk | Jones | Porteous | Dixon | Taylor | Strauss | Squires | Tadman | Dews | Williams |
| 13 | A | 22/10 | QP Rangers | 15,981 | W 2-0 | Tadman 2 | Shortt | Silk | Jones | Porteous | Dixon | Taylor | Strauss | Squires | Tadman | Dews | Williams |
| 14 | H | 29/10 | PRESTON | 32,802 | W 1-0 | Tadman | Shortt | Silk | Jones | Porteous | Dixon | Taylor | Strauss | Squires | Tadman | Dews | Williams |
| 15 | A | 5/11 | Swansea | 27,000 | D 2-2 | Tadman, Squires | Shortt | Silk | Jones | Porteous | Dixon | Taylor | Strauss | Squires | Tadman | Dews | Williams |
| 16 | H | 12/11 | LEEDS | 22,281 | L 1-2 | Tadman | Shortt | Silk | Jones | Porteous | Dixon | Taylor | Strauss | Squires | Tadman | Dews | Williams |
| 17 | A | 19/11 | Southampton | 25,129 | D 3-3 | Dews, Williams, Strauss | Shortt | Silk | Jones | Porteous | Dixon | Taylor | Strauss | Squires | Tadman | Dews | Williams |
| 18 | H | 26/11 | COVENTRY | 20,995 | L 1-2 | Williams | Shortt | Silk | Jones | Porteous | Dixon | Taylor | Strauss | Squires | Bryant | Dews | Williams |
| 19 | A | 3/12 | Luton | 13,273 | D 1-1 | Porteous | Shortt | Silk | Jones | Porteous | Dixon | Taylor | Strauss | Dougall | Edds | Dews | Williams |
| 20 | H | 10/12 | BARNSLEY | 17,315 | D 2-2 | Dews 2 | Shortt | Silk | Jones | Porteous | Dixon | Taylor | Strauss | Dougall | Tadman | Dews | Williams |
| 21 | A | 17/12 | Bradford P A | 7,708 | L 2-3 | Strauss, Williams | Shortt | Silk | Jones | Dougall | Dixon | Taylor | Strauss | Squires | Tadman | Dews | Williams |
| 22 | A | 24/12 | CHESTERFIELD | 19,864 | W 2-1 | Tadman, Squires | Shortt | Silk | Jones | Dougall | Chisholm | McShane | Strauss | Squires | Tadman | Dews | Williams |
| 23 | H | 26/12 | CARDIFF | 29,000 | D 0-0 | | Shortt | Silk | Jones | Dougall | Chisholm | McShane | Strauss | Squires | Tadman | Dews | Williams |
| 24 | A | 27/12 | Cardiff | 35,000 | L 0-1 | | Shortt | Silk | Jones | Dougall | Chisholm | McShane | Astall | Squires | Tadman | Dews | Williams |
| 25 | A | 31/12 | West Ham | 19,000 | D 2-2 | Strauss, Dews | Shortt | Ratcliffe | Jones | Dougall | Chisholm | McShane | Strauss | Squires | Tadman | Dews | Williams |
| 26 | H | 14/1 | Sheffield Wed | 39,316 | W 4-2 | Squires 2, Strauss, Dews | Shortt | Ratcliffe | Jones | Dougall | Chisholm | McShane | Astall | Squires | Tadman | Dews | Strauss |
| 27 | A | 21/1 | HULL | 20,591 | L 1-3 | Squires | Shortt | Ratcliffe | Jones | Dougall | Chisholm | Porteous | Astall | Taylor | Tadman | Dews | Strauss |
| 28 | A | 4/2 | Brentford | 22,343 | D 0-0 | | Shortt | Ratcliffe | Jones | Dougall | Chisholm | Porteous | Astall | Taylor | Tadman | Dews | Williams |
| 29 | H | 11/2 | Leicester | 27,912 | D 0-0 | | Shortt | Ratcliffe | Jones | Dougall | Chisholm | Porteous | Astall | Taylor | Tadman | Dews | Strauss |
| 30 | H | 18/2 | BLACKBURN | 23,139 | L 0-1 | | Shortt | Ratcliffe | Jones | Dougall | Chisholm | Porteous | Strauss | Taylor | Bryant | Dews | Strauss |
| 31 | H | 25/2 | SHEFFIELD UTD | 21,761 | L 0-1 | | Shortt | Ratcliffe | Jones | Dougall | Chisholm | Porteous | Astall | Taylor | Bryant | Dews | Strauss |
| 32 | A | 4/3 | Grimsby | 17,000 | D 2-2 | Dews 2 | Shortt | Ratcliffe | Jones | Dougall | Chisholm | Porteous | Astall | Squires | Dobbie | Dews | Strauss |
| 33 | H | 11/3 | QP RANGERS | 23,380 | L 0-2 | | Shortt | Ratcliffe | Jones | Dougall | Chisholm | Porteous | Astall | Squires | Dobbie | Dews | Williams |
| 34 | A | 18/3 | Preston | 21,000 | D 0-0 | | Shortt | Ratcliffe | Jones | Dougall | Chisholm | Porteous | Astall | Squires | Dobbie | Dews | Strauss |
| 35 | H | 25/3 | SWANSEA | 20,132 | L 0-1 | | Shortt | Ratcliffe | Jones | Dougall | Chisholm | Porteous | Strauss | Squires | Dobbie | Dews | Tadman |
| 36 | A | 1/4 | Coventry | 20,882 | L 0-3 | | Shortt | Ratcliffe | Jones | Dougall | Chisholm | Porteous | Blatchford | Dobbie | Tadman | Williams | Strauss |
| 37 | H | 8/4 | LUTON | 17,191 | D 0-0 | | Shortt | Ratcliffe | Jones | Dougall | Chisholm | Porteous | Strauss | Squires | Tadman | Dews | Williams |
| 38 | H | 10/4 | LEICESTER | 14,576 | W 2-1 | Strauss, Dews | Shortt | Ratcliffe | Jones | Dougall | Chisholm | Porteous | Strauss | Squires | Tadman | Dews | Williams |
| 39 | A | 15/4 | Leeds | 24,000 | D 1-1 | Ratcliffe | Shortt | Ratcliffe | Jones | Dougall | Chisholm | Porteous | Strauss | Squires | Tadman | Dews | Williams |
| 40 | H | 22/4 | SOUTHAMPTON | 22,873 | D 0-0 | | Shortt | Ratcliffe | Jones | Dougall | Chisholm | Porteous | Strauss | Squires | Tadman | Dobbie | Williams |
| 41 | A | 29/4 | Barnsley | 4,399 | L 1-4 | Bryant | Shortt | Ratcliffe | Jones | Dougall | Chisholm | Porteous | Strauss | Bryant | Bryant | Dobbie | Williams |
| 42 | H | 6/5 | BURY | 12,614 | W 2-0 | Bryant, Blatchford | Shortt | Ratcliffe | Jones | Dougall | Chisholm | Porteous | | | | | |

Shortt · Ratcliffe · Jones · Dougall · Chisholm · McShane · Strauss · Squires · Tadman · Dews · Williams
Shortt · Silk · Ratcliffe · Dougall · Chisholm · McShane · Strauss · Squires · Tadman · Dews · Williams

| | P | | Home | | | | | | Away | | | | Pts |
|---|---|---|---|---|---|---|---|---|---|---|---|---|---|
| | | W | D | L | F | A | W | D | L | F | A | | |
| 1 Tottenham | 42 | 15 | 3 | 3 | 51 | 15 | 12 | 4 | 5 | 30 | 20 | | 61 |
| 2 Sheffield W | 42 | 12 | 7 | 2 | 46 | 23 | 7 | 6 | 6 | 21 | 25 | | 52 |
| 3 Sheffield U | 42 | 9 | 10 | 2 | 36 | 19 | 4 | 10 | 7 | 32 | 30 | | 52 |
| 4 Southampton | 42 | 13 | 4 | 4 | 44 | 25 | 6 | 5 | 10 | 20 | 23 | | 47 |
| 5 Leeds | 42 | 11 | 8 | 2 | 33 | 16 | 6 | 4 | 11 | 21 | 29 | | 45 |
| 6 Preston | 42 | 12 | 5 | 4 | 37 | 21 | 4 | 3 | 12 | 23 | 28 | | 45 |
| 7 Hull | 42 | 11 | 8 | 2 | 39 | 25 | 3 | 6 | 12 | 25 | 47 | | 43 |
| 8 Swansea | 42 | 11 | 3 | 7 | 34 | 18 | 4 | 8 | 9 | 19 | 31 | | 43 |
| 9 Brentford | 42 | 11 | 5 | 5 | 21 | 12 | 6 | 6 | 9 | 23 | 37 | | 43 |
| 10 Cardiff | 42 | 11 | 3 | 5 | 28 | 14 | 3 | 7 | 11 | 13 | 30 | | 42 |
| 11 Grimsby | 42 | 13 | 5 | 3 | 53 | 25 | 3 | 3 | 15 | 21 | 48 | | 40 |
| 12 Coventry | 42 | 8 | 6 | 7 | 32 | 24 | 5 | 7 | 9 | 23 | 31 | | 39 |
| 13 Barnsley | 42 | 11 | 6 | 4 | 45 | 28 | 2 | 7 | 12 | 19 | 39 | | 39 |
| 14 Chesterfield | 42 | 12 | 3 | 6 | 28 | 16 | 3 | 6 | 11 | 15 | 31 | | 39 |
| 15 Leicester | 42 | 8 | 9 | 4 | 30 | 25 | 6 | 5 | 12 | 25 | 45 | | 39 |
| 16 Blackburn | 42 | 10 | 5 | 6 | 30 | 15 | 4 | 5 | 12 | 25 | 45 | | 38 |
| 17 Luton | 42 | 8 | 9 | 4 | 28 | 22 | 2 | 9 | 10 | 13 | 29 | | 38 |
| 18 Bury | 42 | 10 | 8 | 3 | 37 | 19 | 4 | 1 | 16 | 23 | 46 | | 37 |
| 19 West Ham | 42 | 8 | 7 | 6 | 30 | 25 | 3 | 5 | 12 | 23 | 36 | | 36 |
| 20 QP Rangers | 42 | 6 | 5 | 10 | 21 | 30 | 5 | 7 | 9 | 19 | 27 | | 34 |
| 21 PLYMOUTH | 42 | 6 | 6 | 9 | 19 | 24 | 2 | 10 | 9 | 25 | 41 | | 32 |
| 22 Bradford P A | 42 | 7 | 6 | 8 | 34 | 34 | 3 | 5 | 13 | 17 | 43 | | 31 |
| | 924 | 225 | 131 | 106 | 756 | 475 | 106 | 131 | 225 | 475 | 756 | | 924 |

| | Appearances | | Goals | | Tot |
|---|---|---|---|---|---|
| | Lge | FAC | Lge | FAC | |
| Astall, Gordon | 11 | | 1 | | 1 |
| Blatchford, Paddy | 2 | | | | |
| Bryant, Eric | 5 | | 2 | | 2 |
| Chisholm, Jack | 21 | 2 | | | |
| Dews, George | 36 | 2 | 9 | | 9 |
| Dixon, Stan | 15 | | | | |
| Dobbie, Harold | 6 | | | | |
| Dougall, Neil | 30 | 2 | | | |
| Edds, Ernie | 3 | | | | |
| Goddard, Ray | 6 | | | | |
| Govan, Alex | 1 | | | | |
| Hartery, John | 1 | | | | |
| Jones, Pat | 42 | 1 | | | |
| Major, Les | 5 | | | | |
| McShane, Tony | 6 | 2 | | | |
| Pengelly, Norman | 2 | | | | |
| Porteous, John | 35 | | 1 | | 1 |
| Ratcliffe, Paddy | 21 | 2 | 1 | | 1 |
| Shortt, Bill | 37 | 2 | | | |
| Silk, George | 20 | 1 | | | |
| Squires, Frank | 33 | 2 | 5 | | 5 |
| Strauss, Bill | 37 | 2 | 10 | | 10 |
| Tadman, Maurice | 29 | 2 | 9 | | 9 |
| Taylor, George | 22 | | 1 | | 1 |
| Williams, Stan | 35 | 2 | 4 | 1 | 5 |
| Willis, George | 1 | | | | |
| (own-goals) | | | 1 | | 1 |
| 26 players used | 462 | 22 | 44 | 1 | 45 |

# LEAGUE DIVISION 3 (SOUTH)  Manager: Jimmy Rae  SEASON 1951-52

| No | | Date | Opponents | Res | F-A | Att | Scorers | 1 | 2 | 3 | 4 | 5 | 6 | 7 | 8 | 9 | 10 | 11 |
|---|---|---|---|---|---|---|---|---|---|---|---|---|---|---|---|---|---|---|
| 1 | A | 18/8 | Leyton Orient | L | 0-1 | 15,000 | | Shortt | Ratcliffe | Jones | McShane | Chisholm | Porteous | Astall | Willis | Dobbie | Rattray | Govan |
| 2 | H | 22/8 | CRYSTAL PALACE | W | 5-0 | 14,388 | Dews 2, Astall, Strauss, Rattray | Shortt | Ratcliffe | Jones | McShane | Chisholm | Porteous | Astall | Dews | Tadman | Rattray | Strauss |
| 3 | H | 25/8 | WALSALL | W | 3-0 | 12,991 | Tadman 2, Astall | Shortt | Ratcliffe | Jones | McShane | Chisholm | Porteous | Astall | Dews | Tadman | Rattray | Strauss |
| 4 | A | 29/8 | Crystal Palace | W | 1-0 | 14,037 | Rattray | Shortt | Ratcliffe | Jones | McShane | Chisholm | Porteous | Astall | Dews | Tadman | Rattray | Strauss |
| 5 | A | 1/9 | Shrewsbury | L | 3-1 | 12,720 | Dews, Tadman, Ratcliffe | Shortt | Ratcliffe | Jones | McShane | Chisholm | Porteous | Astall | Dougall | Tadman | Dews | Strauss |
| 6 | H | 5/9 | COLCHESTER | W | 3-1 | 17,892 | Dews, Tadman, Ratcliffe | Shortt | Ratcliffe | Jones | McShane | Chisholm | Porteous | Astall | Dougall | Tadman | Dews | Strauss |
| 7 | H | 8/9 | ALDERSHOT | W | 2-1 | 18,201 | Dews, Rattray | Shortt | Ratcliffe | Jones | McShane | Chisholm | Porteous | Astall | Dews | Tadman | Rattray | Strauss |
| 8 | A | 13/9 | Colchester | L | 0-1 | 8,105 | | Shortt | Ratcliffe | Jones | McShane | Chisholm | Porteous | Astall | Dougall | Tadman | Dews | Strauss |
| 9 | A | 15/9 | Watford | W | 3-1 | 12,000 | Astall, Govan, Tadman | Shortt | Ratcliffe | Jones | McShane | Chisholm | Porteous | Astall | Dougall | Tadman | Dews | Govan |
| 10 | H | 22/9 | BRISTOL Rov | L | 1-2 | 25,593 | Govan | Shortt | Ratcliffe | Jones | Dougall | Chisholm | McShane | Astall | Dews | Tadman | Rattray | Govan |
| 11 | A | 29/9 | Ipswich | D | 2-2 | 15,633 | Dews, Rattray | Shortt | Ratcliffe | Jones | Dougall | Chisholm | McShane | Astall | Dews | Tadman | Rattray | Govan |
| 12 | H | 6/10 | PORT VALE | W | 3-0 | 18,867 | Astall, Govan, Rattray | Shortt | Ratcliffe | Jones | Dougall | Chisholm | McShane | Astall | Dews | Tadman | Rattray | Govan |
| 13 | A | 13/10 | Northampton | L | 1-3 | 14,661 | Chisholm | Shortt | Ratcliffe | Jones | Dougall | Chisholm | McShane | Astall | Dews | Tadman | Rattray | Govan |
| 14 | H | 20/10 | READING | W | 3-2 | 18,116 | Astall 2, Dews | Major | Ratcliffe | Jones | Dougall | Chisholm | McShane | Astall | Dews | Rattray | Willis | Govan |
| 15 | A | 27/10 | Newport | D | 3-3 | 10,065 | Tadman 2, Astall | Shortt | Ratcliffe | Jones | Dougall | Chisholm | McShane | Astall | Dews | Tadman | Rattray | Govan |
| 16 | H | 3/11 | SOUTHEND | W | 2-0 | 17,627 | Dougall, Tadman | Shortt | Ratcliffe | Jones | Dougall | Chisholm | McShane | Astall | Dews | Tadman | Rattray | Govan |
| 17 | A | 10/11 | Bournemouth | W | 2-1 | 18,618 | Dews, Govan | Shortt | Ratcliffe | Jones | Dougall | Chisholm | McShane | Astall | Dews | Tadman | Rattray | Govan |
| 18 | H | 17/11 | MILLWALL | W | 5-0 | 21,849 | Astall, Rattray, Tad', Dews, Govan | Shortt | Ratcliffe | Jones | Dougall | Chisholm | McShane | Astall | Dews | Tadman | Rattray | Govan |
| 19 | H | 1/12 | GILLINGHAM | W | 4-2 | 18,609 | Rattray 2, Astall, Dougall | Shortt | Ratcliffe | Jones | Dougall | Chisholm | McShane | Astall | Dews | Tadman | Rattray | Govan |
| 20 | A | 8/12 | Torquay | L | 2-3 | 9,987 | Rattray 2 | Shortt | Ratcliffe | Jones | Dougall | Chisholm | McShane | Astall | Dews | Tadman | Rattray | Govan |
| 21 | A | 22/12 | Walsall | W | 5-2 | 7,991 | Tadman 3, Govan, Russon (og) | Shortt | Ratcliffe | Jones | Dougall | Chisholm | Porteous | Astall | Dews | Tadman | Rattray | Govan |
| 22 | H | 25/12 | BRISTOL CITY | D | 2-2 | 17,498 | Rattray 2 | Shortt | Ratcliffe | Jones | Dougall | Chisholm | Porteous | Astall | Dews | Tadman | Rattray | Govan |
| 23 | A | 26/12 | Bristol City | D | 1-1 | 23,365 | Tadman | Shortt | Ratcliffe | Jones | McShane | Chisholm | Porteous | Astall | Dews | Tadman | Rattray | Govan |
| 24 | H | 29/12 | SHREWSBURY | W | 6-1 | 16,840 | Dews 2, Rattray 2, Tad', Govan | Shortt | Ratcliffe | Jones | McShane | Chisholm | Porteous | Astall | Dews | Tadman | Rattray | Govan |
| 25 | A | 5/1 | Aldershot | W | 2-1 | 7,800 | Dews, Tadman | Shortt | Ratcliffe | Jones | Dougall | Chisholm | Porteous | Astall | Dews | Tadman | Rattray | Govan |
| 26 | H | 12/1 | EXETER | W | 2-1 | 25,494 | Dews, Rattray | Shortt | Ratcliffe | Jones | Dougall | Chisholm | Porteous | Astall | Dews | Tadman | Rattray | Govan |
| 27 | H | 16/1 | NORWICH | W | 3-1 | 15,293 | Astall 2, Dews | Shortt | Ratcliffe | Jones | Dougall | Chisholm | Porteous | Astall | Dews | Tadman | Rattray | Govan |
| 28 | A | 19/1 | WATFORD | W | 3-1 | 20,381 | Tadman 2, Astall | Shortt | Ratcliffe | Jones | Dougall | Chisholm | Porteous | Astall | Dews | Tadman | Rattray | Govan |
| 29 | A | 26/1 | Bristol Rov | W | 2-1 | 29,937 | Rattray, Dougall | Shortt | Ratcliffe | Jones | Dougall | Chisholm | Porteous | Strauss | Dews | Tadman | Rattray | Govan |
| 30 | H | 9/2 | IPSWICH | W | 2-0 | 19,039 | Dews, Rattray | Shortt | Ratcliffe | Jones | Dougall | Chisholm | Porteous | Astall | Dews | Tadman | Rattray | Govan |
| 31 | H | 13/2 | SWINDON | W | 3-0 | 13,257 | Astall, Dews, Tadman | Shortt | Ratcliffe | Jones | McShane | Chisholm | Porteous | Astall | Dews | Tadman | Rattray | Govan |
| 32 | A | 16/2 | Port Vale | L | 0-1 | 10,600 | | Shortt | Ratcliffe | Jones | McShane | Chisholm | Porteous | Astall | Dews | Tadman | Rattray | Govan |
| 33 | H | 27/2 | Swindon | D | 2-2 | 8,000 | Dews 2 | Shortt | Ratcliffe | Jones | Dougall | Chisholm | Porteous | Astall | Dews | Tadman | Rattray | Govan |
| 34 | H | 1/3 | NORTHAMPTON | W | 2-0 | 22,046 | Rattray, Tadman | Shortt | Ratcliffe | Jones | Dougall | Chisholm | Porteous | Astall | Dews | Tadman | Rattray | Govan |
| 35 | A | 8/3 | Reading | L | 0-2 | 28,161 | | Shortt | Ratcliffe | Jones | Rundle | Chisholm | Porteous | Astall | Dews | Tadman | Rattray | Strauss |
| 36 | H | 15/3 | NEWPORT | W | 5-0 | 17,939 | Astall 2, Tadman 2, Dews | Major | Ratcliffe | Jones | Rundle | Chisholm | Porteous | Astall | Dews | Tadman | Rattray | Govan |
| 37 | A | 19/3 | LEYTON ORIENT | W | 3-0 | 15,508 | Astall, Rattray, Tadman | Shortt | Ratcliffe | Jones | McShane | Chisholm | Porteous | Astall | Dews | Tadman | Rattray | Govan |
| 38 | A | 22/3 | Southend | D | 1-1 | 15,000 | Tadman | Shortt | Ratcliffe | Jones | McShane | Chisholm | Porteous | Astall | Dews | Tadman | Rattray | Govan |
| 39 | H | 29/3 | BOURNEMOUTH | W | 4-1 | 11,994 | Dews 2, Astall, Govan | Shortt | Ratcliffe | Jones | McShane | Chisholm | Porteous | Astall | Dews | Tadman | Dobbie | Govan |
| 40 | H | 5/4 | Millwall | W | 2-0 | 26,810 | Dews, Tadman | Shortt | Ratcliffe | Jones | McShane | Chisholm | Porteous | Astall | Dews | Tadman | Rattray | Dobbie |
| 41 | H | 12/4 | BRIGHTON | D | 2-2 | 31,755 | Ratcliffe, Tadman | Shortt | Ratcliffe | Jones | McShane | Chisholm | Porteous | Astall | Dews | Tadman | Rattray | Dobbie |
| 42 | H | 14/4 | Exeter | L | 0-1 | 19,000 | | Shortt | Ratcliffe | Jones | McShane | Chisholm | Porteous | Astall | Dews | Tadman | Rattray | Dobbie |
| 43 | A | 19/4 | Gillingham | W | 2-1 | 14,639 | Dews, Tadman | Shortt | Ratcliffe | Jones | McShane | Chisholm | Porteous | Astall | Dews | Tadman | Rattray | Govan |
| 44 | A | 23/4 | Brighton | L | 3-2 | 28,000 | Dews, Govan, Astall | Shortt | Ratcliffe | Jones | McShane | Chisholm | Porteous | Astall | Dews | Tadman | Rattray | Govan |
| 45 | H | 26/4 | TORQUAY | D | 2-2 | 28,738 | Dews, Tadman | Shortt | Ratcliffe | Jones | McShane | Chisholm | Porteous | Astall | Dews | Tadman | Rattray | Govan |

**1 A 25/11 Millwall   26,490 L 0-1**

Players: Shortt · Ratcliffe · Jones · Dougall · Chisholm · McShane · Astall · Dews · Tadman · Rattray · Govan

| | P | Home | | | | | Away | | | | | Pts |
|---|---|---|---|---|---|---|---|---|---|---|---|---|
| | | W | D | L | F | A | W | D | L | F | A | |
| 1 PLYMOUTH | 46 | 19 | 3 | 1 | 70 | 19 | 10 | 5 | 8 | 37 | 34 | 66 |
| 2 Reading | 46 | 19 | 2 | 2 | 73 | 23 | 10 | 1 | 12 | 39 | 37 | 61 |
| 3 Norwich | 46 | 18 | 1 | 4 | 55 | 15 | 8 | 8 | 7 | 34 | 35 | 61 |
| 4 Millwall | 46 | 16 | 5 | 2 | 46 | 21 | 7 | 7 | 9 | 28 | 32 | 58 |
| 5 Brighton | 46 | 15 | 4 | 4 | 57 | 24 | 9 | 6 | 8 | 30 | 39 | 58 |
| 6 Newport | 46 | 13 | 7 | 3 | 45 | 26 | 8 | 5 | 10 | 32 | 50 | 54 |
| 7 Bristol Rov | 46 | 14 | 5 | 4 | 60 | 20 | 6 | 6 | 10 | 29 | 33 | 52 |
| 8 Northampton | 46 | 17 | 1 | 5 | 65 | 31 | 4 | 5 | 14 | 28 | 43 | 49 |
| 9 Southend | 46 | 16 | 6 | 1 | 56 | 17 | 3 | 4 | 16 | 19 | 49 | 48 |
| 10 Colchester | 46 | 12 | 7 | 4 | 32 | 22 | 5 | 5 | 13 | 24 | 55 | 46 |
| 11 Torquay | 46 | 10 | 3 | 10 | 53 | 42 | 7 | 7 | 9 | 33 | 56 | 44 |
| 12 Aldershot | 46 | 11 | 4 | 8 | 40 | 27 | 7 | 4 | 12 | 38 | 62 | 44 |
| 13 Port Vale | 46 | 11 | 11 | 1 | 33 | 16 | 3 | 4 | 16 | 17 | 50 | 43 |
| 14 Bournemouth | 46 | 11 | 4 | 8 | 42 | 30 | 5 | 6 | 12 | 27 | 45 | 42 |
| 15 Bristol City | 46 | 13 | 6 | 4 | 29 | 26 | 2 | 6 | 15 | 14 | 43 | 42 |
| 16 Swindon | 46 | 9 | 9 | 5 | 29 | 22 | 5 | 5 | 13 | 22 | 46 | 42 |
| 17 Ipswich | 46 | 12 | 4 | 7 | 45 | 31 | 4 | 5 | 14 | 18 | 43 | 41 |
| 18 Leyton O | 46 | 12 | 5 | 6 | 39 | 26 | 4 | 4 | 15 | 16 | 42 | 41 |
| 19 Crys Palace | 46 | 9 | 7 | 7 | 32 | 28 | 6 | 2 | 15 | 29 | 52 | 39 |
| 20 Shrewsbury | 46 | 11 | 3 | 9 | 35 | 29 | 2 | 7 | 14 | 27 | 57 | 36 |
| 21 Watford | 46 | 7 | 7 | 9 | 34 | 37 | 6 | 3 | 14 | 23 | 44 | 36 |
| 22 Gillingham | 46 | 10 | 7 | 6 | 47 | 31 | 1 | 6 | 16 | 24 | 50 | 35 |
| 23 Exeter | 46 | 10 | 4 | 9 | 40 | 36 | 3 | 5 | 15 | 25 | 50 | 35 |
| 24 Walsall | 46 | 11 | 3 | 9 | 38 | 31 | 2 | 2 | 19 | 17 | 63 | 31 |
| | 1104 | 306 | 118 | 128 | 1110 | 630 | 128 | 118 | 306 | 630 | 1110 | 1104 |

| | Appearances | | Goals | | Tot |
|---|---|---|---|---|---|
| | Lge | FAC | Lge | FAC | |
| Astall, Gordon | 45 | | 18 | | 18 |
| Chisholm, Jack | 46 | 1 | 1 | | 1 |
| Dews, George | 44 | 1 | 25 | | 25 |
| Dobbie, Harold | 6 | | | | |
| Dougall, Neil | 26 | 1 | 3 | | 3 |
| Govan, Alex | 35 | 1 | 9 | | 9 |
| Jones, Pat | 46 | | | | |
| Major, Les | 2 | | | | |
| McShane, Tony | 34 | 1 | | | |
| Porteous, John | 34 | | | | |
| Ratcliffe, Paddy | 46 | 1 | 3 | | 3 |
| Rattray, Peter | 41 | 1 | 19 | | 19 |
| Rundle, Sid | 2 | | | | |
| Shortt, Bill | 44 | 1 | | | |
| Strauss, Bill | 9 | | 1 | | 1 |
| Tadman, Maurice | 44 | 1 | 27 | | 27 |
| Willis, George | 2 | | | | |
| (own-goals) | | | 1 | | 1 |
| 17 players used | 506 | 11 | 107 | | 107 |

# LEAGUE DIVISION 2 — Manager: Jack Rowley — SEASON 1955-56

| No | H/A | Date | Opponents | Att | F-A | Scorers | 1 | 2 | 3 | 4 | 5 | 6 | 7 | 8 | 9 | 10 | 11 |
|----|-----|------|-----------|-----|-----|---------|---|---|---|---|---|---|---|---|---|----|----|
| 1 | A | 20/8 | Sheffield Wed | 31,716 | L 2-5 | Anderson 2 | Major | Robertson | Jones | Clelland | Lawless | Wetton | Thomas | Crawford | McJarrow | Rowley | Anderson |
| 2 | H | 22/8 | DONCASTER | 21,236 | D 2-2 | Willis, Rowley | Major | Robertson | Jones | Dougall | Lawless | Wetton | Anderson | Willis | Davis | Crawford | Rowley |
| 3 | H | 27/8 | NOTT'M FOREST | 17,955 | L 1-2 | Willis | Major | Robertson | Jones | Dougall | Lawless | Wetton | Davies | Willis | Langman N | Clelland | Anderson |
| 4 | A | 1/9 | Doncaster | 10,000 | L 1-3 | Anderson | Major | Robertson | Jones | Dougall | Lawless | Wetton | Davies | Willis | Langman N | Porteous | Anderson |
| 5 | A | 3/9 | Hull | 17,815 | W 1-0 | Anderson | Shortt | Robertson | Jones | Dougall | Lawless | Wetton | Anderson | Willis | Davis | Porteous | Anderson |
| 6 | H | 5/9 | STOKE | 21,000 | L 0-1 | | Shortt | Robertson | Jones | Dougall | Lawless | Wetton | Davies | Willis | McJarrow | Porteous | Rowley |
| 7 | H | 10/9 | BLACKBURN | 20,500 | W 1-0 | Rowley | Shortt | Robertson | Jones | Dougall | Lawless | Wetton | Davies | Willis | McJarrow | Williams | Rowley |
| 8 | A | 12/9 | Stoke | 17,179 | L 1-4 | Rowley | Shortt | Robertson | Jones | Dougall | Lawless | Wetton | Davies | Willis | McJarrow | Williams | Porteous |
| 9 | A | 17/9 | Lincoln | 13,466 | L 0-1 | | Shortt | Wyatt | Jones | Robertson | Langman P | Wetton | Davies | Crawford | Langman N | Rowley | Stenner |
| 10 | H | 24/9 | LEICESTER | 19,454 | L 0-1 | | Shortt | Wyatt | Jones | Robertson | Langman P | Wetton | Davies | Crawford | Langman N | Rowley | Stenner |
| 11 | A | 1/10 | Liverpool | 34,397 | L 1-4 | Williams | Shortt | Robertson | Jones | Robertson | Langman P | Wetton | Davies | Williams | Williams | Rowley | Stenner |
| 12 | A | 8/10 | West Ham | 19,750 | L 0-4 | | Shortt | Robertson | Jones | Dougall | Langman P | Wetton | Davies | Tilley | Davis | Rowley | Stenner |
| 13 | H | 15/10 | PORT VALE | 16,879 | D 1-1 | Rowley | Shortt | Ratcliffe | Jones | Robertson | Langman P | Dougall | Twissell | Tilley | Williams | Wetton | Rowley |
| 14 | A | 22/10 | Barnsley | 11,246 | W 2-1 | Rowley 2 | Shortt | Ratcliffe | Jones | Dougall | Langman P | McJarrow | Twissell | Tilley | Williams | Wetton | Rowley |
| 15 | H | 29/10 | SWANSEA | 24,070 | L 0-1 | | Shortt | Ratcliffe | Jones | Robertson | Langman P | Dougall | Baker | Tilley | Williams | Wetton | Rowley |
| 16 | A | 5/11 | Notts Co | 12,500 | L 0-3 | | Shortt | Ratcliffe | Jones | Robertson | Langman P | Dougall | Baker | Langman N | Williams | Tilley | Rowley |
| 17 | H | 12/11 | LEEDS | 18,852 | W 4-3 | Willis, Williams, Davis, Dougall | Shortt | Ratcliffe | Jones | Robertson | Langman P | Dougall | Twissell | Williams | Davis | Willis | Baker |
| 18 | A | 19/11 | Fulham | 23,000 | L 1-2 | Dougall | Shortt | Ratcliffe | Jones | Robertson | Langman P | Dougall | Twissell | Williams | Davis | Willis | Baker |
| 19 | H | 26/11 | BURY | 15,474 | L 1-4 | Twissell | Major | Ratcliffe | Jones | Robertson | Langman P | Dougall | Twissell | Willis | Davis | Willis | Baker |
| 20 | A | 3/12 | Rotherham | 11,488 | D 0-0 | | Major | Ratcliffe | Jones | Dougall | Langman P | Dougall | Twissell | Willis | Davis | Williams | Baker |
| 21 | H | 10/12 | MIDDLESBROUGH | 11,415 | W 4-0 | Wet', Davis, Robinson(og), Stenner | Shortt | Robertson | Jones | Dougall | Langman P | Wetton | Baker | Willis | Davis | Williams | Stenner |
| 22 | H | 17/12 | SHEFFIELD WED | 16,500 | D 1-1 | Jones | Shortt | Robertson | Jones | Dougall | Langman P | Wetton | Baker | Williams | Davis | Tilley | Twissell |
| 23 | A | 24/12 | Nott'm Forest | 10,003 | L 1-3 | Twissell | Shortt | Robertson | Jones | Dougall | Langman P | Wetton | Baker | Williams | Davis | Tilley | Twissell |
| 24 | H | 26/12 | BRISTOL CITY | 22,096 | W 5-0 | Davies, Crawf'd 2, Davis, Williams | Shortt | Robertson | Jones | Dougall | Langman P | Wetton | Davies | Crawford | Davis | Williams | Twissell |
| 25 | A | 27/12 | Bristol City | 27,490 | L 0-6 | | Shortt | Robertson | Jones | Robertson | Langman P | Wetton | Davies | Williams | Davis | Crawford | Twissell |
| 26 | H | 31/12 | HULL | 20,130 | D 1-1 | Twissell | Dyer | Robertson | Jones | Dougall | Langman P | Wetton | Davies | Williams | Davis | Crawford | Twissell |
| 27 | A | 14/1 | Blackburn | 18,200 | L 1-2 | Willis | Major | Robertson | Wyatt | Dougall | Langman P | Wetton | Davies | Williams | Porteous | Willis | Twissell |
| 28 | H | 21/1 | LINCOLN | 12,586 | L 1-4 | Robertson | Major | Robertson | Jones | Robertson | Langman P | Wetton | Davies | Williams | Swiggs | Swiggs | Twissell |
| 29 | A | 4/2 | Leicester | 25,000 | L 1-4 | Davis | Major | Robertson | Wyatt | Robertson | Langman P | Wetton | Davies | Crawford | Swiggs | Williams | Stenner |
| 30 | H | 11/2 | LIVERPOOL | 10,250 | W 4-0 | Morgan, Langman N | Major | Robertson | Jones | Dougall | Langman P | Wetton | Twissell | Crawford | Davis | Langman N | Stenner |
| 31 | H | 18/2 | FULHAM | 16,962 | D 0-0 | | Major | Robertson | Jones | Dougall | Langman P | Wetton | Davies | Langman N | Davis | Morgan | Rowley |
| 32 | A | 25/2 | Port Vale | 14,236 | L 1-3 | Langman N | Major | Robertson | Jones | Dougall | Langman P | Wetton | Twissell | Langman N | Davis | Morgan | Rowley |
| 33 | H | 3/3 | BARNSLEY | 11,200 | W 3-0 | Morgan, Langman N, Davies | Major | Robertson | Wyatt | Tilley | Langman P | Wetton | Davies | Williams | Langman N | Morgan | Twissell |
| 34 | A | 10/3 | Middlesbrough | 23,000 | W 2-1 | Davies, Langman N | Major | Robertson | Jones | Tilley | Langman P | Wetton | Davies | Williams | Langman N | Morgan | Twissell |
| 35 | H | 17/3 | NOTTS CO | 19,616 | D 1-1 | Morgan | Major | Robertson | Jones | Tilley | Langman P | Wetton | Davies | Williams | Langman N | Morgan | Twissell |
| 36 | A | 24/3 | Leeds | 12,000 | L 2-4 | Mitchell 2 | Major | Robertson | Jones | Tilley | Langman P | Wetton | Davies | Langman N | Mitchell | Morgan | Stenner |
| 37 | H | 30/3 | Bristol Rov | 27,814 | L 1-2 | Langman N | Major | Robertson | Jones | Robertson | Langman P | Wetton | Davies | Wyatt | Langman N | Morgan | Stenner |
| 38 | H | 31/3 | WEST HAM | 17,555 | L 0-1 | | Shortt | Robertson | Jones | Tilley | Langman P | Wetton | Twissell | Wyatt | Langman N | Morgan | Twissell |
| 39 | A | 2/4 | BRISTOL ROV | 19,181 | L 0-1 | | Shortt | Wyatt | Jones | Robertson | Langman P | Wetton | Davies | Langman N | Davis | Tilley | Stenner |
| 40 | A | 7/4 | Bury | 8,936 | L 1-7 | Wyatt | Dyer | Robertson | Jones | Tilley | Langman P | McJarrow | Davies | Wyatt | Mitchell | Bell | Morgan |
| 41 | H | 14/4 | ROTHERHAM | 6,661 | W 3-1 | Langman N 2, Morgan | Dyer | John | Jones | Robertson | Langman P | Wetton | Davies | Wyatt | Langman N | Langman N | Stenner |

3 A 7/1 Leyton O  15,619 L 0-1

Major | Robertson | Jones | Dougall | Langman P | Wetton | Davies | Williams | Davis | Crawford | Twissell

| | P | | Home | | | | | Away | | | | Pts |
|---|---|---|---|---|---|---|---|---|---|---|---|---|
| | | W | D | L | F | A | W | D | L | F | A | |
| 1 Sheffield W | 42 | 13 | 5 | 3 | 60 | 28 | 8 | 8 | 5 | 41 | 34 | 55 |
| 2 Leeds | 42 | 17 | 3 | 1 | 51 | 18 | 6 | 3 | 12 | 29 | 42 | 52 |
| 3 Liverpool | 42 | 14 | 4 | 3 | 52 | 25 | 8 | 3 | 11 | 33 | 38 | 48 |
| 4 Blackburn | 42 | 13 | 4 | 4 | 55 | 29 | 8 | 2 | 11 | 29 | 36 | 48 |
| 5 Leicester | 42 | 15 | 3 | 3 | 63 | 23 | 6 | 3 | 12 | 31 | 55 | 48 |
| 6 Bristol Rov | 42 | 13 | 3 | 5 | 53 | 33 | 8 | 3 | 10 | 31 | 37 | 48 |
| 7 Nott'm Forest | 42 | 9 | 5 | 7 | 30 | 26 | 4 | 7 | 7 | 38 | 37 | 47 |
| 8 Lincoln | 42 | 14 | 5 | 2 | 49 | 17 | 4 | 5 | 12 | 30 | 48 | 46 |
| 9 Fulham | 42 | 15 | 2 | 4 | 59 | 27 | 5 | 4 | 12 | 30 | 52 | 46 |
| 10 Swansea | 42 | 14 | 4 | 3 | 49 | 23 | 6 | 2 | 13 | 34 | 58 | 46 |
| 11 Bristol City | 42 | 14 | 4 | 3 | 49 | 20 | 5 | 3 | 13 | 31 | 44 | 45 |
| 12 Port Vale | 42 | 12 | 4 | 5 | 38 | 21 | 4 | 9 | 8 | 22 | 35 | 45 |
| 13 Stoke | 42 | 13 | 2 | 6 | 47 | 27 | 7 | 2 | 12 | 24 | 35 | 44 |
| 14 Midd'brough | 42 | 11 | 4 | 6 | 46 | 31 | 5 | 4 | 12 | 30 | 47 | 40 |
| 15 Bury | 42 | 9 | 5 | 7 | 44 | 39 | 7 | 3 | 11 | 42 | 51 | 40 |
| 16 West Ham | 42 | 12 | 4 | 5 | 52 | 27 | 7 | 2 | 12 | 22 | 42 | 39 |
| 17 Doncaster | 42 | 11 | 5 | 5 | 45 | 30 | 1 | 6 | 14 | 24 | 66 | 35 |
| 18 Barnsley | 42 | 10 | 5 | 6 | 33 | 35 | 1 | 7 | 13 | 14 | 49 | 34 |
| 19 Rotherham | 42 | 7 | 5 | 9 | 29 | 34 | 5 | 4 | 12 | 27 | 41 | 33 |
| 20 Notts Co | 42 | 8 | 5 | 8 | 39 | 37 | 3 | 4 | 14 | 16 | 45 | 31 |
| 21 PLYMOUTH | 42 | 7 | 6 | 8 | 33 | 25 | 2 | 2 | 16 | 21 | 62 | 28 |
| 22 Hull | 42 | 6 | 4 | 11 | 32 | 45 | 4 | 2 | 15 | 21 | 52 | 26 |
| | 924 | 257 | 90 | 115 | 1008 | 620 | 115 | 90 | 257 | 620 | 1008 | 924 |

| | Appearances | | Goals | | |
|---|---|---|---|---|---|
| | Lge | FAC | Lge | FAC | Tot |
| Anderson, Peter | 6 | | 4 | | 4 |
| Baker, George | 9 | | | | |
| Bell, Bobby | 2 | | 1 | | 1 |
| Clelland, Crawford | 2 | | | | |
| Crawford, Jimmy | 9 | 1 | 2 | | 2 |
| Davies, Malcolm | 23 | 1 | 4 | | 4 |
| Davis, Eric | 18 | 1 | 4 | | 4 |
| Dougall, Neil | 29 | 1 | 2 | | 2 |
| Dyer, Peter | 4 | | | | |
| John, Dennis | 2 | | | | |
| Jones, Pat | 39 | 1 | 1 | | 1 |
| Langman, Neil | 19 | | 9 | | 9 |
| Langman, Peter | 34 | 1 | | | |
| Lawless, Trevor | 8 | | | | |
| Major, Les | 17 | 1 | | | |
| McJarrow, Hugh | 5 | | | | |
| Mitchell, Ken | 2 | | 2 | | 2 |
| Morgan, Arthur | 12 | | 4 | | 4 |
| Porteous, John | 5 | | | | |
| Ratcliffe, Paddy | 8 | | | | |
| Robertson, George | 41 | 1 | 1 | | 1 |
| Rowley, Jack | 16 | | 6 | | 6 |
| Shortt, Bill | 21 | | | | |
| Stenner, Arthur | 9 | | | | |
| Swiggs, Bob | 2 | | | | |
| Thomas, Keith | 1 | | | | |
| Tilley, Rex | 14 | | | | |
| Twissell, Charlie | 21 | 1 | 3 | | 3 |
| Wetton, Ralph | 36 | 1 | 1 | | 1 |
| Williams, Johnny | 23 | 1 | 3 | | 3 |
| Willis, George | 14 | | 4 | | 4 |
| Wyatt, Reg | 11 | | 1 | | 1 |
| (own-goals) | | | 1 | | 1 |
| 32 players used | 462 | 11 | 54 | | 54 |

# LEAGUE DIVISION 3 (South)

## Manager: Jack Rowley

## SEASON 1957-58

| # | Date | V | Opponents | Att | Res | F-A | Scorers | 1 | 2 | 3 | 4 | 5 | 6 | 7 | 8 | 9 | 10 | 11 |
|---|------|---|-----------|-----|-----|-----|---------|---|---|---|---|---|---|---|---|---|----|----|
| 1 | 24/8 | A | Shrewsbury | 10,092 | L | 0-2 | | Brown | Robertson | Jones | Williams | Wyatt | Tilley | Penk | Carter | Langman N | Dougall | Anderson |
| 2 | 26/8 | H | READING | 20,123 | W | 1-0 | Langman N | Brown | Robertson | Jones | Williams | Wyatt | Tilley | Penk | Carter | Langman N | Kearns | Anderson |
| 3 | 31/8 | H | ALDERSHOT | 20,423 | W | 4-2 | Anderson, Carter 2, Kearns | Brown | Robertson | Jones | Williams | Wyatt | Tilley | Penk | Carter | Langman N | Kearns | Anderson |
| 4 | 4/9 | A | Reading | 10,568 | W | 3-1 | Langman N 3 | Brown | Robertson | Jones | Williams | Wyatt | Tilley | Penk | Carter | Langman N | Kearns | Twissell |
| 5 | 7/9 | A | Swindon | 11,305 | L | 0-1 | | Brown | Robertson | Jones | Williams | Wyatt | Tilley | Penk | Carter | Langman N | Kearns | Twissell |
| 6 | 12/9 | A | Brighton | 13,408 | L | 2-3 | Langman N, Kearns | Brown | Robertson | Jones | Williams | Wyatt | Tilley | Penk | Carter | Langman N | Kearns | Twissell |
| 7 | 14/9 | H | MILLWALL | 18,385 | W | 1-0 | Carter | Brown | Robertson | Jones | Williams | Wyatt | Tilley | Twissell | Carter | Langman N | Quinn | Kearns |
| 8 | 16/9 | H | BRIGHTON | 18,883 | W | 2-1 | Williams, Carter | Brown | Robertson | Jones | Williams | Wyatt | Tilley | Twissell | Carter | Langman N | Quinn | Kearns |
| 9 | 21/9 | A | Gillingham | 9,555 | L | 0-1 | | Brown | Robertson | Jones | Williams | Wyatt | Tilley | Twissell | Carter | Langman N | Quinn | Kearns |
| 10 | 25/9 | H | Southampton | 14,251 | W | 1-0 | Carter | Brown | Robertson | Jones | Williams | Wyatt | Tilley | Penk | Carter | Langman N | Kearns | Anderson |
| 11 | 28/9 | H | EXETER | 23,418 | W | 1-0 | Langman N | Brown | Robertson | Jones | Dougall | Wyatt | Tilley | Penny | Carter | Langman N | Kearns | Penk |
| 12 | 30/9 | H | SOUTHAMPTON | 25,600 | W | 4-0 | Anderson, Carter 2, Kearns | Brown | Robertson | Jones | Williams | Langman P | Tilley | Penk | Carter | Langman N | Kearns | Anderson |
| 13 | 5/10 | A | QP Rangers | 11,222 | L | 0-1 | | Brown | Robertson | Jones | Williams | Wyatt | Tilley | Penk | Carter | Langman N | Kearns | Anderson |
| 14 | 9/10 | H | COLCHESTER | 22,550 | D | 1-1 | Langman N | Brown | Robertson | Jones | Williams | Wyatt | Tilley | Penk | Carter | Langman N | Kearns | Anderson |
| 15 | 12/10 | A | Northampton | 9,422 | L | 0-5 | | Brown | Robertson | Jones | Williams | Wyatt | Dougall | Penk | Carter | Langman N | Barrett | Anderson |
| 16 | 19/10 | H | WATFORD | 17,901 | W | 2-1 | Langman N 2 | Brown | Robertson | Jones | Williams | Wyatt | Tilley | Penk | Carter | Langman N | Kearns | Anderson |
| 17 | 26/10 | A | Crystal Palace | 14,532 | L | 0-3 | | Brown | Robertson | Jones | Williams | Wyatt | Tilley | Penk | Carter | Langman N | Gauld | Anderson |
| 18 | 2/11 | H | TORQUAY | 23,765 | W | 1-0 | Gauld | Brown | Dougall | Wyatt | Williams | Langman P | Tilley | Penk | Carter | Langman N | Gauld | Anderson |
| 19 | 9/11 | H | Brentford | 15,600 | L | 0-2 | | Brown | Dougall | Dougall | Williams | Langman P | Tilley | Penk | Carter | Langman N | Gauld | Anderson |
| 20 | 23/11 | A | Norwich | 20,776 | L | 0-1 | | Barnsley | Robertson | Dougall | Williams | Wyatt | Tilley | Penk | Carter | Barnes | Gauld | Anderson |
| 21 | 30/11 | H | BOURNEMOUTH | 16,892 | W | 3-1 | Rule (og), Gauld, Hughes (og) | Barnsley | Robertson | Dougall | Williams | Wyatt | Tilley | Penk | Gauld | Barnes | Gauld | Anderson |
| 22 | 14/12 | A | COVENTRY | 14,539 | W | 4-0 | Anderson, Barrett 3 | Barnsley | Robertson | Adams | Williams | Wyatt | Barrett | Penk | Gauld | Carter | Kearns | Anderson |
| 23 | 21/12 | H | SHREWSBURY | 13,638 | W | 2-2 | Carter, Barrett | Barnsley | Robertson | Dougall | Tilley | Wyatt | Barrett | Penk | Gauld | Carter | Kearns | Anderson |
| 24 | 25/12 | A | Newport | 10,680 | W | 2-0 | Baker, Gauld | Barnsley | Robertson | Dougall | Williams | Wyatt | Tilley | Penk | Carter | Baker | Gauld | Anderson |
| 25 | 26/12 | H | NEWPORT | 25,936 | W | 1-0 | Carter | Barnsley | Robertson | Dougall | Williams | Wyatt | Tilley | Penk | Carter | Baker | Gauld | Anderson |
| 26 | 28/12 | A | Aldershot | 5,767 | D | 3-3 | Carter 2, Baker | Barnsley | Robertson | Dougall | Williams | Wyatt | Tilley | Penk | Carter | Baker | Gauld | Anderson |
| 27 | 11/1 | H | SWINDON | 16,797 | D | 2-2 | Carter, Baker | Barnsley | Robertson | Timmins | Williams | Wyatt | Tilley | Penk | Carter | Baker | Gauld | Anderson |
| 28 | 18/1 | H | Millwall | 11,338 | W | 1-0 | Baker | Barnsley | Robertson | Timmins | Williams | Wyatt | Barrett | Penk | Carter | Baker | Gauld | Anderson |
| 29 | 1/2 | H | GILLINGHAM | 17,566 | W | 2-1 | Anderson, Carter | Barnsley | Robertson | Timmins | Williams | Wyatt | Barrett | Penk | Carter | Baker | Gauld | Anderson |
| 30 | 8/2 | A | Exeter | 13,599 | L | 2-4 | Penk, Gauld | Barnsley | Robertson | Timmins | Williams | Wyatt | Tilley | Penk | Carter | Baker | Gauld | Anderson |
| 31 | 15/2 | H | QP RANGERS | 17,068 | W | 3-1 | Carter 3 | Barnsley | Robertson | Fulton | Williams | Wyatt | Barrett | Penk | Carter | Baker | Kearns | Anderson |
| 32 | 22/2 | A | NORTHAMPTON | 16,517 | W | 3-0 | Williams, Carter, Baker | Barnsley | Robertson | Fulton | Williams | Wyatt | Barrett | Anderson | Carter | Baker | Kearns | Penk |
| 33 | 1/3 | H | Watford | 10,508 | W | 2-0 | Williams, Baker | Barnsley | Robertson | Fulton | Williams | Wyatt | Barrett | Anderson | Carter | Baker | Kearns | Penk |
| 34 | 3/3 | A | Walsall | 9,393 | W | 2-0 | Carter, Penk | Barnsley | Robertson | Fulton | Williams | Wyatt | Barrett | Anderson | Carter | Baker | Kearns | Penk |
| 35 | 8/3 | H | CRYSTAL PALACE | 18,719 | W | 1-0 | Anderson | Barnsley | Robertson | Fulton | Williams | Wyatt | Barrett | Anderson | Carter | Baker | Kearns | Penk |
| 36 | 15/3 | A | Torquay | 14,609 | W | 2-0 | Carter, Kearns | Barnsley | Robertson | Fulton | Williams | Wyatt | Barrett | Anderson | Carter | Baker | Kearns | Penk |
| 37 | 22/3 | H | NORWICH | 17,018 | L | 0-1 | | Barnsley | Robertson | Fulton | Williams | Wyatt | Barrett | Anderson | Carter | Baker | Kearns | Penk |
| 38 | 29/3 | A | Coventry | 11,563 | D | 1-1 | Carter | Barnsley | Robertson | Fulton | Williams | Wyatt | Barrett | Anderson | Carter | Baker | Kearns | Penk |
| 39 | 4/4 | A | PORT VALE | 22,258 | W | 1-0 | Kearns | Barnsley | Robertson | Jones | Williams | Wyatt | Barrett | Anderson | Carter | Baker | Kearns | Penk |
| 40 | 5/4 | H | BRENTFORD | 19,581 | D | 0-0 | | Brown | Robertson | Jones | Williams | Wyatt | Barrett | Anderson | Dougall | Baker | Kearns | Penk |
| 41 | 7/4 | A | Port Vale | 11,059 | D | 0-0 | | Brown | Robertson | Jones | Williams | Wyatt | Tilley | Anderson | Dougall | Baker | Kearns | Penk |
| 42 | 12/4 | A | Bournemouth | 16,705 | D | 0-0 | | Brown | Robertson | Jones | Williams | Wyatt | Tilley | Dougall | Gauld | Baker | Kearns | Penk |
| 43 | 16/4 | H | Southend | 10,000 | L | 1-2 | Morrison (og) | Brown | Robertson | Jones | Williams | Wyatt | Tilley | Carter | Gauld | Baker | Kearns | Penk |
| 44 | 19/4 | A | WALSALL | 19,081 | W | 2-1 | Carter, Baker | Brown | Robertson | Jones | Williams | Wyatt | Barrett | Baker | Gauld | Gauld | Kearns | Timmins |
| 45 | 21/4 | H | SOUTHEND | 22,000 | L | 2-3 | Carter, Baker | Brown | Robertson | Jones | Williams | Wyatt | Barrett | Anderson | Gauld | Baker | Carter | Penk |

**FA Cup**

| # | | Date | Opponent | Attendance | Result | Scorers |
|---|---|---|---|---|---|---|
| 1 | H | 16/11 | WATFORD | 20,875 | W 6-2 | And'son, Barnes 2, Carter 2, Gauld |
| 2 | H | 7/12 | DORCHESTER | 18,305 | W 5-2 | Penk, Carter 3, Gauld |
| 3 | H | 4/12 | NEWCASTLE | 38,129 | L 1-6 | Carter |

| Match 1 | Match 2 | Match 3 |
|---|---|---|
| Barnsley | Barnsley | Barnsley |
| Robertson | Robertson | Robertson |
| Dougall | Jasper | Dougall |
| Williams | Tilley | Williams |
| Wyatt | Wyatt | Wyatt |
| Tilley | Barrett | Tilley |
| Penk | Penk | Penk |
| Carter | Carter | Carter |
| Barnes | Barnes | Baker |
| Gauld | Gauld | Gauld |
| Anderson | Anderson | Anderson |

| | | P | Home | | | | | Away | | | | | Pts |
|---|---|---|---|---|---|---|---|---|---|---|---|---|---|
| | | | W | D | L | F | A | W | D | L | F | A | |
| 1 | Brighton | 46 | 13 | 6 | 4 | 52 | 30 | 11 | 6 | 6 | 36 | 34 | 60 |
| 2 | Brentford | 46 | 15 | 5 | 3 | 52 | 24 | 9 | 5 | 9 | 30 | 32 | 58 |
| 3 | PLYMOUTH | 46 | 17 | 4 | 2 | 43 | 17 | 8 | 4 | 11 | 24 | 31 | 58 |
| 4 | Swindon | 46 | 14 | 7 | 2 | 47 | 16 | 7 | 8 | 8 | 32 | 34 | 57 |
| 5 | Reading | 46 | 14 | 5 | 4 | 52 | 23 | 7 | 8 | 8 | 27 | 41 | 55 |
| 6 | Southampton | 46 | 16 | 3 | 4 | 78 | 31 | 6 | 7 | 10 | 34 | 32 | 54 |
| 7 | Southend | 46 | 14 | 5 | 4 | 56 | 26 | 7 | 7 | 9 | 34 | 42 | 54 |
| 8 | Norwich | 46 | 11 | 9 | 3 | 41 | 28 | 8 | 6 | 9 | 34 | 42 | 53 |
| 9 | Bournemouth | 46 | 16 | 5 | 2 | 54 | 24 | 5 | 4 | 14 | 27 | 50 | 51 |
| 10 | QP Rangers | 46 | 15 | 6 | 2 | 40 | 14 | 3 | 8 | 12 | 24 | 51 | 51 |
| 11 | Newport | 46 | 12 | 6 | 5 | 40 | 24 | 5 | 8 | 10 | 33 | 43 | 48 |
| 12 | Colchester | 46 | 13 | 5 | 5 | 45 | 27 | 4 | 8 | 11 | 32 | 52 | 47 |
| 13 | Northampton | 46 | 13 | 1 | 9 | 60 | 33 | 6 | 5 | 12 | 27 | 46 | 44 |
| 14 | Crys Palace | 46 | 12 | 5 | 6 | 46 | 30 | 3 | 8 | 12 | 24 | 42 | 43 |
| 15 | Port Vale | 46 | 12 | 6 | 5 | 49 | 24 | 4 | 3 | 15 | 18 | 34 | 42 |
| 16 | Watford | 46 | 9 | 8 | 6 | 34 | 27 | 4 | 8 | 11 | 25 | 50 | 42 |
| 17 | Shrewsbury | 46 | 10 | 6 | 7 | 29 | 25 | 5 | 4 | 14 | 20 | 46 | 40 |
| 18 | Aldershot | 46 | 7 | 9 | 7 | 31 | 34 | 5 | 3 | 11 | 28 | 55 | 40 |
| 19 | Coventry | 46 | 10 | 9 | 4 | 41 | 24 | 3 | 4 | 16 | 20 | 57 | 39 |
| 20 | Walsall | 46 | 10 | 7 | 6 | 37 | 24 | 4 | 2 | 17 | 24 | 51 | 37 |
| 21 | Torquay | 46 | 9 | 7 | 7 | 33 | 34 | 2 | 6 | 15 | 16 | 40 | 35 |
| 22 | Gillingham | 46 | 12 | 5 | 6 | 33 | 24 | 1 | 4 | 18 | 19 | 57 | 35 |
| 23 | Millwall | 46 | 6 | 6 | 11 | 37 | 36 | 5 | 3 | 15 | 26 | 55 | 31 |
| 24 | Exeter | 46 | 10 | 4 | 9 | 37 | 35 | 1 | 5 | 17 | 20 | 64 | 31 |
| | | 1104 | 290 | 139 | 123 | 1067 | 634 | 123 | 139 | 290 | 634 | 1067 | 1104 |

| | Appearances | | Goals | | |
|---|---|---|---|---|---|
| | Lge | FAC | Lge | FAC | Tot |
| Adams, Graham | 1 | | | | |
| Anderson, Peter | 36 | 3 | 5 | 1 | 6 |
| Baker, George | 23 | 1 | 9 | | 9 |
| Barnes, Bernard | 2 | 2 | | 2 | 2 |
| Barnsley, Geoff | 20 | 3 | | | |
| Barrett, Tommy | 18 | 1 | 1 | | 1 |
| Brown, Harry | 26 | | | | |
| Carter, Wilf | 44 | 3 | 26 | 6 | 32 |
| Dougall, Neil | 13 | 2 | | | |
| Fulton, Bryce | 9 | | | | |
| Gauld, Jimmy | 19 | 3 | 4 | 2 | 6 |
| Jasper, Brian | | 1 | | | |
| Jones, Pat | 24 | | | | |
| Kearns, Peter | 30 | | 5 | | 5 |
| Langman, Neil | 19 | | 9 | | 9 |
| Langman, Peter | 3 | | | | |
| Penk, Harry | 42 | 3 | 2 | 1 | 3 |
| Penny, John | 1 | | | | |
| Quinn, Gordon | 3 | | | | |
| Robertson, George | 45 | 3 | | | |
| Tilley, Rex | 28 | 3 | | | |
| Timmins, John | 5 | | | | |
| Twissell, Charlie | 6 | | | | |
| Williams, Johnny | 44 | 2 | 3 | | 3 |
| Wyatt, Reg | 45 | 3 | | | |
| (own-goals) | | | 3 | | 3 |
| 25 players used | 506 | 33 | 67 | 12 | 79 |

# LEAGUE DIVISION 3

## Manager: Jack Rowley

### SEASON 1958-59

| # | Date | | Opponents | Att | F-A | | Scorers | 1 | 2 | 3 | 4 | 5 | 6 | 7 | 8 | 9 | 10 | 11 |
|---|------|---|-----------|-----|-----|---|---------|---|---|---|---|---|---|---|---|---|----|----|
| 1 | 23/8 | A | Hull | 14,318 | 1-1 | D | Gauld | Barnsley | Robertson | Doughty | Williams J | Wyatt | Barrett | Anderson | Gauld | Baker | Carter | Penk |
| 2 | 25/8 | A | Rochdale | 8,442 | 2-0 | W | Carter, Penk | Barnsley | Robertson | Dougall | Williams J | Wyatt | Barrett | Anderson | Gauld | Baker | Carter | Penk |
| 3 | 30/8 | H | TRANMERE | 22,518 | 4-0 | W | Carter 2, Baker, Gauld | Barnsley | Robertson | Dougall | Williams J | Wyatt | Barrett | Anderson | Carter | Baker | Gauld | Penk |
| 4 | 4/9 | H | ROCHDALE | 26,961 | 2-1 | W | Carter, Williams J | Barnsley | Robertson | Dougall | Williams J | Wyatt | Barrett | Penk | Gauld | Baker | Carter | Anderson |
| 5 | 6/9 | A | Stockport | 11,300 | 2-2 | D | Penk, Gauld | Barnsley | Robertson | Dougall | Williams J | Wyatt | Barrett | Anderson | Gauld | Baker | Carter | Penk |
| 6 | 8/9 | A | Bury | 12,189 | 1-1 | D | Anderson | Barnsley | Robertson | Dougall | Williams J | Wyatt | Barrett | Anderson | Gauld | Baker | Carter | Penk |
| 7 | 13/9 | H | READING | 25,966 | 2-2 | D | Carter, Penk | Barnsley | Robertson | Dougall | Williams J | Wyatt | Williams J L | Penk | Gauld | Meyer | Carter | Govan |
| 8 | 18/9 | H | BURY | 27,589 | 3-0 | W | Meyer 2, Gauld | Barnsley | Robertson | Dougall | Williams J | Wyatt | Williams J L | Penk | Gauld | Meyer | Carter | Govan |
| 9 | 20/9 | A | Colchester | 10,038 | 0-2 | L | | Barnsley | Robertson | Dougall | Williams J | Wyatt | Williams J L | Penk | Gauld | Meyer | Carter | Govan |
| 10 | 22/9 | H | DONCASTER | 24,827 | 4-0 | W | Carter 2, Williams J, Govan | Barnsley | Robertson | Dougall | Williams J | Wyatt | Williams J L | Penk | Carter | Meyer | Carter | Govan |
| 11 | 27/9 | H | BOURNEMOUTH | 24,822 | 3-1 | W | Dougall, Meyer, Wyatt | Barnsley | Robertson | Dougall | Williams J | Wyatt | Williams J L | Anderson | Carter | Meyer | Gauld | Govan |
| 12 | 2/10 | A | Doncaster | 5,300 | 6-4 | W | Anderson 3, Meyer 2, Penk | Barnsley | Robertson | Dougall | Williams J | Wyatt | Williams J L | Anderson | Carter | Meyer | Gauld | Penk |
| 13 | 4/10 | A | Norwich | 22,200 | 1-1 | D | Carter | Barnsley | Robertson | Dougall | Williams J | Wyatt | Williams J L | Anderson | Carter | Meyer | Carter | Penk |
| 14 | 8/10 | H | SOUTHEND | 25,349 | 3-1 | W | Costello (og), Williams J, Gauld | Barnsley | Robertson | Dougall | Williams J | Wyatt | Williams J L | Anderson | Gauld | Meyer | Gauld | Penk |
| 15 | 11/10 | H | SWINDON | 26,051 | 3-2 | W | Carter, Gauld 2 | Barnsley | Robertson | Dougall | Williams J | Wyatt | Williams J L | Anderson | Carter | Baker | Gauld | Penk |
| 16 | 18/10 | A | Mansfield | 12,488 | 4-1 | W | Carter 3, Anderson | Barnsley | Robertson | Dougall | Williams J | Wyatt | Williams J L | Anderson | Carter | Baker | Gauld | Penk |
| 17 | 25/10 | H | NOTTS CO | 25,910 | 3-0 | W | Baker, Gauld, Penk | Barnsley | Robertson | Dougall | Williams J | Wyatt | Williams J L | Anderson | Carter | Baker | Gauld | Penk |
| 18 | 1/11 | A | Chesterfield | 10,976 | 2-1 | W | Baker, Carter | Barnsley | Robertson | Dougall | Williams J | Wyatt | Williams J L | Anderson | Carter | Baker | Gauld | Penk |
| 19 | 8/11 | H | NEWPORT | 23,482 | 3-2 | W | Baker, Gauld 2 | Barnsley | Robertson | Dougall | Williams J | Wyatt | Williams J L | Anderson | Carter | Baker | Gauld | Penk |
| 20 | 22/11 | H | WREXHAM | 21,056 | 2-2 | D | Penk, Gauld | Barnsley | Robertson | Dougall | Williams J | Wyatt | Williams J L | Anderson | Gauld | Baker | Meyer | Penk |
| 21 | 29/11 | A | Southampton | 21,830 | 1-5 | L | Carter | Barnsley | Robertson | Fulton | Barrett | Wyatt | Williams J L | Anderson | Carter | Baker | Carter | Penk |
| 22 | 13/12 | A | Bradford C | 11,908 | 0-0 | D | | Barnsley | Robertson | Dougall | Williams J | Wyatt | Williams J L | Anderson | Carter | Baker | Gauld | Penk |
| 23 | 20/12 | H | HULL | 20,305 | 1-1 | D | Carter | Barnsley | Robertson | Dougall | Williams J | Wyatt | Casey | Anderson | Carter | Baker | Gauld | Penk |
| 24 | 26/12 | H | QP RANGERS | 30,036 | 3-2 | W | Carter, Gauld 2 | Barnsley | Robertson | Bellett | Williams J | Wyatt | Casey | Anderson | Carter | Baker | Gauld | Govan |
| 25 | 27/12 | A | QP Rangers | 15,656 | 1-2 | L | Gauld | Barnsley | Robertson | Bellett | Williams J | Wyatt | Casey | Anderson | Carter | Baker | Gauld | Govan |
| 26 | 17/1 | H | STOCKPORT | 10,099 | 2-1 | W | Govan, Baker | Barnsley | Robertson | Bellett | Williams J | Wyatt | Casey | Penk | Carter | Baker | Gauld | Govan |
| 27 | 24/1 | A | Southend | 12,410 | 0-0 | D | | Barnsley | Robertson | Bellett | Williams J | Wyatt | Casey | Penk | Carter | Baker | Gauld | Govan |
| 28 | 31/1 | H | Reading | 13,595 | 2-0 | W | Govan, Baker | Barnsley | Robertson | Bellett | Williams J | Wyatt | Casey | Penk | Carter | Baker | Gauld | Govan |
| 29 | 7/2 | H | COLCHESTER | 22,686 | 1-1 | D | Williams J | Barnsley | Fulton | Bellett | Williams J | Wyatt | Casey | Penk | Carter | Baker | Gauld | Govan |
| 30 | 14/2 | A | Bournemouth | 15,107 | 1-1 | D | Govan | Barnsley | Fulton | Bellett | Williams J | Wyatt | Casey | Penk | Carter | Baker | Gauld | Govan |
| 31 | 21/2 | H | NORWICH | 24,532 | 0-1 | L | | Barnsley | Fulton | Bellett | Williams J | Wyatt | Casey | Penk | Carter | Baker | Gauld | Anderson |
| 32 | 28/2 | A | Swindon | 13,090 | 4-3 | W | Gauld 3, Anderson | Barnsley | Fulton | Bellett | Williams J | Wyatt | Casey | Penk | Carter | Baker | Gauld | Anderson |
| 33 | 4/3 | A | ACCRINGTON S | 12,022 | 2-4 | L | Gauld, Penk | Barnsley | Fulton | Bellett | Williams J | Wyatt | Casey | Penk | Gauld | Jenkins | Gauld | Anderson |
| 34 | 7/3 | H | MANSFIELD | 17,597 | 8-3 | W | Gov', P'k, Wil' 2, G'd, Carr', Swin' (2og) | Barnsley | Fulton | Bellett | Williams J | Wyatt | Casey | Penk | Gauld | Carter | Baker | Govan |
| 35 | 14/3 | A | Notts Co | 7,369 | 2-1 | W | Gauld 2 | Wyllie | Fulton | Bellett | Williams J | Fincham | Casey | Penk | Gauld | Carter | Baker | Govan |
| 36 | 16/3 | H | Tranmere | 15,811 | 0-2 | L | | Wyllie | Fulton | Bellett | Williams J L | Fincham | Casey | Anderson | Williams J | Carter | Gauld | Govan |
| 37 | 21/3 | H | CHESTERFIELD | 17,334 | 2-0 | W | Jenkins, Carter | Wyllie | Fulton | Bellett | Williams J L | Fincham | Casey | Penk | Gauld | Carter | Jenkins | Govan |
| 38 | 27/3 | A | Brentford | 29,000 | 0-3 | L | | Wyllie | Fulton | Wyatt | Williams J L | Fincham | Casey | Baker | Gauld | Carter | Jenkins | Anderson |
| 39 | 28/3 | H | Newport | 8,108 | 1-0 | W | Carter | Barnsley | Fulton | Bellett | Williams J L | Fincham | Casey | Baker | Gauld | Carter | Williams J | Govan |
| 40 | 30/3 | H | BRENTFORD | 27,073 | 1-1 | D | Govan | Barnsley | Fulton | Bellett | Williams J L | Fincham | Casey | Baker | Gauld | Carter | Williams J | Govan |
| 41 | 4/4 | A | HALIFAX | 19,571 | 1-1 | D | Carter | Barnsley | Fulton | Bellett | Williams J L | Fincham | Casey | Baker | Williams J | Carter | Anderson | Govan |
| 42 | 11/4 | A | Wrexham | 8,817 | 1-1 | D | Williams J | Barnsley | Robertson | Wyatt | Williams J L | Fincham | Casey | Baker | Gauld | Carter | Williams J | Govan |
| 43 | 18/4 | H | SOUTHAMPTON | 23,775 | 1-0 | W | Carter | Barnsley | Robertson | Wyatt | Williams J L | Fincham | Casey | Baker | Gauld | Carter | Williams J | Govan |
| 44 | 20/4 | A | Halifax | 8,523 | 1-0 | W | Anderson | Barnsley | Robertson | Wyatt | Williams J L | Fincham | Casey | Anderson | Gauld | Carter | Williams J | Govan |
| 45 | 25/4 | A | Accrington S | 4,000 | 1-1 | D | Penk | Barnsley | Robertson | Wyatt | Williams J L | Fincham | Casey | Anderson | Gauld | Carter | Williams J | Penk |

| | | Date | Opponent | Attendance | Result | Score | Scorers |
|---|---|---|---|---|---|---|---|
| 1 | H | 15/11 | GILLINGHAM | 21,759 | D | 2-2 | Carter, Anderson |
| 1R | A | 19/11 | Gillingham | 10,459 | W | 4-1 | Meyer 3, Gauld |
| 2 | A | 6/12 | Coventry | 27,295 | W | 3-1 | Baker, Carter 2 |
| 3 | H | 10/1 | CARDIFF | 36,247 | L | 0-3 | |

| | | | | | | | | | | |
|---|---|---|---|---|---|---|---|---|---|---|
| Barnsley | Robertson | Dougall | Williams J | Wyatt | Williams JL | Anderson | Carter | Baker | Gauld | Penk |
| Barnsley | Robertson | Dougall | Williams J | Wyatt | Williams JL | Anderson | Gauld | Baker | Meyer | Penk |
| Barnsley | Robertson | Dougall | Williams J | Wyatt | Williams JL | Anderson | Carter | Baker | Gauld | Penk |
| Barnsley | Robertson | Bellett | Casey | Wyatt | Casey | Baker | Carter | Meyer | Gauld | Govan |

| | Appearances | | Goals | | |
|---|---|---|---|---|---|
| | Lge | FAC | Lge | FAC | Tot |
| Anderson, Peter | 30 | 3 | 7 | 1 | 8 |
| Baker, George | 32 | 4 | 6 | 1 | 7 |
| Barnsley, Geoff | 41 | 4 | | | |
| Barrett, Tommy | 8 | 1 | | | |
| Bellett, Wally | 18 | | | | |
| Carter, Wilf | 45 | 3 | 22 | 3 | 25 |
| Casey, Len | 24 | 1 | | | |
| Dougall, Neil | 20 | 3 | 1 | | 1 |
| Doughty, Eric | 1 | | | | |
| Fincham, Gordon | 13 | | | | |
| Fulton, Bryce | 14 | | | | |
| Gauld, Jimmy | 45 | 4 | 21 | 1 | 22 |
| Govan, Alex | 20 | 1 | 6 | | 6 |
| Jenkins, Reg | 4 | | 1 | | 1 |
| Meyer, Barrie | 8 | 2 | 5 | 3 | 8 |
| Penk, Harry | 37 | 3 | 9 | | 9 |
| Robertson, George | 33 | 4 | | | |
| Williams, John L | 24 | 3 | | | |
| Williams, Johnny | 45 | 4 | 7 | | 7 |
| Wyatt, Reg | 39 | 4 | 1 | | 1 |
| Wylie, Robinson | 5 | | | | |
| (own-goals) | | | 3 | | 3 |
| 21 players used | 506 | 44 | 89 | 9 | 98 |

| | P | Home | | | | | Away | | | | | Pts |
|---|---|---|---|---|---|---|---|---|---|---|---|---|
| | | W | D | L | F | A | W | D | L | F | A | |
| 1 PLYMOUTH | 46 | 14 | 7 | 2 | 55 | 27 | 9 | 9 | 5 | 34 | 32 | 62 |
| 2 Hull | 46 | 19 | 3 | 1 | 65 | 21 | 7 | 6 | 10 | 25 | 34 | 61 |
| 3 Brentford | 46 | 15 | 5 | 3 | 49 | 22 | 6 | 10 | 7 | 27 | 27 | 57 |
| 4 Norwich | 46 | 13 | 6 | 4 | 51 | 29 | 9 | 7 | 7 | 38 | 33 | 57 |
| 5 Colchester | 46 | 15 | 2 | 6 | 46 | 31 | 6 | 8 | 9 | 25 | 36 | 52 |
| 6 Reading | 46 | 16 | 4 | 3 | 51 | 21 | 5 | 4 | 14 | 27 | 42 | 50 |
| 7 Tranmere | 46 | 15 | 3 | 5 | 53 | 22 | 6 | 5 | 12 | 29 | 45 | 50 |
| 8 Southend | 46 | 14 | 6 | 3 | 52 | 26 | 7 | 2 | 14 | 33 | 54 | 50 |
| 9 Halifax | 46 | 14 | 5 | 4 | 48 | 25 | 7 | 3 | 13 | 32 | 52 | 50 |
| 10 Bury | 46 | 12 | 9 | 2 | 51 | 24 | 5 | 5 | 13 | 18 | 34 | 48 |
| 11 Bradford C | 46 | 13 | 4 | 6 | 47 | 25 | 5 | 7 | 11 | 37 | 51 | 47 |
| 12 Bournemouth | 46 | 12 | 9 | 2 | 40 | 18 | 5 | 3 | 15 | 29 | 51 | 46 |
| 13 QP Rangers | 46 | 14 | 6 | 3 | 49 | 28 | 5 | 2 | 16 | 25 | 49 | 46 |
| 14 Southampton | 46 | 12 | 7 | 4 | 57 | 33 | 5 | 4 | 14 | 31 | 47 | 45 |
| 15 Swindon | 46 | 13 | 4 | 6 | 39 | 25 | 3 | 9 | 11 | 20 | 32 | 45 |
| 16 Chesterfield | 46 | 12 | 5 | 6 | 40 | 26 | 5 | 5 | 13 | 27 | 38 | 44 |
| 17 Newport | 46 | 15 | 2 | 6 | 43 | 24 | 2 | 7 | 14 | 26 | 44 | 43 |
| 18 Wrexham | 46 | 12 | 6 | 5 | 40 | 30 | 2 | 8 | 13 | 23 | 47 | 42 |
| 19 Accrington S | 46 | 10 | 8 | 5 | 42 | 31 | 5 | 4 | 14 | 29 | 56 | 42 |
| 20 Mansfield | 46 | 11 | 5 | 7 | 38 | 42 | 3 | 8 | 12 | 35 | 56 | 41 |
| 21 Stockport | 46 | 9 | 7 | 7 | 33 | 23 | 4 | 3 | 16 | 32 | 55 | 36 |
| 22 Doncaster | 46 | 13 | 2 | 8 | 40 | 32 | 1 | 3 | 19 | 10 | 58 | 33 |
| 23 Notts Co | 46 | 5 | 9 | 9 | 33 | 39 | 4 | 4 | 16 | 22 | 57 | 29 |
| 24 Rochdale | 46 | 8 | 7 | 8 | 21 | 26 | 0 | 5 | 18 | 16 | 53 | 28 |
| | 1104 | 306 | 131 | 115 | 1083 | 650 | 115 | 131 | 306 | 650 | 1083 | 1104 |

# LEAGUE DIVISION 2

**Manager: Derek Ufton / Billy Bingham**

**SEASON 1967-68**

| # | | Date | Opponents | Att | F-A | Scorers | 1 | 2 | 3 | 4 | 5 | 6 | 7 | 8 | 9 | 10 | 11 | sub |
|---|---|------|-----------|-----|-----|---------|---|---|---|---|---|---|---|---|---|----|----|-----|
| 1 | A | 19/8 | Cardiff | 17,343 | D 1-1 | Mitten | Dunne | Everitt | Baird | Hore | Nelson | Newman | Davey | Tedesco | Etheridge | Piper | Mitten | |
| 2 | H | 23/8 | ASTON VILLA | 20,347 | W 2-1 | Tedesco, Davey | Dunne | Everitt | Baird | Hore | Nelson | Newman | Davey | Tedesco | Etheridge | Piper | Mitten | |
| 3 | H | 26/8 | PORTSMOUTH | 16,979 | L 1-2 | Piper | Dunne | Everitt | Baird | Hore | Nelson | Newman | Davey | Tedesco | Etheridge | Piper | Mitten | Reynolds |
| 4 | A | 28/8 | Aston Villa | 15,108 | W 1-0 | Mitten | Dunne | Rounsevell | Reeves | Everitt | Baird | Hore | Tedesco | Piper | Etheridge | Brimacombe | Mitten | |
| 5 | A | 2/9 | Norwich | 14,452 | L 0-2 | | Dunne | Rounsevell | Reeves | Everitt | Baird | Hore | Tedesco | Piper | Etheridge | Brimacombe | Mitten | |
| 6 | A | 6/9 | Crystal Palace | 16,372 | L 0-5 | | Dunne | Everitt | Baird | Hore | Nelson | Newman | Tedesco | Brimacombe | Etheridge | Piper | Mitten | Penrhyn |
| 7 | H | 9/9 | ROTHERHAM | 9,323 | L 0-1 | | Dunne | Everitt | Baird | Hore | Nelson | Newman | Neale | Tedesco | Etheridge | Piper | Mitten | |
| 8 | A | 16/9 | Derby | 21,516 | L 0-1 | | Dunne | Everitt | Baird | Hore | Nelson | Newman | Davey | Reynolds | Sillett | Piper | Mitten | Rounsevell |
| 9 | H | 23/9 | PRESTON | 10,889 | L 1-2 | Piper | Dunne | Rounsevell | Baird | Hore | Nelson | Newman | Davey | Davey | Sillett | Piper | Harrison | |
| 10 | A | 30/9 | Charlton | 11,208 | L 0-1 | | Dunne | Rounsevell | Everitt | Neale | Nelson | Newman | Sealey | Davey | Reynolds | Piper | Harrison | |
| 11 | H | 7/10 | HUDDERSFIELD | 12,900 | D 1-1 | Reynolds | Dunne | Everitt | Baird | Neale | Nelson | Hore | Sealey | Reynolds | Peacock | Brimacombe | Harrison | Sillett |
| 12 | A | 14/10 | Middlesbrough | 18,025 | L 0-5 | | Dunne | Everitt | Reeves | Piper | Baird | Newman | Sealey | Banks | Peacock | Banks | Reynolds | |
| 13 | H | 21/10 | HULL | 8,577 | L 2-5 | Davey, Harrison | Dunne | Everitt | Baird | Hore | Nelson | Newman | Davey | Piper | Etheridge | Etheridge | Harrison | |
| 14 | A | 28/10 | Millwall | 11,193 | L 0-3 | | Dunne | Everitt | Baird | Piper | Nelson | Newman | Sealey | Piper | Davey | Neale | Harrison | |
| 15 | H | 18/11 | BRISTOL CITY | 11,179 | L 0-1 | | Dunne | Everitt | Baird | Piper | Nelson | Hore | Davey | Bickle | Peacock | Neale | Harrison | |
| 16 | A | 25/11 | Ipswich | 14,919 | D 1-1 | Mitten | Dunne | Sillett | Baird | Neale | Nelson | Hore | Davey | Bickle | Peacock | Neale | Mitten | |
| 17 | H | 2/12 | CARLISLE | 8,791 | W 3-1 | Peacock, Harrison, Bickle | Dunne | Sillett | Baird | Neale | Nelson | Hore | Davey | Bickle | Peacock | Mitten | Harrison | |
| 18 | A | 9/12 | Bolton | 9,309 | W 2-1 | Piper, Bickle | Dunne | Sillett | Baird | Piper | Nelson | Hore | Neale | Bickle | Peacock | Mitten | Harrison | |
| 19 | H | 16/12 | CARDIFF | 10,736 | D 0-0 | | Dunne | Sillett | Baird | Piper | Nelson | Hore | Neale | Bickle | Peacock | Mitten | Harrison | |
| 20 | A | 23/12 | Portsmouth | 24,218 | D 0-0 | | Dunne | Sillett | Baird | Piper | Nelson | Hore | Neale | Bickle | Peacock | Mitten | Harrison | Reynolds |
| 21 | H | 26/12 | QP RANGERS | 21,003 | L 0-1 | | Dunne | Sillett | Baird | Piper | Nelson | Hore | Neale | Bickle | Davey | Mitten | Harrison | |
| 22 | A | 30/12 | QP Rangers | 15,889 | L 1-4 | Bickle | Dunne | Sillett | Baird | Piper | Nelson | Piper | Everitt | Bickle | Peacock | Mitten | Harrison | |
| 23 | H | 10/1 | NORWICH | 7,946 | D 2-2 | Harrison, Bickle | Dunne | Sillett | Baird | Piper | Nelson | Hore | Neale | Bickle | Peacock | Mitten | Harrison | |
| 24 | A | 20/1 | DERBY | 9,026 | L 3-4 | Mitten 2, Bickle | Dunne | Sillett | Baird | Neale | Nelson | Hore | Davey | Bickle | Peacock | Mitten | Harrison | |
| 25 | A | 3/2 | Preston | 13,980 | L 0-2 | | Shearing | Sillett | Reeves | Hore | Nelson | Saxton | Piper | Neale | Bickle | Bloomfield | Mitten | |
| 26 | H | 10/2 | CHARLTON | 9,036 | L 1-4 | Mitten | Dunne | Everitt | Reeves | Neale | Saxton | Mitten | Etheridge | Bickle | Tedesco | Piper | Reynolds | Davey |
| 27 | H | 17/2 | BLACKBURN | 7,986 | W 2-1 | Neale, Davey | Dunne | Sillett | Reeves | Hore | Saxton | Mitten | Davey | Piper | Tedesco | Neale | Bickle | Rounsevell |
| 28 | A | 24/2 | Huddersfield | 6,562 | W 1-0 | Reynolds | Dunne | Everitt | Reeves | Hore | Saxton | Neale | Davey | Piper | Reynolds | Neale | Mitten | |
| 29 | H | 2/3 | MIDDLESBROUGH | 9,040 | L 0-1 | | Dunne | Everitt | Reeves | Hore | Saxton | Mitten | Davey | Piper | Reynolds | Neale | Bickle | Tedesco |
| 30 | A | 9/3 | BLACKPOOL | 8,688 | D 2-2 | Reynolds, Tedesco | Dunne | Sillett | Everitt | Hore | Saxton | Etheridge | Davey | Piper | Tedesco | Reynolds | Mitten | Brimacombe |
| 31 | A | 16/3 | Hull | 11,948 | W 2-0 | Reynolds, Piper | Dunne | Sillett | Brimacombe | Hore | Saxton | Mitten | Davey | Piper | Tedesco | Burnside | Reynolds | |
| 32 | H | 19/3 | Rotherham | 16,350 | L 0-1 | | Dunne | Sillett | Sullivan | Hore | Saxton | Mitten | Davey | Bickle | Tedesco | Burnside | Reynolds | |
| 33 | H | 23/3 | MILLWALL | 7,728 | W 2-1 | Piper 2 | Dunne | Sillett | Sullivan | Hore | Saxton | Mitten | Piper | Piper | Bickle | Burnside | Reynolds | |
| 34 | A | 30/3 | Blackpool | 14,586 | L 0-2 | | Dunne | Sillett | Sullivan | Hore | Saxton | Etheridge | Reynolds | Bickle | Tedesco | Burnside | Harrison | Etheridge |
| 35 | H | 13/4 | Bristol City | 17,076 | L 0-2 | | Dunne | Sillett | Sullivan | Hore | Saxton | Etheridge | Bickle | Piper | Mitten | Burnside | Reynolds | Davey |
| 36 | H | 15/4 | BIRMINGHAM | 13,497 | L 1-2 | Bickle | Dunne | Reeves | Sullivan | Saxton | Nelson | Etheridge | Piper | Burnside | Bickle | Reynolds | Bickle | |
| 37 | A | 16/4 | Birmingham | 29,359 | D 2-2 | Bickle 2 | Dunne | Reeves | Sullivan | Saxton | Nelson | Hore | Reynolds | Piper | Bickle | Etheridge | Burnside | |
| 38 | H | 20/4 | IPSWICH | 9,956 | L 0-1 | | Dunne | Reeves | Sullivan | Saxton | Nelson | Hore | Reynolds | Piper | Bickle | Etheridge | Burnside | |
| 39 | A | 24/4 | Blackburn | 7,465 | D 1-1 | Bickle | Dunne | Reeves | Sullivan | Saxton | Nelson | Hore | Reynolds | Piper | Bickle | Etheridge | Burnside | |
| 40 | H | 27/4 | Carlisle | 5,938 | L 0-2 | | Dunne | Reeves | Sullivan | Saxton | Nelson | Hore | Reynolds | Piper | Bickle | Etheridge | Burnside | |
| 41 | H | 4/5 | BOLTON | 5,371 | L 1-2 | Reynolds | Dunne | Reeves | Sullivan | Hore | Nelson | Hore | Davey | Piper | Bickle | Etheridge | Burnside | |
| 42 | H | 11/5 | CRYSTAL PALACE | 4,768 | W 2-1 | Tomkins (o.g), Bickle | Dunne | Reeves | Reeves | Hore | Saxton | Burnside | Davey | Piper | Bickle | Reynolds | Mitten | |

Team line-ups:

Dunne · Everitt · Baird · Hore · Newman · Nelson · Davey · Tedesco · Bickle · Neale · Piper · Sillett · Mitten

Dunne · Sillett · Everitt · Piper · Nelson · Baird · Neale · Bickle · Bloomfield · Mitten · Peacock · Etheridge

## League Table

| | | | Home | | | | | Away | | | | | | |
|---|---|---|---|---|---|---|---|---|---|---|---|---|---|---|
| | P | W | D | L | F | A | W | D | L | F | A | F | A | Pts |
| 1 Ipswich | 42 | 12 | 7 | 2 | 45 | 20 | 10 | 8 | 3 | 34 | 24 | | | 59 |
| 2 QP Rangers | 42 | 18 | 2 | 1 | 45 | 9 | 7 | 6 | 8 | 22 | 27 | | | 58 |
| 3 Blackpool | 42 | 12 | 6 | 3 | 33 | 16 | 12 | 4 | 5 | 38 | 27 | | | 58 |
| 4 Birmingham | 42 | 12 | 6 | 3 | 54 | 21 | 7 | 8 | 6 | 29 | 30 | | | 52 |
| 5 Portsmouth | 42 | 13 | 6 | 2 | 43 | 18 | 5 | 7 | 9 | 25 | 37 | | | 49 |
| 6 Mid'brough | 42 | 10 | 7 | 4 | 39 | 19 | 7 | 5 | 9 | 21 | 35 | | | 46 |
| 7 Millwall | 42 | 9 | 10 | 2 | 35 | 16 | 5 | 7 | 9 | 27 | 34 | | | 45 |
| 8 Blackburn | 42 | 13 | 5 | 3 | 34 | 16 | 3 | 6 | 12 | 22 | 33 | | | 43 |
| 9 Norwich | 42 | 12 | 4 | 5 | 40 | 30 | 4 | 7 | 10 | 20 | 35 | | | 43 |
| 10 Carlisle | 42 | 9 | 9 | 3 | 38 | 22 | 5 | 4 | 12 | 20 | 30 | | | 41 |
| 11 Crys Palace | 42 | 11 | 4 | 6 | 34 | 19 | 3 | 7 | 11 | 22 | 37 | | | 39 |
| 12 Bolton | 42 | 8 | 6 | 7 | 37 | 28 | 5 | 7 | 9 | 23 | 35 | | | 39 |
| 13 Cardiff | 42 | 9 | 6 | 6 | 35 | 29 | 4 | 6 | 11 | 25 | 37 | | | 38 |
| 14 Huddersfield | 42 | 10 | 6 | 5 | 29 | 23 | 3 | 6 | 12 | 17 | 38 | | | 38 |
| 15 Charlton | 42 | 10 | 6 | 5 | 43 | 25 | 3 | 6 | 12 | 20 | 43 | | | 37 |
| 16 Aston Villa | 42 | 10 | 3 | 8 | 35 | 30 | 5 | 4 | 12 | 19 | 34 | | | 37 |
| 17 Hull | 42 | 6 | 8 | 7 | 25 | 23 | 6 | 5 | 10 | 33 | 50 | | | 37 |
| 18 Derby | 42 | 8 | 5 | 8 | 40 | 35 | 5 | 5 | 11 | 31 | 43 | | | 36 |
| 19 Bristol City | 42 | 8 | 7 | 7 | 26 | 25 | 4 | 3 | 13 | 22 | 37 | | | 36 |
| 20 Preston | 42 | 8 | 7 | 6 | 29 | 24 | 4 | 4 | 13 | 14 | 41 | | | 35 |
| 21 Rotherham | 42 | 7 | 4 | 10 | 22 | 32 | 3 | 7 | 11 | 20 | 44 | | | 31 |
| 22 PLYMOUTH | 42 | 5 | 4 | 12 | 26 | 36 | 4 | 5 | 12 | 12 | 36 | | | 27 |
| | 924 | 219 | 128 | 115 | 787 | 516 | 115 | 128 | 219 | 516 | 787 | | | 924 |

## Appearances and Goals

| | Appearances | | | | | | Goals | | | |
|---|---|---|---|---|---|---|---|---|---|---|
| | Lge | Sub | LC | Sub | FAC | Sub | Lge | LC | FAC | Tot |
| Baird, Doug | 23 | | 1 | | | | | | | |
| Banks, Alan | 2 | | | | | | | | | |
| Bickle, Mike | 25 | 1 | | | | | 10 | | | 10 |
| Bloomfield, Jimmy | 1 | 1 | | | | | | | | |
| Brimacombe, Tony | 5 | 1 | | | | | | | | |
| Burnside, David | 12 | | | | | | | | | |
| Davey, Steve | 20 | 2 | 1 | | | | 3 | | | 3 |
| Dunne, Pat | 41 | | 1 | | 1 | | | | | |
| Etheridge, Keith | 18 | 1 | | | | 1 | | | | |
| Everitt, Mike | 20 | | 1 | | 1 | | | | | |
| Harrison, Mike | 15 | | | | | | 3 | | | 3 |
| Hore, John | 39 | 1 | | | | | | | | |
| Mitten, John | 28 | 1 | 1 | | 1 | | 6 | | | 6 |
| Neale, Duncan | 17 | 1 | 1 | | | | 1 | | | 1 |
| Nelson, Andy | 26 | | | | 1 | | | | | |
| Newman, John | 10 | 1 | | | 1 | | | | | |
| Peacock, Alan | 11 | | | | 1 | | 1 | | | 1 |
| Penrhyn, Norman | | 1 | | | | | | | | |
| Piper, Norman | 41 | | 1 | | 1 | | 6 | | | 6 |
| Reeves, Mike | 16 | | | | | | | | | |
| Reynolds, Richard | 20 | 2 | | | | | 5 | | | 5 |
| Rounsevell, Tony | 4 | 2 | | | | | | | | |
| Saxton, Bobby | 18 | | | | | | | | | |
| Sealey, Alan | 4 | | | | | | | | | |
| Shearing, Peter | 1 | | | | | | | | | |
| Sillett, John | 19 | 1 | 1 | | 1 | | | | | |
| Sullivan, Colin | 11 | | | | | | | | | |
| Tedesco, John | 15 | 1 | | | 1 | | | | | |
| (own-goals) | | | | | | | 2 | | | 2 |
| | | | | | | | 1 | | | 1 |
| 28 players used | 462 | 11 | 11 | | 11 | 1 | 38 | 11 | 11 | 38 |

# LEAGUE DIVISION 3

## Manager: Tony Waiters

## SEASON 1974-75

| # | Date | H/A | Opponents | Att | F-A | | Scorers | 1 | 2 | 3 | 4 | 5 | 6 | 7 | 8 | 9 | 10 | 11 | sub |
|---|------|-----|-----------|-----|-----|---|---------|---|---|---|---|---|---|---|---|---|----|----|-----|
| 1 | 17/8 | A | Preston | 11,663 | 0-1 | L | | Furnell | Darke | Burrows P | Hore | Griffiths | Green | Delve | Davey | Rafferty | Mariner | Burrows H | Pearson |
| 2 | 24/8 | H | GRIMSBY | 8,531 | 2-1 | W | Mariner, Rafferty | Furnell | Darke | Burrows P | Hore | Griffiths | Green | Delve | Davey | Mariner | Rafferty | Burrows H | Pearson |
| 3 | 30/8 | A | Southend | 8,600 | 1-2 | L | Rafferty | Furnell | Darke | Burrows P | Hore | Griffiths | Green | Delve | Davey | Rafferty | Mariner | Burrows H | |
| 4 | 4/9 | A | Aldershot | 3,756 | 3-4 | L | Burrows H, Rafferty, Green | Furnell | Darke | Burrows P | Hore | Griffiths | Green | Delve | Davey | Rafferty | Hardcastle | Burrows H | Mariner |
| 5 | 7/9 | H | TRANMERE | 5,752 | 4-1 | W | Mariner, Rafferty 3 | Furnell | Darke | Burrows P | Delve | Griffiths | Green | Mariner | Davey | Rafferty | Hardcastle | Burrows H | Hore |
| 6 | 14/9 | A | Swindon | 5,495 | 0-2 | L | | Furnell | Darke | Burrows P | Green | Griffiths | Delve | Mariner | Davey | Rafferty | Hardcastle | Randell | |
| 7 | 17/9 | A | Colchester | 5,389 | 0-1 | L | | Furnell | Darke | Provan | Hardcastle | Saxton | Green | Hore | Mariner | Mariner | Saxton | Randell | Davey |
| 8 | 21/9 | H | GILLINGHAM | 5,556 | 1-1 | D | Randell | Furnell | Darke | Provan | Griffiths | Saxton | Green | Delve | Hardcastle | Mariner | Rafferty | Randell | Davey |
| 9 | 24/9 | H | HEREFORD | 5,519 | 1-0 | W | Mariner | Furnell | Darke | Provan | Griffiths | Griffiths | Saxton | Delve | Randell | Mariner | Rafferty | Burrows H | Hardcastle |
| 10 | 28/9 | A | Wrexham | 3,814 | 1-5 | L | Green | Furnell | Darke | Provan | Green | Saxton | Green | Randell | Mariner | Rafferty | Delve | Burrows H | Hardcastle |
| 11 | 1/10 | H | HUDDERSFIELD | 5,324 | 2-0 | W | Randell, Mariner | Furnell | Darke | Provan | Delve | Saxton | Hardcastle | Randell | Hardcastle | Mariner | Hardcastle | Burrows H | Hardcastle |
| 12 | 5/10 | H | WALSALL | 5,765 | 2-1 | W | Rafferty, Delve | Furnell | Darke | Provan | Delve | Saxton | Green | Randell | Mariner | Rafferty | Hardcastle | Burrows H | Hardcastle |
| 13 | 12/10 | A | Port Vale | 3,634 | 0-2 | L | | Furnell | Darke | Provan | Delve | Saxton | Delve | Randell | Hardcastle | Mariner | Rafferty | Burrows H | Hardcastle |
| 14 | 15/10 | H | ALDERSHOT | 5,175 | 1-0 | W | Rafferty | Furnell | Darke | Burrows P | Saxton | Green | Delve | Randell | Hardcastle | Mariner | Rafferty | Johnson | Griffiths |
| 15 | 19/10 | A | PETERBOROUGH | 6,843 | 2-0 | W | Green, Rafferty | Furnell | Darke | Burrows P | Saxton | Green | Delve | Randell | Johnson | Mariner | Johnson | McAuley | |
| 16 | 26/10 | A | Bury | 4,697 | 1-0 | W | Forrest (og) | Furnell | Darke | Burrows P | Delve | Saxton | Delve | Randell | Mariner | Rafferty | Rafferty | McAuley | |
| 17 | 2/11 | H | Charlton | 8,495 | 2-0 | W | Johnson, McAuley | Furnell | Hore | Burrows P | Saxton | Green | Delve | Randell | Johnson | Mariner | Rafferty | McAuley | |
| 18 | 9/11 | H | WATFORD | 8,063 | 1-1 | D | Johnson | Furnell | Darke | Burrows P | Saxton | Green | Delve | Randell | Johnson | Mariner | Rafferty | McAuley | |
| 19 | 16/11 | A | Crystal Palace | 19,308 | 3-3 | D | Rafferty, Johnson, Mariner | Furnell | Darke | Burrows P | Saxton | Green | Delve | Randell | Johnson | Mariner | Rafferty | McAuley | Vassallo |
| 20 | 30/11 | A | Chesterfield | 4,663 | 2-1 | W | Rafferty, Mariner | Furnell | Hore | Burrows P | Delve | Saxton | Delve | Randell | Johnson | Rafferty | Rafferty | McAuley | |
| 21 | 7/12 | H | BOURNEMOUTH | 9,897 | 1-0 | W | Rafferty | Furnell | Hore | Burrows P | Saxton | Green | Delve | Randell | Johnson | Rafferty | Johnson | McAuley | |
| 22 | 21/12 | A | Brighton | 9,193 | 2-2 | D | Rafferty 2 | Furnell | Hore | Burrows P | Delve | Green | Saxton | Randell | Johnson | Mariner | Rafferty | McAuley | |
| 23 | 26/12 | H | SWINDON | 18,027 | 4-3 | W | Randell, Delve, Mariner, Rafferty | Furnell | Hore | Burrows P | Saxton | Green | Delve | Randell | Johnson | Mariner | Johnson | McAuley | Rogers |
| 24 | 28/12 | A | Halifax | 2,063 | 1-1 | D | McAuley | Furnell | Hore | Burrows P | Sutton | Green | Saxton | Johnson | Mariner | Rafferty | Hardcastle | McAuley | |
| 25 | 1/11 | A | Bournemouth | 7,352 | 7-3 | W | Raf', Mar' 2, J'son, McA', Delve, Rand' | Furnell | Hore | Burrows P | Sutton | Green | Delve | Randell | Johnson | Mariner | Rafferty | McAuley | |
| 26 | 18/1 | H | CHESTERFIELD | 13,005 | 3-0 | W | Delve, Mariner, Vassallo | Furnell | Hore | Burrows P | Delve | Green | Delve | Randell | Johnson | Mariner | Rafferty | McAuley | Vassallo |
| 27 | 1/2 | A | Watford | 8,563 | 3-1 | W | Markham (og), Johnson, Mariner | Furnell | Hore | Burrows P | Saxton | Green | Delve | Randell | Johnson | Mariner | Rafferty | McAuley | |
| 28 | 4/2 | H | BLACKBURN | 28,744 | 2-1 | W | Rafferty, Johnson | Furnell | Hore | Burrows P | Saxton | Green | Delve | Randell | Johnson | Mariner | Rafferty | McAuley | |
| 29 | 8/2 | H | CHARLTON | 22,946 | 1-1 | D | Rafferty | Furnell | Hore | Burrows P | Saxton | Green | Delve | Randell | Johnson | Mariner | Rafferty | McAuley | |
| 30 | 15/2 | A | Blackburn | 17,734 | 2-5 | L | McAuley, Jones (og) | Furnell | Hore | Burrows P | Saxton | Green | Delve | Randell | Johnson | Mariner | Rafferty | McAuley | |
| 31 | 22/2 | H | CRYSTAL PALACE | 21,002 | 0-1 | L | | Furnell | Hore | Burrows P | Delve | Saxton | Green | Randell | Johnson | Mariner | Rafferty | McAuley | Vassallo |
| 32 | 28/2 | H | SOUTHEND | 16,321 | 1-0 | W | Mariner | Furnell | Hore | Burrows P | Saxton | Green | Hardcastle | Randell | Vassallo | Mariner | Rafferty | McAuley | Darke |
| 33 | 8/3 | A | Hereford | 9,296 | 5-1 | W | Hardc', Mariner, Rafferty 2, Vassal' | Furnell | Hore | Burrows P | Hardcastle | Green | Saxton | Randell | Johnson | Mariner | Rafferty | McAuley | Vassallo |
| 34 | 15/3 | H | WREXHAM | 14,855 | 0-3 | L | | Furnell | Hore | Burrows P | Delve | Green | Saxton | Randell | Johnson | Mariner | Rafferty | McAuley | |
| 35 | 18/3 | H | PRESTON | 22,063 | 2-1 | W | Mariner 2 | Furnell | Hore | Burrows P | Saxton | Green | Delve | Randell | Johnson | Mariner | Rafferty | McAuley | |
| 36 | 21/3 | A | Tranmere | 3,040 | 3-1 | W | Green, Johnson, Rafferty | Furnell | Hore | Burrows P | Saxton | Green | Delve | Randell | Johnson | Mariner | Rafferty | McAuley | |
| 37 | 28/3 | H | HALIFAX | 19,580 | 2-0 | W | Collings (og), McAuley | Furnell | Hore | Burrows P | Saxton | Green | Delve | Randell | Johnson | Mariner | Rafferty | McAuley | |
| 38 | 29/3 | H | BRIGHTON | 19,396 | 2-2 | D | Green, Mariner | Furnell | Hore | Burrows P | Saxton | Green | Delve | Randell | Johnson | Mariner | Rafferty | McAuley | |
| 39 | 31/3 | A | Gillingham | 11,200 | 2-2 | D | Green, Rafferty | Furnell | Hore | Burrows P | Saxton | Green | Saxton | Vassallo | Johnson | Mariner | Rafferty | McAuley | |
| 40 | 5/4 | H | BURY | 14,940 | 2-1 | W | Rafferty, Johnson | Furnell | Hore | Burrows P | Saxton | Green | Saxton | Vassallo | Johnson | Mariner | Rafferty | McAuley | |
| 41 | 8/4 | A | Huddersfield | 2,947 | 2-0 | W | Mariner 2 | Furnell | Hore | Burrows P | Saxton | Green | Saxton | Vassallo | Johnson | Mariner | Rafferty | McAuley | Darke |
| 42 | 12/4 | A | Walsall | 7,404 | 0-0 | D | | Furnell | Hore | Burrows P | Delve | Green | Delve | Vassallo | Johnson | Mariner | Rafferty | McAuley | |
| 43 | 15/4 | H | COLCHESTER | 23,551 | 1-0 | W | Mariner | Furnell | Hore | Burrows P | Saxton | Green | Delve | Randell | Johnson | Mariner | Rafferty | McAuley | |
| 44 | 19/4 | H | PORT VALE | 22,447 | 1-1 | D | Delve | Furnell | Hore | Burrows P | Saxton | Green | Delve | Randell | Johnson | Mariner | Rafferty | McAuley | |
| 45 | 22/4 | A | Grimsby | 9,052 | 1-1 | D | Mariner | Furnell | Hore | Burrows P | Saxton | Green | Delve | Randell | Johnson | Mariner | Rafferty | McAuley | |

## LEAGUE CUP

| | | Date | Opponent | Att | Res | Score | Scorers |
|---|---|---|---|---|---|---|---|
| 1 | A | 20/8 | Bristol Rov | 8,974 | D | 0-0 | |
| 1R | H | 27/8 | BRISTOL ROV | 11,213 | L | 0-1 | |

## FA CUP

| | | Date | Opponent | Att | Res | Score | Scorers |
|---|---|---|---|---|---|---|---|
| 1 | A | 23/11 | Dartford | 4,384 | W | 3-2 | Randell 2, Mariner |
| 2 | H | 14/12 | CRYSTAL PALACE | 17,473 | W | 2-1 | Green, Rafferty |
| 3 | H | 3/1 | BLACKPOOL | 23,143 | W | 2-0 | Rafferty 2 |
| 4 | H | 24/1 | EVERTON | 38,000 | L | 1-3 | Vassallo |

### Team selections

League Cup (positions 1–12):

|  | | | | | | | | | | | | |
|---|---|---|---|---|---|---|---|---|---|---|---|---|
| LC 1 | Furnell | Darke | Burrows P | Hore | Griffiths | Green | Delve | Davey | Rafferty | Mariner | Burrows H | Pearson |
| LC 1R | Furnell | Darke | Burrows P | Hore | Griffiths | Green | Delve | Davey | Rafferty | Mariner | Burrows H | |

FA Cup (positions 1–12):

|  | | | | | | | | | | | | |
|---|---|---|---|---|---|---|---|---|---|---|---|---|
| FA 1 | Furnell | Hore | Burrows P | Delve | Saxton | Green | Randell | Rafferty | Mariner | Johnson | McAuley | Rogers |
| FA 2 | Furnell | Hore | Burrows P | Saxton | Green | Delve | Randell | Johnson | Mariner | Rafferty | McAuley | Rogers |
| FA 3 | Furnell | Hore | Burrows P | Delve | Green | Saxton | Johnson | Mariner | Rafferty | Hardcastle | McAuley | Rogers |
| FA 4 | Furnell | Saxton | Burrows P | Saxton | Green | Delve | Randell | Johnson | Vassallo | Rafferty | McAuley | |

### Final Table

| Pos | Team | P | Home W | D | L | F | A | Away W | D | L | F | A | Pts |
|---|---|---|---|---|---|---|---|---|---|---|---|---|---|
| 1 | Blackburn | 46 | 15 | 7 | 1 | 40 | 16 | 7 | 9 | 7 | 28 | 29 | 60 |
| 2 | PLYMOUTH | 46 | 16 | 5 | 2 | 38 | 19 | 6 | 6 | 9 | 41 | 39 | 59 |
| 3 | Charlton | 46 | 15 | 5 | 3 | 51 | 29 | 7 | 6 | 10 | 25 | 32 | 55 |
| 4 | Swindon | 46 | 18 | 3 | 2 | 43 | 17 | 3 | 8 | 12 | 21 | 41 | 53 |
| 5 | Crys Palace | 46 | 14 | 8 | 1 | 48 | 22 | 4 | 7 | 12 | 18 | 35 | 51 |
| 6 | Port Vale | 46 | 15 | 6 | 2 | 37 | 19 | 3 | 9 | 11 | 24 | 35 | 51 |
| 7 | Peterborough | 46 | 10 | 9 | 4 | 24 | 17 | 9 | 3 | 11 | 23 | 36 | 50 |
| 8 | Walsall | 46 | 15 | 5 | 3 | 46 | 13 | 3 | 8 | 12 | 21 | 39 | 49 |
| 9 | Preston | 46 | 16 | 5 | 2 | 42 | 19 | 3 | 6 | 14 | 21 | 37 | 49 |
| 10 | Gillingham | 46 | 14 | 6 | 3 | 43 | 23 | 3 | 8 | 12 | 22 | 37 | 48 |
| 11 | Colchester | 46 | 13 | 7 | 3 | 45 | 22 | 4 | 6 | 13 | 25 | 41 | 47 |
| 12 | Hereford | 46 | 14 | 6 | 3 | 42 | 21 | 2 | 8 | 13 | 22 | 45 | 46 |
| 13 | Wrexham | 46 | 10 | 8 | 5 | 41 | 23 | 5 | 7 | 11 | 24 | 32 | 45 |
| 14 | Bury | 46 | 13 | 6 | 4 | 38 | 17 | 3 | 6 | 14 | 15 | 33 | 44 |
| 15 | Chesterfield | 46 | 11 | 7 | 5 | 37 | 25 | 5 | 5 | 13 | 25 | 41 | 44 |
| 16 | Grimsby | 46 | 12 | 8 | 3 | 35 | 19 | 2 | 5 | 15 | 20 | 45 | 43 |
| 17 | Halifax | 46 | 11 | 10 | 2 | 33 | 20 | 2 | 7 | 14 | 16 | 45 | 43 |
| 18 | Southend | 46 | 11 | 9 | 3 | 32 | 17 | 2 | 7 | 14 | 14 | 34 | 42 |
| 19 | Brighton | 46 | 14 | 7 | 2 | 38 | 21 | 2 | 3 | 18 | 18 | 43 | 42 |
| 20 | Aldershot* | 46 | 13 | 5 | 5 | 40 | 21 | 1 | 6 | 16 | 13 | 42 | 38 |
| 21 | Bournemouth | 46 | 9 | 6 | 8 | 27 | 25 | 4 | 6 | 13 | 17 | 33 | 38 |
| 22 | Tranmere | 46 | 12 | 4 | 7 | 39 | 21 | 2 | 5 | 16 | 16 | 36 | 37 |
| 23 | Watford | 46 | 9 | 7 | 7 | 30 | 31 | 1 | 10 | 12 | 22 | 44 | 37 |
| 24 | Huddersfield | 46 | 9 | 6 | 8 | 32 | 29 | 2 | 4 | 17 | 15 | 47 | 32 |
| | | 1104 | 309 | 155 | 88 | 921 | 506 | 88 | 155 | 309 | 506 | 921 | 1103 |

* deducted 1 pt

### Appearances and Goals

| Player | Lge | Sub | LC | Sub | FAC | Sub | Goals Lge | LC | FAC | Tot |
|---|---|---|---|---|---|---|---|---|---|---|
| Burrows, Harry | 10 | | 2 | | | | 1 | | | 1 |
| Burrows, Phil | 39 | | 2 | | 4 | | | | | |
| Darke, Peter | 19 | 2 | 2 | | | | | | | |
| Davey, Steve | 6 | 2 | 2 | | | | | | | |
| Delve, John | 42 | | 2 | | 4 | | 5 | | | 5 |
| Furnell, Jim | 46 | | 2 | | 4 | | | | | |
| Green, Mike | 46 | | 2 | | 4 | | 6 | | 1 | 7 |
| Griffiths, Clive | 10 | 1 | 2 | | | | | | | |
| Hardcastle, Peter | 12 | 1 | | | 1 | | 1 | | | 1 |
| Hore, John | 33 | 1 | 2 | | 4 | | | | | |
| Johnson, Brian | 32 | | | | 4 | | | | | |
| Mariner, Paul | 45 | 1 | 2 | | 3 | | 8 | | | 8 |
| McAuley, Hugh | 32 | | 2 | | 4 | | 20 | | 1 | 21 |
| Pearson, Ian | 7 | 2 | | 1 | 1 | | 5 | | | 5 |
| Provan, David | 7 | | | | | | | | | |
| Rafferty, Bill | 46 | | 2 | | 4 | | 23 | | 3 | 26 |
| Randell, Colin | 36 | | | | 3 | | 4 | | 2 | 6 |
| Rogers, Alan | 38 | 1 | | | 3 | 3 | | | | |
| Saxton, Bobby | 38 | | | | 4 | | | | | |
| Sutton, Dave | 2 | | | | | | | | | |
| Vassallo, Barrie | 5 | 5 | | | 1 | | 2 | | 1 | 3 |
| (own-goals) | | | | | | | 4 | | | 4 |
| 21 players used | 506 | 16 | 22 | 1 | 44 | 3 | 79 | | 8 | 87 |

# LEAGUE DIVISION 2

**Manager: Tony Waiters / Mike Kelly**  **SEASON 1976-77**

| # | H/A | Date | Opponents | Att | Res | F-A | Scorers | 1 | 2 | 3 | 4 | 5 | 6 | 7 | 8 | 9 | 10 | 11 | sub |
|---|-----|------|-----------|-----|-----|-----|---------|---|---|---|---|---|---|---|---|---|----|----|-----|
| 1 | A | 21/8 | Oldham | 7,378 | D | 2-2 | Mariner, Johnson | Ramsbottom | Darke | Horswill | Harrison | Sutton | Green | Hall | Johnson | Mariner | Collins | McAuley | |
| 2 | H | 24/8 | BLACKBURN | 13,553 | W | 4-0 | Johnson, Collins, Hall, Mariner | Ramsbottom | Darke | Horswill | Harrison | Sutton | Green | Johnson | Hall | Mariner | Collins | McAuley | Delve |
| 3 | H | 28/8 | NOTTS CO | 14,539 | L | 1-2 | Mariner | Ramsbottom | Darke | Horswill | Harrison | Sutton | Green | Hall | Johnson | Mariner | Collins | McAuley | Rogers |
| 4 | A | 4/9 | Orient | 4,808 | D | 2-2 | Green, Mariner | Ramsbottom | Darke | Horswill | Harrison | Sutton | Green | Delve | Johnson | Mariner | Collins | McAuley | Delve |
| 5 | H | 11/9 | CHELSEA | 18,356 | L | 2-3 | Hall, Mariner | Ramsbottom | Randell | Horswill | Harrison | Sutton | Green | Delve | Johnson | Mariner | Hall | Hall | Hamilton |
| 6 | A | 18/9 | Millwall | 9,883 | L | 0-3 | | Ramsbottom | Randell | Horswill | Delve | Sutton | Green | Hall | Hall | Mariner | Johnson | Rogers | Foster |
| 7 | H | 25/9 | BOLTON | 12,564 | D | 1-1 | Mariner | Ramsbottom | Randell | Horswill | Delve | Sutton | Green | Johnson | Harrison | Mariner | Johnson | Collins | Rogers |
| 8 | H | 2/10 | LUTON | 12,187 | W | 1-0 | Johnson | Ramsbottom | Randell | Horswill | Delve | Sutton | Green | Hall | Johnson | Mariner | Johnson | Hall | |
| 9 | A | 9/10 | Blackpool | 12,647 | W | 2-0 | Collins, Horswill | Ramsbottom | Randell | Horswill | Delve | Sutton | Green | Hall | Johnson | Mariner | Collins | Harrison | Hamilton |
| 10 | H | 16/10 | CARDIFF | 14,198 | D | 2-2 | Mariner, Hall | Barron | Randell | Horswill | Delve | Sutton | Green | Hall | Harrison | Mariner | Collins | Hamilton | Hamilton |
| 11 | A | 23/10 | Bristol Rov | 10,258 | D | 1-1 | Hall | Ramsbottom | Randell | Horswill | Delve | Sutton | Green | Hall | Hamilton | Trusson | Harrison | Collins | Johnson |
| 12 | H | 30/10 | BURNLEY | 14,704 | L | 0-1 | | Ramsbottom | Randell | Horswill | Delve | Sutton | Peddelty | Hall | Harrison | Austin | Collins | Hamilton | Johnson |
| 13 | A | 5/11 | Charlton | 13,617 | L | 1-3 | Hall | Ramsbottom | Randell | Horswill | Delve | Sutton | Peddelty | Hall | Hamilton | Hamilton | Harrison | Johnson | |
| 14 | H | 13/11 | FULHAM | 25,335 | D | 2-2 | Austin, Johnson | Barron | Randell | Horswill | Collins | Sutton | Peddelty | Hall | Hamilton | Austin | Harrison | Collins | |
| 15 | A | 20/11 | Hull | 8,161 | L | 1-3 | Harrison | Barron | Randell | Horswill | Johnson | Sutton | Peddelty | Hall | Hamilton | Austin | Harrison | Collins | Delve |
| 16 | H | 27/11 | CARLISLE | 10,204 | L | 0-1 | | Ramsbottom | Randell | Horswill | Johnson | Sutton | Green | Hall | Harrison | Austin | Foster | Collins | McAuley |
| 17 | A | 4/12 | Wolves | 16,370 | L | 0-4 | | Ramsbottom | Randell | Horswill | Delve | Sutton | Green | Hall | Harrison | Austin | Foster | Collins | |
| 18 | H | 11/12 | SHEFFIELD UTD | 8,827 | D | 0-0 | | Ramsbottom | Randell | Horswill | Delve | Sutton | Green | Hall | Peddelty | Austin | Collins | Trusson | |
| 19 | A | 18/12 | Nott'm Forest | 15,180 | L | 1-1 | Austin | Ramsbottom | Randell | Horswill | Delve | Sutton | Green | Hall | Peddelty | Austin | Bannister | Collins | |
| 20 | H | 27/12 | SOUTHAMPTON | 24,787 | L | 1-1 | Bannister | Ramsbottom | Randell | Horswill | Delve | Sutton | Peddelty | Hall | Green | Austin | Bannister | Collins | |
| 21 | H | 1/1 | CHARLTON | 13,445 | W | 1-0 | Austin | Ramsbottom | Randell | Horswill | Peddelty | Sutton | Green | Hall | Delve | Austin | Bannister | Collins | |
| 22 | A | 3/1 | Burnley | 10,399 | W | 2-0 | Green, Austin | Ramsbottom | Randell | Horswill | Delve | Sutton | Green | Hall | Harrison | Austin | Bannister | Collins | |
| 23 | H | 22/1 | OLDHAM | 9,200 | D | 2-2 | Austin, Craven | Ramsbottom | Randell | Horswill | Craven | Peddelty | Green | Hall | Harrison | Austin | Bannister | Rogers | |
| 24 | A | 5/2 | Notts Co | 9,079 | L | 0-2 | | Ramsbottom | Randell | Horswill | Craven | Peddelty | Green | Hall | Harrison | Austin | Bannister | Rogers | |
| 25 | A | 9/2 | Hereford | 5,002 | D | 1-1 | Hall | Ramsbottom | Randell | Horswill | Craven | Peddelty | Green | Hall | Delve | Austin | Bannister | Rogers | |
| 26 | H | 12/2 | ORIENT | 9,551 | L | 1-2 | Rogers | Ramsbottom | Randell | Horswill | Delve | Craven | Peddelty | Hall | Collins | Austin | Bannister | Rogers | Banton |
| 27 | A | 19/2 | Chelsea | 22,154 | D | 2-2 | Austin, Bannister | Ramsbottom | Randell | Horswill | Green | Green | Peddelty | Hall | Craven | Austin | Bannister | Rogers | |
| 28 | H | 26/2 | MILLWALL | 10,437 | D | 2-2 | Hall 2 | Ramsbottom | Randell | Darke | Craven | Sutton | Hall | Hall | Delve | Austin | Bannister | Rogers | |
| 29 | A | 2/3 | Blackburn | 7,755 | L | 0-2 | | Ramsbottom | Randell | Darke | Sutton | Peddelty | Green | Delve | Craven | Austin | Bannister | Rogers | Collins |
| 30 | A | 5/3 | Bolton | 18,496 | L | 0-3 | | Ramsbottom | Peddelty | Darke | Delve | Sutton | Green | Hall | Harrison | Austin | Bannister | Collins | Rogers |
| 31 | H | 12/3 | Luton | 12,793 | D | 1-1 | Foster | Ramsbottom | Smart | Darke | Peddelty | Sutton | Horswill | Randell | Foster | Austin | Bannister | Rogers | |
| 32 | H | 19/3 | BLACKPOOL | 8,893 | W | 2-0 | Foster, Bannister | Ramsbottom | Smart | Darke | Horswill | Sutton | Peddelty | Randell | Foster | Austin | Bannister | Rogers | |
| 33 | A | 26/3 | Cardiff | 9,587 | W | 1-0 | Austin | Ramsbottom | Smart | Smart | Horswill | Sutton | Peddelty | Randell | Foster | Austin | Bannister | Rogers | |
| 34 | A | 2/4 | BRISTOL ROV | 10,307 | L | 1-1 | Peddelty | Ramsbottom | Smart | Darke | Horswill | Sutton | Peddelty | Randell | Foster | Austin | Bannister | Rogers | |
| 35 | H | 8/4 | Southampton | 20,914 | L | 1-4 | Bannister | Ramsbottom | Smart | Darke | Craven | Sutton | Peddelty | Foster | Randell | Austin | Bannister | Delve | Rogers |
| 36 | H | 9/4 | HEREFORD | 9,787 | W | 2-1 | Bannister 2 | Ramsbottom | Randell | Darke | Craven | Sutton | Peddelty | Hall | Foster | Trusson | Bannister | Rogers | Delve |
| 37 | A | 11/4 | Fulham | 11,710 | L | 0-2 | | Ramsbottom | Darke | Horswill | Craven | Sutton | Peddelty | Hall | Foster | Austin | Bannister | Rogers | |
| 38 | H | 16/4 | HULL | 8,694 | L | 1-2 | Hall | Ramsbottom | Darke | Horswill | Craven | Sutton | Peddelty | Hall | Foster | Trusson | Bannister | Delve | Johnson |
| 39 | A | 23/4 | Carlisle | 7,751 | L | 1-3 | Hall | Ramsbottom | Smart | Horswill | Craven | Sutton | Peddelty | Hall | Foster | Austin | Bannister | Delve | Randell |
| 40 | H | 30/4 | WOLVES | 16,795 | D | 0-0 | | Ramsbottom | Smart | Horswill | Delve | Craven | Randell | Hall | Foster | Austin | Bannister | Randell | |
| 41 | H | 2/5 | NOTT'M FOREST | 13,542 | L | 1-2 | Bannister | Ramsbottom | Smart | Horswill | Craven | Peddelty | Randell | Foster | Delve | Austin | Bannister | Delve | Johnson |
| 42 | A | 7/5 | Sheffield Utd | 12,227 | L | 0-1 | Hall | Ramsbottom | Smart | Horswill | Craven | Peddelty | Randell | Foster | Delve | Austin | Bannister | Rogers | Hall |

| | | | | | | | | | | | | | |
|---|---|---|---|---|---|---|---|---|---|---|---|---|---|
| 1:1 | H | 14/8 | EXETER | 8,688 | L | 0-1 | Barron | Ramsbottom | Darke | Horswill | Randell | Sutton | Green | Hall | Harrison | Mariner | Collins | McAuley | Johnson |
| 1:2 | A | 17/8 | Exeter | 8,859 | L | 0-1 | | Ramsbottom | Darke | Horswill | Randell | Sutton | Green | Johnson | Mariner | Collins | McAuley | Johnson |

**FA CUP**

| | | | | | | | | | | | | | | | | |
|---|---|---|---|---|---|---|---|---|---|---|---|---|---|---|---|---|
| 3 | A | 8/1 | Oldham | 9,889 | L | 0-3 | Ramsbottom | Delve | Horswill | Peddelty | Sutton | Green | Hall | Harrison | Austin | Bannister | Johnson |

| | P | W | D | L | F | A | W | D | L | F | A | Pts |
|---|---|---|---|---|---|---|---|---|---|---|---|---|
| | | | | Home | | | | | Away | | | |
| 1 Wolves | 42 | 15 | 3 | 3 | 48 | 21 | 7 | 10 | 4 | 36 | 24 | 57 |
| 2 Chelsea | 42 | 15 | 6 | 0 | 51 | 22 | 6 | 7 | 8 | 22 | 31 | 55 |
| 3 Nott'm Forest | 42 | 14 | 3 | 4 | 53 | 22 | 7 | 7 | 7 | 24 | 21 | 52 |
| 4 Bolton | 42 | 15 | 2 | 4 | 46 | 21 | 5 | 9 | 7 | 29 | 33 | 51 |
| 5 Blackpool | 42 | 11 | 7 | 3 | 29 | 17 | 6 | 10 | 5 | 29 | 25 | 51 |
| 6 Luton | 42 | 13 | 5 | 3 | 39 | 17 | 8 | 1 | 12 | 28 | 31 | 48 |
| 7 Charlton | 42 | 14 | 2 | 5 | 52 | 27 | 2 | 11 | 8 | 19 | 31 | 48 |
| 8 Notts Co | 42 | 11 | 5 | 5 | 29 | 20 | 8 | 5 | 8 | 36 | 40 | 48 |
| 9 Southampton | 42 | 12 | 6 | 3 | 40 | 24 | 5 | 4 | 12 | 32 | 43 | 44 |
| 10 Millwall | 42 | 9 | 6 | 6 | 31 | 22 | 6 | 7 | 8 | 26 | 31 | 43 |
| 11 Sheffield Utd | 42 | 9 | 8 | 4 | 32 | 25 | 5 | 4 | 12 | 22 | 38 | 40 |
| 12 Blackburn | 42 | 12 | 4 | 5 | 31 | 18 | 3 | 5 | 13 | 11 | 36 | 39 |
| 13 Oldham | 42 | 11 | 6 | 4 | 37 | 23 | 3 | 4 | 14 | 15 | 41 | 38 |
| 14 Hull | 42 | 9 | 8 | 4 | 31 | 17 | 1 | 9 | 11 | 14 | 41 | 37 |
| 15 Bristol Rov | 42 | 8 | 9 | 4 | 32 | 27 | 4 | 4 | 13 | 21 | 44 | 37 |
| 16 Burnley | 42 | 8 | 9 | 4 | 27 | 20 | 3 | 5 | 13 | 19 | 44 | 36 |
| 17 Fulham | 42 | 9 | 7 | 5 | 39 | 25 | 2 | 6 | 13 | 15 | 36 | 35 |
| 18 Cardiff | 42 | 7 | 6 | 8 | 30 | 30 | 5 | 4 | 12 | 26 | 37 | 34 |
| 19 Orient | 42 | 4 | 8 | 9 | 18 | 23 | 5 | 8 | 8 | 19 | 32 | 34 |
| 20 Carlisle | 42 | 7 | 7 | 7 | 31 | 33 | 4 | 5 | 12 | 18 | 42 | 34 |
| 21 PLYMOUTH | 42 | 5 | 9 | 7 | 27 | 25 | 3 | 7 | 11 | 19 | 40 | 32 |
| 22 Hereford | 42 | 6 | 9 | 6 | 28 | 30 | 2 | 6 | 13 | 29 | 48 | 31 |
| | 924 | 224 | 138 | 100 | 781 | 509 | 100 | 138 | 224 | 509 | 781 | 924 |

| | Appearances | | | | | | Goals | | | |
|---|---|---|---|---|---|---|---|---|---|---|
| | Lge | Sub | LC | Sub | FAC | Sub | Lge | LC | FAC | Tot |
| Austin, Terry | 29 | | | | 1 | | 7 | | | 7 |
| Bannister, Bruce | 24 | | | | 1 | | 7 | | | 7 |
| Banton, Geoff | | 1 | | | | 1 | | | | |
| Barron, Paul | 3 | | 1 | | | | | | | |
| Collins, Doug | 22 | 1 | 2 | | | | 2 | | | 2 |
| Craven, John | 15 | | 2 | | | | | | | |
| Darke, Peter | 15 | | | | | | 1 | | | 1 |
| Delve, John | 28 | 4 | | | 1 | | | | | |
| Foster, George | 14 | 1 | | | | | | | | |
| Green, Mike | 22 | | 2 | | 1 | | 2 | | | 2 |
| Hall, Brian | 36 | 1 | 2 | | 1 | | 10 | | | 10 |
| Hamilton, Jim | 6 | 2 | | | | | | | | |
| Harrison, Chris | 21 | | 1 | | 1 | | 1 | | | 1 |
| Horswill, Mick | 37 | | 2 | | 1 | | 1 | | | 1 |
| Johnson, Brian | 12 | 3 | 1 | 1 | 1 | | 4 | | | 4 |
| Mariner, Paul | 10 | | 2 | | | | 7 | | | 7 |
| McAuley, Hugh | 4 | 1 | 2 | | | | | | | |
| Peddelty, John | 29 | | | | 1 | | | | | |
| Ramsbottom, Neil | 39 | | 1 | | 1 | | | | | |
| Randell, Colin | 34 | 1 | 2 | | | | | | | |
| Rogers, Alan | 15 | 4 | | | | | 1 | | | 1 |
| Smart, Kevin | 9 | | | | | | | | | |
| Sutton, Dave | 34 | | 2 | | 1 | | | | | |
| Trusson, Mike | 4 | | | | | | | | | |
| 24 players used | 462 | 19 | 22 | 1 | 11 | | 46 | | | 46 |

# LEAGUE DIVISION 3    Manager: Dave Smith    SEASON 1985-86

| # | | Date | Opponents | Att | | F-A | Scorers | 1 | 2 | 3 | 4 | 5 | 6 | 7 | 8 | 9 | 10 | 11 | sub |
|---|---|------|-----------|-----|---|-----|---------|---|---|---|---|---|---|---|---|---|----|----|-----|
| 1 | A | 17/8 | York | 4,246 | L | 1-3 | McElhinney | Crudgington | Nisbet | Goodyear | Uzzell | McElhinney | Matthews | Hodges | Coughlin | Cooper S | Rowbotham | Nelson | |
| 2 | H | 24/8 | READING | 4,261 | L | 0-1 | | Crudgington | Nisbet | Uzzell | Goodyear | McElhinney | Matthews | Hodges | Coughlin | Cooper S | Cooper L | Nelson | |
| 3 | A | 26/8 | Swansea | 3,906 | W | 2-0 | McElhinney, Cooper S | Crudgington | Nisbet | Uzzell | Goodyear | McElhinney | Matthews | Hodges | Coughlin | Cooper S | Cooper L | Nelson | |
| 4 | H | 31/8 | NOTTS CO | 5,105 | L | 0-1 | | Crudgington | Nisbet | Cooper L | Burrows | McElhinney | Matthews | Hodges | Coughlin | Cooper S | Clayton | Nelson | |
| 5 | A | 7/9 | Brentford | 3,927 | D | 1-1 | Cooper S | Crudgington | Nisbet | Cooper L | Burrows | McElhinney | Matthews | Hodges | Coughlin | Cooper S | Clayton | Nelson | |
| 6 | H | 14/9 | NEWPORT | 3,686 | W | 2-0 | Burrows, Nelson | Crudgington | Nisbet | Goodyear | Burrows | McElhinney | Rowbotham | Hodges | Coughlin | Cooper S | Clayton | Nelson | Rowbotham |
| 7 | A | 17/9 | Doncaster | 2,904 | L | 0-1 | | Crudgington | Nisbet | Goodyear | Burrows | McElhinney | Matthews | Hodges | Coughlin | Cooper S | Clayton | Nelson | Rowbotham |
| 8 | H | 21/9 | WOLVES | 5,241 | W | 3-1 | Cooper S, Nelson 2 | Crudgington | Nisbet | Goodyear | Burrows | McElhinney | Matthews | Hodges | Coughlin | Cooper S | Clayton | Nelson | |
| 9 | A | 28/9 | Bolton | 4,270 | L | 1-3 | Clayton | Crudgington | Nisbet | Goodyear | Goodyear | McElhinney | Matthews | Hodges | Coughlin | Cooper S | Clayton | Nelson | |
| 10 | H | 1/10 | GILLINGHAM | 4,135 | W | 3-0 | Hodges, Nelson, Cooper S | Crudgington | Nisbet | Cooper L | Goodyear | McElhinney | Matthews | Hodges | Coughlin | Cooper S | Clayton | Nelson | |
| 11 | H | 5/10 | BRISTOL ROV | 5,662 | W | 4-2 | Clayt', Cough', Hodges, Parkin (og) | Crudgington | Nisbet | Cooper L | Goodyear | McElhinney | Matthews | Hodges | Coughlin | Cooper S | Clayton | Nelson | Summerfield |
| 12 | A | 12/10 | Walsall | 4,253 | D | 2-2 | Nelson 2 | Crudgington | Nisbet | Cooper L | Goodyear | McElhinney | Matthews | Hodges | Coughlin | Cooper S | Clayton | Nelson | |
| 13 | A | 19/10 | Rotherham | 2,942 | D | 1-1 | Hodges | Crudgington | Nisbet | Cooper L | Goodyear | McElhinney | Matthews | Hodges | Coughlin | Cooper S | Clayton | Nelson | |
| 14 | H | 22/10 | LINCOLN | 6,552 | W | 2-1 | Hodges, Nelson | Crudgington | Nisbet | Cooper L | Goodyear | McElhinney | Matthews | Hodges | Coughlin | Cooper S | Clayton | Nelson | |
| 15 | A | 26/10 | Derby | 11,433 | W | 2-1 | Hodges, Goodyear | Crudgington | Nisbet | Cooper L | Goodyear | McElhinney | Matthews | Hodges | Coughlin | Cooper S | Clayton | Nelson | |
| 16 | H | 2/11 | CHESTERFIELD | 7,522 | W | 2-1 | Hodges, Cooper S | Crudgington | Nisbet | Cooper L | Goodyear | McElhinney | Matthews | Hodges | Coughlin | Cooper S | Clayton | Nelson | Rowbotham |
| 17 | H | 5/11 | BOURNEMOUTH | 6,186 | W | 2-1 | Clayton | Crudgington | Nisbet | Cooper L | Goodyear | McElhinney | Summerfield | Hodges | Coughlin | Cooper S | Clayton | Nelson | |
| 18 | A | 9/11 | Bury | 2,975 | W | 1-0 | Clayton | Crudgington | Nisbet | Cooper L | Goodyear | McElhinney | Matthews | Hodges | Coughlin | Cooper S | Clayton | Nelson | Summerfield |
| 19 | H | 23/11 | WIGAN | 6,714 | W | 2-1 | Summerfield, Coughlin | Crudgington | Nisbet | Cooper L | Goodyear | McElhinney | Summerfield | Hodges | Coughlin | Cooper S | Clayton | Nelson | Matthews |
| 20 | A | 30/11 | Blackpool | 6,184 | D | 1-1 | Nelson | Crudgington | Nisbet | Cooper L | Goodyear | McElhinney | Matthews | Hodges | Coughlin | Cooper S | Clayton | Nelson | |
| 21 | H | 14/12 | DARLINGTON | 6,036 | W | 4-2 | Hodges 2, Cooper S, Summerfield | Crudgington | Nisbet | Cooper L | Goodyear | McElhinney | Summerfield | Hodges | Coughlin | Cooper S | Clayton | Nelson | Rowbotham |
| 22 | A | 21/12 | Reading | 8,512 | L | 3-4 | Hodges, Cooper S, Clayton | Crudgington | Nisbet | Cooper L | Goodyear | McElhinney | Summerfield | Hodges | Coughlin | Cooper S | Clayton | Nelson | |
| 23 | A | 26/12 | Bristol City | 8,298 | L | 0-2 | | Crudgington | Nisbet | Cooper L | Goodyear | McElhinney | Summerfield | Hodges | Coughlin | Cooper S | Clayton | Nelson | Rowbotham |
| 24 | H | 28/12 | SWANSEA | 8,622 | W | 2-0 | Clayton 2 | Crudgington | Nisbet | Cooper L | Goodyear | McElhinney | Summerfield | Hodges | Coughlin | Cooper S | Clayton | Nelson | |
| 25 | H | 1/1 | CARDIFF | 8,920 | D | 4-4 | Nelson, Sum'field, Clayton, Hodges | Crudgington | Nisbet | Cooper L | Goodyear | McElhinney | Summerfield | Hodges | Summerfield | Cooper S | Clayton | Nelson | Matthews |
| 26 | A | 11/1 | Notts Co | 4,953 | L | 0-2 | | Crudgington | Nisbet | Uzzell | Brimacombe | McElhinney | Matthews | Hodges | Summerfield | Cooper S | Clayton | Nelson | Coughlin |
| 27 | H | 18/1 | YORK | 5,942 | D | 2-2 | Brimacombe, Coughlin | Crudgington | Nisbet | Cooper L | Brimacombe | McElhinney | Matthews | Hodges | Coughlin | Summerfield | Clayton | Nelson | Cooper L |
| 28 | A | 25/1 | Newport | 3,007 | L | 1-3 | Clayton | Crudgington | Nisbet | Cooper L | Goodyear | McElhinney | Matthews | Hodges | Coughlin | Cooper S | Clayton | Nelson | |
| 29 | H | 1/2 | BRENTFORD | 4,873 | W | 2-0 | Nelson 2 | Crudgington | Nisbet | Cooper L | Goodyear | McElhinney | Matthews | Hodges | Coughlin | Cooper S | Clayton | Nelson | |
| 30 | H | 15/2 | DONCASTER | 4,827 | L | 0-1 | | Crudgington | Nisbet | Cooper L | Goodyear | McElhinney | Matthews | Hodges | Coughlin | Cooper S | Clayton | Nelson | |
| 31 | A | 4/3 | Gillingham | 3,490 | D | 1-1 | Summerfield | Crudgington | Nisbet | Cooper L | Goodyear | McElhinney | Summerfield | Hodges | Coughlin | Godfrey | Clayton | Nelson | |
| 32 | A | 8/3 | Bristol Rov | 4,667 | W | 2-1 | Coughlin, Godfrey | Crudgington | Nisbet | Cooper L | Goodyear | McElhinney | Summerfield | Hodges | Coughlin | Godfrey | Clayton | Nelson | |
| 33 | H | 11/3 | WOLVES | 2,367 | W | 3-0 | Coughlin, Summerfield, Clayton | Crudgington | Nisbet | Cooper L | Goodyear | McElhinney | Summerfield | Hodges | Coughlin | Godfrey | Clayton | Nelson | |
| 34 | H | 15/3 | WALSALL | 6,097 | W | 2-0 | Cooper L, Coughlin | Crudgington | Nisbet | Cooper L | Goodyear | McElhinney | Summerfield | Hodges | Coughlin | Godfrey | Clayton | Nelson | |
| 35 | A | 18/3 | Chesterfield | 1,828 | W | 2-1 | Summerfield, Goodyear | Crudgington | Nisbet | Cooper L | Goodyear | Uzzell | Summerfield | Hodges | Coughlin | Godfrey | Clayton | Nelson | Rowbotham |
| 36 | H | 22/3 | DERBY | 11,769 | W | 4-1 | Clayton 2, Rowbotham, Hodges | Crudgington | Nisbet | Cooper L | Uzzell | McElhinney | Summerfield | Hodges | Coughlin | Godfrey | Clayton | Rowbotham | Cooper S |
| 37 | A | 28/3 | Cardiff | 3,834 | W | 2-1 | Hodges, Matthews | Crudgington | Nisbet | Cooper L | Uzzell | McElhinney | Summerfield | Hodges | Matthews | Godfrey | Clayton | Rowbotham | Cooper S |
| 38 | H | 5/4 | Bournemouth | 5,351 | W | 3-1 | Cooper S, Coughlin, Hodges | Crudgington | Nisbet | Cooper L | Uzzell | McElhinney | Coughlin | Hodges | Matthews | Tynan | Cooper S | Rowbotham | Cooper S |
| 39 | H | 8/4 | ROTHERHAM | 13,034 | W | 4-0 | Pickering (og), Tynan 2, Summer'fld | Crudgington | Nisbet | Cooper L | Goodyear | McElhinney | Matthews | Hodges | Coughlin | Tynan | Cooper S | Rowbotham | Nelson |
| 40 | H | 12/4 | BURY | 13,625 | W | 3-0 | Hodges, Tynan 2 | Crudgington | Nisbet | Cooper L | Goodyear | McElhinney | Matthews | Hodges | Coughlin | Tynan | Cooper S | Nelson | Summerfield |
| 41 | H | 16/4 | Lincoln | 2,297 | D | 1-1 | Tynan | Crudgington | Nisbet | Cooper L | Goodyear | McElhinney | Matthews | Hodges | Coughlin | Tynan | Cooper S | Nelson | |
| 42 | A | 19/4 | Wigan | 9,485 | L | 0-3 | | Crudgington | Nisbet | Cooper L | Goodyear | McElhinney | Matthews | Hodges | Coughlin | Tynan | Cooper S | Nelson | |
| 43 | H | 22/4 | BOLTON | 12,183 | W | 4-1 | Hodges, Coughlin, Tynan, Burrows | Crudgington | Nisbet | Cooper L | Goodyear | Burrows | Summerfield | Hodges | Coughlin | Tynan | Clayton | Nelson | Summerfield |
| 44 | A | 26/4 | BLACKPOOL | 14,975 | W | 3-1 | Nelson, Coughlin, Tynan | Crudgington | Nisbet | Cooper L | Goodyear | Burrows | Summerfield | Hodges | Coughlin | Tynan | Clayton | Nelson | Summerfield |
| 45 | H | 29/4 | BRISTOL CITY | 20,000 | W | 4-0 | Tynan 2, Nelson, Coughlin | Crudgington | Nisbet | Cooper L | Goodyear | McElhinney | Matthews | Hodges | Coughlin | Tynan | Summerfield | Nelson | Summerfield |

| | | | | | Result | Scorers |
|---|---|---|---|---|---|---|
| 1:1 | H | 20/8 | EXETER | 4,754 | W 2-1 | Summerfield, McElhinney |
| 1:2 | A | 4/9 | Exeter | 3,362 | L 0-2 | |

**FA CUP**

| | | | | | Result | Scorers |
|---|---|---|---|---|---|---|
| 1 | H | 16/11 | ALDERSHOT | 7,209 | W 1-0 | Coughlin |
| 2 | H | 7/12 | MAIDSTONE | 7,597 | W 3-0 | Cooper L, Nelson, Summerfield |
| 3 | A | 4/1 | Hull | 6,776 | D 2-2 | Clayton, Cooper S |
| 3R | H | 7/1 | HULL | 13,940 | L 0-1 | |

**Cup line-ups**

| | LC 1:1 EXETER | LC 1:2 Exeter | FA 1 ALDERSHOT | FA 2 MAIDSTONE | FA 3 Hull | FA 3R HULL |
|---|---|---|---|---|---|---|
| 1 | Crudgington | Crudgington | Crudgington | Crudgington | Philp | Philp |
| 2 | Nisbet | Nisbet | Nisbet | Nisbet | Burrows | Burrows |
| 3 | Cooper L | Cooper L | Cooper L | Cooper L | Cooper L | Cooper L |
| 4 | Goodyear | Burrows | Goodyear | Goodyear | Goodyear | Goodyear |
| 5 | McElhinney | McElhinney | McElhinney | McElhinney | McElhinney | McElhinney |
| 6 | Matthews | Matthews | Summerfield | Summerfield | Summerfield | Matthews |
| 7 | Coughlin | Coughlin | Coughlin | Coughlin | Matthews | Summerfield |
| 8 | Hodges | Hodges | Hodges | Hodges | Hodges | Hodges |
| 9 | Nelson | Nelson | Nelson | Nelson | Nelson | Nelson |
| 10 | Summerfield | Clayton | Clayton | Clayton | Clayton | Clayton |
| 11 | Cooper S | Cooper S | Cooper S | Cooper S | Cooper S | Cooper S |
| Sub | | Goodyear | Rowbotham | | Uzzell | Uzzell |

**League table**

| | | P | Home | | | | | Away | | | | | Pts |
|---|---|---|---|---|---|---|---|---|---|---|---|---|---|
| | | | W | D | L | F | A | W | D | L | F | A | |
| 1 | Reading | 46 | 16 | 3 | 4 | 39 | 22 | 13 | 4 | 6 | 28 | 29 | 94 |
| 2 | PLYMOUTH | 46 | 17 | 3 | 3 | 56 | 20 | 9 | 6 | 8 | 32 | 33 | 87 |
| 3 | Derby | 46 | 13 | 7 | 3 | 45 | 20 | 10 | 8 | 5 | 35 | 21 | 84 |
| 4 | Wigan | 46 | 17 | 4 | 2 | 54 | 17 | 6 | 10 | 7 | 28 | 31 | 83 |
| 5 | Gillingham | 46 | 14 | 5 | 4 | 48 | 17 | 8 | 8 | 7 | 33 | 37 | 79 |
| 6 | Walsall | 46 | 15 | 7 | 1 | 59 | 23 | 7 | 4 | 12 | 31 | 41 | 75 |
| 7 | York | 46 | 16 | 4 | 3 | 49 | 17 | 4 | 7 | 12 | 28 | 34 | 71 |
| 8 | Notts Co | 46 | 12 | 6 | 5 | 42 | 26 | 7 | 8 | 8 | 29 | 34 | 71 |
| 9 | Bristol City | 46 | 14 | 5 | 4 | 43 | 19 | 4 | 9 | 10 | 26 | 41 | 68 |
| 10 | Brentford | 46 | 8 | 8 | 7 | 29 | 29 | 10 | 4 | 9 | 29 | 32 | 66 |
| 11 | Doncaster | 46 | 7 | 10 | 6 | 20 | 21 | 9 | 6 | 8 | 25 | 31 | 64 |
| 12 | Blackpool | 46 | 11 | 6 | 6 | 38 | 19 | 6 | 6 | 11 | 28 | 36 | 63 |
| 13 | Darlington | 46 | 10 | 7 | 6 | 39 | 33 | 6 | 6 | 12 | 22 | 45 | 58 |
| 14 | Rotherham | 46 | 13 | 5 | 5 | 44 | 18 | 2 | 7 | 14 | 17 | 41 | 57 |
| 15 | Bournemouth | 46 | 9 | 6 | 8 | 41 | 31 | 6 | 5 | 12 | 24 | 41 | 54 |
| 16 | Bristol Rov | 46 | 9 | 8 | 6 | 27 | 21 | 5 | 4 | 14 | 24 | 54 | 54 |
| 17 | Chesterfield | 46 | 10 | 6 | 7 | 41 | 30 | 3 | 8 | 12 | 20 | 34 | 53 |
| 18 | Bolton | 46 | 10 | 4 | 9 | 35 | 30 | 5 | 4 | 14 | 19 | 38 | 53 |
| 19 | Newport | 46 | 7 | 8 | 8 | 35 | 33 | 4 | 10 | 9 | 17 | 32 | 51 |
| 20 | Bury | 46 | 11 | 7 | 5 | 46 | 26 | 4 | 6 | 16 | 17 | 41 | 49 |
| 21 | Lincoln | 46 | 7 | 9 | 7 | 33 | 34 | 3 | 7 | 13 | 22 | 43 | 46 |
| 22 | Cardiff | 46 | 7 | 5 | 11 | 22 | 29 | 5 | 4 | 14 | 31 | 54 | 45 |
| 23 | Wolves | 46 | 6 | 6 | 11 | 29 | 47 | 5 | 4 | 14 | 28 | 51 | 43 |
| 24 | Swansea | 46 | 9 | 6 | 8 | 27 | 27 | 2 | 4 | 17 | 16 | 60 | 43 |
| | | 1104 | 268 | 145 | 139 | 941 | 609 | 139 | 145 | 268 | 609 | 941 | 1511 |

**Appearances and Goals**

| | Appearances | | | | | | Goals | | | |
|---|---|---|---|---|---|---|---|---|---|---|
| | Lge | Sub | LC | Sub | FAC | Sub | Lge | LC | FAC | Tot |
| Brimacombe, John | 1 | | | | | | 1 | | | 1 |
| Burrows, Adrian | 7 | | 1 | | 2 | | 2 | | | 2 |
| Clayton, John | 36 | | 1 | | 4 | | 11 | | 1 | 12 |
| Cooper, Leigh | 39 | 1 | 2 | | 4 | | 1 | | 1 | 2 |
| Cooper, Steve | 34 | 4 | 2 | | 4 | | 8 | | 1 | 9 |
| Coughlin, Russell | 44 | 1 | 2 | | 2 | | 10 | | 1 | 11 |
| Crudgington, Geoff | 46 | | 2 | | 2 | | | | | |
| Godfrey, Kevin | 7 | | | | | | 1 | | | 1 |
| Goodyear, Clive | 41 | | 1 | 1 | 4 | | 2 | | | 2 |
| Hodges, Kevin | 46 | | 2 | | 4 | | 16 | | | 16 |
| Matthews, John | 29 | 2 | 2 | | 2 | | 1 | | | 1 |
| McElhinney, Gerry | 44 | | 2 | | 4 | | 2 | 1 | | 3 |
| Nelson, Garry | 41 | 1 | 2 | | 4 | | 13 | | 1 | 14 |
| Nisbet, Gordon | 46 | | 2 | | 2 | | | | | |
| Philp, Dave | | | | | 2 | | | | | |
| Rowbotham, Darren | 7 | 7 | | | | 1 | 1 | | | 1 |
| Summerfield, Kevin | 21 | 5 | 1 | | 4 | | 7 | 1 | 1 | 9 |
| Tynan, Tommy | 9 | | | | | | 10 | | | 10 |
| Uzzell, John | 8 | | | | | 1 | 2 | | | 2 |
| (own-goals) | | | | | | | 2 | | | 2 |
| 19 players used | 506 | 21 | 22 | 1 | 44 | 2 | 88 | 2 | 6 | 96 |

# LEAGUE DIVISION 2

**Manager: Kemp / Gillett & Nisbet /Shilton**

## SEASON 1991-92

| No | | Date | Opponents | Att | F-A | | Scorers | 1 | 2 | 3 | 4 | 5 | 6 | 7 | 8 | 9 | 10 | 11 | Subs (2) |
|----|---|------|-----------|-----|-----|---|---------|---|---|---|---|---|---|---|---|---|----|----|----------|
| 1 | H | 17/8 | BARNSLEY | 6,352 | 2-1 | W | Marshall, Turner | Wilmot | Salman | Spearing | Marker | Cross | Morgan | Barlow | Marshall | Turner | Morrison | Fiore | Clement |
| 2 | A | 24/8 | Leicester | 11,852 | 0-2 | L | | Wilmot | Salman | Spearing | Marker | Cross | Morgan | Quamina | Marshall | Turner | Morrison | Clement | Barlow/Fiore |
| 3 | H | 31/8 | MILLWALL | 5,369 | 3-2 | W | Marshall, Burrows, Wood (og) | Wilmot | Clement | Spearing | Marker | Burrows | Morgan | Barlow | Marshall | Turner | Morrison | Evans | Scott/Edworthy |
| 4 | A | 4/9 | Newcastle | 19,543 | 2-2 | D | Salman, Marshall | Wilmot | Clement | Spearing | Marker | Burrows | Morgan | Barlow | Marshall | Turner | Morrison | Evans | Salman |
| 5 | H | 7/9 | CHARLTON | 5,602 | 0-2 | L | | Walter | Clement | Spearing | Marker | Burrows | Morgan | Barlow | Marshall | Scott | Morrison | Edworthy | Scott/Edworthy |
| 6 | A | 14/9 | Grimsby | 5,432 | 1-2 | L | Burrows | Walter | Salman | Spearing | Marker | Burrows | Morgan | Barlow | Marshall | Scott | Morrison | Edworthy | Fiore/Clement |
| 7 | A | 17/9 | Southend | 4,585 | 1-2 | L | Burrows | Walter | Salman | Spearing | Marker | Burrows | Morgan | Barlow | Marshall | Scott | Morrison | Clement | |
| 8 | H | 21/9 | MIDDLESBROUGH | 5,280 | 1-1 | D | Burrows | Walter | Clement | Spearing | Marker | Burrows | Morgan | Barlow | Marshall | Scott | Quamina | Fiore | Clement |
| 9 | A | 28/9 | Oxford | 3,726 | 2-3 | L | Fiore, Barlow | Wilmot | Salman | Spearing | Marker | Burrows | Morgan | Barlow | Marshall | Turner | Quamina | Fiore | |
| 10 | H | 5/10 | SWINDON | 6,208 | 0-4 | L | | Wilmot | Salman | Spearing | Marker | Burrows | Morgan | Barlow | Marshall | Scott | Quamina | Fiore | Damerell |
| 11 | A | 12/10 | Blackburn | 10,830 | 2-5 | L | Marshall, Barlow | Wilmot | Salman | Clement | Marker | Burrows | Morgan | Barlow | Marshall | Turner | Cross | Fiore | Quamina/Evans |
| 12 | H | 19/10 | Bristol Rov | 5,049 | 0-0 | D | | Wilmot | Salman | Clement | Marker | Evans | Morgan | Barlow | Marshall | Turner | Morrison | Cross | Edworthy |
| 13 | H | 26/10 | WATFORD | 4,090 | 0-1 | L | | Wilmot | Salman | Clement | Marker | Hopkins | Morgan | Barlow | Marshall | Evans | Fiore | Cross | Hodges |
| 14 | A | 2/11 | WOLVES | 4,200 | 1-0 | W | Marshall | Wilmot | Salman | Clement | Marker | Hopkins | Morgan | Garner | Marshall | Scott | Fiore | Cross | Evans/Edworthy |
| 15 | A | 5/11 | Bristol City | 7,735 | 0-2 | L | | Wilmot | Salman | Clement | Marker | Hopkins | Morgan | Edworthy | Marshall | Evans | Fiore | Cross | Scott/Barlow |
| 16 | H | 8/11 | Tranmere | 7,490 | 0-1 | L | | Wilmot | Salman | Clement | Marker | Hopkins | Morgan | Barlow | Marshall | Regis | Fiore | Edworthy | |
| 17 | H | 16/11 | PORT VALE | 4,363 | 1-0 | W | Marshall | Wilmot | Spearing | Clement | Marker | Hopkins | Morgan | Barlow | Marshall | Regis | Fiore | Turner | Edworthy/Jones |
| 18 | A | 23/11 | SUNDERLAND | 6,007 | 1-0 | W | Fiore | Wilmot | Spearing | Clement | Marker | Hopkins | Morgan | Meaker | Marshall | Regis | Fiore | Turner | |
| 19 | A | 30/11 | Brighton | 6,713 | 0-1 | L | | Wilmot | Spearing | Clement | Marker | Hopkins | Morgan | Meaker | Marshall | Regis | Fiore | Turner | Barlow |
| 20 | H | 7/12 | IPSWICH | 4,986 | 1-0 | W | Fiore | Wilmot | Spearing | Clement | Marker | Morrison | Morgan | Meaker | Marshall | Regis | Fiore | Turner | Morrison |
| 21 | A | 20/12 | NEWCASTLE | 5,048 | 2-0 | W | Regis, Barlow | Wilmot | Spearing | Salman | Marker | Morrison | Morgan | Barlow | Marshall | Regis | Fiore | Turner | Barlow |
| 22 | A | 26/12 | Cambridge | 7,105 | 1-1 | D | Turner | Wilmot | Spearing | Salman | Marker | Morrison | Morgan | Barlow | Marshall | Regis | Fiore | Turner | Smith/Clement |
| 23 | A | 28/12 | Millwall | 6,980 | 1-2 | L | Morgan | Wilmot | Spearing | Salman | Marker | Morrison | Morgan | Barlow | Marshall | Regis | Fiore | Turner | Edworthy/Clement |
| 24 | H | 1/1 | PORTSMOUTH | 8,887 | 3-2 | W | Turner, Morrison, Marshall | Wilmot | Spearing | Salman | Marker | Morrison | Morgan | Barlow | Marshall | Regis | Fiore | Turner | Edworthy |
| 25 | H | 11/1 | LEICESTER | 5,846 | 2-2 | D | Witter | Wilmot | Spearing | Clement | Witter | Morrison | Morgan | Barlow | Marshall | Regis | Fiore | Turner | Salman |
| 26 | A | 18/1 | Barnsley | 5,322 | 3-1 | W | Marshall 3 | Wilmot | Spearing | Clement | Marker | Morrison | Morgan | Barlow | Marshall | Regis | Fiore | Turner | Fiore |
| 27 | H | 1/2 | BRISTOL ROV | 6,631 | 0-0 | D | | Wilmot | Spearing | Clement | Marker | Fiore | Morgan | Barlow | Marshall | Regis | Salman | Turner | Edworthy |
| 28 | A | 4/2 | Portsmouth | 10,467 | 1-4 | L | Regis | Wilmot | Spearing | Clement | Marker | Edworthy | Morgan | Witter | Marshall | Regis | Salman | Turner | Garner |
| 29 | A | 8/2 | Watford | 7,260 | 0-1 | L | | Wilmot | Spearing | Smith | Marker | Edworthy | Morrison | Garner | Marshall | Regis | Salman | Turner | Fiore |
| 30 | H | 11/2 | CAMBRIDGE | 4,290 | 0-1 | L | | Wilmot | Salman | Salman | Marker | van Rossum | Morrison | Morrison | Marshall | Smith | Fiore | Turner | Regis |
| 31 | A | 22/2 | Brighton | 5,259 | 1-1 | D | Smith | Wilmot | Salman | Fiore | Marker | Burrows | Morgan | Barlow | Morrison | Smith | Marshall | Turner | Barlow/Clement |
| 32 | A | 29/2 | Ipswich | 12,852 | 1-2 | L | Morrison | Wilmot | Spearing | Morrison | Marker | van Rossum | Morgan | Hodges | Garner | Regis | Smith | Turner | Smith/Hodges |
| 33 | H | 7/3 | DERBY | 8,864 | 0-1 | L | | Wilmot | Salman | Spearing | Edworthy | Morrison | Marker | van Rossum | Garner | Regis | Marshall | Morgan | |
| 34 | A | 10/3 | BRISTOL CITY | 9,734 | 1-0 | W | Marshall | Wilmot | Salman | Spearing | van Rossum | Morrison | Marker | Hodges | Garner | Regis | Marshall | Morgan | Garner/Burrows |
| 35 | A | 14/3 | Wolves | 11,556 | 0-1 | L | | Wilmot | Salman | Spearing | van Rossum | Morrison | Marker | Hodges | Fiore | Smith | Marshall | Morgan | |
| 36 | H | 21/3 | TRANMERE | 7,447 | 1-0 | W | Morgan | Wilmot | Hodges | Spearing | van Rossum | Morrison | Marker | Hodges | Smith | Regis | Marshall | Morgan | Smith/Nugent |
| 37 | A | 24/3 | Derby | 13,799 | 0-2 | L | | Wilmot | Hodges | Spearing | van Rossum | Morrison | Marker | Barlow | Fiore | Regis | Marshall | Morgan | Smith/Regis |
| 38 | H | 28/3 | PORT VALE | 5,310 | 0-3 | L | | Shilton | Hodges | Morgan | Lee | Marker | van Rossum | Barlow | McCall | Nugent | Marshall | Morgan | |
| 39 | H | 31/3 | GRIMSBY | 6,274 | 1-2 | L | McCall | Shilton | Hodges | Morgan | Burrows | Marker | van Rossum | Lee | McCall | Nugent | Marshall | Morgan | |
| 40 | A | 4/4 | Charlton | 6,787 | 0-0 | D | | Shilton | Hodges | Morgan | Morrison | Marker | Burrows | Lee | McCall | Nugent | Marshall | Smith | Fiore |
| 41 | H | 11/4 | SOUTHEND | 7,060 | 0-2 | L | | Shilton | Cross | Morgan | Morrison | Marker | Burrows | Lee | McCall | Regis | Marshall | Smith | Fiore/Pickard |
| 42 | A | 16/4 | Sunderland | 28,813 | 1-0 | W | Marshall | Shilton | Cross | Morgan | Lee | Burrows | Fiore | Hodges | McCall | Regis | Marshall | Smith | |
| 43 | A | 18/4 | Middlesbrough | 15,086 | 1-2 | L | Marshall | Shilton | Cross | Morgan | Morrison | Marker | Lee | Garner | McCall | Evans | Marshall | Smith | |
| 44 | A | 20/4 | OXFORD | 9,735 | 3-1 | W | Morrison, Marker, Lee | Shilton | Cross | Morgan | Morrison | Marker | Lee | Garner | McCall | Evans | Marshall | Smith | Pickard |
| 45 | A | 25/4 | Swindon | 10,463 | 0-1 | L | | Shilton | Cross | Morgan | Morrison | Marker | Lee | Garner | McCall | Evans | Fiore | Smith | Regis/Hodges |

| | | | Att | | Score | Scorers | | | | | | | | | | | |
|---|---|---|---|---|---|---|---|---|---|---|---|---|---|---|---|---|---|
| 1:1 | A | 20/8 | Shrewsbury | 2,152 | D | 1-1 | Morrison |
| 1:2 | H | 27/8 | SHREWSBURY | 3,580 | D | 2-2 | Barlow, Turner |

**FA CUP**

| | | | Att | | Score | |
|---|---|---|---|---|---|---|
| 3 | A | 5/1 | Bristol R | 6,767 | L | 0-5 |

Line-ups:

| 1:1 | Wilmot | Salman | Spearing | Marker | Cross | Morgan | Turner | Marshall | Barlow | Morrison | Fiore | Clement |
| 1:2 | Wilmot | Salman | Spearing | Marker | Cross | Morgan | Turner | Marshall | Barlow | Morrison | Fiore | Clement/Scott |
| 3 | Wilmot | Spearing | Salman | Burrows | Morrison | Morgan | Turner | Marshall | Barlow | Fiore | Turner | Edworthy |

## League table

| | | P | | Home | | | | | | Away | | | | | Pts |
|---|---|---|---|---|---|---|---|---|---|---|---|---|---|---|---|
| | | | W | D | L | F | A | W | D | L | F | A | | | |
| 1 | Ipswich | 46 | 16 | 3 | 4 | 42 | 22 | 8 | 9 | 6 | 28 | 28 | | | 84 |
| 2 | Midd'brough | 46 | 15 | 6 | 2 | 37 | 13 | 8 | 5 | 10 | 21 | 28 | | | 80 |
| 3 | Derby | 46 | 11 | 4 | 8 | 35 | 24 | 12 | 5 | 6 | 34 | 27 | | | 78 |
| 4 | Leicester | 46 | 14 | 4 | 5 | 41 | 24 | 9 | 4 | 10 | 21 | 31 | | | 77 |
| 5 | Cambridge | 46 | 10 | 9 | 4 | 34 | 19 | 9 | 8 | 6 | 31 | 28 | | | 74 |
| 6 | Blackburn * | 46 | 14 | 5 | 4 | 41 | 21 | 7 | 6 | 10 | 29 | 32 | | | 74 |
| 7 | Charlton | 46 | 9 | 7 | 7 | 25 | 23 | 11 | 4 | 8 | 29 | 25 | | | 71 |
| 8 | Swindon | 46 | 15 | 3 | 5 | 38 | 22 | 3 | 12 | 8 | 31 | 33 | | | 69 |
| 9 | Portsmouth | 46 | 15 | 6 | 2 | 41 | 12 | 4 | 6 | 13 | 24 | 39 | | | 69 |
| 10 | Watford | 46 | 9 | 5 | 9 | 25 | 23 | 9 | 6 | 8 | 26 | 25 | | | 65 |
| 11 | Wolves | 46 | 11 | 6 | 6 | 36 | 24 | 7 | 4 | 12 | 25 | 30 | | | 64 |
| 12 | Southend | 46 | 11 | 5 | 7 | 37 | 26 | 6 | 6 | 11 | 26 | 37 | | | 62 |
| 13 | Bristol Rov | 46 | 11 | 9 | 3 | 43 | 29 | 5 | 5 | 13 | 17 | 34 | | | 62 |
| 14 | Tranmere | 46 | 9 | 9 | 5 | 37 | 32 | 5 | 10 | 8 | 19 | 24 | | | 61 |
| 15 | Millwall | 46 | 10 | 4 | 9 | 32 | 32 | 7 | 6 | 10 | 32 | 39 | | | 61 |
| 16 | Barnsley | 46 | 11 | 4 | 8 | 27 | 25 | 5 | 7 | 11 | 19 | 32 | | | 59 |
| 17 | Bristol City | 46 | 10 | 8 | 5 | 30 | 24 | 3 | 7 | 13 | 25 | 47 | | | 54 |
| 18 | Sunderland | 46 | 10 | 8 | 5 | 36 | 23 | 4 | 3 | 16 | 25 | 42 | | | 53 |
| 19 | Grimsby | 46 | 7 | 5 | 11 | 28 | 28 | 7 | 6 | 10 | 22 | 34 | | | 53 |
| 20 | Newcastle | 46 | 9 | 8 | 6 | 38 | 30 | 4 | 5 | 14 | 28 | 54 | | | 52 |
| 21 | Oxford | 46 | 10 | 6 | 7 | 39 | 30 | 3 | 5 | 15 | 27 | 43 | | | 50 |
| 22 | PLYMOUTH | 46 | 11 | 5 | 7 | 26 | 26 | 2 | 4 | 17 | 16 | 38 | | | 48 |
| 23 | Brighton | 46 | 7 | 7 | 9 | 36 | 37 | 6 | 4 | 14 | 20 | 40 | | | 47 |
| 24 | Port Vale | 46 | 7 | 8 | 8 | 23 | 25 | 3 | 7 | 13 | 19 | 34 | | | 45 |
| | | 1104 | 262 | 144 | 146 | 824 | 594 | 146 | 144 | 262 | 594 | 824 | | | 1512 |

* promoted p/o

## Appearances / Goals

| | Appearances | | | | | | Goals | | | |
|---|---|---|---|---|---|---|---|---|---|---|
| | Lge | Sub | LC | Sub | FAC | Sub | Lge | LC | FAC | Tot |
| Barlow, Martin | 23 | 5 | 2 | | | | 3 | | 1 | 4 |
| Burrows, Adrian | 14 | 1 | | | 1 | | 3 | | | 3 |
| Clement, Andy | 20 | 6 | 2 | | 2 | | | | | |
| Cross, Ryan | 12 | | 2 | | | | | | | |
| Damerell, Mark | | 1 | | | | 1 | | | | |
| Edworthy, Marc | 7 | 8 | | | | 1 | | | | |
| Evans, Michael | 11 | 2 | | | | | | | | |
| Fiore, Mark | 25 | 7 | 2 | | 1 | | 4 | | | 4 |
| Garner, Darren | 8 | 2 | | | | | | | | |
| Hodges, Kevin | 11 | 3 | | | | | | | | |
| Hopkins, Jeff | 8 | | | | | | | | | |
| Jones, Steve | | 1 | | | | | | | | |
| Lee, David | 9 | | | | | | 1 | | | 1 |
| Marker, Nicky | 44 | | 2 | | 1 | | 1 | | | 1 |
| Marshall, Dwight | 44 | | 2 | | 1 | | 14 | | | 14 |
| McCall, Steve | 9 | | | | | | 1 | | | 1 |
| Meaker, Michael | 4 | | | | | | | | | |
| Morgan, Steve | 45 | | 2 | | 1 | | 2 | | | 2 |
| Morrison, Andy | 29 | 1 | 2 | | 1 | | 3 | | 1 | 4 |
| Nugent, Kevin | 2 | 2 | | | 2 | | | | | |
| Pickard, Owen | | 2 | | | | | | | | |
| Quamina, Mark | 4 | 1 | | | | | | | | |
| Regis, Dave | 21 | 3 | 2 | | 1 | | 2 | | | 2 |
| Salman, Danis | 26 | 2 | 2 | | 1 | | 1 | | | 1 |
| Scott, Morrys | 3 | 3 | | | | 1 | | | | |
| Shilton, Peter | 7 | | | | | | | | | |
| Smith, David | 14 | 4 | | | | | | | | |
| Spearing, Tony | 30 | | 2 | | 1 | | 2 | | | 2 |
| Turner, Robbie | 25 | | 2 | | 1 | | 3 | | 1 | 4 |
| van Rossum, Erik | 9 | | | | | | | | | |
| Walter, Dave | 5 | | | | | | | | | |
| Wilmot, Rhys | 34 | | 2 | | 1 | | | | | |
| Witter, Tony | 3 | | | | | | 1 | | | 1 |
| (own-goals) | | | | | | | 1 | | | 1 |
| 33 players used | 506 | 54 | 22 | 3 | 11 | 1 | 42 | | 3 | 45 |

# LEAGUE DIVISION 2

## Manager: Shilton / McCall / Osman

## SEASON 1994-95

| # | | Date | Opponents | | Att | F-A | Scorers | 1 | 2 | 3 | 4 | 5 | 6 | 7 | 8 | 9 | 10 | 11 | Subs (2) |
|---|---|---|---|---|---|---|---|---|---|---|---|---|---|---|---|---|---|---|---|
| 1 | H | 13/8 | BRENTFORD | L | 7,976 | 1-5 | Swan | Hodge | Patterson | Hill | Comyn | Swan | Payne | Barlow | Burnett | Nugent | Evans | Skinner | Edworthy/Landon |
| 2 | A | 20/8 | Brighton | D | 8,309 | 1-1 | Bradshaw | Hodge | Edworthy | Naylor | Comyn | Swan | Hill | Barlow | Bradshaw | Nugent | Evans | Dalton | Burnett |
| 3 | H | 27/8 | BRADFORD C | L | 6,469 | 1-5 | Dalton | Hodge | Edworthy | Naylor | Comyn | Swan | Bradshaw | Barlow | Castle | Nugent | Shaw | Dalton | Twiddy |
| 4 | A | 30/8 | Hull | L | 3,384 | 0-2 | | Hodge | Patterson | Naylor | Hill | Swan | Bradshaw | Burnett | Castle | Nugent | Shaw | Dalton | Twiddy |
| 5 | A | 3/9 | Birmingham | L | 13,202 | 2-4 | Castle, Nugent | Hodge | Patterson | Naylor | Comyn | Swan | Hill | Barlow | Castle | Nugent | Shaw | Twiddy | Bradshaw |
| 6 | H | 10/9 | HUDDERSFIELD | L | 5,464 | 0-3 | | Hodge | Bradshaw | Naylor | Comyn | Swan | Burnett | Barlow | Castle | Nugent | Shaw | Twiddy | Hill/Nicholls |
| 7 | H | 13/9 | CAMBRIDGE | D | 3,824 | 0-0 | | Nicholls | Patterson | Naylor | Hill | Comyn | Burnett | Barlow | Castle | Nugent | Shaw | Twiddy | |
| 8 | A | 17/9 | Cardiff | W | 5,674 | 1-0 | Castle | Nicholls | Patterson | Naylor | Hill | Comyn | Burnett | Barlow | Morgan | Nugent | Landon | Twiddy | Swan/Landon |
| 9 | H | 24/9 | CHESTER | W | 5,329 | 1-0 | Twiddy | Hodge | Patterson | Naylor | Hill | Comyn | Burnett | Barlow | Morgan | Nugent | Shaw | Twiddy | Swan/Evans |
| 10 | A | 1/10 | Leyton Orient | W | 4,140 | 2-0 | Landon 2 | Nicholls | Patterson | Naylor | Hill | Comyn | Burnett | Barlow | Morgan | Skinner | Landon | Twiddy | Edworthy |
| 11 | A | 8/10 | Oxford | L | 6,550 | 0-1 | | Nicholls | Patterson | Naylor | Swan | Comyn | Burnett | Barlow | Morgan | Skinner | Landon | Twiddy | Nugent/Edworthy |
| 12 | H | 15/10 | WYCOMBE | D | 6,864 | 2-2 | Skinner, Barlow | Nicholls | Patterson | Naylor | Hill | Comyn | Burnett | Barlow | Morgan | Skinner | Landon | Twiddy | O'Hagan |
| 13 | H | 22/10 | Stockport | W | 5,652 | 4-2 | Edworthy, O'Hagan, Landon 2 | Nicholls | Patterson | Naylor | Hill | Comyn | Burnett | Barlow | Edworthy | Skinner | Landon | Twiddy | O'Hagan/Dungey |
| 14 | H | 29/10 | BLACKPOOL | L | 6,285 | 0-2 | | Nicholls | Patterson | Naylor | Edworthy | Comyn | Burnett | Barlow | O'Hagan | Crocker | Landon | Twiddy | Crocker |
| 15 | H | 1/11 | PETERBOROUGH | L | 4,145 | 0-1 | | Nicholls | Patterson | Naylor | Edworthy | Comyn | Burnett | Barlow | Morgan | Crocker | Landon | Twiddy | Nugent |
| 16 | A | 5/11 | Rotherham | L | 2,848 | 1-3 | Skinner | Hodge | Patterson | Naylor | Edworthy | Comyn | Burnett | Barlow | Morgan | Nugent | Crocker | Skinner | Evans/Landon |
| 17 | H | 19/11 | WREXHAM | W | 6,936 | 4-1 | Hughes (og), Bur , Phillips (og), Barlow | Nicholls | Patterson | Naylor | Edworthy | Comyn | Burnett | Barlow | Skinner | Nugent | Quinn | Evans | Morgan |
| 18 | H | 26/11 | York | L | 3,185 | 0-1 | | Nicholls | Patterson | Naylor | Edworthy | Comyn | Burnett | Barlow | Dawe | Evans | Twiddy | Twiddy | Swan/Ross |
| 19 | H | 10/12 | BRIGHTON | L | 6,091 | 0-3 | | Nicholls | Patterson | Naylor | Edworthy | Comyn | Burnett | Barlow | Nugent | Quinn | Shilton | Shilton | Evans |
| 20 | A | 17/12 | Brentford | L | 4,492 | 0-7 | | Hodge | Patterson | Dawe | Swan | Comyn | Burnett | Barlow | Dawe | Quinn | Ross | Crocker | Shilton |
| 21 | A | 26/12 | Swansea | L | 4,859 | 0-3 | | Nicholls | Patterson | Hill | Swan | Comyn | Burnett | Barlow | Nugent | Evans | Ross | Barber | Nugent/Crocker |
| 22 | H | 2/1 | CREWE | W | 6,802 | 3-2 | Patterson, Evans 2 | Nicholls | Patterson | Naylor | Swan | Hill | Edworthy | Barlow | Skinner | Evans | Ross | Barber | Evans |
| 23 | A | 14/1 | Bournemouth | D | 4,913 | 0-0 | | Nicholls | Edworthy | Naylor | Hill | Comyn | Burnett | Barlow | Skinner | Nugent | Evans | Barber | Landon/Dawe |
| 24 | A | 21/1 | ROTHERHAM | D | 5,484 | 0-0 | | Nicholls | Edworthy | Naylor | Hill | Comyn | Burnett | Barlow | Barlow | Landon | Evans | Barber | Dalton |
| 25 | A | 28/1 | Blackpool | L | 3,599 | 2-5 | Patterson, Dalton | Nicholls | Patterson | Naylor | Hill | Comyn | Edworthy | Skinner | Barlow | Landon | Landon | McCall | Burnett/Dalton |
| 26 | H | 4/2 | YORK | L | 5,572 | 1-2 | Skinner | Nicholls | Patterson | Naylor | Hill | Comyn | McCall | Skinner | Barlow | Gee | Burnett | Burnett | Evans/Dalton |
| 27 | H | 7/2 | Shrewsbury | L | 3,029 | 2-3 | Nugent, Evans | Nicholls | Patterson | Naylor | Hill | Swan | McCall | Barlow | Wotton | Gee | Nugent | Dalton | Evans/Castle |
| 28 | A | 11/2 | Peterborough | W | 4,318 | 2-1 | McCall, Nugent | Nicholls | Patterson | Naylor | Hill | Swan | McCall | Barlow | Wotton | Evans | Nugent | Dalton | Skinner/Castle |
| 29 | H | 18/2 | BOURNEMOUTH | L | 5,435 | 0-1 | | Hodge | Patterson | Naylor | Hill | Swan | McCall | Barlow | Wotton | Gee | Nugent | Dalton | Evans/Wotton |
| 30 | A | 21/2 | Wrexham | L | 3,030 | 1-3 | Castle | Hodge | Patterson | Naylor | Hill | Comyn | Wotton | Barlow | Castle | Landon | Landon | Dalton | Skinner |
| 31 | H | 25/2 | LEYTON ORIENT | W | 5,173 | 1-0 | Landon | Hodge | Patterson | Naylor | Hill | Comyn | Twiddy | Barlow | Castle | Landon | Gee | Dalton | Burnett/Skinner |
| 32 | H | 4/3 | Chester | L | 1,823 | 0-1 | | Hodge | Patterson | Naylor | Hill | Comyn | Burnett | Barlow | Castle | Nugent | Landon | Dalton | Evans/Wotton |
| 33 | A | 11/3 | Bradford C | L | 5,399 | 0-2 | | Hodge | Edworthy | Naylor | Swan | Comyn | Burnett | Wotton | Castle | Nugent | Evans | Dalton | Morgan/Ross |
| 34 | H | 18/3 | HULL | W | 4,839 | 2-1 | Nugent, Evans | Hodge | Edworthy | Naylor | Swan | Comyn | Barlow | Evans | Castle | Nugent | Ross | Dalton | |
| 35 | H | 21/3 | Huddersfield | L | 12,099 | 0-2 | | Hodge | Edworthy | Naylor | Swan | Comyn | Burnett | Evans | Castle | Nugent | Ross | Dalton | Barlow/Patterson |
| 36 | H | 25/3 | CARDIFF | D | 5,611 | 0-0 | | Hodge | Patterson | Naylor | Swan | Edworthy | Barlow | Evans | Castle | Nugent | Ross | Dalton | Hill |
| 37 | H | 28/3 | STOCKPORT | L | 4,618 | 0-2 | | Hodge | Patterson | Naylor | Swan | Edworthy | Wotton | Barlow | Castle | Nugent | Ross | Dalton | Evans |
| 38 | A | 1/4 | Cambridge | D | 3,913 | 1-1 | Landon | Nicholls | Patterson | Naylor | Swan | Edworthy | Hill | Barlow | Castle | Landon | Ross | Dalton | Burnett/Ross |
| 39 | H | 4/4 | BRISTOL ROV | D | 6,743 | 1-1 | Nugent | Nicholls | Patterson | Naylor | Swan | Edworthy | Hill | Barlow | Barlow | Nugent | Landon | Dalton | Burnett/Ross |
| 40 | H | 8/4 | SHREWSBURY | W | 5,089 | 1-0 | Patterson | Nicholls | Patterson | Naylor | McCall | Edworthy | Hill | Barlow | Barlow | Nugent | Landon | Dalton | Castle/Ross |
| 41 | A | 15/4 | Bristol Rov | L | 7,068 | 0-2 | | Nicholls | Patterson | Castle | Burnett | Edworthy | Hill | Skinner | Castle | Nugent | Landon | Dalton | Ross |
| 42 | H | 17/4 | SWANSEA | W | 5,890 | 2-1 | Swan, Nugent | Nicholls | Patterson | Naylor | Swan | Edworthy | Hill | Skinner | Castle | Nugent | Ross | Dalton | Barlow |
| 43 | H | 19/4 | BIRMINGHAM | L | 8,550 | 1-3 | Dalton | Nicholls | Patterson | Naylor | Swan | Edworthy | Hill | Skinner | Castle | Nugent | Ross | Dalton | Landon |
| 44 | A | 22/4 | Crewe | D | 3,786 | 2-2 | Gardiner (og), Dalton | Dungey | Patterson | Naylor | Swan | Barlow | Hill | Skinner | Castle | Nugent | Ross | Dalton | Burnett/Landon |
| 45 | A | 29/4 | Wycombe | W | 6,850 | 2-1 | Hill, Landon | Dungey | Patterson | Naylor | Hill | Edworthy | Barlow | Skinner | Castle | Nugent | Landon | Dalton | Evans |

## LEAGUE CUP

| | | | | Att | Result | Scorers |
|---|---|---|---|---|---|---|
| 1:1 | A | 16/8 | Walsall | 2,810 | L 0-4 | |
| 1:2 | H | 23/8 | WALSALL | 2,801 | W 2-1 | Swan, Castle |

## FA CUP

| | | | | Att | Result | Scorers |
|---|---|---|---|---|---|---|
| 1 | A | 13/11 | Kettering | 4,602 | W 1-0 | Skinner |
| 2 | H | 3/12 | BOURNEMOUTH | 6,739 | W 2-1 | Ross 2 |
| 3 | A | 7/1 | Nottingham F | 19,821 | L 0-2 | |

### Line-ups

| | LC 1:1 | LC 1:2 | FAC 1 | FAC 2 | FAC 3 |
|---|---|---|---|---|---|
| | Hodge | Hodge | Hodge | Nicholls | Nicholls |
| | Barlow | Barlow | Barlow | Barlow | Barlow |
| | Payne | Bradshaw | Patterson | Edworthy | Patterson |
| | Comyn | Comyn | Edworthy | Swan | Swan |
| | Edworthy | Edworthy | Naylor | Naylor | Naylor |
| | Swan | Swan | Comyn | Comyn | Hill |
| | Comyn | Comyn | Burnett | Burnett | Edworthy |
| | Barlow | Barlow | Barlow | Barlow | Barlow |
| | Burnett | Castle | Skinner | Patterson | Skinner |
| | Nugent | Nugent | Nugent | Nugent | Nugent |
| | Morgan | Twiddy/Landon | Landon/Shilton | Evans | Morgan |
| subs | Evans | Evans | Skinner Dalton Twiddy Evans Barber | Evans Ross Burnett | Burnett Burnett Edworthy |

## League Table

| | | P | W | D | L | F | A | W | D | L | F | A | Pts |
|---|---|---|---|---|---|---|---|---|---|---|---|---|---|
| | | | | **Home** | | | | | **Away** | | | | |
| 1 | Birmingham | 46 | 15 | 6 | 2 | 53 | 18 | 10 | 8 | 5 | 31 | 19 | 89 |
| 2 | Brentford | 46 | 14 | 4 | 5 | 44 | 15 | 11 | 6 | 6 | 37 | 24 | 85 |
| 3 | Crewe | 46 | 14 | 3 | 6 | 46 | 33 | 11 | 5 | 7 | 34 | 35 | 83 |
| 4 | Bristol Rov | 46 | 15 | 7 | 1 | 48 | 20 | 7 | 9 | 7 | 22 | 20 | 82 |
| 5 | Huddersfield* | 46 | 14 | 5 | 4 | 45 | 21 | 8 | 10 | 5 | 34 | 28 | 81 |
| 6 | Wycombe | 46 | 13 | 7 | 3 | 36 | 19 | 8 | 7 | 8 | 24 | 27 | 78 |
| 7 | Oxford | 46 | 13 | 6 | 4 | 30 | 18 | 8 | 6 | 9 | 36 | 34 | 75 |
| 8 | Hull | 46 | 13 | 6 | 4 | 40 | 18 | 8 | 5 | 10 | 30 | 39 | 74 |
| 9 | York | 46 | 13 | 4 | 6 | 37 | 21 | 8 | 5 | 10 | 30 | 30 | 72 |
| 10 | Swansea | 46 | 10 | 8 | 5 | 23 | 13 | 9 | 6 | 8 | 34 | 32 | 71 |
| 11 | Stockport | 46 | 12 | 3 | 8 | 40 | 29 | 7 | 5 | 11 | 23 | 31 | 65 |
| 12 | Blackpool | 46 | 11 | 4 | 8 | 40 | 36 | 7 | 6 | 10 | 24 | 34 | 64 |
| 13 | Wrexham | 46 | 10 | 7 | 6 | 38 | 27 | 6 | 8 | 9 | 27 | 37 | 63 |
| 14 | Bradford C | 46 | 8 | 6 | 9 | 29 | 32 | 8 | 6 | 6 | 28 | 32 | 60 |
| 15 | Peterborough | 46 | 7 | 11 | 5 | 26 | 29 | 7 | 9 | 7 | 28 | 40 | 60 |
| 16 | Brighton | 46 | 9 | 10 | 4 | 25 | 15 | 5 | 7 | 11 | 29 | 38 | 59 |
| 17 | Rotherham | 46 | 12 | 6 | 5 | 36 | 26 | 2 | 8 | 13 | 21 | 35 | 56 |
| 18 | Shrewsbury | 46 | 9 | 9 | 5 | 34 | 27 | 4 | 5 | 14 | 20 | 35 | 53 |
| 19 | Bournemouth | 46 | 9 | 4 | 10 | 30 | 34 | 4 | 7 | 12 | 19 | 35 | 50 |
| 20 | Cambridge | 46 | 8 | 9 | 6 | 33 | 28 | 3 | 6 | 14 | 19 | 41 | 48 |
| 21 | PLYMOUTH | 46 | 7 | 6 | 10 | 25 | 36 | 5 | 4 | 14 | 23 | 47 | 46 |
| 22 | Cardiff | 46 | 5 | 6 | 12 | 25 | 31 | 4 | 5 | 14 | 21 | 43 | 38 |
| 23 | Chester | 46 | 5 | 6 | 12 | 23 | 42 | 0 | 5 | 17 | 14 | 42 | 29 |
| 24 | Leyton O | 46 | 6 | 6 | 11 | 21 | 29 | 2 | 2 | 21 | 9 | 46 | 26 |
| | | 1104 | 252 | 149 | 151 | 824 | 617 | 151 | 149 | 252 | 617 | 824 | 1507 |

\* promoted p/o

## Appearances and Goals

| Player | Lge | Sub | LC | Sub | FAC | Sub | Goals Lge | LC | FAC | Tot |
|---|---|---|---|---|---|---|---|---|---|---|
| Barber, Phil | 4 | | 1 | | | | | | | |
| Barlow, Martin | 40 | 2 | 2 | | 3 | | 2 | | | 2 |
| Bradshaw, Darren | 5 | 1 | 1 | | | | 1 | | | 1 |
| Burnett, Wayne | 25 | 7 | 1 | | 3 | | 1 | | | 1 |
| Castle, Steve | 23 | 3 | 1 | | 1 | | 3 | 1 | | 4 |
| Comyn, Andy | 30 | | 2 | | 2 | | | | | |
| Crocker, Marcus | 3 | 2 | | | | | | | | |
| Dalton, Paul | 23 | 3 | 1 | | 2 | | 4 | | | 4 |
| Dawe, Simon | 3 | 1 | | | | | | | | |
| Dungey, James | 3 | | | | | | | | | |
| Edworthy, Marc | 24 | 3 | 2 | | 3 | | 1 | | | 1 |
| Evans, Michael | 12 | 11 | 2 | | 2 | 1 | 4 | | | 4 |
| Gee, Phil | 6 | | | | | | | | | |
| Hill, Keith | 32 | 2 | 2 | | 1 | | 1 | | | 1 |
| Hodge, Martin | 17 | | 2 | | 1 | | | | | |
| Landon, Richard | 18 | 6 | | 1 | | 1 | 7 | | | 7 |
| McCall, Steve | 7 | | | | | | | | | |
| Morgan, Jamie | 6 | 2 | | | | 1 | 1 | | | 1 |
| Naylor, Dominic | 42 | | | | 3 | | | | | |
| Nicholls, Alan | 26 | 1 | | | 2 | | | | | |
| Nugent, Kevin | 34 | 3 | 2 | | 3 | | 7 | | | 7 |
| O'Hagan, Danny | 1 | 2 | | | | | 1 | | | 1 |
| Patterson, Mark | 37 | 1 | 1 | | 3 | | 3 | | | 3 |
| Payne, Ian | 1 | | | | 1 | | | | | |
| Quinn, Mick | 3 | | | | | | | | | |
| Ross, Micky | 11 | 6 | | | 1 | | | | 2 | 2 |
| Shaw, Graham | 6 | | | | | | | | | |
| Shilton, Sam | 1 | | 1 | | | | | | | |
| Skinner, Craig | 21 | 3 | 1 | | 2 | | 3 | | 1 | 4 |
| Swan, Peter | 24 | 3 | 2 | | 2 | | 2 | 1 | | 3 |
| Twiddy, Chris | 13 | 2 | 1 | | 1 | | 1 | | | 1 |
| Wotton, Paul | 5 | 2 | | | | | | | | |
| (own-goals) | | | | | | | 3 | | | 3 |
| 32 players used | 506 | 68 | 22 | 3 | 33 | 3 | 45 | 2 | 3 | 50 |

# LEAGUE DIVISION 3

## Manager: Neil Warnock

## SEASON 1995-96

| # | | Date | Opponents | Att | | F-A | Scorers | 1 | 2 | 3 | 4 | 5 | 6 | 7 | 8 | 9 | 10 | 11 | Subs (3) |
|---|---|---|---|---|---|---|---|---|---|---|---|---|---|---|---|---|---|---|---|
| 1 | A | 12/8 | Colchester | 3,585 | L | 1-2 | Littlejohn | Hammond | Patterson | Williams | Burnett | Heathcote | Hill | Billy | Mauge | Littlejohn | Nugent | Leadbitter | Twiddy/Evans/Hodgson |
| 2 | H | 19/8 | PRESTON | 6,862 | L | 0-2 | | Hammond | Patterson | Williams | Burnett | Heathcote | Hill | Billy | Mauge | Littlejohn | Nugent | Clayton | Leadbitter/Evans/Hodgson |
| 3 | A | 26/8 | Chester | 2,660 | L | 1-3 | Heathcote | Hammond | Twiddy | Williams | Burnett | Heathcote | Hill | Billy | Mauge | Littlejohn | Nugent | Clayton | Leadbitter/Evans/O'Hagan |
| 4 | H | 29/8 | HEREFORD | 5,608 | L | 0-1 | | Hammond | Saunders | Williams | Clayton | Heathcote | Hodgson | Billy | Mauge | Littlejohn | Nugent | Leadbitter | Patterson/Evans/O'Hagan |
| 5 | A | 2/9 | Bury | 3,040 | W | 5-0 | Evans 2, Clayton, Billy, Littlejohn | Blackwell | Patterson | Williams | Clayton | Heathcote | Hodgson | Billy | Mauge | Littlejohn | Evans | Leadbitter | Saunders/O'Hagan |
| 6 | H | 9/9 | LEYTON ORIENT | 6,292 | D | 1-1 | Evans | Blackwell | Patterson | Williams | Clayton | Heathcote | Hodgson | Billy | Mauge | Littlejohn | Evans | Leadbitter | O'Hagan/Saunders/Shilton |
| 7 | H | 12/9 | DONCASTER | 4,858 | W | 3-1 | Evans, Billy, Littlejohn | Blackwell | Patterson | Williams | Burnett | Heathcote | Hill | Billy | Mauge | Littlejohn | Evans | Leadbitter | |
| 8 | A | 16/9 | Barnet | 2,557 | W | 2-1 | Evans (p), Littlejohn | Blackwell | Patterson | Williams | Burnett | Heathcote | Hill | Billy | Mauge | Littlejohn | Evans | Leadbitter | Nugent/Saunders |
| 9 | A | 23/9 | Wigan | 2,631 | W | 1-0 | Littlejohn | Blackwell | Patterson | Williams | Barlow | Heathcote | Hill | Billy | Mauge | Littlejohn | Evans | Leadbitter | Nugent/Saunders |
| 10 | H | 30/9 | LINCOLN | 6,643 | W | 3-0 | Minett (og), Evans, Littlejohn | Blackwell | Patterson | Williams | Barlow | Heathcote | Hill | Baird | Mauge | Littlejohn | Evans | Leadbitter | Clayton/Magee |
| 11 | H | 7/10 | FULHAM | 6,681 | W | 3-0 | Littlejohn, Baird 2 | Blackwell | Patterson | Williams | Clayton | Heathcote | Hill | Baird | Mauge | Littlejohn | Evans | Leadbitter | Clayton |
| 12 | A | 14/10 | Mansfield | 3,164 | D | 1-1 | Heathcote | Blackwell | Patterson | Williams | Barlow | Heathcote | Hill | Baird | Mauge | Littlejohn | Evans | Leadbitter | Clayton |
| 13 | H | 21/10 | TORQUAY | 11,695 | W | 4-3 | Littlejohn 3, Mauge | Blackwell | Patterson | Williams | Clayton | Heathcote | Hill | Baird | Mauge | Littlejohn | Evans | Leadbitter | Clayton/Magee |
| 14 | A | 28/10 | Darlington | 2,352 | L | 0-2 | | Blackwell | Patterson | Williams | Clayton | Logan | Hill | Barlow | Mauge | Littlejohn | Evans | Leadbitter | Barlow/Magee/Logan |
| 15 | A | 31/10 | Scarborough | 1,876 | D | 2-2 | Littlejohn 2 | Blackwell | Patterson | Williams | Clayton | Logan | Hill | Barlow | Mauge | Littlejohn | Evans | Leadbitter | Baird/Wotton |
| 16 | H | 4/11 | CARDIFF | 7,434 | D | 0-0 | | Blackwell | Patterson | Williams | Clayton | Heathcote | Hill | Baird | Mauge | Littlejohn | Evans | Leadbitter | Billy/Magee |
| 17 | A | 18/11 | Hartlepool | 1,830 | D | 2-2 | Evans (p), Mauge | Blackwell | Patterson | Williams | Clayton | Heathcote | Hill | Billy | Mauge | Littlejohn | Evans | Leadbitter | Logan |
| 18 | H | 25/11 | ROCHDALE | 6,558 | W | 2-0 | Littlejohn, Evans | Blackwell | Patterson | Williams | Clayton | Heathcote | Hill | Billy | Mauge | Littlejohn | Evans | Leadbitter | Saunders/Baird |
| 19 | H | 9/12 | WIGAN | 5,931 | W | 3-1 | Barlow, Littlejohn 2 | Blackwell | Patterson | Williams | Clayton | Heathcote | Hill | Baird | Barlow | Littlejohn | Evans | Leadbitter | Billy/Magee |
| 20 | A | 16/12 | Lincoln | 2,801 | D | 0-0 | | Blackwell | Patterson | Williams | Clayton | Heathcote | Hill | Baird | Logan | Littlejohn | Evans | Leadbitter | |
| 21 | H | 23/12 | CAMBRIDGE | 7,135 | W | 1-0 | Mauge | Blackwell | Patterson | Williams | Clayton | Heathcote | Hill | Baird | Mauge | Littlejohn | Evans | Leadbitter | Logan/Curran |
| 22 | A | 26/12 | Gillingham | 9,651 | L | 0-1 | | Blackwell | Patterson | Williams | Clayton | Heathcote | Hill | Baird | Mauge | Littlejohn | Evans | Leadbitter | Billy/Logan |
| 23 | H | 1/1 | EXETER | 12,427 | D | 2-2 | Mauge, Baird | Blackwell | Patterson | Williams | Clayton | Heathcote | Hill | Baird | Mauge | Littlejohn | Evans | Leadbitter | Billy/Logan/Curran |
| 24 | A | 13/1 | Preston | 11,126 | L | 2-3 | Heathcote, Saunders | Blackwell | Billy | Williams | Logan | Heathcote | Hill | Saunders | Mauge | Littlejohn | Evans | Leadbitter | Baird |
| 25 | H | 20/1 | COLCHESTER | 5,800 | D | 1-1 | Baird | Patterson | Billy | Williams | Logan | Heathcote | Curran | Baird | Mauge | Littlejohn | Evans | Leadbitter | Hill/Saunders |
| 26 | H | 23/1 | SCUNTHORPE | 4,712 | L | 1-3 | Logan | Patterson | Patterson | Williams | Saunders | Heathcote | Curran | Baird | Mauge | Littlejohn | Evans | Billy | Logan/Barlow/Partridge |
| 27 | A | 30/1 | Northampton | 3,911 | L | 0-1 | | Patterson | Patterson | Williams | Saunders | Heathcote | Curran | Baird | Mauge | Partridge | Evans | Barlow | Billy |
| 28 | H | 3/2 | CHESTER | 5,114 | W | 4-2 | Barlow, Mauge, Partridge, Williams | Patterson | Patterson | Williams | Mauge | Heathcote | Clayton | Baird | Logan | Partridge | Evans | Barlow | Billy/O'Hagan |
| 29 | A | 10/2 | Scunthorpe | 2,789 | D | 1-1 | Evans | Patterson | Patterson | Williams | Mauge | Heathcote | Clayton | Baird | Logan | Partridge | Evans | Barlow | Billy |
| 30 | A | 17/2 | Doncaster | 2,338 | D | 0-0 | | Patterson | Patterson | Williams | Mauge | Heathcote | Clayton | Baird | Logan | Partridge | Evans | Barlow | Billy |
| 31 | H | 20/2 | BURY | 4,536 | W | 1-0 | Heathcote | Cherry | Patterson | Williams | Mauge | Heathcote | Clayton | Baird | Logan | Partridge | Evans | Barlow | Billy/Littlejohn |
| 32 | H | 24/2 | BARNET | 6,426 | D | 1-1 | Partridge | Cherry | Patterson | Williams | Mauge | Heathcote | Clayton | Baird | Logan | Partridge | Evans | Barlow | |
| 33 | A | 27/2 | Leyton Orient | 3,374 | W | 1-0 | Logan | Cherry | Patterson | Williams | Mauge | Heathcote | Clayton | Baird | Logan | Partridge | Evans | Barlow | |
| 34 | H | 2/3 | GILLINGHAM | 8,485 | W | 1-0 | Barlow | Cherry | Patterson | Williams | Mauge | Heathcote | Clayton | Baird | Logan | Littlejohn | Evans | Barlow | |
| 35 | A | 9/3 | Cambridge | 2,785 | W | 3-2 | Billy, Logan, Baird | Cherry | Patterson | Williams | Billy | Heathcote | Clayton | Baird | Logan | Littlejohn | Evans | Barlow | Leadbitter |
| 36 | H | 16/3 | NORTHAMPTON | 7,001 | W | 1-0 | Evans | Cherry | Patterson | Williams | Billy | Heathcote | Clayton | Baird | Logan | Littlejohn | Evans | Barlow | |
| 37 | A | 23/3 | Exeter | 6,185 | D | 1-1 | Clayton | Cherry | Patterson | Williams | Billy | Heathcote | Clayton | Baird | Logan | Littlejohn | Evans | Barlow | |
| 38 | A | 30/3 | Fulham | 5,667 | W | 1-0 | Corazzin(p) | Cherry | Patterson | Williams | Billy | Heathcote | Clayton | Baird | Logan | Littlejohn | Evans | Barlow | Hill/Corazzin |
| 39 | H | 2/4 | MANSFIELD | 6,375 | W | 1-0 | | Cherry | Patterson | Williams | Mauge | Heathcote | Hill | Billy | Logan | Littlejohn | Evans | Barlow | Corazzin/McCall |
| 40 | H | 6/4 | DARLINGTON | 8,990 | L | 0-1 | | Cherry | Patterson | Williams | Mauge | Heathcote | Hill | McCall | Logan | Corazzin | Evans | Barlow | Billy/Littlejohn/Leadbitter |
| 41 | A | 8/4 | Torquay | 4,269 | W | 2-0 | Mauge, Littlejohn | Cherry | Patterson | Williams | Mauge | Heathcote | Clayton | Leadbitter | Logan | Littlejohn | Evans | Barlow | Billy/Corazzin/McCall |
| 42 | H | 13/4 | SCARBOROUGH | 6,949 | W | 5-1 | Mauge, Barlow 2, Littlejohn 2 | Cherry | Patterson | Williams | Mauge | Heathcote | Clayton | Leadbitter | Logan | Littlejohn | Evans | Barlow | Billy/Corazzin/Leadbitter |
| 43 | A | 16/4 | Hereford | 4,739 | L | 0-3 | | Cherry | Patterson | Williams | Billy | Heathcote | McCall | Leadbitter | Logan | Littlejohn | Evans | Barlow | Hill/Billy/Corazzin |
| 44 | A | 20/4 | Cardiff | 3,374 | W | 1-0 | Evans | Cherry | Patterson | Williams | Billy | Heathcote | Clayton | Leadbitter | Logan | Littlejohn | Evans | Curran | |
| 45 | A | 27/4 | Rochdale | 2,355 | W | 1-0 | Evans | Cherry | Patterson | Williams | Billy | Heathcote | Clayton | Leadbitter | Logan | Littlejohn | Evans | Curran | Barlow |

## PLAY-OFFS

| Round | | Date | Opponent | Att | Result | Scorers |
|---|---|---|---|---|---|---|
| SF | A | 12/5 | Colchester | 6,511 | L 0-1 | |
| SF | H | 15/5 | COLCHESTER | 14,525 | W 3-1 | Evans, Leadbitter, Williams |
| F | N | 25/5 | Darlington | 43,431 | W 1-0 | Mauge |

Line-ups:

| Match | 1 | 2 | 3 | 4 | 5 | 6 | 7 | 8 | 9 | 10 | 11 | Subs |
|---|---|---|---|---|---|---|---|---|---|---|---|---|
| SF A Colchester | Cherry | Patterson | Williams | Billy | Heathcote | Leadbitter | Littlejohn | Logan | Evans | Curran | Barlow | Mauge |
| SF H COLCHESTER | Cherry | Patterson | Williams | Mauge | Heathcote | Leadbitter | Littlejohn | Logan | Evans | Curran | Barlow | |
| F N Darlington | Cherry | Patterson | Williams | Mauge | Heathcote | Leadbitter | Littlejohn | Logan | Evans | Curran | Barlow | |

## LEAGUE CUP

| Round | | Date | Opponent | Att | Result | Scorers |
|---|---|---|---|---|---|---|
| 1:1 | A | 15/8 | Birmingham | 7,964 | L 0-1 | |
| 1:2 | H | 22/8 | BIRMINGHAM | 6,529 | L 1-2 | Heathcote |

Line-ups:

| Match | 1 | 2 | 3 | 4 | 5 | 6 | 7 | 8 | 9 | 10 | 11 | Subs |
|---|---|---|---|---|---|---|---|---|---|---|---|---|
| 1:1 Birmingham | Hammond | Patterson | Williams | Burnett | Heathcote | Billy | Littlejohn | Mauge | Nugent | Clayton | Hill | O'Hagan/Saunders/Evans |
| 1:2 BIRMINGHAM | Hammond | Twiddy | Williams | Burnett | Heathcote | Billy | Littlejohn | Mauge | Nugent | Clayton | Hill | |

## FA CUP

| Round | | Date | Opponent | Att | Result | Scorers |
|---|---|---|---|---|---|---|
| 1 | A | 11/11 | Slough | 3,030 | W 2-0 | Harvey (og), Heathcote |
| 2 | A | 3/12 | Kingstonian | 2,961 | W 2-1 | Leadbitter, Littlejohn |
| 3 | H | 6/1 | COVENTRY | 17,721 | L 1-3 | Baird |

Line-ups:

| Match | 1 | 2 | 3 | 4 | 5 | 6 | 7 | 8 | 9 | 10 | 11 | Subs |
|---|---|---|---|---|---|---|---|---|---|---|---|---|
| 1 Slough | Blackwell | Patterson | Williams | Clayton | Heathcote | Billy | Littlejohn | Mauge | Evans | Leadbitter | Hill | Logan |
| 2 Kingstonian | Blackwell | Patterson | Williams | Clayton | Heathcote | Billy | Littlejohn | Mauge | Evans | Leadbitter | Hill | Baird/Magee/Logan |
| 3 COVENTRY | Blackwell | Billy | Williams | Logan | Heathcote | Baird | Littlejohn | Mauge | Evans | Leadbitter | Hill | Twiddy/Saunders |

## League table

| Pos | Team | P | W | D | L | F | A | W | D | L | F | A | Pts |
|---|---|---|---|---|---|---|---|---|---|---|---|---|---|
| | | | | Home | | | | | Away | | | | |
| 1 | Preston | 46 | 11 | 8 | 4 | 44 | 22 | 12 | 9 | 2 | 34 | 16 | 86 |
| 2 | Gillingham | 46 | 16 | 6 | 1 | 33 | 6 | 11 | 6 | 6 | 16 | 14 | 83 |
| 3 | Bury | 46 | 11 | 6 | 6 | 33 | 21 | 11 | 7 | 5 | 27 | 27 | 79 |
| 4 | PLYMOUTH * | 46 | 14 | 5 | 4 | 41 | 20 | 8 | 7 | 8 | 27 | 29 | 78 |
| 5 | Darlington | 46 | 10 | 6 | 7 | 30 | 21 | 10 | 12 | 1 | 30 | 21 | 78 |
| 6 | Hereford | 46 | 13 | 5 | 5 | 25 | 22 | 9 | 7 | 9 | 25 | 25 | 74 |
| 7 | Colchester | 46 | 13 | 7 | 3 | 37 | 22 | 5 | 11 | 7 | 24 | 29 | 72 |
| 8 | Chester | 46 | 11 | 9 | 3 | 45 | 22 | 7 | 7 | 9 | 27 | 31 | 70 |
| 9 | Barnet | 46 | 13 | 6 | 4 | 40 | 19 | 5 | 10 | 8 | 25 | 26 | 70 |
| 10 | Wigan | 46 | 15 | 3 | 5 | 36 | 21 | 5 | 7 | 11 | 26 | 35 | 70 |
| 11 | Northampton | 46 | 9 | 10 | 4 | 32 | 22 | 9 | 3 | 11 | 19 | 22 | 67 |
| 12 | Scunthorpe | 46 | 8 | 8 | 7 | 36 | 30 | 7 | 7 | 9 | 31 | 31 | 60 |
| 13 | Doncaster | 46 | 11 | 6 | 6 | 25 | 19 | 5 | 5 | 13 | 24 | 41 | 59 |
| 14 | Exeter | 46 | 9 | 9 | 5 | 22 | 22 | 4 | 9 | 10 | 21 | 31 | 57 |
| 15 | Rochdale | 46 | 7 | 8 | 8 | 32 | 33 | 7 | 5 | 11 | 25 | 28 | 55 |
| 16 | Cambridge | 46 | 8 | 8 | 7 | 34 | 30 | 6 | 4 | 13 | 27 | 41 | 54 |
| 17 | Fulham | 46 | 10 | 9 | 4 | 39 | 26 | 2 | 8 | 13 | 18 | 37 | 53 |
| 18 | Lincoln | 46 | 8 | 7 | 8 | 32 | 26 | 5 | 7 | 11 | 25 | 47 | 53 |
| 19 | Mansfield | 46 | 6 | 10 | 7 | 25 | 29 | 5 | 10 | 8 | 29 | 35 | 53 |
| 20 | Hartlepool | 46 | 8 | 9 | 6 | 30 | 24 | 4 | 4 | 15 | 17 | 43 | 49 |
| 21 | Leyton O | 46 | 11 | 4 | 8 | 29 | 22 | 1 | 7 | 15 | 15 | 41 | 47 |
| 22 | Cardiff | 46 | 8 | 6 | 9 | 24 | 22 | 3 | 6 | 14 | 17 | 42 | 45 |
| 23 | Scarborough | 46 | 5 | 11 | 7 | 22 | 28 | 3 | 5 | 15 | 17 | 41 | 40 |
| 24 | Torquay | 46 | 4 | 9 | 10 | 17 | 36 | 1 | 5 | 17 | 13 | 48 | 29 |
| | | 1104 | 239 | 175 | 138 | 781 | 565 | 138 | 175 | 239 | 565 | 781 | 1481 |

* promoted p/o

## Appearances and Goals

| Player | Lge | Sub | LC | Sub | FAC | Sub | Goals Lge | LC | FAC | Tot |
|---|---|---|---|---|---|---|---|---|---|---|
| Baird, Ian | 24 | 3 | | | 1 | 1 | 5 | | 1 | 6 |
| Barlow, Martin | 25 | 3 | | | | | 5 | | | 5 |
| Billy, Chris | 22 | 10 | 2 | | 3 | | 4 | | | 4 |
| Blackwell, Kevin | 20 | | | | 3 | | | | | |
| Burnett, Wayne | 6 | 2 | 2 | | | | | | | |
| Cherry, Steve | 16 | | | | | | | | | |
| Clayton, Gary | 32 | 4 | 2 | | 2 | | 2 | | | 2 |
| Corazzin, Carlo | 1 | 5 | | | | | 1 | | | 1 |
| Curran, Chris | 6 | 2 | | | | | | | | |
| Evans, Michael | 41 | 4 | | 1 | 3 | | 12 | | | 12 |
| Hammond, Nicky | 4 | 2 | 2 | | | | | | | |
| Heathcote, Mick | 44 | | 2 | | 3 | | 4 | 1 | 1 | 6 |
| Hill, Keith | 21 | 3 | 2 | | 3 | | | | | |
| Hodgson, Doug | 3 | 2 | | | | | | | | |
| Leadbitter, Chris | 29 | 4 | | | 3 | | 1 | | 1 | 2 |
| Littlejohn, Adrian | 40 | 2 | 2 | | 3 | | 17 | | 1 | 18 |
| Logan, Richard | 25 | 6 | | | 1 | 2 | 4 | | | 4 |
| Magee, Kevin | 4 | 4 | | | | 1 | 1 | | | 1 |
| Mauge, Ronnie | 36 | 2 | 2 | | 3 | | 7 | | | 7 |
| McCall, Steve | 2 | 2 | | | | | | | | |
| Nugent, Kevin | 4 | 2 | 2 | | | | | | | |
| O'Hagan, Danny | 6 | 1 | | 1 | | | | | | |
| Partridge, Scott | 6 | 1 | | | | 1 | | | | |
| Patterson, Mark | 42 | 1 | 1 | | 2 | | 2 | | | 2 |
| Patterson, Andy | 6 | | | | | | | | | |
| Saunders, Mark | 4 | 6 | | 1 | | 1 | 1 | | | 1 |
| Shilton, Sam | 1 | | | | | | | | | |
| Twiddy, Chris | 1 | 1 | 1 | | | 1 | | | | |
| Williams, Paul | 46 | | 2 | | 3 | | 2 | | | 2 |
| Wotton, Paul | 1 | | | | | | | | | |
| (own-goals) | | | | | | | 1 | | 1 | 2 |
| 30 players used | 506 | 74 | 22 | 3 | 33 | 6 | 68 | 1 | 5 | 74 |

# LEAGUE DIVISION 2  Manager: Mick Jones  SEASON 1997-98

| # | H/A | Date | Opponents | Att | | F-A | Scorers | 1 | 2 | 3 | 4 | 5 | 6 | 7 | 8 | 9 | 10 | 11 | Subs (3) |
|---|---|---|---|---|---|---|---|---|---|---|---|---|---|---|---|---|---|---|---|
| 1 | A | 9/8 | Bristol Rov | 7,386 | D | 1-1 | Heathcote | Sheffield | Collins | Williams | Ro'botham | Heathcote | Wotton | Billy | Logan | Littlejohn | Corazzin | Anthony | Jean |
| 2 | H | 16/8 | GRIMSBY | 6,002 | D | 2-2 | Logan, Littlejohn | Sheffield | Billy | Williams | Mauge | Heathcote | Wotton | Ro'botham | Logan | Littlejohn | Corazzin | Anthony | Jean/Clayton |
| 3 | A | 23/8 | Wigan | 3,761 | D | 1-1 | Logan | Sheffield | Billy | Williams | Mauge | Heathcote | Wotton | Anthony | Logan | Littlejohn | Jean | Anthony | Wilson |
| 4 | H | 30/8 | CHESTERFIELD | 5,284 | L | 0-1 | | Sheffield | Billy | Williams | Mauge | Heathcote | Wotton | Anthony | Logan | Littlejohn | Jean | Wilson | Illman |
| 5 | A | 2/9 | WATFORD | 5,141 | L | 0-1 | Jean | Sheffield | Billy | Williams | Mauge | Heathcote | Wotton | Barlow | Logan | Littlejohn | Jean | Wilson | Barlow/Illman |
| 6 | H | 9/9 | Fulham | 8,961 | L | 0-2 | | Sheffield | Billy | Williams | Mauge | Heathcote | Wotton | Barlow | Logan | Littlejohn | Jean | Illman | Collins/Wilson |
| 7 | A | 13/9 | BRENTFORD | 4,394 | D | 0-0 | | Sheffield | Billy | Williams | Mauge | Heathcote | Wotton | Barlow | Logan | Littlejohn | Jean | Illman | Illman |
| 8 | H | 20/9 | Carlisle | 5,667 | D | 2-2 | Littlejohn, Wilson | Sheffield | Billy | Williams | Mauge | Heathcote | Wotton | Barlow | Saunders | Littlejohn | Corazzin | Wilson | Saunders |
| 9 | H | 27/9 | WALSALL | 6,207 | W | 2-1 | Barlow 2 | Sheffield | Billy | Williams | Mauge | Heathcote | Wotton | Barlow | Saunders | Littlejohn | Corazzin | Wilson | |
| 10 | A | 4/10 | York | 2,894 | L | 0-1 | | Sheffield | Billy | Williams | Mauge | Heathcote | Wotton | Barlow | Saunders | Littlejohn | Corazzin | Wilson | Jean |
| 11 | H | 11/10 | Luton | 4,931 | L | 0-3 | | Sheffield | Collins | Williams | Mauge | Heathcote | Wotton | Barlow | Saunders | Littlejohn | Billy | Wilson | Jean |
| 12 | A | 18/10 | SOUTHEND | 3,430 | L | 2-3 | Littlejohn, Corazzin | Sheffield | Collins | Williams | Mauge | Heathcote | Wotton | Barlow | Saunders | Littlejohn | Corazzin | Billy | Jean |
| 13 | H | 21/10 | BURNLEY | 3,003 | D | 2-2 | Jean, Heathcote | Sheffield | Collins | Williams | Mauge | Heathcote | Wotton | Barlow | Jean | Littlejohn | Corazzin | Billy | |
| 14 | A | 25/10 | Gillingham | 6,679 | L | 1-2 | Jean | Sheffield | Collins | Williams | Mauge | Saunders | Wotton | Barlow | Jean | Littlejohn | Corazzin | Billy | Illman/Wilson/Besweth'ck |
| 15 | H | 1/11 | Preston | 8,405 | W | 1-0 | Corazzin | Sheffield | Collins | Williams | Mauge | Saunders | Wotton | Barlow | Jean | Littlejohn | Corazzin | Billy | |
| 16 | H | 4/11 | WYCOMBE | 3,030 | W | 4-2 | Corazzin 2 (1p), Littlejohn, Mauge | Sheffield | Collins | Williams | Mauge | Saunders | Wotton | Barlow | Jean | Littlejohn | Corazzin | Billy | Illman |
| 17 | H | 8/11 | BOURNEMOUTH | 5,067 | W | 3-0 | Jean, Littlejohn 2 | Sheffield | Collins | Williams | Hodges | Saunders | Wotton | Barlow | Jean | Littlejohn | O'Hagan | Billy | |
| 18 | A | 18/11 | Bristol City | 10,267 | L | 1-2 | Corazzin | Sheffield | Collins | Williams | Hodges | Mauge | Wotton | Barlow | Jean | Littlejohn | Corazzin | Billy | Saunders/Wilson |
| 19 | A | 22/11 | Wrexham | 3,641 | D | 1-1 | Corazzin | Sheffield | Logan | Williams | Hodges | Mauge | Wotton | Barlow | Jean | Littlejohn | Corazzin | Billy | O'Hagan |
| 20 | H | 29/11 | OLDHAM | 5,452 | L | 0-2 | | Sheffield | Logan | Williams | Mauge | Hodges | Wotton | Barlow | Jean | Littlejohn | Corazzin | Billy | Saunders/O'Hagan |
| 21 | A | 2/12 | Blackpool | 3,281 | D | 0-0 | | Sheffield | Ro'botham | Williams | Hodges | Saunders | Collins | Barlow | Logan | Littlejohn | Corazzin | Billy | O'Hagan |
| 22 | H | 13/12 | MILLWALL | 4,460 | W | 3-0 | Collins, Billy, Corazzin (p) | Sheffield | Ro'botham | Williams | Hodges | Saunders | Collins | Barlow | Logan | Littlejohn | Corazzin | Billy | Wotton/Jean/Besweth'ck |
| 23 | A | 20/12 | Northampton | 5,546 | L | 1-2 | Corazzin | Sheffield | Ro'botham | Williams | Hodges | Saunders | Collins | Barlow | Logan | O'Hagan | Corazzin | Billy | Jean |
| 24 | H | 26/12 | FULHAM | 9,469 | L | 1-4 | Barlow | Sheffield | Collins | Williams | Hodges | Heathcote | Saunders | Barlow | Logan | O'Hagan | Corazzin | Billy | Littlejohn/Jean/Mauge |
| 25 | A | 28/12 | Watford | 11,594 | D | 1-1 | Saunders | Sheffield | Collins | Williams | Mauge | Heathcote | Saunders | Barlow | Hodges | Littlejohn | Corazzin | Billy | Jean |
| 26 | H | 10/1 | BRISTOL ROV | 6,850 | L | 1-2 | Corazzin | Sheffield | Collins | Williams | Mauge | Heathcote | Saunders | Barlow | Jean | O'Hagan | Corazzin | Ro'botham | O'Hagan/Phillips |
| 27 | A | 17/1 | Chesterfield | 3,879 | L | 1-2 | Corazzin (p) | Sheffield | Collins | Williams | Mauge | Heathcote | Saunders | Barlow | Wotton | O'Hagan | Corazzin | Ro'botham | Logan/Jean |
| 28 | H | 24/1 | WIGAN | 4,345 | W | 3-2 | Saunders, Barlow, Collins | Sheffield | Collins | Williams | Mauge | Heathcote | Ro'botham | Barlow | Saunders | Littlejohn | Corazzin | Billy | Logan/Jean |
| 29 | A | 31/1 | Brentford | 4,783 | L | 1-3 | Corazzin | Sheffield | Collins | Williams | Mauge | Heathcote | Ro'botham | Barlow | Saunders | Littlejohn | Corazzin | Billy | Logan/Jean/Phillips |
| 30 | H | 7/2 | CARLISLE | 4,540 | W | 2-1 | Heathcote, Corazzin | Sheffield | Collins | Williams | Mauge | Heathcote | Ro'botham | Barlow | Saunders | Jean | Corazzin | Billy | Littlejohn/Phillips |
| 31 | H | 14/2 | YORK | 4,382 | D | 0-0 | | Sheffield | Collins | Williams | Logan | Heathcote | Ro'botham | Barlow | Phillips | Corazzin | Corazzin | Billy | Mauge |
| 32 | A | 21/2 | Walsall | 4,612 | W | 1-0 | Heathcote | Sheffield | Collins | Williams | Saunders | Heathcote | Wotton | Barlow | Phillips | Littlejohn | Corazzin | Billy | Jean |
| 33 | A | 24/2 | Southend | 4,363 | L | 0-3 | | Sheffield | Collins | Williams | Saunders | Heathcote | Wotton | Barlow | Conlon | Jean | Corazzin | Billy | Logan/Wotton |
| 34 | H | 28/2 | LUTON | 4,846 | L | 0-2 | | Sheffield | Collins | Williams | Saunders | Heathcote | Wotton | Barlow | Logan | Littlejohn | Corazzin | Billy | Wotton |
| 35 | A | 3/3 | Bournemouth | 3,545 | D | 3-3 | Saunders, Logan, Corazzin | Sheffield | Collins | Williams | Saunders | Heathcote | Wotton | Barlow | Logan | Littlejohn | Corazzin | Billy | Ro'botham/Littlejohn |
| 36 | H | 7/3 | PRESTON | 4,201 | W | 2-0 | Wotton, Conlon | Sheffield | Collins | Ro'botham | Ro'botham | Heathcote | Wotton | Barlow | Logan | Conlon | Corazzin | Billy | |
| 37 | A | 14/3 | Wycombe | 5,508 | L | 1-5 | Corazzin | Sheffield | Collins | Williams | Saunders | Heathcote | Wotton | Barlow | Starbuck | Conlon | Corazzin | Billy | Littlejohn/Jean |
| 38 | H | 21/3 | BRISTOL CITY | 7,622 | W | 2-0 | Saunders, Conlon | Sheffield | Collins | Ro'botham | Saunders | Heathcote | Wotton | Barlow | Starbuck | Conlon | Corazzin | Billy | Ro'botham/Phillips |
| 39 | A | 24/3 | Grimsby | 4,661 | L | 0-1 | | Sheffield | Collins | Williams | Saunders | Heathcote | Wotton | Barlow | Starbuck | Conlon | Logan | Billy | Mauge/Phillips |
| 40 | H | 28/3 | WREXHAM | 4,759 | W | 2-0 | Corazzin, Saunders | Sheffield | Woods | Ro'botham | Saunders | Heathcote | Wotton | Barlow | Starbuck | Conlon | Corazzin | Billy | Phillips/Currie |
| 41 | A | 4/4 | Oldham | 4,244 | L | 0-2 | | Sheffield | Woods | Williams | Saunders | Heathcote | Wotton | Barlow | Starbuck | Conlon | Corazzin | Billy | Phillips/Currie |
| 42 | H | 11/4 | BLACKPOOL | 5,655 | W | 3-1 | Butler(og), Logan, Corazzin (p) | Sheffield | Collins | Ro'botham | Saunders | Heathcote | Logan | Barlow | Conlon | Conlon | Corazzin | Collins | Jean/Phillips/Currie |
| 43 | H | 13/4 | Millwall | 5,496 | D | 1-1 | Corazzin | Sheffield | Wotton | Williams | Saunders | Heathcote | Logan | Barlow | Conlon | Conlon | Corazzin | Currie | Jean/Mauge |
| 44 | A | 18/4 | NORTHAMPTON | 6,389 | L | 1-3 | Saunders | Sheffield | Wotton | Williams | Saunders | Heathcote | Logan | Barlow | Currie | Conlon | Corazzin | Billy | Jean/Mauge/Woods |
| 45 | H | 25/4 | GILLINGHAM | 7,941 | L | 0-1 | | Sheffield | Collins | Williams | Saunders | Saunders | Woods | Barlow | Currie | Conlon | Corazzin | Billy | Jean/Mauge/Starbuck |

## League Cup

| | | Date | Opponent | Att. | Result | Scorers |
|---|---|---|---|---|---|---|
| 1:1 | A | 12/8 | Oxford | 5,083 | L 0-2 | |
| 1:2 | H | 26/8 | OXFORD | 3,037 | L 3-5 | Wilson, Logan, Smith (og) |

## FA CUP

| | | Date | Opponent | Att. | Result | Scorers |
|---|---|---|---|---|---|---|
| 1 | H | 15/11 | CAMBRIDGE | 4,793 | D 0-0 | |
| 1R | A | 24/11 | Cambridge | 3,139 | L 2-3 | Mauge, Jean |

**Line-ups**

- 1:1 — Sheffield, Collins, Williams, Mauge, Heathcote, Wotton, Logan, Ro'botham, Littlejohn, Corazzin, Anthony, Wilson
- 1:2 — Sheffield, Billy, Williams, Wilson, Heathcote, Wotton, Logan, Ro'botham, Littlejohn, Jean, Anthony, Illman/Ashton
- FA 1 — Sheffield, Wilson, Williams, Mauge, Saunders, Wotton, Jean, Barlow, Littlejohn, Corazzin, Billy, Illman
- FA 1R — Sheffield, Logan, Williams, Mauge, Saunders, Wotton, Jean, Barlow, Littlejohn, Corazzin, Billy, Wilson/Ro'botham

## League Table

| | Team | P | Home | | | | | Away | | | | | Pts |
|---|---|---|---|---|---|---|---|---|---|---|---|---|---|
| | | | W | D | L | F | A | W | D | L | F | A | |
| 1 | Watford | 46 | 13 | 7 | 3 | 36 | 22 | 11 | 9 | 3 | 31 | 19 | 88 |
| 2 | Bristol City | 46 | 16 | 5 | 2 | 41 | 17 | 9 | 5 | 9 | 28 | 22 | 85 |
| 3 | Grimsby * | 46 | 11 | 7 | 5 | 30 | 14 | 8 | 8 | 7 | 25 | 23 | 72 |
| 4 | Northampton | 46 | 14 | 5 | 4 | 33 | 17 | 4 | 12 | 7 | 19 | 20 | 71 |
| 5 | Bristol Rov | 46 | 13 | 6 | 4 | 43 | 33 | 7 | 8 | 8 | 27 | 31 | 70 |
| 6 | Fulham | 46 | 12 | 7 | 4 | 31 | 14 | 8 | 3 | 12 | 29 | 29 | 70 |
| 7 | Wrexham | 46 | 10 | 10 | 3 | 30 | 23 | 8 | 6 | 9 | 24 | 28 | 70 |
| 8 | Gillingham | 46 | 13 | 7 | 3 | 30 | 18 | 6 | 6 | 11 | 22 | 29 | 70 |
| 9 | Bournemouth | 46 | 11 | 8 | 4 | 28 | 15 | 7 | 4 | 12 | 29 | 37 | 66 |
| 10 | Chesterfield | 46 | 13 | 7 | 3 | 31 | 19 | 3 | 10 | 10 | 15 | 25 | 65 |
| 11 | Wigan | 46 | 12 | 5 | 6 | 41 | 31 | 5 | 6 | 12 | 23 | 35 | 62 |
| 12 | Blackpool | 46 | 13 | 6 | 4 | 43 | 24 | 4 | 5 | 14 | 24 | 43 | 62 |
| 13 | Oldham | 46 | 13 | 7 | 3 | 43 | 23 | 2 | 9 | 12 | 19 | 31 | 61 |
| 14 | Wycombe | 46 | 10 | 10 | 3 | 32 | 20 | 4 | 8 | 11 | 19 | 33 | 60 |
| 15 | Preston | 46 | 10 | 6 | 7 | 29 | 26 | 5 | 10 | 8 | 27 | 30 | 59 |
| 16 | York | 46 | 9 | 7 | 7 | 26 | 21 | 7 | 5 | 10 | 26 | 26 | 59 |
| 17 | Luton | 46 | 7 | 7 | 9 | 35 | 38 | 7 | 8 | 8 | 25 | 26 | 57 |
| 18 | Millwall | 46 | 7 | 8 | 8 | 23 | 23 | 7 | 5 | 11 | 20 | 31 | 55 |
| 19 | Walsall | 46 | 10 | 8 | 5 | 26 | 16 | 4 | 4 | 15 | 17 | 36 | 54 |
| 20 | Burnley | 46 | 10 | 9 | 4 | 34 | 23 | 4 | 4 | 16 | 21 | 42 | 52 |
| 21 | Brentford | 46 | 9 | 7 | 7 | 33 | 29 | 2 | 10 | 11 | 17 | 42 | 50 |
| 22 | PLYMOUTH | 46 | 10 | 5 | 8 | 36 | 30 | 2 | 8 | 13 | 19 | 40 | 49 |
| 23 | Carlisle | 46 | 8 | 5 | 10 | 27 | 28 | 4 | 3 | 16 | 30 | 45 | 44 |
| 24 | Southend | 46 | 8 | 7 | 8 | 29 | 30 | 3 | 3 | 17 | 18 | 49 | 43 |
| | | 1104 | 262 | 162 | 128 | 783 | 554 | 128 | 162 | 262 | 554 | 783 | 1494 |

* promoted p/o

## Appearances and Goals

| Player | Appearances | | | | | | Goals | | | |
|---|---|---|---|---|---|---|---|---|---|---|
| | Lge | Sub | LC | Sub | FAC | Sub | Lge | LC | FAC | Tot |
| Anthony, Graham | 5 | | 2 | | | | | | | |
| Ashton, Jon | | | | 1 | | | | | | |
| Barlow, Martin | 41 | 1 | | | 2 | | 4 | | | 4 |
| Beswetherick, Jon | | 2 | | | | | | | | |
| Billy, Chris | 41 | 1 | 1 | | 2 | | 2 | | | 2 |
| Clayton, Gary | | 1 | | | | | | | | |
| Collins, Simon | 30 | 2 | 1 | | | | 2 | | | 2 |
| Conlon, Barry | 13 | | | | | | 2 | | | 2 |
| Corazzin, Carlo | 38 | | 1 | | 2 | | 16 | | | 16 |
| Currie, Darren | 5 | 2 | | | | | | | | |
| Heathcote, Mick | 36 | | 2 | | | | 4 | | | 4 |
| Hodges, Lee | 9 | | | | | | | | | |
| Illman, Neil | 1 | 5 | | 1 | | 1 | | | | |
| Jean, Earl | 16 | 20 | 1 | | 2 | | 4 | | 1 | 5 |
| Littlejohn, Adrian | 27 | 4 | 2 | | 2 | | 6 | | | 6 |
| Logan, Richard | 23 | 8 | 2 | | 1 | | 4 | 1 | | 5 |
| Mauge, Ronnie | 23 | | 1 | | 2 | | 1 | | 1 | 2 |
| O'Hagan, Danny | 5 | 4 | | | | | | | | |
| Phillips, Lee | 3 | 7 | | | | | | | | |
| Rowbotham, Jason | 23 | 2 | 2 | | | 1 | | | | |
| Saunders, Mark | 34 | 3 | | | 2 | | 7 | | | 7 |
| Sheffield, Jon | 46 | | 2 | | 2 | | | | | |
| Starbuck, Phil | 6 | 1 | | | | | | | | |
| Willaims, Paul | 39 | | 2 | | 2 | | | | | |
| Wilson, Padi | 7 | 4 | 1 | 1 | 1 | 1 | 1 | 1 | | 2 |
| Woods, Stephen | 4 | 1 | | | | | | | | |
| Wotton, Paul | 31 | 3 | 2 | | 2 | | 1 | | | 1 |
| (own-goals) | | | | | | | 1 | 1 | | 2 |
| 27 players used | 506 | 74 | 22 | 3 | 22 | 3 | 55 | 3 | 2 | 60 |

# LEAGUE DIVISION 3

## Manager: Paul Sturrock

## SEASON 2001-02

| # | H/A | Date | Opponents | Att | F-A | Scorers | 1 | 2 | 3 | 4 | 5 | 6 | 7 | 8 | 9 | 10 | 11 | Subs (3) |
|---|---|---|---|---|---|---|---|---|---|---|---|---|---|---|---|---|---|---|
| 1 | H | 11/8 | SHREWSBURY | 5,087 | L 0-1 | | Larrieu | Adams | Besweth'k | Friio | Wotton | Coughlan | Wills | McGlinchey | Evans | Ston'bridge | Phillips | Crowe/Gritton/Evers |
| 2 | A | 18/8 | Hull | 10,755 | D 0-0 | | Larrieu | Adams | Besweth'k | Friio | Wotton | Coughlan | Evers | McGlinchey | Evans | Hodges | Phillips | Broad/Stonebridge |
| 3 | H | 25/8 | ROCHDALE | 4,198 | L 1-2 | Coleman(og) | Larrieu | Worrell | McGlinchey | Adams | Wotton | Coughlan | Phillips | Evers | Evans | Ston'bridge | Hodges | Besweth'k |
| 4 | A | 27/8 | Rushden & D | 4,414 | W 3-2 | Evans, Coughlan, McGlinchey | Larrieu | Adams | Besweth'k | Broad | Wotton | Coughlan | Phillips | Wills | Evans | Hodges | McGlinchey | Gritton |
| 5 | A | 8/9 | Torquay | 4,217 | W 1-0 | Friio | Larrieu | Worrell | Besweth'k | Friio | Wotton | Coughlan | Phillips | Adams | Evans | Ston'bridge | McGlinchey | McGlinchey/Banger |
| 6 | H | 11/9 | SWANSEA | 3,850 | W 3-1 | Wotton (p), Banger, Phillips | Larrieu | Worrell | Besweth'k | Friio | Wotton | Coughlan | Phillips | Adams | Evans | Banger | McGlinchey | Hodges |
| 7 | A | 15/9 | Kidderminster | 2,801 | D 0-0 | | Larrieu | Worrell | Besweth'k | Friio | Wotton | Coughlan | Phillips | Adams | Evans | Wills | Hodges | BangerMcGlinchey/S'bridg |
| 8 | A | 18/9 | Exeter | 5,756 | W 3-2 | Phillips, Evans, Stonebridge | Larrieu | Worrell | McGlinchey | Friio | Wotton | Coughlan | Phillips | Adams | Evans | Banger | McGlinchey | Hodges/Ston'bridge |
| 9 | H | 22/9 | MACCLESFIELD | 4,227 | W 2-0 | Hodges, Friio | Larrieu | Worrell | McGlinchey | Friio | Wotton | Coughlan | Phillips | Adams | Evans | Ston'bridge | Hodges | Bent |
| 10 | A | 25/9 | York | 2,282 | D 0-0 | | Larrieu | Worrell | McGlinchey | Friio | Wotton | Coughlan | Phillips | Adams | Evans | Wills | Hodges | Ston'bridge |
| 11 | H | 29/9 | LUTON | 5,782 | W 2-1 | Phillips, Friio | Larrieu | Worrell | McGlinchey | Friio | Wotton | Coughlan | Phillips | Bent | Evans | Ston'bridge | Adams | Hodges/Wills |
| 12 | H | 6/10 | Oxford | 6,017 | D 1-1 | Banger | Larrieu | Worrell | McGlinchey | Friio | Wotton | Coughlan | Phillips | Bent | Banger | Adams | Hodges | Ston'bridge/Banger/Wills |
| 13 | H | 13/10 | HALIFAX | 5,065 | W 3-0 | Coughlan, Phillips, Hodges | Larrieu | Worrell | McGlinchey | Friio | Wotton | Coughlan | Phillips | Bent | Evans | Ston'bridge | Hodges | Evans/Adams |
| 14 | A | 20/10 | Mansfield | 4,621 | W 2-0 | Evans, Friio, Stonebridge | Larrieu | Worrell | McGlinchey | Friio | Wotton | Coughlan | Phillips | Adams | Evans | Wills | Hodges | B'weth'ck/Broad/S'bridge |
| 15 | A | 23/10 | LINCOLN | 6,572 | W 2-0 | Friio, Coughlan | Larrieu | Worrell | McGlinchey | Friio | Wotton | Coughlan | Phillips | Bent | Evans | Ston'bridge | Hodges | Adams/Banger |
| 16 | H | 28/10 | Bristol Rov | 6,889 | W 2-1 | Phillips, Hodges | Larrieu | Worrell | McGlinchey | Friio | Wotton | Coughlan | Phillips | Bent | Evans | Wills | Hodges | S'bridge/Bent/B'weth'ck |
| 17 | H | 3/11 | HARTLEPOOL | 5,723 | W 1-0 | Friio | Larrieu | Worrell | McGlinchey | Friio | Wotton | Coughlan | Phillips | Bent | Evans | Ston'bridge | Hodges | Banger/Adams |
| 18 | A | 9/11 | Cheltenham | 5,035 | D 0-0 | | Larrieu | Worrell | McGlinchey | Friio | Wotton | Coughlan | Phillips | Bent | Evans | Adams | Hodges | Ston'bridge/Banger/Wills |
| 19 | A | 20/11 | Southend | 3,716 | W 1-0 | Adams | Larrieu | Worrell | Besweth'k | Friio | Wotton | Coughlan | Wills | Bent | Evans | Ston'bridge | Hodges | Besweth'ck/KeithAdams |
| 20 | H | 24/11 | CARLISLE | 5,870 | W 3-0 | Evans, Bent, Phillips | Larrieu | Worrell | McGlinchey | Friio | Wotton | Coughlan | Phillips | Bent | Evans | Ston'bridge | Adams | Evers |
| 21 | A | 1/12 | Leyton Orient | 6,342 | D 0-0 | | Larrieu | Worrell | Besweth'k | Adams | Wotton | Coughlan | Phillips | Wills | Evans | Hodges | McGlinchey | Keith/Adams/Sturrock |
| 22 | H | 15/12 | DARLINGTON | 5,041 | W 1-0 | Friio | Larrieu | Worrell | McGlinchey | Friio | Wotton | Coughlan | Phillips | Bent | Ston'bridge | Hodges | Besweth'k | Keith/Sturrock |
| 23 | A | 22/12 | Scunthorpe | 3,602 | L 1-2 | Coughlan | Larrieu | Worrell | McGlinchey | Friio | Wotton | Coughlan | Phillips | Wills | Ston'bridge | Adams | Hodges | Sturrock/Heaney/Wills |
| 24 | H | 26/12 | TORQUAY | 13,677 | D 2-2 | Coughlan, Stonebridge | Larrieu | Worrell | McGlinchey | Friio | Wotton | Coughlan | Phillips | Adams | Keith | Ston'bridge | Hodges | Sturrock/Evers |
| 25 | H | 29/12 | RUSHDEN & D | 9,503 | W 1-0 | Keith | Larrieu | Worrell | McGlinchey | Friio | Wotton | Coughlan | Phillips | Adams | Keith | Ston'bridge | Hodges | Evans/Bent |
| 26 | H | 12/1 | HULL | 9,134 | W 1-0 | Stonebridge | Adamson | Worrell | McGlinchey | Friio | Wotton | Coughlan | Phillips | Adams | Keith | Evers | Hodges | Keith/Ston'bridge/Heaney |
| 27 | A | 19/1 | Shrewsbury | 4,796 | L 1-3 | Evans | Larrieu | Worrell | Besweth'k | Friio | Wotton | Coughlan | Phillips | Adams | Keith | Ston'bridge | Hodges | Besweth'k/Evans |
| 28 | A | 22/1 | SCUNTHORPE | 5,804 | W 2-1 | Wotton (p), Keith | Larrieu | Worrell | Besweth'k | Friio | Wotton | Coughlan | Phillips | Adams | Keith | Ston'bridge | Hodges | Evans |
| 29 | H | 26/1 | OXFORD | 8,239 | W 4-2 | Coughlan, Hodges, Stonebridge 2 | Larrieu | Worrell | Besweth'k | Friio | Wotton | Coughlan | Phillips | Adams | Keith | Sturrock | Hodges | Evers/Evans/Heaney |
| 30 | A | 2/2 | Luton | 9,585 | L 0-2 | | Larrieu | Bent | Besweth'k | Friio | Wotton | Coughlan | Heaney | Adams | Evans | Ston'bridge | Hodges | Ston'bridge/Broad |
| 31 | H | 5/2 | Swansea | 4,060 | W 1-0 | Sturrock | Larrieu | Worrell | Besweth'k | Friio | Wotton | Coughlan | Phillips | Adams | Sturrock | Sturrock | Hodges | Keith/Sturrock/Heaney |
| 32 | H | 9/2 | MANSFIELD | 14,716 | W 2-0 | Friio | Larrieu | Worrell | Besweth'k | Friio | Wotton | Coughlan | Wills | Adams | Evans | Ston'bridge | Hodges | BroadPhillips |
| 33 | A | 16/2 | Halifax | 2,330 | W 2-0 | Hodges, Wotton (p) | Larrieu | Worrell | Besweth'k | Friio | Wotton | Coughlan | Phillips | Adams | Sturrock | Ston'bridge | Hodges | Sturrock/Heaney/Keith |
| 34 | A | 23/2 | KIDDERMINSTER | 8,758 | W 2-1 | Coughlan, Wotton (p) | Larrieu | Worrell | Besweth'k | Friio | Wotton | Coughlan | Phillips | Adams | Keith | Ston'bridge | Hodges | Sturrock/Wills/Heaney |
| 35 | A | 26/2 | EXETER | 16,369 | W 3-0 | Adams, Keith 2 | Larrieu | Worrell | Besweth'k | Friio | Wotton | Coughlan | Phillips | Adams | Sturrock | Ston'bridge | Hodges | Broad/Keith |
| 36 | A | 2/3 | Macclesfield | 2,557 | D 1-1 | Coughlan | Larrieu | Worrell | Besweth'k | Friio | Wotton | Coughlan | Wills | Adams | Keith | Ston'bridge | Hodges | Taylor/Sturrock |
| 37 | H | 5/3 | YORK | 10,801 | W 1-0 | Potter (og) | Larrieu | Worrell | Besweth'k | Friio | Wotton | Coughlan | Phillips | Adams | Keith | Ston'bridge | Hodges | Evans/Bent/Sturrock |
| 38 | H | 16/3 | LEYTON ORIENT | 9,438 | W 3-0 | Stonebridge, Coughlan, Evans | Larrieu | Worrell | Besweth'k | Friio | Wotton | Coughlan | Phillips | Adams | Evans | Ston'bridge | Hodges | Ston'bridge/Sturrock |
| 39 | A | 23/3 | Lincoln | 4,019 | W 1-0 | Stonebridge | Larrieu | Bent | Besweth'k | Friio | Wotton | Coughlan | Phillips | Adams | Keith | Wills | Hodges | Sturrock |
| 40 | H | 26/3 | Rochdale | 4,457 | W 3-1 | Keith, Coughlan, Hodges | Larrieu | Worrell | Besweth'k | Friio | Wotton | Coughlan | Bent | Adams | Evans | Ston'bridge | Hodges | Keith/Ston'bridge/Heaney |
| 41 | H | 30/3 | BRISTOL ROV | 15,732 | W 1-0 | Keith | Larrieu | Worrell | Besweth'k | Friio | Wotton | Coughlan | Bent | Adams | Keith | Ston'bridge | Hodges | Evans/Bent/Sturrock |
| 42 | A | 1/4 | Hartlepool | 3,725 | L 0-1 | | Larrieu | Worrell | Besweth'k | Friio | Wotton | Coughlan | Bent | Adams | Evans | Wills | Hodges | Sturrock/S'bridge/Keith |
| 43 | H | 6/4 | SOUTHEND | 10,021 | D 0-0 | | Larrieu | Worrell | Besweth'k | Bent | Wotton | Coughlan | Keith | Bent | Evans | Ston'bridge | Hodges | Sturrock/KeithAdams |
| 44 | A | 13/4 | Carlisle | 3,080 | W 2-0 | Keith, Wotton | Larrieu | Worrell | Besweth'k | Bent | Wotton | Coughlan | Keith | Adams | Evans | Ston'bridge | Hodges | |
| 45 | H | 15/4 | Darlington | 4,089 | W 4-1 | Evans, Keith 2, Bent | Larrieu | Worrell | Besweth'k | Bent | Wotton | Coughlan | Keith | Adams | Evans | Ston'bridge | Hodges | Sturrock/Phillips/McG'y |

| 1 | A | 21/8 | Watford | 9,230 | L | 0-1 | | Larrieu | Adams | McGlinchey | Friio | Wotton | Coughlan | Wills | Phillips | Hodges | Evans | Evers | Broad/Gritton/Ston'bridge |
|---|---|---|---|---|---|---|---|---|---|---|---|---|---|---|---|---|---|---|---|

## FA CUP

| 1 | A | 17/11 | Whitby | 2,202 | D | 1-1 | Phillips | Larrieu | Worrell | McGlinchey | Friio | Wotton | Coughlan | Phillips | Ston'bridge | Hodges | Evans | Bent | Adams/Besweth'ck |
|---|---|---|---|---|---|---|---|---|---|---|---|---|---|---|---|---|---|---|
| 1R | H | 27/11 | WHITBY | 5,914 | W | 3-2 | Bent, Stonebridge, Phillips | Larrieu | Worrell | McGlinchey | Friio | Wotton | Coughlan | Phillips | Ston'bridge | Hodges | Evans | Bent | Adams/B'weth'k/Sturrock |
| 2 | H | 8/12 | BRISTOL ROV | 6,141 | D | 1-1 | Wotton | Larrieu | Worrell | McGlinchey | Friio | Wotton | Coughlan | Phillips | Ston'bridge | Adams | Ston'bridge | Wills | Keith/Sturrock/Evers |
| 2R | A | 18/12 | Bristol Rov | 5,763 | L | 2-3 | Friio 2 | Larrieu | Worrell | McGlinchey | Friio | Wotton | Coughlan | Phillips | Phillips | Hodges | Ston'bridge | Wills | |

## League Table

| | | P | | Home | | | | | | Away | | | | | Pts |
|---|---|---|---|---|---|---|---|---|---|---|---|---|---|---|---|
| | | | W | D | L | F | A | | W | D | L | F | A | | |
| 1 | PLYMOUTH | 46 | 19 | 2 | 2 | 41 | 11 | | 12 | 7 | 4 | 30 | 17 | | 102 |
| 2 | Luton | 46 | 15 | 5 | 3 | 50 | 18 | | 15 | 2 | 6 | 46 | 30 | | 97 |
| 3 | Mansfield | 46 | 17 | 3 | 3 | 49 | 24 | | 7 | 4 | 12 | 23 | 36 | | 79 |
| 4 | Cheltenham * | 46 | 11 | 11 | 1 | 40 | 20 | | 4 | 9 | | 26 | 29 | | 78 |
| 5 | Rochdale | 46 | 13 | 8 | 2 | 41 | 22 | | 8 | 8 | | 24 | 30 | | 78 |
| 6 | Rushden & D | 46 | 14 | 5 | 4 | 40 | 20 | | 6 | 8 | 9 | 29 | 33 | | 73 |
| 7 | Hartlepool | 46 | 12 | 6 | 5 | 53 | 23 | | 5 | 10 | | 21 | 25 | | 71 |
| 8 | Scunthorpe | 46 | 14 | 5 | 4 | 43 | 22 | | 5 | 9 | 9 | 31 | 34 | | 71 |
| 9 | Shrewsbury | 46 | 13 | 4 | 6 | 36 | 19 | | 7 | 6 | 10 | 28 | 34 | | 70 |
| 10 | Kidderminster | 46 | 13 | 6 | 4 | 35 | 17 | | 6 | 3 | 14 | 21 | 30 | | 66 |
| 11 | Hull | 46 | 12 | 6 | 5 | 38 | 18 | | 4 | 7 | 12 | 19 | 33 | | 61 |
| 12 | Southend | 46 | 12 | 5 | 6 | 36 | 22 | | 3 | 8 | 12 | 15 | 32 | | 58 |
| 13 | Macclesfield | 46 | 7 | 7 | 9 | 23 | 25 | | 8 | 6 | 9 | 18 | 27 | | 58 |
| 14 | York | 46 | 11 | 5 | 7 | 26 | 20 | | 5 | 4 | 14 | 28 | 47 | | 57 |
| 15 | Darlington | 46 | 11 | 6 | 6 | 26 | 25 | | 4 | 5 | 14 | 23 | 46 | | 56 |
| 16 | Exeter | 46 | 7 | 9 | 7 | 25 | 32 | | 7 | 4 | 12 | 23 | 41 | | 55 |
| 17 | Carlisle | 46 | 11 | 5 | 7 | 31 | 21 | | 1 | 11 | 11 | 18 | 35 | | 52 |
| 18 | Leyton O | 46 | 10 | 7 | 6 | 37 | 25 | | 3 | 6 | 14 | 18 | 46 | | 52 |
| 19 | Torquay | 46 | 8 | 6 | 9 | 27 | 31 | | 4 | 4 | 10 | 19 | 32 | | 51 |
| 20 | Swansea | 46 | 7 | 8 | 8 | 26 | 26 | | 6 | 4 | 13 | 27 | 51 | | 51 |
| 21 | Oxford | 46 | 8 | 7 | 8 | 34 | 28 | | 3 | 7 | 13 | 19 | 34 | | 47 |
| 22 | Lincoln | 46 | 8 | 4 | 11 | 25 | 27 | | 2 | 12 | 9 | 19 | 35 | | 46 |
| 23 | Bristol Rov | 46 | 8 | 7 | 8 | 28 | 28 | | 3 | 5 | 15 | 12 | 32 | | 45 |
| 24 | Halifax | 46 | 5 | 9 | 9 | 24 | 28 | | 3 | 3 | 17 | 15 | 56 | | 36 |
| | | 1104 | 266 | 146 | 140 | 845 | 552 | | 140 | 146 | 266 | 552 | 845 | | 1510 |

promoted p/o

## Appearances / Goals

| | Appearances | | | | | | Goals | | | |
|---|---|---|---|---|---|---|---|---|---|---|
| | Lge | Sub | LC | Sub | FAC | Sub | Lge | LC | FAC | Tot |
| Adams, Steve | 40 | 6 | 1 | | 2 | 2 | 2 | | | 2 |
| Adamson, Chris | 1 | | | | | | | | | |
| Banger, Nicky | 3 | 7 | | | | | 2 | | | 2 |
| Bent, Jason | 16 | 5 | | | 2 | 1 | 3 | | 1 | 4 |
| Beswetherick, Jon | 27 | 5 | | | 1 | 2 | | | | |
| Broad, Joe | 1 | 6 | | | 1 | | | | | |
| Coughlan, Graham | 46 | | 1 | | 4 | | 11 | | | 11 |
| Crowe, Dean | | 1 | | | | | | | | |
| Evans, Michael | 30 | 8 | 1 | | 3 | | 7 | | | 7 |
| Evers, Sean | 3 | 4 | | | 1 | | | | | |
| Friio, David | 41 | | 1 | | 4 | | 8 | | 2 | 10 |
| Gritton, Martin | | 2 | | | | 1 | | | | |
| Heaney, Neil | 1 | 7 | | | | | | | | |
| Hodges, Lee | 42 | 3 | 1 | | 4 | | 6 | | | 6 |
| Keith, Marino | 13 | 10 | | | | 2 | 9 | | | 9 |
| Larrieu, Romain | 45 | | 1 | | 4 | | | | | |
| McGlinchey, Brian | 26 | 3 | 1 | | 3 | | 1 | | | 1 |
| Phillips, Martin | 37 | 2 | 1 | | 4 | | 6 | 2 | | 8 |
| Stonebridge, Ian | 29 | 13 | 1 | | 4 | | 8 | 1 | | 9 |
| Sturrock, Blair | 4 | 15 | | | | 2 | 1 | | | 1 |
| Taylor, Craig | | 1 | | | | | | | | |
| Wills, Kevin | 13 | 5 | 1 | | | 1 | | | | |
| Worrell, David | 42 | | 1 | | 4 | | | | | |
| Wotton, Paul | 46 | | | | 4 | | 5 | | 1 | 6 |
| (own-goals) | | | | | | | 2 | | | 2 |
| 24 players used | 506 | 103 | 11 | 3 | 44 | 11 | 71 | | 7 | 78 |

# LEAGUE DIVISION 2

## Manager: Sturrock / Sum'field / Williamson — SEASON 2003-04

| # | H/A | Date | Opponents | Res | F-A | Att | Scorers | 1 | 2 | 3 | 4 | 5 | 6 | 7 | 8 | 9 | 10 | 11 | Subs (3) |
|---|-----|------|-----------|-----|-----|-----|---------|---|---|---|---|---|---|---|---|---|----|----|----------|
| 1 | H | 9/8 | GRIMSBY | D | 2-2 | 9,590 | Keith, Coughlan | Larrieu | Worrell | Hodges | Friio | Wotton | Coughlan | Norris | Bent | Keith | St'bridge | Capaldi | Evans/Adams/Lowndes |
| 2 | A | 16/8 | Rushden & D | L | 1-2 | 4,045 | Capaldi | Larrieu | Worrell | Hodges | Friio | Wotton | Coughlan | Norris | Bent | Evans | Keith | Capaldi | St'bridge/Lowndes/Adams |
| 3 | H | 23/8 | STOCKPORT | W | 3-1 | 7,954 | Keith, Hodges, Bent | Larrieu | Worrell | Hodges | Friio | Wotton | Coughlan | Norris | Bent | Keith | St'bridge | Capaldi | Adams/Evans/Lowndes |
| 4 | A | 25/8 | Chesterfield | D | 1-1 | 4,089 | Friio | Larrieu | Worrell | Hodges | Friio | Wotton | Coughlan | Adams | Bent | Keith | St'bridge | Capaldi | Evans/Norris/Lowndes |
| 5 | H | 30/8 | BRIGHTON | D | 3-3 | 9,289 | Coughlan, Stonebridge, Friio | Larrieu | Connolly | Gilbert | Friio | Wotton | Coughlan | Norris | Adams | Evans | St'bridge | Capaldi | Sturrock/Adams/Ber'ford |
| 6 | A | 6/9 | Brentford | W | 3-1 | 5,688 | Stonebridge, Evans 2 | Larrieu | Worrell | Gilbert | Friio | Wotton | Coughlan | Norris | Adams | Evans | St'bridge | Hodges | Connolly/Sturrock/Aljofree |
| 7 | H | 13/9 | LUTON | W | 2-1 | 9,894 | Evans, Friio | McCormick | Worrell | Gilbert | Friio | Wotton | Coughlan | Norris | Bent | Evans | St'bridge | Capaldi | Keith/Sturrock/Bent |
| 8 | A | 16/9 | Peterborough | D | 2-2 | 4,183 | Wotton (p), Capaldi | McCormick | Worrell | Hodges | Adams | Wotton | Coughlan | Norris | Bent | Keith | St'bridge | Capaldi | Adams/Keith/Sturrock |
| 9 | A | 20/9 | Wrexham | D | 2-2 | 3,947 | Norris, Capaldi | McCormick | Worrell | Hodges | Adams | Wotton | Coughlan | Norris | Bent | Evans | St'bridge | Capaldi | Evans/Sturrock |
| 10 | H | 27/9 | BARNSLEY | W | 2-0 | 8,695 | Coughlan, Evans | McCormick | Worrell | Gilbert | Adams | Wotton | Coughlan | Norris | Bent | Evans | Keith | Capaldi | Sturrock/Hodges |
| 11 | H | 30/9 | BRISTOL CITY | L | 0-1 | 13,923 | | McCormick | Worrell | Gilbert | Adams | Wotton | Coughlan | Norris | Bent | Evans | Keith | Capaldi | Sturrock/St'bridge/Hodges |
| 12 | A | 4/10 | Wycombe | D | 0-0 | 5,708 | | McCormick | Worrell | Gilbert | Friio | Wotton | Coughlan | Norris | Bent | Evans | Keith | Capaldi | Hodges/Stonebridge |
| 13 | H | 11/10 | TRANMERE | W | 6-0 | 7,610 | Friio, Wot', Gilb', Keith, Evans, Norris | McCormick | Worrell | Gilbert | Friio | Wotton | Coughlan | Norris | Adams | Evans | Keith | St'bridge | Hodges/Sturrock/Lowndes |
| 14 | A | 18/10 | Port Vale | W | 5-1 | 5,786 | Keith, Friio 2, Adams, Wotton | McCormick | Worrell | Gilbert | Friio | Wotton | Coughlan | Norris | Adams | Evans | Keith | St'bridge | Capaldi/Bent/Aljofree |
| 15 | A | 22/10 | Sheffield Wed | W | 3-1 | 20,090 | Friio 2, Wotton (p) | McCormick | Worrell | Gilbert | Friio | Wotton | Coughlan | Norris | Adams | Evans | Keith | St'bridge | Bent/Capaldi |
| 16 | A | 25/10 | BLACKPOOL | W | 1-0 | 12,372 | Keith | McCormick | Worrell | Gilbert | Friio | Wotton | Coughlan | Norris | Adams | Evans | Keith | St'bridge | Bent/Lowndes/Capaldi |
| 17 | H | 1/11 | OLDHAM | D | 2-2 | 11,205 | Wotton, Evans | McCormick | Worrell | Gilbert | Friio | Wotton | Coughlan | Norris | Bent | Evans | Keith | St'bridge | Capaldi/Lowndes/Capaldi |
| 18 | H | 15/11 | QP Rangers | L | 0-3 | 17,049 | | McCormick | Worrell | Gilbert | Adams | Wotton | Coughlan | Norris | Bent | Evans | Hodges | St'bridge | Keith/Lowndes |
| 19 | H | 22/11 | HARTLEPOOL | W | 2-0 | 9,000 | Keith, Lowndes | McCormick | Connolly | Gilbert | Wotton | Coughlan | Aljofree | Norris | Hodges | Lowndes | Keith | Capaldi | Wotton/Sturrock/St'bridge |
| 20 | A | 29/11 | Colchester | W | 2-0 | 4,332 | Capaldi, Keith | McCormick | Connolly | Gilbert | Wotton | Coughlan | Aljofree | Norris | Hodges | Lowndes | Keith | Capaldi | Evans |
| 21 | A | 13/12 | Swindon | W | 3-2 | 9,374 | Capaldi, Norris, Keith | McCormick | Connolly | Gilbert | Wotton | Coughlan | Aljofree | Norris | Hodges | Lowndes | Keith | Capaldi | Evans |
| 22 | H | 20/12 | NOTTS CO | W | 3-0 | 9,923 | Lowndes, Evans 2 | McCormick | Connolly | Gilbert | Friio | Coughlan | Aljofree | Norris | Hodges | Lowndes | Keith | Capaldi | Sturrock/Friio/Evans |
| 23 | A | 26/12 | Bournemouth | W | 2-0 | 8,901 | Wotton, Norris | McCormick | Connolly | Gilbert | Friio | Coughlan | Aljofree | Norris | Wotton | Lowndes | Keith | Hodges | Evans/Sturrock/Adams |
| 24 | H | 28/12 | BRENTFORD | W | 2-0 | 17,882 | Capaldi, Lowndes | McCormick | Connolly | Gilbert | Friio | Coughlan | Aljofree | Phillips | Hodges | Evans | Lowndes | Capaldi | Stonebridge/Sturrock |
| 25 | H | 3/1 | CHESTERFIELD | W | 7-0 | 13,109 | Hodges, Capaldi, Lowndes 2, Friio 3 | McCormick | Connolly | Gilbert | Friio | Coughlan | Aljofree | Phillips | Hodges | Evans | Lowndes | Capaldi | Norris/St'bridge/Keith |
| 26 | A | 10/1 | Grimsby | D | 0-0 | 5,007 | | McCormick | Connolly | Gilbert | Friio | Coughlan | Aljofree | Norris | Hodges | Evans | Lowndes | Capaldi | Norris/Wotton/Keith |
| 27 | H | 17/1 | RUSHDEN & D | W | 3-0 | 13,021 | Coughlan, Stonebridge, Wotton | McCormick | Connolly | Gilbert | Friio | Coughlan | Aljofree | Norris | Hodges | Evans | Lowndes | St'bridge | Keith/Wotton |
| 28 | A | 24/1 | Stockport | W | 2-0 | 6,608 | Friio, Coughlan | McCormick | Connolly | Gilbert | Friio | Coughlan | Aljofree | Norris | Hodges | Evans | Lowndes | St'bridge | Wotton/Sturrock/St'bridge |
| 29 | H | 31/1 | Brighton | L | 1-2 | 6,379 | Lowndes | McCormick | Connolly | Gilbert | Friio | Coughlan | Aljofree | Norris | Wotton | Evans | Lowndes | Capaldi | Adams/Keith/Sturrock |
| 30 | H | 7/2 | BOURNEMOUTH | D | 0-0 | 13,371 | | McCormick | Connolly | Gilbert | Friio | Coughlan | Aljofree | Norris | Adams | Evans | Lowndes | Hodges | Keith/Wotton/Phillips |
| 31 | A | 17/2 | Tranmere | L | 0-3 | 7,948 | | McCormick | Connolly | Gilbert | Friio | Coughlan | Aljofree | Norris | Adams | Evans | Lowndes | St'bridge | Phillips/Wotton/Sturrock |
| 32 | A | 21/2 | PORT VALE | W | 2-1 | 11,330 | Phillips, Stonebridge | McCormick | Connolly | Gilbert | Friio | Coughlan | Coughlan | Norris | Adams | Evans | Lowndes | Capaldi | Phillips/St'bridge/Sturrock |
| 33 | A | 28/2 | Blackpool | W | 1-0 | 7,253 | Stonebridge | McCormick | Connolly | Gilbert | Friio | Coughlan | Coughlan | Norris | Adams | Evans | Lowndes | St'bridge | St'bridge/Hodges/Sturrock |
| 34 | H | 2/3 | SHEFFIELD WED | W | 2-0 | 17,218 | Evans, Coughlan | McCormick | Connolly | Gilbert | Friio | Coughlan | Coughlan | Norris | Adams | Evans | Lowndes | St'bridge | Hodges/Sturrock |
| 35 | A | 6/3 | Notts Co | D | 0-0 | 8,057 | | McCormick | Connolly | Gilbert | Friio | Coughlan | Coughlan | Norris | Adams | Evans | Keith | St'bridge | Hodges/Sturrock/Lowndes |
| 36 | H | 13/3 | SWINDON | W | 2-1 | 16,080 | Keith, Evans R (og) | McCormick | Connolly | Gilbert | Friio | Wotton | Coughlan | Norris | Adams | Evans | Keith | Capaldi | Lowndes/Bent/Sturrock |
| 37 | H | 16/3 | PETERBOROUGH | W | 2-0 | 13,110 | Lowndes, Wotton(p) | McCormick | Connolly | Gilbert | Friio | Wotton | Coughlan | Norris | Adams | Evans | Keith | Capaldi | Lowndes/Hodges |
| 38 | A | 20/3 | Luton | D | 1-1 | 8,499 | Adams | McCormick | Connolly | Gilbert | Friio | Wotton | Coughlan | Norris | Adams | Evans | Lowndes | St'bridge | Phillips/Keith/Sturrock |
| 39 | H | 27/3 | WREXHAM | D | 0-0 | 12,275 | | McCormick | Connolly | Gilbert | Friio | Wotton | Coughlan | Norris | Adams | Evans | Lowndes | Capaldi | Phillips/Hodges/Keith |
| 40 | H | 3/4 | Barnsley | L | 0-1 | 9,226 | | McCormick | Connolly | Gilbert | Friio | Wotton | Coughlan | Norris | Adams | Keith | St'bridge | Hodges | Evans/Sturrock |
| 41 | H | 10/4 | WYCOMBE | W | 2-1 | 14,806 | Coughlan, Evans | McCormick | Connolly | Gilbert | Friio | Wotton | Coughlan | Norris | Hodges | Evans | Keith | Capaldi | Adams/Lowndes/Sturrock |
| 42 | H | 13/4 | Bristol City | L | 0-1 | 19,045 | | McCormick | Connolly | Gilbert | Adams | Wotton | Coughlan | Norris | Bent | Evans | Hodges | Capaldi | Aljofree/Lowndes/Keith |
| 43 | A | 17/4 | Oldham | L | 1-4 | 6,924 | Wotton | McCormick | Connolly | Gilbert | Friio | Coughlan | Aljofree | Norris | Hodges | Evans | Keith | Capaldi | Phillips/Aljofree/Adams |
| 44 | A | 24/4 | QP RANGERS | W | 2-0 | 19,888 | Evans, Friio | McCormick | Connolly | Gilbert | Friio | Wotton | Aljofree | Norris | Hodges | Evans | Keith | Capaldi | Lowndes |
| 45 | A | 1/5 | Hartlepool | W | 3-1 | 7,437 | Hodges, Lowndes, Tinkler (og) | McCormick | Worrell | Gilbert | Adams | Coughlan | Aljofree | Norris | Hodges | Lowndes | Keith | Capaldi | St'bridge/Sturrock/Wotton |

| | | | Match | | Att | Res | Scorers |
|---|---|---|---|---|---|---|---|
| 1 | A | 12/8 | Colchester | | 2,367 | L 1-2 | Evans |
| 1 | A | 8/11 | Northampton | | 4,385 | L 2-3 | Friio, Stonebridge |

Line-ups (by column): Larrieu, McCormick, Worrell, Gilbert, Friio, Adams, Coughlan, Wotton, Coughlan, Aljofree, Norris, Bent, Evans, Norris, Aljofree, Adams, Gilbert, Worrell, Larrieu

Subs: Capaldi / St'bridge, Keith / Keith, Bent / Bent, Friio/Wotton/Stonebridge, Hodges/Phillips/Lowndes

## League Table

| | | | Home | | | | | Away | | | | | |
|---|---|---|---|---|---|---|---|---|---|---|---|---|---|
| | P | W | D | L | F | A | W | D | L | F | A | Pts |
| 1 PLYMOUTH | 46 | 17 | 5 | 1 | 52 | 13 | 9 | 7 | 7 | 33 | 28 | 90 |
| 2 QP Rangers | 46 | 16 | 7 | 0 | 47 | 12 | 6 | 10 | 7 | 33 | 33 | 83 |
| 3 Bristol City | 46 | 15 | 6 | 2 | 34 | 12 | 8 | 7 | 8 | 24 | 25 | 82 |
| 4 Brighton * | 46 | 17 | 4 | 2 | 39 | 11 | 5 | 7 | 11 | 25 | 32 | 77 |
| 5 Swindon | 46 | 12 | 7 | 4 | 41 | 23 | 8 | 6 | 9 | 35 | 35 | 73 |
| 6 Hartlepool | 46 | 10 | 8 | 5 | 39 | 24 | 10 | 5 | 8 | 37 | 37 | 73 |
| 7 Port Vale | 46 | 15 | 6 | 2 | 45 | 28 | 6 | 4 | 13 | 28 | 35 | 73 |
| 8 Tranmere | 46 | 13 | 7 | 3 | 36 | 18 | 4 | 9 | 10 | 23 | 38 | 67 |
| 9 Bournemouth | 46 | 11 | 8 | 4 | 35 | 25 | 6 | 7 | 10 | 21 | 26 | 66 |
| 10 Luton | 46 | 14 | 6 | 3 | 44 | 27 | 3 | 9 | 11 | 25 | 39 | 66 |
| 11 Colchester | 46 | 11 | 8 | 4 | 33 | 23 | 6 | 5 | 12 | 19 | 33 | 64 |
| 12 Barnsley | 46 | 7 | 12 | 4 | 25 | 19 | 8 | 5 | 10 | 29 | 39 | 62 |
| 13 Wrexham | 46 | 9 | 6 | 8 | 27 | 21 | 7 | 6 | 10 | 23 | 39 | 60 |
| 14 Blackpool | 46 | 9 | 5 | 9 | 31 | 28 | 7 | 6 | 10 | 27 | 35 | 59 |
| 15 Oldham | 46 | 9 | 8 | 6 | 37 | 25 | 3 | 13 | 7 | 29 | 35 | 57 |
| 16 Sheffield W | 46 | 7 | 9 | 7 | 25 | 26 | 6 | 5 | 12 | 23 | 38 | 53 |
| 17 Brentford | 46 | 9 | 5 | 9 | 34 | 38 | 5 | 6 | 12 | 18 | 31 | 53 |
| 18 Peterborough | 46 | 5 | 8 | 10 | 36 | 33 | 7 | 8 | 8 | 22 | 25 | 52 |
| 19 Stockport | 46 | 6 | 8 | 9 | 31 | 36 | 5 | 11 | 7 | 31 | 34 | 52 |
| 20 Chesterfield | 46 | 9 | 7 | 7 | 34 | 31 | 3 | 8 | 12 | 15 | 40 | 51 |
| 21 Grimsby | 46 | 10 | 5 | 8 | 36 | 26 | 3 | 6 | 14 | 19 | 55 | 50 |
| 22 Rushden & D | 46 | 9 | 5 | 9 | 37 | 34 | 4 | 4 | 15 | 23 | 40 | 48 |
| 23 Notts Co | 46 | 6 | 9 | 8 | 32 | 27 | 4 | 3 | 16 | 18 | 51 | 42 |
| 24 Wycombe | 46 | 5 | 7 | 11 | 31 | 39 | 1 | 12 | 10 | 19 | 36 | 37 |
| | 1104 | 251 | 166 | 135 | 861 | 599 | 135 | 166 | 251 | 599 | 861 | 1490 |

* promoted p/o

## Appearances and Goals

| | Appearances | | | | | | Goals | | | |
|---|---|---|---|---|---|---|---|---|---|---|
| | Lge | *Sub* | LC | *Sub* | FAC | *Sub* | Lge | LC | FAC | Tot |
| Adams, Steve | 25 | *11* | 1 | | | | 2 | | | 2 |
| Aljofree, Hasney | 20 | *4* | 1 | | 1 | | | | | |
| Bent, Jason | 13 | *5* | 1 | | 1 | | 1 | | | 1 |
| Beresford, David | | *1* | | | | | | | | |
| Capaldi, Tony | 29 | *4* | 1 | | 1 | | 7 | | | 7 |
| Connolly, Paul | 28 | *2* | | | | | | | | |
| Coughlan, Graham | 46 | | 1 | | 1 | | 7 | | | 7 |
| Evans, Michael | 35 | *9* | 1 | | 1 | | 11 | 1 | | 12 |
| Friio, David | 35 | *1* | | *1* | 1 | | 14 | | 1 | 15 |
| Gilbert, Peter | 40 | | 1 | | 1 | | 1 | | | 1 |
| Hodges, Lee | 28 | *9* | | *1* | | *1* | 3 | | | 3 |
| Keith, Marino | 28 | *12* | 1 | *1* | | | 9 | | | 9 |
| Larrieu, Romain | 6 | | | | | | | | | |
| Lowndes, Nathan | 18 | *15* | | *1* | | *1* | 8 | | | 8 |
| McCormick, Luke | 40 | | | *1* | | | | | | |
| Norris, David | 42 | *3* | 1 | | 1 | | 5 | | | 5 |
| Phillips, Martin | 3 | *6* | | | | | 1 | | | 1 |
| Stonebridge, Ian | 21 | *9* | 1 | *1* | 1 | | 5 | | 1 | 6 |
| Sturrock, Blair | | *23* | | | | | | | | |
| Worrell, David | 18 | *1* | 1 | | 1 | | | | | |
| Wotton, Paul | 31 | *7* | 1 | | 1 | | 9 | | | 9 |
| Yetton, Stewart | | *1* | | | | | | | | |
| (own-goals) | | | | | | | 2 | | | 2 |
| 22 players used | 506 | *122* | 11 | *3* | 11 | *3* | 85 | 1 | 2 | 88 |

| Subscribers | Scorer of Best Goal | Opposition | Season | Competition |
|---|---|---|---|---|
| *Paul 'Grizzly' Adams* | Garry Nelson | Bristol City | 1985-86 | League |
| *Christopher Archer-Lock* | Wayne Burnett | Exeter | 1993-94 | League |
| *K M Arthur* | Ronnie Mauge | Darlington | 1995-96 | Play-off |
| *Mike Arthur* | Mickey Evans | QPR | 2003-04 | League |
| *Nigel Aston* | Garry Nelson | Bristol City | 1985-86 | League |
| *Peter Batchelor* | Billy Rafferty | Sunderland | 1975-76 | League |
| *Robert F Bennett* | Pat Jones | Sheffield Wed | 1955-56 | League |
| *Steve Billing* | Ronnie Mauge | Darlington | 1995-96 | Play-off |
| *John C Blithe* | David Friio | Port Vale | 2003-04 | League |
| *Barry Bowden* | Mickey Evans | QPR | 2003-04 | League |
| *Jon Brain* | David Friio | Port Vale | 2003-04 | League |
| *Bernie Bright* | Paul Dalton | Barnsley | 1993-94 | FA Cup |
| *David Brown* | Paul Williams | Colchester | 1995-96 | Play-off |
| *Stuart Bulley* | Hughie Reed | Torquay | 1971-72 | League |
| *Peter Cannan* | Hughie Reed | Torquay | 1971-72 | League |
| *Roger Cawse* | Paul Wotton | Rushden | 2003-04 | League |
| *Nick Colbourne* | | | | |
| *Jeff Cole* | Paul Wotton | Bournemouth | 2003-04 | League |
| *David Coles* | Stan Williams | Wolves | 1949-50 | FA Cup |
| *Ian William Collins* | Dwight Marshall | Barnsley | 1993-94 | FA Cup |
| *John Condon* | Wayne Burnett | Exeter | 1993-94 | League |
| *Gordon Couch* | | | | |
| *Philip Crossman* | Micky Lill | Preston | 1962-63 | League |
| *Paul A S Docking* | Ronnie Mauge | Darlington | 1995-96 | Play-off |
| *Callum E M Douglas* | | | | |
| *Jeff Down* | | | | |
| *Mark Dunstan* | David Friio | Port Vale | 2003-04 | League |
| *Peter Dunstan* | Mickey Evans | QPR | 2003-04 | League |
| *John D Eales* | Andy Rogers | Derby Co | 1983-84 | FA Cup |
| *Paul Edmonds* | Steve Davey | Birmingham | 1973-74 | L'gue Cup |
| *Harry Farr* | Ronnie Mauge | Darlington | 1995-96 | Play-off |
| *Bob Foale* | Paul Wotton | Brighton | 1996-97 | AutoWind' |
| *Ivor W H Francis* | Stan Williams | Wolves | 1949-50 | FA Cup |
| *Warwick Franklin* | David Friio | Port Vale | 2003-04 | League |
| *Keith Gale* | Gordon Nisbet | WBA | 1986-87 | League |
| *Bernard Gillbard* | Ronnie Mauge | Darlington | 1995-96 | Play-off |
| *Blake Hall* | Paul Williams | Colchester | 1995-96 | Play-off |
| *Colin James Hall* | Ronnie Mauge | Darlington | 1995-96 | Play-off |
| *James Hancock* | Andy Rogers | Derby Co | 1983-84 | FA Cup |

| Subscribers | Scorer of Best Goal | Opposition | Season | Competition |
|---|---|---|---|---|
| *Bill Hansford* | Dwight Marshall | Barnsley | 1993-94 | FA Cup |
| *David Harding* | Tommy Tynan | WBA | 1983-84 | FA Cup |
| *James Harries* | Martin Barlow | Shrewsbury | 1996-97 | League |
| *David Harris* | Mickey Evans | Colchester | 1995-96 | Play-off |
| *Peter Head* | Kevin Summerfield | Ipswich | 1987-88 | League |
| *Dale Heath* | Kevin Summerfield | Ipswich | 1987-88 | League |
| *Alec Henderson* | Tommy Tynan | Bristol City | 1985-86 | League |
| *Kevin C Hoare* | Alan Welsh | Birmingham | 1973-74 | L'gue Cup |
| *P M Hollow* | Jimmy Gauld | Swindon | 1958-59 | League |
| *Michael Hoskin* | David Friio | Port Vale | 2003-04 | League |
| *Kevin Ireland* | Ronnie Mauge | Darlington | 1995-96 | Play-off |
| *Ian Jackson* | Tommy Tynan | Bristol City | 1985-86 | League |
| *Brian Jervis* | | | | |
| *Mark Joannes* | Ronnie Mauge | Darlington | 1995-96 | Play-off |
| *Peter Job* | Dwight Marshall | Barnsley | 1993-94 | FA Cup |
| *Toby Jones* | Dwight Marshall | Barnsley | 1991-92 | League |
| *Barry Jury* | Paul Wotton | Bournemouth | 2003-04 | League |
| *David Keogh* | Ronnie Mauge | Darlington | 1995-96 | Play-off |
| *Tony Keogh* | Andy Morrison | Swindon | 1990-91 | League |
| *A G Knox* | | | | |
| *Jon Leask* | Nathan Lowndes | Hartlepool | 2003-04 | League |
| *Matthew Lee* | Mickey Evans | QPR | 2003-04 | League |
| *Philip Lee* | Garry Nelson | Bristol City | 1985-86 | League |
| *Geoffrey Luke* | Tommy Tynan | WBA | 1984-85 | FA Cup |
| *Marks Family in Madrid* | | | | |
| *Glenn Martin* | Billy Rafferty | Blackpool | 1974-75 | FA Cup |
| *Robert Martin* | Billy Rafferty | Sunderland | 1975-76 | League |
| *Derek Vivian May* | Gordon Nisbet | WBA | 1986-87 | League |
| *Charles Mills* | Ronnie Mauge | Darlington | 1995-96 | Play-off |
| *David Moor* | Paul Williams | Colchester | 1995-96 | Play-off |
| *M Northcott* | Andy Rogers | Derby Co | 1983-84 | FA Cup |
| *Pete Ogley* | | | | |
| *Raymond John Owens* | | | | |
| *Derek & Gary Palmer* | Steve Davey | Birmingham | 1973-74 | L'gue Cup |
| *Colin Parsons* | Johnny Williams | West Ham | 1961-62 | FA Cup |
| *Andy Perrow* | Mickey Evans | QPR | 2003-04 | League |
| *David J Perry* | Ronnie Mauge | Darlington | 1995-96 | Play-off |
| *John A Pitts* | Steve Davey | Manchester C | 1973-74 | L'gue Cup |
| *Julian Pitts* | Tommy Tynan | WBA | 1983-84 | FA Cup |

| Subscribers | Scorer of Best Goal | Opposition | Season | Competition |
|---|---|---|---|---|
| Margaret Prior | | | | |
| Kevin Quinn | Johnny Williams | West Ham | 1961-62 | FA Cup |
| R J Rapson | Mickey Evans | QPR | 2003-04 | League |
| David Revell | Mickey Evans | QPR | 2003-04 | League |
| Jim Richards | Johnny Williams | Aston Villa | 1959-60 | League |
| Barry Richardson | Johnny Porteous | West Ham | 1953-54 | League |
| Colin Ridge | | | | |
| Chris Ridley | Marino Keith | Exeter | 2001-02 | League |
| Martin Rogers | Mickey Evans | QPR | 2003-04 | League |
| Ed Rundle | | | | |
| Mike Rundle | | | | |
| Trevor Scallan | Ian Stonebridge | Exeter | 2001-02 | League |
| Vim Smart | Hughie Reed | Torquay | 1971-72 | League |
| Richard Stocken | | | | |
| Alderman Joan Stopporton | Ronnie Mauge | Darlington | 1995-96 | Play-off |
| J I Street | Marino Keith | Exeter | 2001-02 | League |
| Irving Sweet | Gordon Nisbet | WBA | 1986-87 | League |
| Malcolm A Townrow | Paul Wotton | Bournemouth | 2003-04 | League |
| John Treleven | | | | |
| Simon Veale | Paul Wotton | Bournemouth | 2003-04 | League |
| Jan Walaszkowski | Kevin Summerfield | Ipswich | 1987-88 | League |
| James Wallace | Marino Keith | Exeter | 2001-02 | League |
| Chris Warren | Hughie Reed | Torquay | 1971-72 | League |
| David Whiteman | Keith Etheridge | Hull | 1966-67 | League |
| Clive Willis | | | | |
| Graham Wilton | Paul Wotton | Bournemouth | 2003-04 | League |
| Chris Wise | Mickey Evans | QPR | 2003-04 | League |
| Marc & Andrea Woodward | Mickey Evans | QPR | 2003-04 | League |
| Peter Yolland | | | | |
| Pap Zoltan | Ronnie Mauge | Brentford | 1996-97 | League |

*34 different goals were chosen*

| | | | | |
|---|---|---|---|---|
| 1st | Ronnie Mauge | Darlington | 1995-96 | Play-off |
| 2nd | Mickey Evans | QPR | 2003-04 | League |
| 3rd = | David Friio | Port Vale | 2003-04 | League |
| 3rd = | Paul Wotton | Bournemouth | 2003-04 | League |